Bearing YHWH's Name at Sinai

Bulletin for Biblical Research Supplements

1. *Bridging the Gap: Ritual and Ritual Texts in the Bible*, by Gerald A. Klingbeil
2. *War in the Bible and Terrorism in the Twenty-First Century*, edited by Richard S. Hess and Elmer A. Martens
3. *Critical Issues in Early Israelite History*, edited by Richard S. Hess, Gerald A. Klingbeil, and Paul J. Ray Jr.
4. *Poetic Imagination in Proverbs: Variant Repetitions and the Nature of Poetry*, by Knut Martin Heim
5. *Divine Sabbath Work*, by Michael H. Burer
6. *The Iron Age I Structure on Mt. Ebal: Excavation and Interpretation*, by Ralph K. Hawkins
7. *Toward a Poetics of Genesis 1–11: Reading Genesis 4:17–22 in Its Near Eastern Context*, by Daniel DeWitt Lowery
8. *Melchizedek's Alternative Priestly Order: A Compositional Analysis of Genesis 14:18–20 and Its Echoes throughout the Tanak*, by Joshua G. Mathews
9. *Sacred Ritual: A Study of the West Semitic Ritual Calendars in Leviticus 23 and the Akkadian Text Emar 446*, by Bryan C. Babcock
10. *Wrestling with the Violence of God: Soundings in the Old Testament*, edited by M. Daniel Carroll R. and J. Blair Wilgus
11. *Wealth in Ancient Ephesus and the First Letter to Timothy: Fresh Insights from* Ephesiaca *by Xenophon of Ephesus*, by Gary G. Hoag
12. *Paul and His Mortality: Imitating Christ in the Face of Death*, by R. Gregory Jenks
13. *"Did I Not Bring Israel Out of Egypt?" Biblical, Archaeological, and Egyptological Perspectives on the Exodus Narratives*, edited by James K. Hoffmeier, Alan R. Millard, and Gary A. Rendsburg
14. *Honor, Shame, and Guilt: Social Scientific Approaches to the Book of Ezekiel*, by Daniel Y. Wu
15. *Hostility in the House of God: An Investigation of the Opponents in 1 and 2 Timothy*, by Dillon T. Thornton
16. *Hope for a Tender Sprig: Jehoiachin in Biblical Theology*, by Matthew H. Patton
17. *Making Sense of the Divine Name in Exodus: From Etymology to Literary Onomastics*, by Austin Surls
18. *Trees and Kings: A Comparative Analysis of Tree Imagery in Israel's Prophetic Tradition and the Ancient Near East*, by William R. Osborne
19. *Bearing YHWH's Name at Sinai: A Reexamination of the Name Command of the Decalogue*, by Carmen Joy Imes

Bearing YHWH*'s Name at Sinai*

A Reexamination of the Name Command of the Decalogue

by

Carmen Joy Imes

Eisenbrauns
University Park, Pennsylvania

Library of Congress Cataloging-in-Publication Data

Names: Imes, Carmen Joy, 1977– author.
Title: Bearing Yhwh's name at Sinai : a reexamination of the name command of the Decalogue / by Carmen Joy Imes.
Description: University Park, Pennsylvania : Eisenbrauns, [2017] | Includes Bibliographical references and index.
Summary: "Explores the Name Command in the Decalogue by examining its expression in Jewish rituals and their associated metaphorical concepts"—Provided by publisher.
Identifiers: LCCN 2017058616 | ISBN 9781575067728 (cloth : alk. paper)
Subjects: LCSH: Ten commandments—Name of God. God—Name—Biblical teaching.
Classification: LCC BV4664+
LC record available at https://lccn.loc.gov/2017058616

Printed in the United States of America
Published by The Pennsylvania State University Press, University Park, PA 16802–1003

Eisenbrauns is an imprint of The Pennsylvania State University Press.

The Pennsylvania State University Press is a member of the Association of University Presses.

It is the policy of The Pennsylvania State University Press to use acid-free paper. Publications on uncoated stock satisfy the minimum requirements of American National Standard for Information Sciences—Permanence of Paper for Printed Library Material, ANSI Z39.48–1992.

To my mentors in biblical studies.
You bear the name of YHWH with honor—
not only in the classroom and the academy, but also
at home, in the public square, and in the church worldwide.

Karl Neerhof

Ray Lubeck

Karl Kutz

Rollin Grams

Karen Jobes

Sandra Richter

Daniel Block

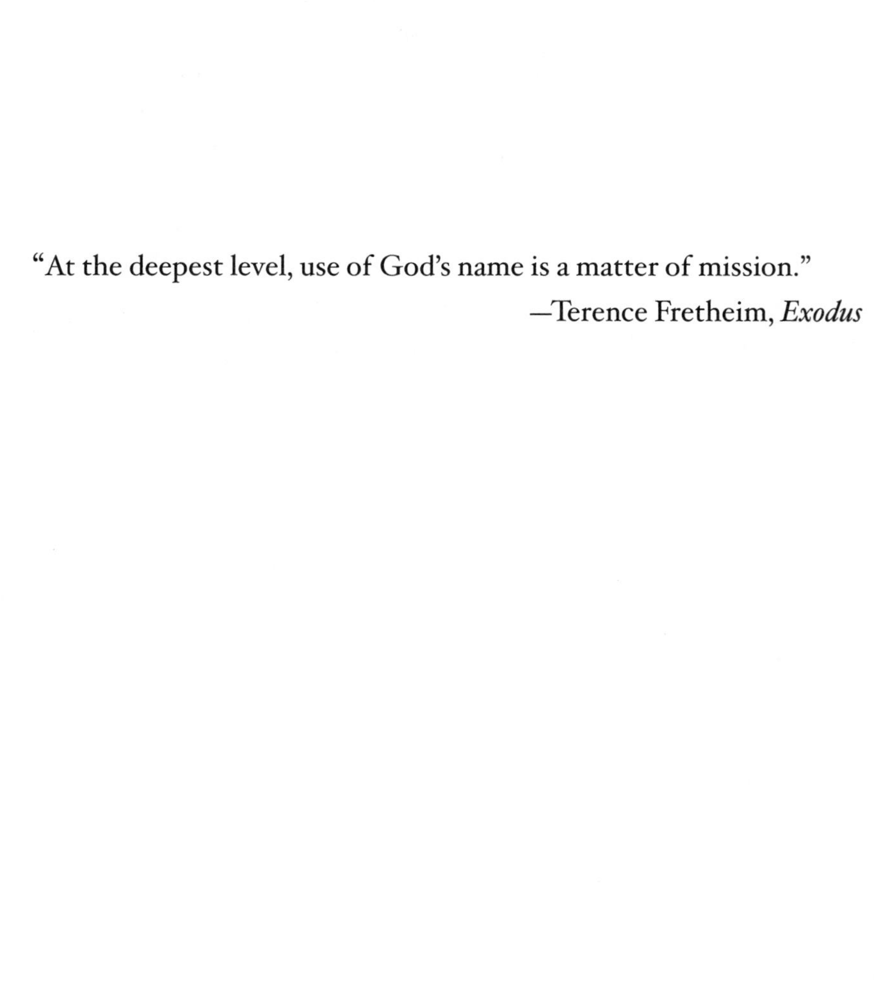

"At the deepest level, use of God's name is a matter of mission."

—Terence Fretheim, *Exodus*

Contents

List of Figures

List of Tables

Foreword

"You shall not bear the name of Yhwh your God in vain." I grew up thinking this command prohibited verbal profanity, specifically the use of any divine epithets or derivatives from these epithets ("Gosh," "Golly," "Gee whiz," "Geez") as oral exclamation marks. Later, I learned that other traditions (for example, Jewish) interpreted this as the flippant use of the divine name in oaths, or even the mistaken pronunciation of the divine name. Common to all these interpretations is the assumption that the command concerns primarily speech acts, that is, taking the name of Yhwh on one's lips or uttering it with the tongue.

Later, much later, on closer examination, it dawned on me that the locution in the command, specifically the Hebrew verb נָשָׂא, does not readily lend itself to a verbal interpretation. The invitation to deliver the sermon at the morning worship service sponsored by the Institute for Biblical Research in the context of the Society for Biblical Literature annual meetings on November 22, 2009, afforded me an opportunity for my first foray into this fascinating but under-researched subject. The address was eventually published under the heading "Bearing the Name of the Lord with Honor: A Homily on the Second Command of the Decalogue," in *Bibliotheca Sacra*. However, this was an initial exploration, cast as a hypothesis with profound theological and homiletical significance. I am delighted that Carmen Imes accepted my invitation to test my hypothesis by exploring the subject more thoroughly. The present volume presents the results of her investigation.

Many have commented on the Name Command in essays and commentaries, and almost 20 years ago, Thomas R. Elßner published a monograph on the subject (*Das Namensmißbrauch-Verbot*, 1999), though his conversation partners were primarily German. However, this is the first English-language dissertation on the subject in more than a century. Carmen's work stands out particularly for the thoroughness of her investigation into the history of the command's interpretation before launching into her own assessment of that history. Paying careful attention to the lexemes that make up the command and exploring its significance within its literary (as a part of the Decalogue) and covenantal contexts, Carmen offers a sensitive and respectful critique of traditional interpretations and then argues for a compelling alternative. Although the command may indeed prohibit certain speech acts involving the utterance of the divine name, she amasses the evidence for a metaphorical interpretation. This command assumes that, as the covenant people of Yhwh, the Israelites bore his name. On the one hand, this means that Yhwh had marked them as his own, and on the other hand, that everywhere they went they represented him. For the Israelites to bear Yhwh's name in vain meant to claim to belong to him but in their actions display allegiance to another god or gods, and in so doing misrepresent Yhwh.

Carmen's study helps us understand the complementary significance of the first two commands of the Decalogue (by the traditional Catholic and Lutheran numbering), which taken together allude to the two basic clauses of the "covenant formula": "I will be your God, and you shall be my people." With the first command, the Israelites recognized Yhwh's grace in presenting himself as the personal deity of the covenant people; with the second, they recognized the obverse and reciprocal fact—they belonged to Yhwh. Carmen's work also helps us grasp the significance of a series of biblical idioms involving the divine name, including "to place the name upon" (שִׂים שֵׁם עַל) and "to call the name over" (or "to read the name on"; קָרָא שֵׁם עַל). These are metaphorical idioms that suggest that Israel or some object that bore his name had been virtually branded with Yhwh's name and thereby claimed as his possession. It is not difficult to see how this notion spills over into the New Testament with its references to "baptism into the name of Christ" and "suffering for the name," and other expressions.

This volume offers Hebrew scholars, biblical and systematic theologians, and preachers a fresh and profoundly theological perspective on one of the most familiar statements of Scripture. We are indebted to Carmen Imes for her groundbreaking study, to Rick Hess for accepting the manuscript for publication in the Bulletin for Biblical Research Supplement series, and to Jim Eisenbraun and his publishing house for making it available in print. May this work inspire all who claim to be the Lord's people to represent him with honor and integrity.

Daniel I. Block
Gunther H. Knoedler Professor Emeritus of Old Testament
Wheaton College
October 31, 2017

Acknowledgments

This project began as a doctoral dissertation under the supervision of Daniel Block at Wheaton College. He has been an ideal mentor, from those first days of dreaming up a topic together through the long years of work to bring this book to press. He has modeled a generous and hospitable scholarship, improved my writing abilities, and pushed me beyond what I thought I could do. I will always be grateful for the privilege of working so closely with him. Karen Jobes went above and beyond the call of duty for a second reader. Her personal and academic encouragement helped to make the first years of work a joyful journey. Sandra Richter generously agreed to take over as second reader late in the project when Karen retired. Her expertise helped me vanquish that mortal enemy, illegitimate totality transfer, and sharpened many a fuzzy sentence, bringing clarity throughout.

Other scholars at Wheaton shaped my thinking in important ways: John Walton, Daniel Treier, Lynn Cohick, Michael Graves, Richard Schultz, Kevin Vanhoozer, and Adam Miglio. I am also grateful to the many fine scholars I have met through IBR and SBL who have shared their unpublished work and/or stimulated my research in new directions through personal conversation: Andrea Weiss, Alison Gray, Monica Phillips, Jacob Lauinger, Jeffrey Stackert, Carly Crouch, Anne Knafl, Alan Harman, Jason DeRouchie, Joseph Lam, Richard Averbeck, Scott Morschauser, Travis Bott, and my fellow members of the "Clothing in the Hebrew Bible Research Group" in the Pacific Northwest Region of SBL: Tony Finitsis, Ian Wilson, Shawn Flynn, Scott Starbuck, Josh Spoelstra, Sara Koenig, Ehud Ben Zvi, and Sean Cook. As series editor, Rick Hess's timely and insightful feedback strengthened the work in many areas and helped the dissertation become a monograph.

I am also indebted to a host of friends, too many to name here, whose skill in other languages enhanced my research, especially Chris Ansberry (Egyptian), the late Harry Hoffner (Hittite), and Austin Surls, who cheerfully helped with Akkadian, Hebrew (both classical and modern), and Aramaic on countless occasions and then thanked me for asking him.

My dear family—Danny, Eliana, Emma, and Easton—fought with me for every page, pushing me to write, and celebrating when each was written. I cannot imagine a stronger support team. My children have grown up with the Name Command and will happily explain what it means if you ask them. They have also kept me grounded in the heady world of academia. Words cannot express what Danny's support has meant to me. He laid down his life for me, hour after hour, so that I could faithfully answer God's calling. His sweat shows on every page. His partnership is every scholar's dream.

And finally, six remarkable couples should take satisfaction in the completion and publication of this project: Dan and Verna Camfferman, Phil and Julie Parshall, Chuck and Vicki Kinnaman, Mike and Maggie Rowe, Dan and Ellen Block, Willy and Angela Brandle. While a whole host of people have encouraged us on this journey, without each of you we could not have finished. Thank you.

In spite of help from all these fantastic people, mistakes undoubtedly remain. My gratitude for the expertise of so many should not be interpreted as their endorsement of my conclusions. May the weaknesses of this project not reflect on any of these fine mentors and friends, who rescued me from countless errors. *Soli deo gloria*!

Carmen Joy Imes
January 2017

Abbreviations

General

A	Codex Alexandrinus (LXX)
ANE	ancient Near East
Ant.	Josephus, *Jewish Antiquities*
AT	author's translation
b. ʿAbod. Zar.	*Babylonian (Talmud) ʿAbodah Zarah*
b. Ber.	*Babylonian (Talmud) Berakot*
b. Ḥag	*Babylonian (Talmud) Ḥagigah*
b. Ned.	*Babylonian (Talmud) Nedarim*
b. Pesaḥ	*Babylonian (Talmud) Pesaḥim*
b. Šabb.	*Babylonian (Talmud) Šabbat*
b. Šebu	*Babylonian (Talmud) Šebuʿot*
b. Tamid	*Babylonian (Talmud) Tamid*
b. Tem.	*Babylonian (Talmud) Temurah*
b. Yoma	*Babylonian (Talmud) Yoma*
DH	Deuteronomistic History
ESV	English Standard Version
Herm. Sim.	Hermas, *Similitudes*
KJV	King James Version
Mek.	*Mekhilta*
LXX	Septuagint
MT	Masoretic Text
NC	Name Command (Exod 20:7; Deut 5:11)
NET	New English Translation
NIV	New International Version
NJPS	*Tanakh: The Holy Scriptures. The New JPS Translation according to the Traditional Hebrew Text*
NLT	New Living Translation
NRSV	New Revised Standard Version
Pesiq. Rab.	*Pesiqta Rabbati*
SP	Samaritan Pentateuch
ST	Samaritan Targum
Syr.	Syriac
Tg(s).	*Targum(s)*
Tg. Onq.	*Targum Onqelos*
Tg. Ps.-J.	*Targum Pseudo-Jonathan*
TH	Theodotion (LXX)
TO	*Targum Onqelos*
y. Ber.	*Jerusalem (Talmud) Berakot*

Reference Works

AB	Anchor Bible
ABD	Freedman, D. N., editor. *The Anchor Bible Dictionary*. 6 vols. Garden City, NY: Doubleday, 1992
ABRL	Anchor Bible Reference Library
ABS	Archaeology and Biblical Studies
ACT	Ancient Christian Texts
AfO	Archiv für Orientforschung
AHI	Davies, G. I., editor. *Ancient Hebrew Inscriptions.* 2 vols. Cambridge: Cambridge University Press, 1991–2004
AHw	von Soden, W. *Akkadisches Handwörterbuch*. 3 vols. Wiesbaden: Harrassowitz, 1965–81
AIL	Ancient Israel and Its Literature
AnBib	Analecta biblica
ANET[2]	Pritchard, J. B., editor. *Ancient Near Eastern Texts Relating to the Old Testament.* 2nd ed. Princeton: Princeton University Press, 1955
ANF	Roberts, A., and Donaldson, J., editors. *The Ante-Nicene Fathers: Translations of the Writings of the Fathers down to a.d. 325*. 10 vols. Grand Rapids: Eerdmans, 1978–79
AOAT	Alter Orient und Altes Testament
AOTC	Apollos Old Testament Commentary
ArBib	The Aramaic Bible
ATANT	Abhandlungen zur Theologie des Alten und Neuen Testaments
ATSHB	Sparks, Kenton L. *Ancient Texts for the Study of the Hebrew Bible: A Guide to the Background Literature.* Peabody, MA: Hendrickson, 2005
BASOR	*Bulletin of the American Schools of Oriental Research*
BBR	*Bulletin for Biblical Research*
BBRSup	Bulletin for Biblical Research Supplement Series
BCOT	Baker Commentary on the Old Testament
BDAG	Bauer, W. *Greek-English Lexicon of the New Testament and Other Early Christian Literature.* 3rd ed. of BAGD revised by F. W. Danker. Chicago: University of Chicago Press, 2000
BeO	*Bibbia e oriente*
BETL	Bibliotheca ephemeridum theologicarum lovaniensium
BHQ	*Biblia Hebraica Quinta.* Stuttgart: Deutsche Bibelgesellschaft, 2004–
BHS	Elliger, K., and Rudolph, W., editors. *Biblia Hebraica Stuttgartensia.* Stuttgart: Deutsche Bibelgesellschaft, 1984
BIS	Biblical Interpretation Series
BJS	Brown Judaic Studies
BJSUCSD	Biblical and Judaic Studies from the University of California, San Diego
BN	*Biblische Notizen*
BRLJ	Brill Reference Library of Judaism
BSac	*Bibliotheca sacra*
BTCB	Brazos Theological Commentary on the Bible
BZABR	Beihefte zur Zeitschrift für altorientalische und biblische Rechtsgeschichte
BZAW	Beihefte zur Zeitschrift für die alttestamentliche Wissenschaft

CAD	Gelb, Ignace J., et al., editors. *The Assyrian Dictionary of the Oriental Institute of the University of Chicago*. 21 vols. (A–Z). Chicago: Oriental Institute, 1956–2011
CBQ	*Catholic Biblical Quarterly*
CC	*Calvin's Commentaries*
CC	Continental Commentaries
CHANE	Culture and History of the Ancient Near East
ConBOT	Coniectanea biblica: Old Testament Series
COS	Hallo, W. W., and K. L. Younger Jr., editors. *The Context of Scripture.* 3 vols. Leiden: Brill, 1997–2003
CTH	Laroche, E., editor. *Catalogue des textes hittites.* Etudes et commentaries 75. Paris: Gabalda, 1971
DCH	Clines, D. J. A., editor. *Dictionary of Classical Hebrew.* 9 vols. Sheffield: Sheffield Phoenix, 1993–2014
DDD	Van der Toorn, K.; Becking, B.; and van der Horst, P. W., editors. *Dictionary of Deities and Demons in the Bible.* Leiden: Brill, 1995
DNWSI	Hoftijzer, J., and Jongeling, K. *Dictionary of the North-West Semitic Inscriptions.* 2 vols. Leiden: Brill, 1995
DOTP	Alexander, T. Desmond, and David W. Baker, editors. *Dictionary of the Old Testament: Pentateuch.* Downers Grove, IL: InterVarsity, 2003
DTIB	Vanhoozer, Kevin J., editor. *Dictionary for Theological Interpretation of the Bible.* Grand Rapids: Eerdmans, 2005
EA	Schniedewind, W. M., editor. *The El-Amarna Correspondence: A New Edition of the Cuneiform Letters from the Site of El-Amarna based on Collations of all Extant Tablets.* Collated, Transcribed and Translated by Anson F. Rainey. Leiden: Brill, 2015
EBC	Longman, Tremper, III, and David E. Garland, editors. *The Expositor's Bible Commentary*. Grand Rapids: Baker, 2006–12
ECC	Eerdmans Critical Commentary
EdF	Erträge der Forschung
EDNT	Balz, H., and G. Schneider, editors. *Exegetical Dictionary of the New Testament.* ET. Grand Rapids: Eerdmans, 1990–93
EJ	Roth, Cecil, editor. *Encyclopaedia Judaica.* 16 vols. Jerusalem: Keter, 1972
EPSC	Evangelical Press Study Commentaries
ExpTim	*Expository Times*
FAT	Forschungen zum Alten Testament
FOTL	Forms of the Old Testament Literature
GCS	Die griechische christliche Schriftsteller der ersten [drei] Jahrhunderte
GTJ	*Grace Theological Journal*
HALOT	Koehler, L.; Baumgartner, W.; and Stamm, J. J. *The Hebrew and Aramaic Lexicon of the Old Testament.* Translated and edited under supervision of M. E. J. Richardson. 5 vols. Leiden: Brill, 1994–2000
HCOT	Historical Commentary on the Old Testament
HDT	Beckman, Gary, and Harold A. Hoffner, editors. *Hittite Diplomatic Texts.* SBLWAW 7. Atlanta: SBL, 1999
HKAT	Handkommentar zum Alten Testament

HRCS	Hatch, E., and H. A. Redpath. *Concordance to the Septuagint and Other Greek Versions of the Old Testament.* 2 vols. Oxford: Oxford University Press, 1897. Suppl., 1906
HSM	Harvard Semitic Monographs
HSS	Harvard Semitic Studies
HUCA	*Hebrew Union College Annual*
IBHS	Waltke, B. K., and O'Connor, M. *An Introduction to Biblical Hebrew Syntax*. Winona Lake, IN: Eisenbrauns, 1990
ICC	International Critical Commentary
Int	Interpretation
Int	*Interpretation*
IVP	InterVarsity Press
JANES	*Journal of the Ancient Near Eastern Society*
JAOS	*Journal of the American Oriental Society*
Jastrow	Jastrow, M. *A Dictionary of the Targumim, the Talmud Babli and Yerushalmi, and the Midrashic Literature.* 2nd ed. Peabody, MA: Hendrickson, 2006
JBL	*Journal of Biblical Literature*
JBTh	*Jahrbuch für Biblische Theologie*
JETS	*Journal of the Evangelical Theological Society*
JNES	*Journal of Near Eastern Studies*
Joüon	Joüon, P. *A Grammar of Biblical Hebrew.* Translated and revised by T. Muraoka. Subsidia Biblica 27. Rome: Pontifical Biblical Institute, 2006
JQR	*Jewish Quarterly Review*
JSOT	*Journal for the Study of the Old Testament*
JSOTSup	Journal for the Study of the Old Testament: Supplement Series
KAI	Donner, H., and Röllig, W. *Kanaanäische und aramäische Inschriften.* 3 vols. Wiesbaden: Harrassowitz, 1962–64
KTU	Dietrich, M.; Loretz, O.; and Sanmartín, J., editors. *Die Keilalphabetischen Texte aus Ugarit.* Alter Orient und Altes Testament 24. Kevelaer: Butzon & Bercker / Neukirchen-Vluyn: Neukirchener Verlag, 1976
LAI	Library of Ancient Israel
LCC	Library of Christian Classics
LCL	Loeb Classical Library
LEC	Library of Early Christianity
LH	Laws of Hammurabi
LHBOTS	Library of Hebrew Bible / Old Testament Studies
LSAWS	Linguistic Studies in Ancient West Semitic
LSJ	Liddell, H. G., and Scott, R. *Greek-English Lexicon*. 9th ed. with revised supplement. Revised by H. S. Jones and R. McKenzie. Oxford: Clarendon, 1996
LSTS	Library of Second Temple Studies
LW	*Luther's Works.* Edited by J. Pelikan and H. T. Lehmann. 55 vols. St. Louis: Concordia; Philadelphia: Fortress, 1955–86
NAC	New American Commentary
NCBC	New Century Bible Commentary
NIB	*New Interpreter's Bible*

NIBCOT	New International Biblical Commentary: Old Testament Series
NICOT	New International Commentary on the Old Testament
NIDB	Sakenfeld, K. editor. *New Interpreter's Dictionary of the Bible.* Nashville: Abingdon, 2009
NIDOTTE	VanGemeren, W. A., editor. *New International Dictionary of Old Testament Theology and Exegesis*. 5 vols. Grand Rapids: Zondervan, 1997
NIVAC	NIV Application Commentary
OEAE	Redford, Donald B., editor. *Oxford Encyclopedia of Ancient Egypt*. 3 vols. Oxford: Oxford University Press, 2001
OEANE	Meyers, E. M., editor. *The Oxford Encyclopedia of Archaeology in the Near East.* 5 vols. New York: Oxford University Press, 1997
OED	*Oxford English Dictionary.* 2nd ed. 20 vols. Oxford: Clarendon / New York: Oxford University Press, 1989
OTL	Old Testament Library
Pol. *Phil.*	Polycarp, *To the Philippians.* In *The Apostolic Fathers*, edited and translated by Michael W. Holmes. Grand Rapids: Baker Academic, 2007
QD	Quaestiones disputatae
Rab.	Freedman, H., and Maruice Simon, editors. *Midrash Rabbah*. 3rd ed. New York: Soncino, 1983
RB	*Revue biblique*
RBL	*Review of Biblical Literature*
RIH	Ras Ibn Hani
RIMA	Royal Inscriptions of Mesopotamia: Assyrian Periods
RlA	Ebeling, E., et al., editors. *Reallexikon der Assyriologie*. Berlin: de Gruyter, 1928–
SAA	State Archives of Assyria
SBL	Society of Biblical Literature
SBLDS	Society of Biblical Literature Dissertation Series
SBLWAW	Society of Biblical Literature Writings from the Ancient World
SBS	Stuttgarter Bibelstudien
SBTS	Sources for Biblical and Theological Study
SC	Sources chrétiennes
SHBC	Smyth & Helwys Bible Commentary
SVG	Supplements to Vigiliae Christianae
ST	*Summa Theologiæ*
TBS	Tools for Biblical Study
TDNT	Kittel, G., and Friedrich, G., editors. *Theological Dictionary of the New Testament*. 10 vols. Grand Rapids: Eerdmans, 1964–76
TDOT	Botterweck, G. J., and Ringgren, H., editors. *Theological Dictionary of the Old Testament*. Grand Rapids: Eerdmans, 1974–2006
TLOT	*Theological Lexicon of the Old Testament.* Edited by E. Jenni, with assistance from C. Westermann. Translated by M. E. Biddle. 3 vols. Peabody, MA: Hendrickson, 1997
TOTC	Tyndale Old Testament Commentaries
TWOT	Harris, R. L., and G. L. Archer Jr., editors. *Theological Wordbook of the Old Testament.* 2 vols. Chicago: University of Chicago Press, 1980
TynBul	*Tyndale Bulletin*
VT	*Vetus Testamentum*

VTE	Vassal Treaties of Esarhaddon
VTSup	Supplements to Vetus Testamentum
WBC	Word Biblical Commentary
WC	Westminster Commentaries
Webster	Agnes, M., editor. *Webster's New World College Dictionary.* 4th ed. Cleveland: Wiley, 2008
WSA	*Works of Saint Augustine*. New York: New City, 1990–2009
WTJ	*Westminster Theological Journal*
WUNT	Wissenschaftliche Untersuchungen zum Neuen Testament
YOS	Yale Oriental Series
ZAW	*Zeitschrift für die alttestamentliche Wissenschaft*
ZIBBCOT	Walton, J. H., editor. *Zondervan Illustrated Bible Background Commentary: Old Testament.* 5 vols. Grand Rapids: Baker, 2009

Chapter 1

Introduction

> It is the remarkable impact of the Ten Commandments as a whole on two millennia of religious and, to be sure, cultural history that has so impressed readers and has drawn their attention more to these sixteen verses than to any other single block of biblical laws—perhaps more than to any other part of the Hebrew Bible.
>
> —Douglas Knight, *Law, Power, and Justice in Ancient Israel*

Given the widespread familiarity with the Decalogue in Western culture, it may come as a surprise that it is often misunderstood. This is especially true with the Name Command (Exod 20:7; Deut 5:11; hereafter, NC).[1] When asked what it means "to take the LORD's name in vain," a typical response is, "It means you shouldn't swear." In popular parlance, "to swear" is to utter profanity. Indeed, whether on reality TV, on the basketball court, or in a crowded high school hallway, God's name is frequently used for this kind of "swearing." However, most scholars recognize that, while the flippant use of God's name is objectionable, the NC addresses something else. Many agree that the meaning of the NC is uncertain, but this is where agreement ends. The number of meanings proposed for the NC is more than twice the number of words it contains.[2] I contend that the failure to interpret this command properly arises from a neglect of the natural meaning of the Hebrew in its immediate literary context on the one hand, and inattention to the conceptual metaphors that motivated its unusual phraseology on the other. The NC is expressed identically in both versions of the Decalogue:

1. Most introductions to the Decalogue acknowledge the difficulty of numbering the commands. For discussion, see Jason S. DeRouchie, "Counting the Ten: An Investigation into the Numbering of the Decalogue," in *For Our Good Always: Studies on the Message and Influence of Deuteronomy in Honor of Daniel I. Block*, ed. Jason S. DeRouchie, Jason Gile, and Kenneth J. Turner (Winona Lake, IN: Eisenbrauns, 2013), 93–125. Some traditions call Exod 20:7 the "Second Commandment" and others refer to it as the "Third Commandment." See discussion below, pp. 130–135. To avoid confusion, I will use the designation "Name Command," abbreviated NC. Unless otherwise noted, all English translations of biblical or other texts are my own.

2. Exodus 20:7 contains 17 words. Due to repetition, only 10 lexemes are utilized, but at least 23 different meanings have been proposed.

Exodus 20:7 // Deuteronomy 5:11

לא תשא את־שם־יהוה אלהיך	You shall not bear the name of Yhwh, your God,
לשוא כי לא ינקה יהוה	in vain, for Yhwh will not acquit
את אשר־ישא את־שמו לשוא	one who bears his[3] name in vain.

The word תשא is a 2ms *qal* imperfect of נשא, which typically means "to lift up, carry, or bear." The marked direct object—what the recipients of this command were prohibited from bearing, לשוא—is את־שם־יהוה אלהיך, Yhwh's name.[4] The word לשוא indicates the manner in which the name is not to be borne, with the *lamed* prefix lending the noun שוא an adverbial sense: "in vain." Failure to heed this warning precludes acquittal (לא ינקה); Yhwh treats an infraction with utmost seriousness.

The translation of the NC proposed here requires no exegetical gymnastics, and yet this natural rendering is usually set aside by interpreters, who evidently cannot work out what it means. The clearest biblical instance of the expression נשא שם outside the NC refers to the high priestly garments. The high priest was to "bear the names" of the 12 tribes on his person to signify his role as their authorized representative before Yhwh (Exod 28:29).[5] While he physically carried, or bore, their names, he served as an analog to Israel's bearing of Yhwh's name, which was conferred on them by the high priest when he blessed them (Num 6:27). As Yhwh's chosen people and "kingdom of priests" (Exod 19:5), they represented him among the nations. While the high priestly analogue is not essential to the meaning of the NC, since it relies on a plain-sense reading of the Hebrew text, the high priest provides a convenient visual lexicon or model of Israel's vocation, unlocking a rich network of theological associations. These will be explored in ch. 5.

Scope and Need for Research

This project engages recent scholarly literature as well as significant older works on the Decalogue as a whole, in addition to a thorough survey of publications on the NC in particular. Chapter 2 explores the range of interpretive options advocated by scholars across the ages, focusing on representatives whose exposition is sufficiently detailed to merit close interaction. A survey such as this will prepare the ground for the constructive proj-

3. In keeping with Hebrew convention, I will use masculine pronouns to refer to Yhwh. This grammatical representation of Yhwh is not to be construed as a claim of God's anthropomorphic gender identity. I have adopted this gendered language primarily for the sake of smooth prose.

4. The word אלהיך ("your God") functions epexegetically.

5. Most interpreters routinely overlook these passages. For example, Miller (*The Ten Commandments*, Int [Louisville: Westminster John Knox, 2009], 68) dismisses Exod 28 as "not relevant" to the interpretation of the NC without explanation, even though the description of Aaron's high priestly garments offers the closest lexical and contextual parallels to the NC.

ect that follows. The diversity of approaches and the general puzzlement expressed by many commentators justifies this full-length exploration.

Most interpreters have read the NC as elliptical in nature. A literary ellipsis occurs when some syntactically essential component of the sentence is implied rather than stated explicitly. Ellipses are especially common in the second line of poetic parallelism, but they can appear in other genres when the author feels that a complete statement is unnecessary. For example, in Hos 1:2, YHWH instructs Hosea, "Go. Take for yourself a woman of prostitution and [. . .] children of prostitution." Here, the verb "to bear" (ילד) is implicit.[6] An elliptical reading of the NC supposes that the phrase נשׂא שׁם is shorthand for a longer expression or that some information is assumed. Only a handful have championed an alternative, nonelliptical reading of this command, which accepts נשׂא שׁם as a complete expression. This project will refer to the nonelliptical interpretation as "representational" because it reads the NC as prohibiting the mis*representation* of YHWH by those who bear his name. However, rather than ruling out other interpretations, this alternate reading both includes them and offers a firmer exegetical basis for broader application. The representational view widens the field of reference beyond matters of speech to include behavior that "takes his name in vain" (to use the English idiom).[7] This is the first attempt in English to examine thoroughly the various interpretations and their relationship with each other.[8] It is also the first extended exploration of the minority view that reads the command nonelliptically, as "bearing the name," rather than as an ellipsis for speaking it.[9] Although others have adopted the representational reading of the NC, this project is the first to test this hypothesis systematically for its literary, lexical, grammatical, historical, and theological plausibility. Furthermore, cognitive linguistics has not been previously employed as a helpful model for understanding the NC. While the representational interpretation is not the only possible reading, it offers a more satisfying explanation of the data than other interpretations.

6. Cf. E. W. Bullinger, *Figures of Speech Used in the Bible* (Grand Rapids: Baker, 1968), 1; Luis Alonso Schökel, *A Manual of Hebrew Poetics*, Subsidia Biblica 11 (Rome: Pontifical Biblical Institute, 1988), 166–67. As another example, 2 Sam 6:6 reads, "when they arrived at the threashing floor of Nakon, Uzzah stretched out [*his hand*] to the altar of God and grasped it." As a transitive verb, שׁלח ("stretched out") is usually followed by an object (often יד ["hand"]). Here, "hand" is assumed but not stated. See *DCH* 8:381.

7. On the history of this unusual English idiom, see p. 181.

8. Thomas Elßner's historical survey (*Das Namensmißbrauch-Verbot (Ex 20,7 / Dtn 5,11): Bedeutung, Entstehung und frühe Wirkungsgeschichte*, ETS 75 [Leipzig: St. Benno, 1999], 32–33) includes only German interpreters and categorizes them according to whether they conceived of the NC as specific or general.

9. To my knowledge, the only extended treatments of the NC to date are Elßner, *Das Namensmißbrauch-Verbot*, and Fulton Johnson Coffin, *The Third Commandment* (Ph.D. diss., University of Chicago, 1898). A 22-page version of Coffin's work was released in 1900 ("The Third Commandment," *JBL* 19 [1900]: 166–88).

Historical and Theological Presuppositions

Critical scholars struggle to identify a *Sitz im Leben* for biblical commands, especially the Decalogue, given the internal lack of historical reference.[10] Some see it as one of the oldest parts of the Hebrew Bible, others as one of the most recent.[11] Attempts to recover the original Decalogue have tended to reduce it to a series of brief, negative statements, excising material

10. On the impossibility of determining the date of origin for apodictic law, see Rifat Sonsino, "Law; Forms of Biblical Law," *ABD* 4:254. The date of the Decalogue is notoriously controversial. See, e.g., Douglas Knight, *Law, Power, and Justice in Ancient Israel*, LAI (Louisville: Westminster John Knox, 2011), 24.

11. Conservative or progressive leanings do not necessarily determine one's conclusion on the compositional dating of the Decalogue. See Dennis McCarthy, *Treaty and Covenant: A Study in Form in the Ancient Oriental Documents and in the Old Testament*, AnBib 21A (Rome: Biblical Institute, 1978), 249 n. 8. Those who favor a late date include Axel Graupner, "Die zehn Gebote im Rahmen alttestamentlicher Ethik: Anmerkungen zum gegenwärtigen Stand der Forschung," in *Weisheit, Ethos und Gebot: Weisheits- und Dekalogtraditionen in der Bibel und im frühen Judentum*, Biblisch-Theologische Studien 43 (Neukirchen-Vluyn: Neukirchener Verlag, 2001), 62; Albertus van den Branden, "Le Décalogue," *BeO* 33:2 (1991): 93–124; Eduard Nielsen, *The Ten Commandments in New Perspective* (London: SCM, 1968), 131; Eckhart Otto, *Theologische Ethik des Alten Testaments*, Theologische Wissenschaft (Stuttgart: Kohlhammer, 1994), 212, 218; John Van Seters, "'Comparing Scripture with Scripture': Some Observations on the Sinai Pericope of Exodus 19–24," in *Canon, Theology and Old Testament Interpretation: Essays in Honor of Brevard S. Childs*, ed. G. M. Tucker (Philadelphia: Fortress, 1988), 111–30; Joëlle Ferry, "Le Décalogue, une loi pour l'homme?" *Transversalités* 80 (2001): 155–70; Raymond F. Collins, "Ten Commandments," *ABD* 6:384.

Whether the Exodus or Deuteronomy version came first is unclear. Arguing for the latter are Ronald E. Clements, *Old Testament Theology: A Fresh Approach* (Atlanta: John Knox, 1978), 119–20; Frank Crüsemann, *The Torah: Theology and Social History of Old Testament Law*, trans. A. W. Mahnke (Minneapolis: Fortress, 1996), 355; Ludger Schwienhorst-Schönberger, "Das Verhältnis von Dekalog und Bundesbuch," in *Die Zehn Worte: der Dekalog als Testfall der Pentateuchkritik*, ed. Michael Konkel, Christian Frevel, and Johannes Schnocks, QD 212 (Freiburg im Breisgau: Herder, 2005), 71. Many suspect a long and complicated development culminating in the present versions, including Hendrik Bosman, "Adultery, Prophetic Tradition, and the Decalogue," in *The Ten Commandments: The Reciprocity of Faithfulness*, ed. William P. Brown (Louisville: Westminster John Knox, 2004), 274; Joseph Blenkinsopp, *The Pentateuch: An Introduction to the First Five Books of the Bible*, ABRL (New York: Doubleday, 1992), 209; Frank Moore Cross, *Canaanite Myth and Hebrew Epic: Essays in the History of the Religion of Israel* (Cambridge, MA: Harvard University Press, 1973), 312.

Those who insist on the plausibility of Mosaic origin include J. Durham, *Exodus*, WBC (Waco, TX: Word, 1987), 282; J. J. Stamm, *The Ten Commandments in Recent Research*, trans. M. E. Andrew, SBT 2/2 (Naperville, IL: Allenson, 1967), 39; Kenneth A. Kitchen, *On the Reliability of the Old Testament* (Grand Rapids: Eerdmans, 2006), 287–88; Walther Eichrodt, *Theology of the Old Testament*, trans. J. A. Baker, OTL (Philadelphia: Westminster, 1961), 70–74. Those arguing for the antiquity of part of it include Cornelis Houtman, *Exodus*, trans. Sierd Woudstra, HCOT (Leuven: Peeters, 2000), 3:9; Walter J. Harrelson, *The Ten Commandments and Human Rights*, rev. ed. (Macon, GA: Mercer University Press, 1997), 35.

that interrupts the apodictic cadence. Those who favor this Ur-Decalogue fail to explain why later redactors should have tampered with the symmetry they propose. On the other hand, Werner Kessler's literary analysis of each Decalogic command leads him to conclude that the Decalogue must have arisen during the pre-Monarchic period. Not only do the lexemes and concepts fit an older period, but the blending of civil and religious concerns seems out of place for later times.[12]

Ultimately, any explanation must be held lightly. While not irrelevant to the meaning of the Decalogue, questions of composition and dating are in large part unsolvable, at least given the current state of knowledge. Since firm answers regarding these issues are elusive, the final form of the text will be our object of study. Careful attention to the way the Decalogue functions in both of its narrative settings (but especially at Sinai) will illuminate its significance for Israel's faith and life.[13]

Method and Aims

John Barton rightly affirms that each "method" of critical study offers an angle from which to view the text, and each has both benefits and liabilities.[14] For that reason, this project approaches the NC from many different angles, attempting to read *with* the grain of the text rather than against it. Linguistic (both lexical and cognitive), narrative, historical, and theological

Others deem the quest for an Ur-Decalogue hopeless. For example, Collins, "Ten Commandments," *ABD* 6:383; Umberto Cassuto, *A Commentary on the Book of Exodus*, trans. Israel Abrahams (Jerusalem: Magnes, 1967), 236. Meredith Kline (*Treaty of the Great King: The Covenant Structure of Deuteronomy: Studies and Commentary* [Grand Rapids: Eerdmans, 1963], 21) finds historical-critical proposals for a short original form of the Decalogue "unsatisfactory" because the covenantal elements that best fit the historical occasion are stripped away.

12. Kessler, "Die literarische, historische und theologische Problematik des Dekalogs," *VT* 7 (1957): 13–14.

13. I have intentionally avoided asking, "What was its role in ancient Israel?" Little information survives about the *uses* of the Decalogue in ancient Israel, though this does not prevent some from making specific claims about its liturgical origins. See, e.g., Kessler (ibid., 4), who agrees with Mowinckel that the Decalogue arose in the ancient cult for ceremonial recitation. Given the paucity of clear allusions to the Decalogue as a whole, it seems prudent to limit analysis to what we *can* know—namely, the place of the Decalogue in its current *textual* settings in Exodus and Deuteronomy at the head of the rest of Israel's laws. The Torah in its present canonical setting is the fullest expression of Israelite faith in YHWH, rooted in his concrete historical acts on their behalf. Those inclined to dismiss these accounts as fictitious can at least agree on the literary and theological significance of the texts Israel preserved and transmitted as its Scriptures. On the scarcity of allusions to the Decalogue, see Daniel I. Block, "The Decalogue in the Hebrew Scriptures," in *The Decalogue through the Centuries*, ed. Jeffrey P. Greenman and Timothy Larsen (Louisville: Westminster John Knox, 2012), 21.

14. John Barton, *Reading the Old Testament: Method in Biblical Study*, rev. ed. (Louisville, KY: Westminster John Knox, 1996), 4–6. This project has not adopted all his categories.

angles each provide important insights, facilitating a more natural and historically defensible reading.

Following the history of interpretation in ch. 2, ch. 3 explores the lexical and syntactical features of the NC in conversation with the relevant history and language of the ANE. The historical data on divine names provide a helpful context for the way the Hebrew Bible speaks of YHWH's name. Exhaustive studies of the key terms in the NC provide a basis for identifying related idioms. Chapter 4 assesses the genre of the Decalogue as the immediate literary context of the NC and its place in the overall narratives of Exodus and Deuteronomy, with special focus on the Sinai narratives. In ch. 5, these results are coordinated and discussed in light of conceptual metaphor theory with special reference to Israel's high priest as a visual lexicon of key concepts.

A fuller discussion of each method appears in the chapter where that method is employed. As a whole, the argument is cumulative rather than linear. This project considers the NC from various angles, collecting evidence and answering potential objections. I begin by demonstrating the problems with each of the other views and then build a case for the representational view by accumulating support from various modes of inquiry. The end result is an interpretation of the NC anchored in the literary, historical, and theological contexts of the Bible.

Chapter 2

A History of the Interpretation of the Name Command

> There are no three words in the Hebrew language that have a greater variety of meanings. . . . By the combination of these meanings an immense number of interpretations can be put upon the passage; and, as a matter of fact, the history of exegesis shows that nearly every possible theory has been tried at one time or another.
>
> —Lewis Paton, "The Meaning of Exodus XX. 7"

The variety of ways in which the NC has been understood throughout history is almost dizzying. At least 23 distinct interpretations of Exod 20:7 have been proposed. Most interpreters assume that the Hebrew expression נשׂא שׁם ("lift up the name") is elliptical and ultimately that it has something to do with *speaking* the name. Differences in interpretation depend on which biblical or extrabiblical passages are used to fill in the supposed omission, or ellipsis. Another factor is the interpretation of the enigmatic לשׁוא ("in vain") that stands at the end of the clause. The NC is remarkably pliable, in part because its three key words (נשׂא, שׁם, and שׁוא) exhibit such a wide range of meanings, depending on the context. As Paton noted above, the collocation of these words in the NC has produced numerous proposals for this or that elliptical or idiomatic expression.[1]

This chapter surveys these proposals, beginning with the most common (fig. 1, p. 8). Significantly, these readings of the NC cut across religious, geographic, and chronological lines. While one might trace interpretations as they developed over time, most are represented throughout history, making such an approach repetitive. Neither can these interpretations be effectively organized on the basis of religious affiliation. Jews and Christians, Catholics and Protestants, have often agreed across confessional lines even while disagreeing within their own traditions. Accordingly, this survey presents the advocates of a particular interpretation together—regardless of provenance or religion—with prominence given to those offering an extended rationale for their interpretation.

One interpreter deserves special mention at the outset as the only one to offer a full-length monograph on this command. In his published

1. While Paton exaggerated, many scholars acknowledge the ambiguity of the NC. See Lewis Paton, "The Meaning of Exodus XX. 7," *JBL* 22 (1903): 201.

Interpretive Options for the Name Command

I. Elliptical Expression
  A. You shall not lift [*your hand to*] the name
    1. You shall not swear oaths falsely
      a. by affirming an untruth
      b. by disavowing a truth
      c. by failing to keep a promise
        • to do something
        • not to do something
    2. You shall not swear oaths unnecessarily
      a. by blessing unnecessarily
      b. by affirming an obvious truth
      c. by swearing habitually
    3. You shall not swear oaths with evil intent
      a. to trick someone
      b. to do evil
      c. selfishly
    4. You shall not swear oaths by a false god
  B. You shall not lift the name [*on your lips*]
    1. You shall not say the name:
      a. presumptuously
      b. irreverently
      c. unnecessarily
      d. incorrectly
    2. You shall not use the name:
      a. to teach falsely
      b. without authorization
      c. maliciously
      d. in magic
    3. You shall not call upon:
      a. an idol in the name
      b. the name without a sacrifice
      c. the name hypocritically
  C. Some combination of the above
II. Nonelliptical Expression: You shall not bear the name in vain

Figure 1. Outline of interpretive options for the Name Command

dissertation, Thomas Elßner carefully assembles and analyses texts (both biblical and extrabiblical) that are potentially related, offering an extended rationale for his conclusion that the NC is a late post-deuteronomic (exilic or early postexilic) addition to the Decalogue. Elßner also organizes past interpreters topically, dividing between advocates of a specific, a variable, or a "deliberately abstract" prohibition.[2] While helpful in many ways, Elßner's analysis of the data is at times undependable, and he has neglected to consider some of the most important parallel passages.

The ambiguity of the NC is generally recognized, with some scholars going so far as to suggest that we cannot know with precision what it meant in its original context.[3] Herbert Huffmon argues that the Decalogue is *deliberately* ambiguous, stemming from its nature as a "foundational" law code.[4] Whether the NC is actually ambiguous or intentionally broad remains to be seen. One thing is certain: interpreters have been persistent and creative in explicating this command.

The Name Command as an Elliptical Expression

Most scholars assume the NC is elliptical in some way, though they disagree over what has been left out. לא תשׂא את־שׁם־יהוה אלהיך לשׁוא (lit., "You shall not lift up the name of Yhwh, your God, in vain") does not seem to make sense on its own. Some have proposed that the missing words are "your hand," resulting in the reading, "You shall not lift up [*your hand to*] the name of Yhwh in vain." Lifting the hand is understood as an idiom for taking an oath.[5] Others supply "to your lips," with the result, "You shall not lift up the name of Yhwh [*to your lips*] in vain," that is, *say* it for vain purposes or in a vain manner (fig. 2, p. 10).[6] Since most fail to consider the possibility that נשׂא שׁם is coherent as it stands, the strongest arguments for an elliptical interpretation will be treated first.

The decision to read the NC elliptically by inserting a word or phrase is only the beginning. Each interpretation is further differentiated from the

2. Elßner, *Das Namensmißbrauch-Verbot*, 12. His analysis of contemporary interpreters is limited to German scholarship.

3. See Moshe Weinfeld, *Deuteronomy 1–11*, AB 5 (New York: Doubleday, 1991), 278; Miller, *The Ten Commandments*, 68; Ulrich Kellermann, "Der Dekalog in den Schriften des Frühjudentums: Ein Überblick," in *Weisheit, Ethos und Gebot: Weisheits- und Dekalogtraditionen in der Bibel und im frühen Judentum*, Biblisch-Theologische Studien 43 (Neukirchen-Vluyn: Neukirchener Verlag, 2001), 167; Paul Grimley Kuntz, *The Ten Commandments in History: Mosaic Paradigms for a Well-Ordered Society*, ed. Thomas D'Evelyn, Emory University Studies in Law and Religion (Grand Rapids: Eerdmans, 2004), 6. For an especially pessimistic view, see Waldemar Janzen, *Exodus*, Believers Church Bible Commentary (Scottdale, PA: Herald, 2000), 257.

4. Herbert B. Huffmon, "The Fundamental Code Illustrated: The Third Commandment," in *The Ten Commandments: The Reciprocity of Faithfulness*, ed. William Brown (Louisville: Westminster John Knox, 2004), 205–12.

5. Raising the hand is a gesture typical of oath taking (e.g., Deut 32:40). Representatives of these views will be named below.

6. Figure 2 distinguishes between these two elliptical approaches by the use of different type (not italicized for oath taking; italicized for other types of speech). They appear together in the same text boxes based on corresponding meanings for שׁוא.

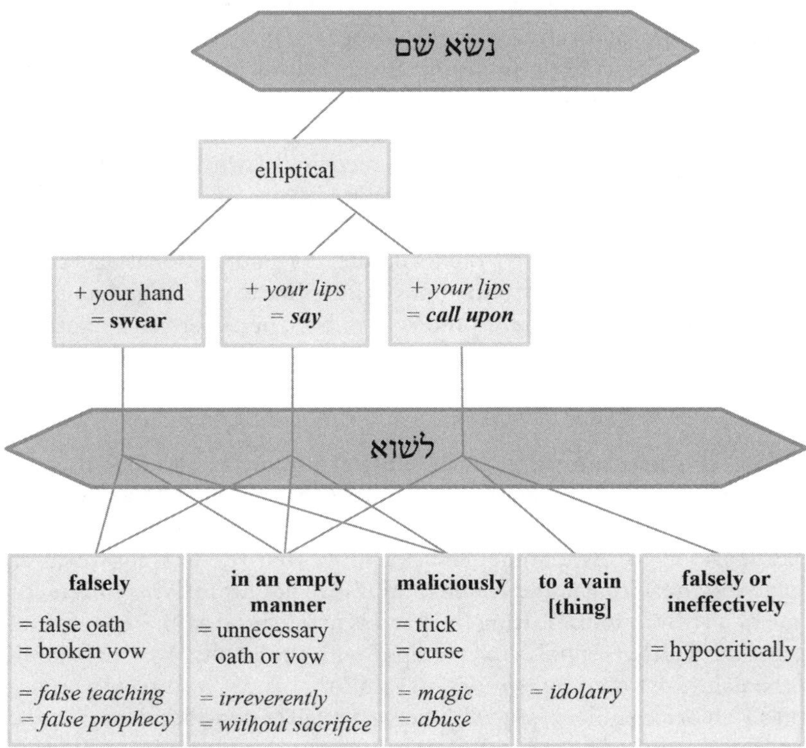

Figure 2. Elliptical interpretations of the Name Command

others by how לשׁוא is understood. It may be taken nominally ("to a vain thing") or adverbially ("vainly"), and at least three distinct adverbial senses have been proposed based on etymology and context: *empty*, *false*, or *malicious*.[7] Given its wide semantic range, שׁוא functions as a prism through which each interpretation is refracted, resulting in a wide array of interpretations (fig. 2). Now we turn to an analysis of the first elliptical possibility and its associated meanings.

You Shall Not Lift Your Hand *to the Name*

The vast majority of interpreters through the ages have thought the NC prohibits a certain kind of oath, but they support this interpretation exegetically by different means. Some supply the missing words "your hand"[8] and interpret "lifting the hand" as an idiom for taking an oath, while others

7. See *HALOT* 2:1424–26. For a full discussion of שׁוא, see pp. 47–87.

8. Recent interpreters include Timo Veijola ("Das dritte Gebot [Namenverbot] im Lichte einer ägyptischen Parallele," *ZAW* 103 [1991]: 8) and Huffmon ("The Fundamental Code Illustrated," 207), though Huffmon suggests a second verb: "You must not lift up (your hand and speak) the name of the Lord your God falsely/frivolously."

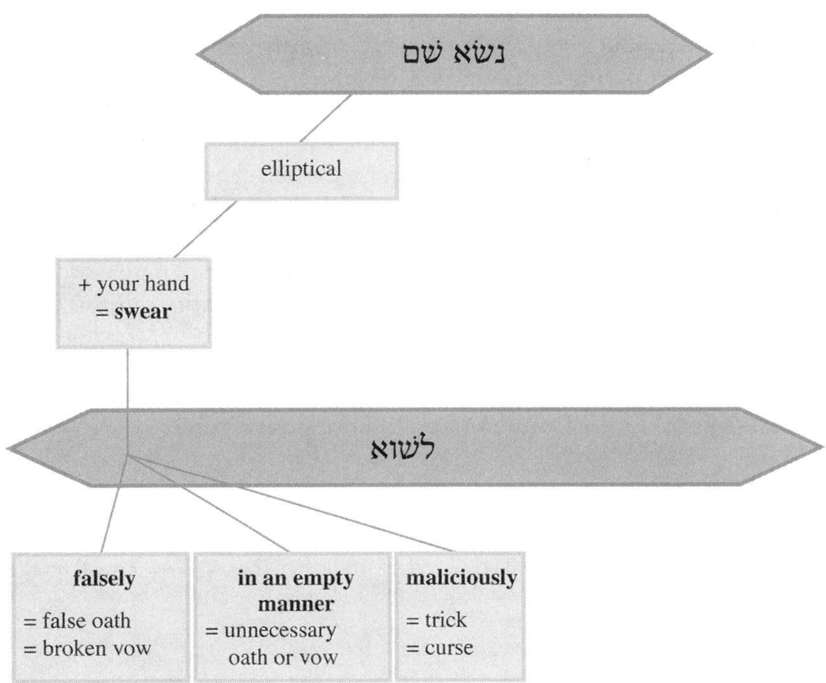

Figure 3. Elliptical interpretations of the Name Command, oaths

think of it as "you shall not lift the name . . . *to your lips*,"[9] but still see oath taking as the primary referent of the resulting metaphor. To simplify the discussion, all who advocate oath taking as the referent are grouped under this first branch of the diagram, regardless of the "missing words" they supply or whether they acknowledge the ellipsis (fig. 3).[10]

False or Unnecessary Oaths

Jewish scholars in particular have usually understood the NC to prohibit improper oaths.[11] Most have either seen these oaths as "false" or "frivolous,"

9. Notable advocates include Weinfeld, *Deuteronomy 1–11*, 278–79; Werner H. Schmidt, *Die Zehn Gebote im Rahmen alttestamentlicher Ethik*, ed. Holger Delkurt and Axel Graupner, EdF 281 (Darmstadt: Wissenschaftliche Buchgesellschaft, 1993), 80; Jeffrey Tigay, *Deuteronomy [Devarim]*, JPS Torah Commentary (Philadelphia: Jewish Publication Society, 1996), 357 n. 79; Nahum Sarna, *Exodus [Shemot]*, JPS Torah Commentary (Philadelphia: Jewish Publication Society, 1991), 111. Ramban (*Commentary on the Torah: Exodus*, trans. Charles B. Chavel [New York: Shilo, 1973], 303) opts for "voice" rather than "lips."

10. The word יד could also be nonidiomatic to indicate the gesture preceding a blessing or oath (Lev 9:22; Ps 134:2). For examples of hand-raising during oath taking where נשא is the operative verb, see Blane Conklin, *Oath Formulas in Biblical Hebrew*, LSAWS 5 (Winona Lake, IN: Eisenbrauns, 2011), 16.

11. Rashi sees a double prohibition (reckless oaths and false oaths), most likely following *Tg. Onq.*, which uses word substitution to arrive at this interpretation. For

though many other nuances have been suggested.[12] Under the reading "you shall not swear oaths . . . falsely" at least three different meanings are possible: (1) affirming an untruth,[13] (2) disavowing a truth, and (3) failing to keep a promise. The last may involve failing to do what one promised to do or doing what one promised *not* to do.[14] While in the first two cases the oath is a lie,[15] for the other the oath becomes false when subsequent actions do not fulfill a promise (unless the intention of the swearer was never to keep the oath, which makes it a lie from the beginning). Many scholars have advocated one or another of these readings, or all of them combined.[16] Still others include oath taking in a longer list of possible violations of this command.[17] An affirmation of an obvious truth might also be a "frivolous" or

discussion, see Elßner, *Das Namensmißbrauch-Verbot*, 12. Other examples include *Tg. Ps.-J.* on Deut 5:11; *Tg. Onq.* on Exod 20:7 and Deut 5:11; *Lev. Rab.* 33.6 on Lev. 25:1, 14; *Ecc. Rab.* 8.1 on Ecc 8:2; *Num. Rab.* 8.4 on Num 5:6; *y. Ber.* 1.4; *b. Pesaḥ.* 63b; *b. Šabb.* 120a. Other Jewish interpreters who read the NC as regarding oaths include Josephus, *Ant.* 3.91 (LCL 242); *Mekhilta according to Rabbi Ishmael: An Analytical Translation*, trans. Jacob Neusner, BJS 148 (Atlanta: Scholars Press, 1988), Bahodesh 7, 2:77–78; Joseph Dana, "The '*Piyyuṭ*' on the Ten Commandments Ascribed to Saadiah Gaon," *JQR* n.s. 86:3–4 (1996): 5a, 367.

12. See Veijola, "Das dritte Gebot," 14.

13. See, e.g., *Num. Rab.* 9.12 (on Num 5:14); *b. Šebu* 20b.

14. For the former, see *b. Pesaḥ.* 63b; *b. Šabb.* 32b; Ibn Ezra, *Commentary on the Pentateuch: Exodus (Shemot)*, trans. H. Norman Strickman and Arthur M. Silver (New York: Menorah, 1996), 423–24; Dana, "The '*Piyyuṭ*' on the Ten Commandments," 5a, 367; Sarna, *Exodus*, 111. For the latter (improper vows), see *b. Tem.* 3a–b and *b. Šabb.* 32b.

15. Rashi (M. Rosenbaum and A. M. Silbermann, trans., *Pentateuch with Targum Onkelos, Haphtaroth and Prayers for Sabbath and Rashi's Commentary* [London: Shapiro, Vallentine, 1948], 1:104) calls this "declaring something . . . to be different *from what it is.*"

16. Jewish scholars who speak of the NC as swearing falsely include Philo, *On the Decalogue* 7.82–95, trans. F. H. Colson, LCL 320 (Cambridge, MA: Harvard University Press; London: St. Edmundsbury, 1937), 49–55; *b. Šeb.* 20b, 38b–39b; *y. Šeb.* 3.10; *y. Ber.* 1.4; *Mekhilta according to Rabbi Ishmael*, Bahodesh 7, 78; Ramban, *Commentary on the Torah: Exodus*, 303; Benno Jacob, *The Second Book of the Bible: Exodus*, trans. Walter Jacob (Hoboken, NJ: Ktav, 1992), 558; Michael Fishbane, *Biblical Interpretation in Ancient Israel* (Oxford: Clarendon, 1988), 344; Tigay, *Deuteronomy*, 67; Sarna, *Exodus*, 111. For a helpful survey of the history of this interpretation, see James L. Kugel, *The Bible as It Was* (Cambridge, MA: Belknap, 1997), 391–93.

Other advocates include Hilaire of Poitiers, *Sur Matthieu I* 4,23, trans. Jean Doignon, SC 254 (Paris: du Cerf, 2007), 143; Cyprian, *Testimonies* 12, *ANF* 5:536; Aquinas, *ST* 2a2æ 100.11; Calvin, *Institutes,* II.8.22; ed. John T. McNeill, trans. Ford Lewis Battles, LCC 20 (Philadelphia: Westminster, 1967); *John Calvin's Sermons on the Ten Commandments*, trans. Benjamin W. Farley (Grand Rapids: Baker, 1980), 84; and more recently Schwienhorst-Schönberger, "Das Verhältnis von Dekalog und Bundesbuch," 59; William H. C. Propp, *Exodus 19–40*, AB 2A (New York: Doubleday, 2006), 174; Dominik Markl, *Der Dekalog als Verfassung des Gottesvolkes: die Brennpunkte einer narrativen Rechtshermeneutik des Pentateuch in Exodus 19–24* und Deuteronomium 5 (Freiberg: Herder, 2007), 112; Telford Work, *Deuteronomy*, BTCB (Grand Rapids: Brazos, 2009), 79.

17. Those who suggest that the command applies broadly will be treated below under the heading "all of the above."

"unnecessary" oath.[18] The apocryphal book of Sirach prohibits habitual and false swearing in the name; the statement, "the one who swears and uses names all the time will never be cleansed from sin" (ἀπὸ ἁμαρτίας οὐ μὴ καθαρισθῃ; Sir 23:9), may allude to the sanction expressed in the NC (μὴ καθαρίσῃ; LXX Exod 20:7). According to the Talmud, even an unnecessary blessing in YHWH's name was proscribed (*b. Ber.* 33a; *b. Yoma* 70a; cf. *b. Tamid* 33b).

Malicious Oaths

Based on proposed Arabic (*sâʾa* = "to be bad") and Ethiopic (*săyĕʾ* = "crime") cognates, some suggest a malicious sense for שׁוא.[19] On this basis, they claim the NC prohibits swearing oaths *with evil intent*, that is, to trick someone, to promise to do evil, or to be selfish.[20] Alternatively, J. A. Motyer treats שׁוא as a noun meaning "idol," arguing that the command warns against swearing oaths "by a false god."[21] The inadequacies of these readings will be explored below.

The Evidence for Oaths: ANE Parallels

The case for oath taking has been founded on two major lines of evidence: ANE parallels and biblical parallels. Timo Veijola notes an Egyptian votive stela dating to the 13th century BCE that preserves the prayer of a workman named Neferʾabu who "swore falsely" and "mispronounced" the name of his god, Ptah (see table 1, p. 14). For this grave sin, Neferʾabu was blinded, either literally or figuratively.[22] Like the NC, mistreatment of

18. See Josephus, *Ant.* 3.91 (LCL 242); Clement of Alexandria, *Paedagogus* 3.79.1, trans. Claude Modésert and Chantal Matray, SC 158 (Paris: du Cerf, 2008), 279, line 28; Ramban, *Commentary on the Torah: Exodus*, 303; Maimonides, *Sefer Ha-Mitzvoth of Maimonides*, trans. Charles B. Chavel (New York: Soncino, 1967), 60; Calvin *Harm. Pent. 2*, *CC* 2:408; Calvin, *John Calvin's Sermons on the Ten Commandments*, 84–85; Kellermann, "Tora für die Völker," 180; John J. Collins, *Introduction to the Hebrew Bible* (Minneapolis: Fortress, 2004), 129.

19. The principal similarities between these words and שׁוא consist of an s-class consonant in first position and a glottal stop in last position (*hamza* in Arabic, *ʾalep* in Hebrew, and *alf* in Ethiopic). The bilateral Old South Arabic root took a medial ו in Hebrew and a medial *jaman* (= *yod*) in Ethiopic. For brief discussions, see Sigmund Mowinckel, *Psalmenstudien I* (Amsterdam: Schippers, 1961), 56; and Coffin, "The Third Commandment," 168. M. A. Klopfenstein (*Die Lüge nach dem Alten Testament* [Zürich: Gotthelf, 1964], 315) regards the etymological relationship with Arabic and Ethiopic as certain, though he erroneously transcribes the Arabic as *sāʿa*, with an *ʿain* rather than *ʾalif*.

20. On tricky oaths, see *b. ʿAbod. Zar.* 28a and *b. Yoma* 84a. I discuss imprecatory curses below. For לשׁוא as "selfishly," see George A. F. Knight, *Theology as Narration: A Commentary on the Book of Exodus* (Edinburgh: Handsel, 1976), 137.

21. J. A. Motyer, *The Message of Exodus: The Days of Our Pilgrimage* (Downers Grove, IL: InterVarsity, 2005), 224.

22. Veijola, "Das dritte Gebot," 4–5. Also noted by Schmidt, *Die Zehn Gebote*, 81. For an English translation, see Elizabeth Frood, *Biographical Texts from Ramessid Egypt*, SBLWAW 26 (Atlanta: SBL, 2007), 223–25. The hieroglyphic text appears as no. 589 in T. G. H. James, *Hieroglyphic Texts from Egyptian Stelae, etc.*, part 9 (London: Trustees of the British Museum, 1970), Plate 31, 36 and 31A.

Table 1. ANE Texts Related to False or Frivolous Oaths

Provenance	*Text*	*Transliteration*	*Translation*
13th c. BCE Egypt	Nefer'abu Stela from Deir El-Medina[23]	*ink s ʿrḳ m ʿḏꜣ n Ptḥ . . . dm* ***rn*** *n Ptḥ m ʿḏꜣ*	I am a man who swore **falsely** by Ptah. . . . [Stop] pronouncing the **name** of Ptah **falsely**.
12th c. BCE Assyria	Middle Assyrian Palace Decree, §10	***šu[m il]e ana masikte*** *taz= zakrūni*	**blasphemously** swear by the **name of the god**
12th c. BCE Assyria	Middle Assyrian Palace Decree, §11	***ana la kitte . . . šu]m ile*** *lu la izakkar*	**not in truth** . . . he shall not swear by the **name of the god**.
10th–7th c. BCE Assyria	*Dinger.šà.dib.ba* Incantations, 1.24[24]	*niš-ka kab-tu* ***qal-liš*** *[a]z-za-kar*	a solemn oath I **lightly** uttered/swore
10th–7th c. BCE Sumeria	*Dinger.šà.dib.ba* Incantations, 1.87[25]	*[k]i-ma ša nīš*(mu) ***ili****-šú kab-tu* ***q[à-liš]*** *iz-ku-ru*	like the one who **lightly** swore a solemn oath by his **god**
10th–7th c. BCE Assyria	*Dinger.šà.dib.ba*, "Eršaḫunga Prayer," 12[26]	*Ki-ma šá ni-iš* ***ili****-šú* ***qal-liš*** *[iz-ku-ru*	as from one who **lightly** swore an oath by his **god**
14th–12th c. BCE Mesopotamia	"Poem of the Righteous Sufferer," 2.21–22[27]	*niš* ***ili****-šú kab-ti* ***qal-liš*** *iz-kur*	he **lightly** swore a solemn oath by his **god**

a god's name resulted in punishment. Furthermore, the syntactical structure of Nefer'abu's prayer is comparable to the NC (neutral transitive verb + direct object ["name"] + divine name + pejorative prepositional phrase). However, aside from a concern with the divine name, this syntactical shell lacks lexico-semantic parallels.[28] Nefer-abu's prayer employs a *verbum dicendi* that relates his offense specifically to swearing, while the NC is worded more generally, using a verb that does not normally denote speaking.[29]

23. Bibliography on the first three texts is listed above. All transliterations appear in the form presented by the source, with the exception of bold text, which highlights key words relevant for this discussion.

24. Lambert, "*Dinger.šà.dib.ba* Incantations," 274. Most manuscripts were found in Assyria but may be translations of older Sumerian texts. See *ATSHB*, 102. See also Alan Lenzi, ed., *Reading Akkadian Prayers and Hymns*, ANEM 3 (Atlanta: SBL, 2011), 434–35, 442–43, where this line reads, "I repeatedly swore a solemn oath on your life in vain."

25. Lambert, "*Dinger.šà.dib.ba* Incantations," 278. This text reflects an Akkadian translation of a Sumerian original. See discussion in ibid., 270.

26. Ibid., 289.

27. Idem, *Babylonian Wisdom Literature*, 39. For an alternate English translation, see "The Poem of the Righteous Sufferer," trans. Benjamin R. Foster, *COS* 1.153:488.

28. For further discussion, see Elßner, *Das Namensmißbrauch-Verbot*, 168.

29. *Verbum dicendi* is Elßner's term of choice for speech-related verbs.

Huffmon adduces several similar examples from ancient Mesopotamia in which people are said to have "sworn frivolously" by their gods (table 1).[30] Elßner notes at least two others.[31] One text deals with harem laws of the Assyrian court, assigning the death penalty to a quarreling woman who swears blasphemously in the name of god. Four other texts represent prayers to an angry god, protesting innocence or ignorance of sin. A Sumerian proverb makes a similar statement. Like Nefer'abu's prayer, the problem with these so-called parallels is that the syntactical similarities with the NC veil the virtual absence of lexical cognates (aside from the "name of god" in the harem text, and "god" in most of the other examples), such as the Egyptian *šw*. In principle, the Egyptian *cḏ*$_3$ ("falsely") or the Akkadian *qalliš* ("lightly") or *ana la kitte* ("not in truth") might serve as a functional cognate to the Hebrew שׁוא. However, each of these texts clearly refers to speech, the "false" or "frivolous" words are explicitly oaths, and none uses a verbal idiom analogous to נשׂא שׁם to express this.[32] Since the chief ambiguity of the NC is the meaning of the phrase נשׂא שׁם, none of these texts is able to clarify its meaning, other than to illustrate a shared cognitive world in which divine names deserved respect.

We can only call these parallel texts if we first establish on other grounds that the expression נשׂא שׁם ("lift up the name") in the NC means "to swear an oath." If so, these ANE texts would be very close conceptually.

The Evidence for Oaths: Biblical Parallels

In order to establish that נשׂא שׁם means "to swear an oath," many interpreters appeal to potential parallels in the Hebrew Bible. Most commonly cited are Lev 19:12, Exod 23:1, Pss 16:4 and 24:4, Hos 4:2, Zech 5:3–4, and Jer 7:9.[33] I will examine each of these and evaluate their suitability as parallels to the NC, beginning with Lev 19:12.

Leviticus 19:12

ולא־תשׁבעו בשׁמי לשׁקר	And you shall not swear by my name falsely
וחללת את־שׁם אלהיך	and [thereby] profane the name of your God.
אני יהוה	I am YHWH.

30. Huffmon, "The Fundamental Code Illustrated," 209. For texts, see W. G. Lambert, "*Dinger.šà.dib.ba* Incantations," *JNES* 33:3 (1974): 274.24, 278.87, 289.12; idem, *Babylonian Wisdom Literature* (Oxford: Clarendon, 1960), 39.21–22.

31. Elßner, *Das Namensmißbrauch-Verbot*, 155–69.

32. Elßner (*Das Namensmißbrauch-Verbot*, 168, 283) suggests that the Egyptian text is syntactically parallel to the NC but admits that the former contains a *verbum dicendi* while the latter does not. For other examples of divine names in oaths, see Bendt Alster, "The Instructions of Urninurta and Related Compositions," *Orientalia* 60 (1991): 150; lines 19, 22–23, 32; Itamar Singer, *Hittite Prayers*, SBLWAW 11 (Atlanta: SBL, 2002), 32, no. 4a (CTH 373), §3; 43, no. 5 (CTH 375), §29–30; Erica Reiner, *Šurpu: A Collection of Sumerian and Akkadian Incantations*, AfO 11 (Osnabrück: Biblio, 1970), 20, line 44; 27–28, line 87; 42, line 60.

33. Less frequently cited are Num 14:30; Deut 5:20; 1 Kgs 8:31; 2 Sam 14:11; Isa 48:1; 59:4; Hos 10:4; Ps 15:3; 59:13; 139:20; 144:8; and Prov 30:9.

Leviticus 19:12 prohibits false swearing in YHWH's name. It mirrors the NC syntactically[34] and shares a similar context: laws communicated to Israel by Moses at Sinai (Lev 19:1), including several that recapitulate Decalogic commands.[35] Since Lev 19:12 indicates that YHWH's name is at stake, the impulse to connect it with the NC is natural.[36] However, apparent similarities between Lev 19 and the Decalogue should not blind us to their unique emphases. Leviticus 19:12 explicitly and unambiguously condemns false oaths with the verb שׁבע ("to swear an oath")[37] and the phrase לשׁקר ("falsely"). Since neither שׁבע nor שׁקר appears in the NC, we would need to establish on other grounds that the NC concerns "false swearing."[38]

Exodus 23:1

לא תשׂא שׁמע שׁוא	You shall not bear a false report.
אל־תשת ידך עם־רשׁע	You shall not set your hand with the wicked
להית עד חמס	to become a malicious witness.

At first glance, Exod 23:1 appears a more likely parallel to the NC. As part of the Book of the Covenant given at Sinai, it shares the lexemes נשׂא and שׁוא with the NC, as well as the negative particle לא. Though it lacks שׁם, שׁמע ("report" or "hearsay") is linked assonantally and could echo the NC through an intertextual play on words.[39] This possibility is reinforced by syntax that mimics an abbreviated NC.[40] However, unlike the NC, the center of gravity for Exod 23:1 rests on interpersonal relationships and lacks

34. Negative particle לא + 2mp verb + שׁם + prepositional phrase with ל prefix.

35. The commands have variations in wording but cover many of the same issues: honor parents and observe Sabbaths (v. 3), no idols (v. 4), no stealing or deception (v. 11), no slander (v. 16), no endangering a neighbor's life (v. 16).

36. Benjamin Kilchör (*Mosetora und Jahwetora: Das Verhältnis von Deuteronomium 12–26 zu Exodus, Levitikus und Numeri*, BZABR 21 [Wiesbaden: Harrassowitz, 2015], 56) is among those who associate the NC with Lev 19:12. However, he later demonstrates that the NC concerns far more than oral invocation of YHWH's name (ibid., 106). Unfortunately, his vague translation of נשׂא ("mißbrauchen"; ibid., 96) obscures this conclusion.

37. LXX manuscripts preserve several variants for ὀμεῖσθε (= שׁבע) regarding theft rather than swearing (John William Wevers, ed., *Leviticus*, Septuaginta: Vetus Testamentum Graecum 2/2 [Göttingen: Vandenhoeck & Ruprecht, 1986], 212).

38. We might conclude preliminarily that Lev 19:12 and the NC are related, in that both concern proper use of YHWH's name, but that the NC applies more broadly. Milgrom (*Leviticus 17–22*, AB 3A [New York: Doubleday, 2000], 1634) agrees that Lev 19:12 is "not equivalent" to the NC but concerns a particular violation of it. He suggests (ibid., 1602) that Leviticus disconnects this statement from those alluding to other Decalogic commands (vv. 3–4) in order to facilitate this application. The link between theft and false oaths in vv. 11–12 suggests the influence of Lev 5:21–24[6:2–5], where the two misdeeds are also linked. However, see Richard Averbeck, "אָשָׁם," in *NIDOTTE* 1:560.

39. The Hebrew text appears stable here (*BHS*). Note the phonological parallelism in the first two lines of Exod 23:1: אל־תשת exhibits a metathesis of לא תשׂא, while עם־רשׁע echoes שׁמע שׁוא. Word choice could have been influenced by sound pairing.

40. Negative particle לא + *qal* imperfect 2ms of נשׂא (with imperatival force) + noun direct object. Exodus 23:1 lacks the direct object marker (את) as well as the prefixed

a Godward focus (cf. Exod 22:27[28]). Instead of "the name of YHWH, your God," the direct object in Exod 23:1 is "a false report"; the name of God does not seem to be at stake.[41] Interestingly, LXX Exod 23:1 renders נשׂא as παραδέξῃ, meaning "receive" or "accept." If this translation is accurate, then the prohibition is not to *listen to* unfounded rumors.[42] This interpretation fits the contextual warning not to "pervert justice" by joining wicked people against the innocent or accepting bribes (23:2–8). Exodus 23:1 therefore provides a closer semantic parallel to the command against false witness (20:16) than to the NC.[43]

Psalm 16:4

ירבו עצבותם אחר מהרו	They multiply their pains, exchange other [gods],[44]
בל־אסיך נסכיהם מדם	I will not pour out their drink offerings of blood,[45]
ובל־אשׂא את־שׁמותם על־שׂפתי	nor will I lift up their names upon my lips.

The collocation of the key lexemes נשׂא and שׁם in this psalm invites comparison with the NC. The structure of the verse is also remarkably similar: a negated form of נשׂא + direct object marker את + a form of שׁם + a prepositional phrase. Given these rare syntactical and lexical parallels with the NC, some interpreters posit that Ps 16:4 clarifies what is elliptical in the NC by specifying that the names are carried on the lips, thereby proscribing a speech-related offense.[46] Although Ps 16:4 does not explicitly mention swearing, some further suggest that the expression "lift up their

preposition ל. As a result, שׁוא appears as a noun construct with the direct object rather than the object of a preposition functioning adverbially, as in the NC.

41. For discussion of the *Sitz im Leben*, see Propp, *Exodus 19–40*, 273.

42. See LXX, *Tgs.*, *Mek. kaspāʾ* 2 and *b. Pesaḥ* 118a (ibid.).

43. The potential allusion to the NC may emphasize that responsibility for a neighbor's reputation (Exod 20:15; 23:1) is analogous to the charge not to misrepresent YHWH (Exod 20:7). However, neither passage explicitly concerns oaths.

44. Rashi (Mayer I. Gruber, *Rashi's Commentary on Psalms*, BRLJ 18 [Boston: Brill, 2004], 226) translates, "May there increase the sorrows of those who are disloyal to You, [and] who are zealous in and devoted to the service of another god." Charles Briggs (*A Critical and Exegetical Commentary on the Book of Psalms*, ICC [Edinburgh: T&T Clark, 1906], 1:119–20) suggests, "They shall multiply their sorrows, who hurry backwards." He prefers to think of these apostate worshipers as the antecedent of "their names." The psalmist refuses to have anything to do with them.

45. This verse is supremely difficult to translate, as all commentators acknowledge. For example, Erhard Gerstenberger, *Psalms: Part 1 with an Introduction to Cultic Poetry*, FOTL 14 (Grand Rapids: Eerdmans, 1988), 89. With characteristic creativity, Mitchell Dahood (*Psalms I: 1–50*, AB [Garden City, NY: Doubleday, 1965], 88) suggests that מדם consists of a partitive followed by a "Northern contracted dual for 'hands'" to yield "I surely will not pour libations to them from my hands." However, Hans-Joachim Kraus (*Psalms 1–59*, CC [Minneapolis: Fortress, 1993], 237) points out that pagan blood rituals are known to us from Isa 66:3, so we need not seek emendation.

46. Elßner (*Das Namensmißbrauch-Verbot*, 42, 277) notes נשׂא is not ingressive but refers to the whole utterance, unlike other occasions in which נשׂא is speech-related.

names upon my lips" is metonymical for taking an oath in the names of other gods.[47]

However, divine names were invoked for a wide variety of purposes, not just swearing (see Josh 23:7). Furthermore, the verb נשׂא is capable of a variety of senses when used idiomatically. Sometimes the same collocation is capable of vastly different meanings.[48] Context is key to determining meaning. In Ps 16:4b, a pagan cultic ritual seems to be in view.[49] The psalmist seeks to identify with faithful worshipers (v. 3) while dissociating from the apostate (v. 4).[50] In this context, limitation to oaths demands stronger justification. Neither can we rationalize limiting the NC to speech in general on the basis of this passage.[51] Psalm 16 is a poetic text far removed from the Sinai narratives, which mitigates its usefulness as a parallel.[52]

Psalm 24:4

נקי כפים	One with innocent hands
ובר־לבב	and a pure heart,
אשר לא־נשׂא לשׁוא נפשׁי	who does not lift up my soul[53] in vain
ולא נשׁבע למרמה	and does not swear deceitfully.

On the other hand, Ps 24:4 may justify a limitation to false oaths. The description of the righteous supplicant seems to echo the NC with the collocation of לא, נשׂא and לשׁוא, and supplies a parallel line describing the

47. See Markl, *Der Dekalog als Verfassung des Gottesvolkes*, 111.

48. An extreme example, נשׂא ראשׁ (Gen 40:13, 19) can mean "to reinstate" or "to behead"!

49. See Kraus, *Psalms 1–59*, 235. Gerstenberger (*Psalms: Part 1*, XIV:91) concludes it is a "loyal decision against idolatry."

50. For discussion, see Nancy deClaissé-Walford, Rolf A. Jacobson, and Beth LaNeel Tanner, *The Book of Psalms*, NICOT (Grand Rapids: Eerdmans, 2014), 179.

51. For discussion, see below, p. 23.

52. Another barrier to comparison is that the pejorative connotation of the phrase נשׂא שׁם in the NC is dependent on שׁוא, which is invariably negative. Psalm 16:4 lacks a marker indicating that the speech act is inherently pejorative. The problem the psalmist seeks to avoid is speaking the names at all, thereby calling them to remembrance. In that case, a parallel with the NC is more difficult to understand; what would it mean to pronounce Yhwh's name, or call him to remembrance לשׁוא?

53. This translation follows the *kethib* reading of BHS (נפשׁי), but a number of manuscripts prefer נפשׁו ("his soul"). If the latter is accepted, then Ps 24:4 may describe the righteous supplicant as one who does not appeal to Yhwh in an empty manner ("lift up his [own] soul in vain"; cf. Ps 25:1). Any connection with the NC would then be remote. However, if Yhwh is taken to be the speaker in v. 4, responding to the liturgical question of v. 3, then נפשׁי is a poetic pronoun of self-reference by Yhwh (cf. Lev 26:11; Isa 1:14; Ezek 23:18). A third voice responds in v. 6b, addressing Yhwh directly, which implies his participation. Though שׁם does not appear in v. 4 and נפשׁ is not strictly a synonym of שׁם , both words can function metonymically to refer to Yhwh (e.g., Deut 28:58; Isa 30:27). Craig Broyles (*Psalms*, NIBCOT [Peabody, MA: Hendrickson, 1999], 132) concurs that נפשׁי is the correct reading in light of the parallel with the NC. Contra Elßner, *Das Namensmißbrauch-Verbot*, 110.

righteous as one who does not "swear deceitfully."[54] For many, this pairing provides sufficient evidence to argue that the NC also prohibits false swearing.[55] However, the case for synonymous parallelism demands reexamination. Psalm 24:4 consists of two pairs of lines, each answering the questions, "Who may go up on the mountain of YHWH? And who may stand in the place of his holiness?" (v. 3). The first two bicola are cast in precise grammatical parallelism, each focusing on one body part modified by one adjective.[56] The last two lines are longer, consisting of a negative particle + verb + adverb, and has seven syllables. *Structurally* and *grammatically*, the AA'BB' pattern is clear, but this does not mean that lines B and B' are *semantically* parallel.[57] Our interpretive work does not end when we identify parallel lines; it begins there, as we wrestle with their interplay.

In the case of Ps 24:4, lines A and A′ are related, but not identical. The righteous are characterized by "innocent hands" (signifying righteous *behavior*) as well as by "purity of heart" (signifying righteous *intentions*).[58] Both inwardly and outwardly the righteous are free from hypocrisy.[59] Perhaps line 3 further describes the results of inner purity by describing the righteous as

---

54. Both LXX Ps 24:4 and LXX NC employ ἐπὶ ματαίῳ, found nowhere else in the LXX, to translate לשוא. Both passages also contain forms of καθαρὸς and λαμβάνω. While these similarities cannot prove a relationship between them, they point to the possibility of a history of reading them together. See Elßner, *Das Namensmißbrauch-Verbot*, 110. Others who argue for a relationship between Ps 24:4 and the NC include Rolf Rendtorff, *The Canonical Hebrew Bible: A Theology of the Old Testament*, trans. David E. Orton, TBS 7 (Leiden: Deo, 2005), 487; J. Clinton McCann, "The Book of Psalms," in *NIB* 4:773; A. Anderson, *The Book of Psalms: Psalms (1–72)*, NCBC (Grand Rapids: Eerdmans, 1981), 1:203; Avrohom Chaim Feuer, *Sēfer Tehillîm: A New Translation with a Commentary Anthologized from Talmudic, Midrashic and Rabbinic Sources* (Brooklyn: Mesorah, 1995), 299.

55. For example, M. R. Lehmann, "Biblical Oaths," *ZAW* 81 (1969): 80; Herbert Chanan Brichto, *The Problem of "Curse" in the Hebrew Bible*, JBL Monograph 13 (Philadelphia: SBL, 1963), 65; Schmidt, *Die Zehn Gebote*, 81; David Stec, ed., *The Targum of Psalms*, ArBib 16 (Collegeville, MN: Liturgical Press, 2004), 62 n. 3; Propp, *Exodus 19–40*, 174.

56. Cf. David Hirsch and Nehama Aschkenasy, "Translatable Structure, Untranslatable Poem: Psalm 24," *Modern Language Studies* 12:4 (1982): 26.

57. On the dynamic function of parallelism, see James Kugel, *The Idea of Biblical Poetry: Parallelism and Its History* (Baltimore: Johns Hopkins University Press, 1998), 52; Adele Berlin, *The Dynamics of Biblical Parallelism*, rev. ed. (Grand Rapids: Eerdmans, 2008), 135. Structurally parallel lines are not necessarily semantically parallel. Grammatically related lines provoke deeper thought about the dynamics of their semantic relationship. See also Robert Alter, *The Art of Biblical Poetry* (New York: Basic Books, 1985), 9–10; Knut Martin Heim, *Poetic Imagination in Proverbs: Variant Repetitions and the Nature of Poetry*, BBRSup 4 (Winona Lake, IN: Eisenbrauns, 2013), 27.

58. Among those who have noted these complementary referents is Christopher Wright, *Old Testament Ethics for the People of God* (Downers Grove, IL: IVP Academic, 2004), 376. Neither בר nor נקי connotes ritual purity; the concern is moral. For discussion, see deClaissé-Walford, Jacobson, and Tanner, *Psalms*, 250.

59. See also Rodney K. Duke, "Form and Meaning: Multi-layered Balanced Thought Structures in Psalm 24:4," *TynBul* 62:2 (2011): 215–32.

"loyal to God," while line 4 indicates a neighborly disposition: the righteous have "no intention of harming or misleading their neighbor."[60] Semantically, this interpretation results in an ABB′A′ chiasm. The nature of this parallel should caution us against reading the meaning of line 4 back into line 3, as many have done.[61] Psalm 24:4 does not prove that the NC prohibits false oaths. We must decide on other grounds what it means to "lift a name" or "lift a soul."[62]

Hosea 4:2

אלה וכחש ורצח וגנב ונאף	Cursing and lying and murder and stealing and adultery
פרצו ודמים בדמים נגעו׃	They break through and bloodshed follows bloodshed.

Hosea 4:2 lists five violations of covenant faithfulness (see 4:1), all of which relate to the neighbor: cursing, lying, murder, stealing, and adultery. The latter three use the same lexemes as the Decalogue, though in a different order, while אלה ("cursing") and כחש ("lying") are unique.[63] Given the potential that Hos 4:2 echoes the Decalogue, it is fair to ask whether either of these unique terms alludes to the NC. In principle, אלה ("cursing") could relate to the NC, but it offers no direct links.[64] As an objectionable speech-act, אלה is most likely a curse pronounced on a neighbor without warrant (see, e.g., Ps 10:7; 1 Sam 14:24), or a binding agreement made under pretense (see Hos 10:4). Here, the association with lying (4:2) and emptiness (10:4) suggests that it could involve false testimony under oath against someone (cf. Lev 5:1), making it probable that the command against false witness is in view (Exod 20:16; Deut 5:20).[65] Hosea 4:2 offers no decisive gloss for the NC.

60. Broyles, *Psalms*, 129.

61. Some argue that נשׂא ("lift up") is a synonym for שׁבע ("swear"). For example, Lehmann, "Biblical Oaths," 80; John Currid, *A Study Commentary on Exodus*, vol. 2: *Exodus 19–40*, EPSC (Webster, NY: Evangelical, 2000), 40; Thomas B. Dozeman, *Commentary on Exodus*, ECC (Grand Rapids: Eerdmans, 2009), 487–88; *b. Ḥag* 14a. However, even if Ps 24:4 echoes the NC, the parallel lines describe two *different* qualities of the righteous supplicant, leaving no reason to equate נשׂא and שׁבע.

62. The righteous either do not exalt YHWH falsely in worship (cf. Ps 25:1) or they do not bear him before others hypocritically. For a defense of the latter option, see de-Claissé-Walford, Jacobson, and Tanner, *Psalms*, 250–51.

63. Murder, stealing, and adultery (ורצח וגנב ונאף) correspond lexically to the three shortest decalogic commands, though the order is different; adultery precedes stealing in the Decalogue (לא תרצח, לא תנאף, and לא תגנב). Hosea's order is both unique and stable in the MSS. See Joseph Ziegler, *Duodecim prophetae*, Septuaginta: Vetus Testamentum Graecum 13 (Göttingen: Vandenhoeck & Ruprecht, 1984), 153–54.

64. In the Hebrew Bible, אלה typically refers to a curse resulting from breach of a covenant agreement (Isa 24:6; Jer 23:10). However, sometimes the covenant itself is called an אלה by way of synecdoche (Gen 26:28; Ezek 16:59), as is an adjuration to testify in a legal setting (Lev 5:1; Prov 29:24), because both are accompanied by a curse.

65. The Exodus version of the command condemns falsehood (שׁקר), while in Deuteronomy the witness is merely "empty" (שׁוא; cf. Hos 10:4).

Zechariah 5:4a

הוצאתיה [האלה]	"I will make [the curse] go forth,"
נאם יהוה צבאות	declares YHWH of hosts.
ובאה אל־בית הגנב	"And it will enter the house of the one stealing
ואל־בית הנשבע בשמי לשקר	and the house of the one swearing falsely by my name."

In Zech 5:4, a curse (אלה; cf. Hos 4:2) resulting from covenant disobedience will destroy those who steal or "swear falsely by my name" (הנשבע בשמי לשקר).[66] While YHWH's "name" may seem reminiscent of the NC, this is a standard oath formula (cf. Deut 6:13; Isa 48:1) and therefore suffers from the same problems as the other supposed parallels.[67]

Jeremiah 7:9–10

הגנב רצח ונאף	"Will you steal, murder, and commit adultery,
והשבע לשקר וקטר לבעל	and swear falsely, and burn incense to Baʿal
והלך אחרי אלהים אחרים	and walk after other gods
אשר לא־ידעתם:	whom you have not known,
ובאתם ועמדתם לפני בבית הזה	then come and stand before me in this house
אשר נקרא־שמי עליו	over which my name has been proclaimed,[68]
ואמרתם נצלנו	and say, 'We are delivered!'—
למען עשות את כל־התועבות האלה:	in order to do all these abominations?"

Jeremiah 7:9 condemns a list of crimes similar to Hos 4:2 (theft, murder, adultery, and false swearing), with the addition of idolatrous worship.[69]

---

66. Among those who see here a clear allusion to the NC is Thomas McComiskey, "Zechariah," in *The Minor Prophets: An Exegetical and Expository Commentary*, ed. Thomas McComiskey (Grand Rapids: Baker Academic, 2009), 1095. Contra Elßner (*Das Namensmißbrauch-Verbot*, 139–40), who says the two lack shared vocabulary or concerns.

67. Deuteronomy 6:13 reads ובשמו תשבע, clarifying that oaths are to be taken "by (means of) his name" (cf. 10:20). Here, the prefix ב is instrumental, as in Lev 19:12; Deut 10:20; 1 Sam 20:42; Isa 48:1; Jer 12:16; Zech 5:3–4. See *DCH* 8:241. To take an oath by the name of YHWH is to call on him as a witness. YHWH's שם is not the only guarantor of an oath in the Hebrew Bible. Oaths are also sworn by YHWH directly (e.g., Josh 2:12), by אלהים (e.g., Gen 21:23), and by the "life of the eternal one" (בחי העולם; Dan 12:7). On oath formulas, see Conklin, *Oath Formulas*.

Advocates of the "false swearing" view also assume שוא ("vain") and שקר ("false") are interchangeable. They usually support this lexical claim by comparing both versions of the command against false witness; while Exod 20:16 reads שקר, Deut 5:20 reads שוא. For example, Veijola, "Das dritte Gebot," 8. I discuss שוא further in ch. 3.

68. I justify this translation below.

69. The order of violations in MT Jer 7:9 (theft, murder, adultery) is unique, departing from virtually every other known list of Decalogic prohibitions, with the exception of a single Greek MS 84 of Exodus. See John William Wevers, ed., *Exodus*, Septuaginta: Vetus Testamentum Graecum 2/1 (Göttingen: Vandenhoeck & Ruprecht, 1991), 243. However, most MSS of LXX Jer 7:9 (except for Origen's Syrohexaplaric recension and the Lucianic recension) correct to the order of the MT Decalogue. See Joseph Ziegler, ed., *Jeremias, Baruch, Threni, Epistula Jeremiae*, 2nd ed., Septuaginta: Vetus Testamentum Graecum 15 (Göttingen: Vandenhoeck & Ruprecht, 1976), 184. Perhaps Greek MS 84 offers a witness to the Vorlage known by Jeremiah.

Jeremiah's concern was religious hypocrisy: the Israelites regularly violated covenant stipulations, all the while assuming that YHWH's temple guaranteed indemnity. The order of these crimes in MT Jer 7:9 differs from the MT Decalogue (theft is moved from third to first place). However, in LXX Jer 7:9, the order has been adjusted to mimic the MT Decalogue (murder, adultery, theft, unjust swearing). However, "swearing" remains in fourth position, suggesting a possible correspondence to the command against false witness rather than the NC. This impression is bolstered by other biblical passages where murder, adultery, and theft are mentioned, followed by false witness (cf. Matt 19:18; Mark 10:19).[70] Furthermore, both MT Jer 7:9 and Exod 20:16 use the adjective שקר to describe the objectionable speech. Therefore, Jeremiah's "false swearing" likely echoes the command against false witness, rather than the NC.

Although oath-related interpretations of the NC are common, the approach is problematic. Without unambiguous support from the passages usually cited (Lev 19:12, Exod 23:1, Pss 16:4 and 24:4, Hos 4:2, Jer 7:9, or Zech 5:3–4), the exegetical argument for oath taking seems tenuous. To interpret the NC as prohibiting "false swearing," interpreters must conclude that נשׂא שׁם is an elliptical expression or an idiom that refers to taking oaths. If נשׂא שׁם was an idiom, we would expect to see it in oath-taking contexts. However, neither the Hebrew Bible nor other ANE texts provide any clear examples. If the statement had intended to prohibit inappropriate oaths, it could have been expressed more transparently, as, for example, in Lev 19:12. Furthermore, the oath-taking interpretation of the NC creates a possible contradiction with Lev 5:20–26[6:1–7], which explicitly provides acquittal for those who swear falsely.[71] In the NC, acquittal is expressly denied.

Other Problems with Oaths

The NC also poses a syntactical problem for the oath-taking view. To disambiguate the allegedly elliptical expression, interpreters supply an object such as יד ("hand") for the verb נשׂא. However, נשׂא already has a marked direct object, את־שׁם־יהוה. To supply another object one must disconnect את from שׁם and make שׁם the object of a missing preposition, without which the sentence is unintelligible ("You shall not lift up *the hand* [to/in] the name"). This solution is far more complicated than the representational reading proposed here.[72]

In addition to these lexical and syntactical issues, the oath-taking view is difficult contextually. It overlooks the wide range of practices associated with YHWH's "name" in the Sinai narratives, as well as the rest of the He-

70. Luke 18:20 corroborates the order of LXX Deuteronomy Decalogue as well.

71. Victor P. Hamilton, *Exodus: An Exegetical Commentary* (Grand Rapids: Baker Academic, 2011), 335.

72. Supplying "your lips" rather than "your hand" avoids the syntactical problem just noted because the addition is an indirect rather than direct object. However, it raises other problems.

brew Bible.[73] Furthermore, the prophets implicate a wide range of objectionable behavior, not just false swearing, when they decry the profanation of the name.[74]

In sum, exegetical support for the oath-taking interpretation of the NC is weak.[75] Those who interpret it as an elliptical expression referring to oaths often appeal to supposed ANE or biblical parallels, but these are only legitimate parallels if one first establishes that נשׂא שׁם refers to oaths. While this interpretation is possible, the oath-taking view overlooks the most straightforward meaning of the expression and the closest lexical parallels.[76]

You Shall Not Say the Name

Nonpronunciation

Some who see a broader frame of reference for the NC posit that it refers to speaking, using, or calling upon the name of YHWH by lifting it *to* or *on the lips*.[77] The most often cited evidence for this reading is Ps 16:4: "Nor

73. Moses speaks in his name (Exod 5:23; cf. 3:15) and proclaims the name (Deut 32:3). Through Israel YHWH makes his name known (Exod 9:16); they are to remember his name (Exod 20:24; cf. 23:13); swear by his name (Deut 6:13; 10:20); and come to the place for his name (Deut 12:5, 11). The Levites are to bless in his name (Deut 10:8; 21:5) and minister in his name (Deut 18:5, 7). Prophets speak in his name (Deut 18:19, 20, 22). The people have had his name proclaimed over them (Deut 28:10) and must fear the name (Deut 28:58).

74. See, e.g., Isa 52:5–6; 48:9–11; Jer 34:15–16; Mal 1:6–14; Ezek 20:9, 14, 22; 36:20; cf. Jer 14:14–15; 23:16–17, 25.

75. For a similar critique, see Elßner, *Das Namensmißbrauch-Verbot*, 17, 271–72. Though Conklin (*Oath Formulas*) did not discuss the NC, two of his examples illustrate why it cannot be elliptical for "raise the hand and swear." Ezekiel 36:7 exhibits a direct object marker appended to "hand." In Ezek 20:5–6, the one to whom the oath was made is preceded by a *lamed* prefix rather than a direct object marker. Neither is grammatically compatible with the NC.

76. Though interpreters eagerly adduce parallel passages to explain the NC, few discuss Exod 28:12, 29, 36–38, which prescribe the names the high priest is to bear, even though it shares a narrative setting with the Decalogue in the instructions at Sinai.

77. Assuming the ritual potency of a name, Erik Hornung (*Conceptions of God in Ancient Egypt: The One and the Many*, trans. John Baines [Ithaca, NY: Cornell University Press, 1971], 88) suggested that pronunciation of some divine names was forbidden. Siegfried Morenz (*Egyptian Religion*, trans. Ann E. Keep [Ithaca, NY: Cornell University Press, 1973], 21–22) agreed that some "secret" names were dangerous to pronounce. He mistakenly based this conclusion on the supposed taboo surrounding the name YHWH. In his view, since YHWH was clearly a personal name and should not be pronounced, this suggested that Egyptian deities were also known by their real names. Morenz's argument was flawed in several respects: (1) He assumed, rather than proved, that ancient Israelites were not to pronounce YHWH's name. (2) He based this conclusion on late evidence (Masoretic vowel pointing). (3) He assumed continuity between the Egyptian pantheon and Israelite worship of YHWH, despite fundamental differences. (4) He assumed that the name YHWH is equivalent to the secret names of Egyptian gods, even though YHWH's name was openly revealed to the Israelites, whereas the Egyptian gods had both secret and public names by which they were known.

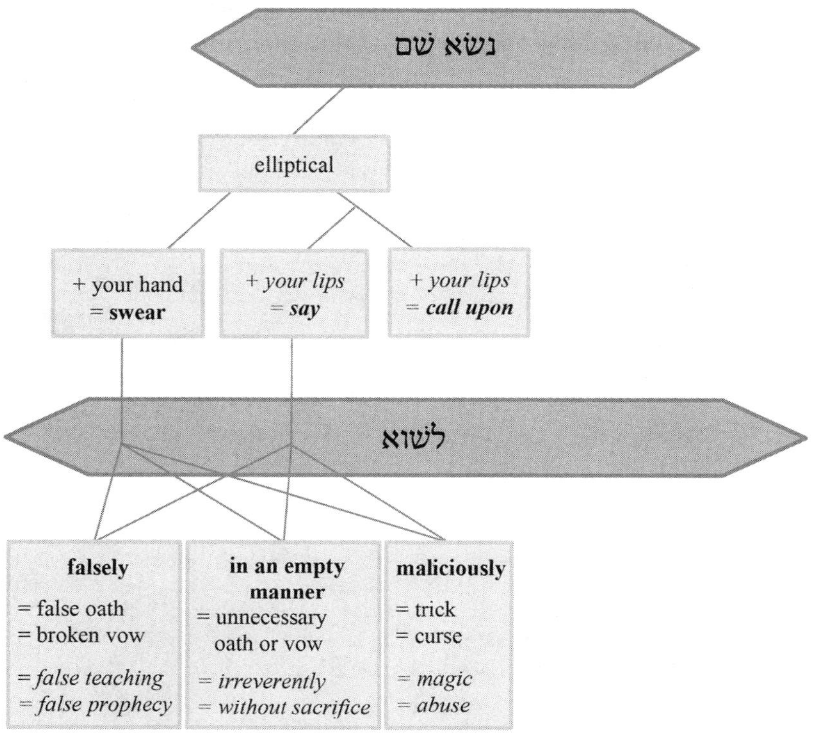

Figure 4. Elliptical interpretations of the Name Command, speech

will I lift up their names on my lips" (ובל־אשׂא את־שׁמותם על־שׂפתי).[78] This proposed parallel avoids the syntactical problems associated with the oath-taking interpretation (the double direct object) because, like the NC, the verb נשׂא has שׁם as the marked direct object. In Ps 16:4, this phrase is further modified by על־שׂפתי ("upon my lips"). Since Ps 16:4 presumably refers to the names of other gods, the contexts are sufficiently similar to warrant a comparison.[79]

However, we need not limit the NC to speech on the basis of this potential parallel by supposing that the NC contains an ellipsis of a longer expression, נשׂא שׁם [על־שׂפת]. Just as probably, Ps 16:4 narrows the application of the phrase נשׂא שׁם hyperbolically to speech with the *addition* of על־שׂפת, underscoring loyalty to YHWH: "nor will I [*even*] lift their names to my lips."[80]

78. See, e.g., Schmidt, *Die Zehn Gebote*, 80; Elßner, *Das Namensmißbrauch-Verbot*, 41, 101, 277.

79. The text is laconic, leaving ambiguity about what names the psalmist refuses to speak. The names could be those of the wicked or their gods.

80. Advocates of this interpretation include F. Crüsemann, *Bewahrung der Freiheit: Das Thema des Dekalogs in sozialgeschichtlicher Perspektive*, Kaiser Traktate 78 (Munich: Chr. Kaiser, 1983), 51; John Goldingay, *Psalms 1–41*, BCOT (Grand Rapids: Baker Academic,

Nonetheless, many have read the NC in light of Ps 16:4, which allows for a variety of interpretations, depending on whether one translates שוא as "falsely," "emptily," or "maliciously," or as a substantive, meaning "idol." The results denoted here in italic type correspond roughly to those under the category of oath taking above (fig. 4).

Some argue the NC warns Israelites not to say the name presumptuously or irreverently.[81] The Talmud preserves lengthy discussions regarding proper occasions when the name might be pronounced. Many Rabbis contended that any pronunciation of the name outside the temple by anyone other than a priest was unnecessary and therefore constituted a violation of the NC.[82] In effect, any utterance of the name by laypeople incurred guilt.[83]

This view is not limited to Jewish scholars. Fifth-century Christian theologian Theodoret of Cyrus argued that the command proscribed unnecessary use of God's name "outside of teaching or prayer or apart from some urgent need."[84] John Calvin included oath taking as a common frivolous use of God's name, but he extended it to any use of God's name that detracts from his character.[85]

The nonpronunciation of God's name as a sign of reverence arose late in Israel's history.[86] For the NC to prohibit the pronunciation of the name,

---

2006), 230. Because the psalmist refuses idolatry, he is able to "drink of the cup of blessing provided by God" in v. 5. See Peter Craigie, *Psalms 1–50*, 2nd ed., WBC (Nashville: Nelson, 2004), 157. For another example of an implied "even," see Exod 21:4: "If a man acts presumptuously toward his neighbor so as to kill him craftily, you are to take him *even* from my altar, so that he may die." Such an offender must face his consequences no matter where he may be found. Elßner's discussion (*Das Namensmißbrauch-Verbot*, 99–100) of this passage is problematic. He notes structural parallels with the NC and concludes that in neither case was the name to be mentioned ("raised"). However, the NC assumes the name *will* be raised, and warns covenant members not to do so falsely.

81. Work, *Deuteronomy*, 79; John Sailhamer, *The Pentateuch as Narrative: A Biblical-Theological Commentary* (Grand Rapids: Zondervan, 1995), 286; James Burton Coffman, *The Ten Commandments: Yesterday and Today* (Westwood, NJ: Revell, 1961), 45; Geerhardus Vos, *Biblical Theology: Old and New Testaments* (Carlisle, PA: Versa, 2007), 138.

82. *B. Ned.* 7b, 8b, 10a–b; *b. Ber.* 33a; *b. Yoma* 70a.

83. *B. ʿAbod. Zar.* 18a; *b. Tamid* 33b; *b. Tem.* 3a–b. Cf. Moshe Weinfeld, "The Decalogue: Its Significance, Uniqueness, and Place in Israel's Tradition," in *Religion and Law: Biblical-Judaic and Islamic Perspectives*, ed. E. B. Firmage, B. G. Weiss, and J. W. Welch (Winona Lake, IN: Eisenbrauns, 1990), 6. Tigay (*Deuteronomy*, 431) insists that the Jewish practice of nonpronunciation derives elsewhere. However, the rabbis discussed penalties for wrongful pronunciation in light of the NC.

84. Theodoret of Cyrus, *The Questions on the Octateuch: On Genesis and Exodus, Question 41*, ed. John F. Peiruccione, trans. Robert C. Hill, LEC 1 (Washington, DC: Catholic University of America Press, 2007), 293; cf. Victor P. Hamilton, "שָׁוְא," *TWOT* 908.

85. Calvin, *Harm. Pent., CC* 2:409; *John Calvin's Sermons on the Ten Commandments*, 96.

86. Reticence to use the name Yhwh in Ecclesiastes, Esther, and the Elohistic Psalter can be explained without reference to the NC. For discussion, see Elßner, *Das Namensmißbrauch-Verbot*, 194–204, 286–87. On the absence of the Tetragrammaton in the New Testament, see R. Kendall Soulen, *The Divine Name(s) and the Holy Trinity: Distinguishing the Voices* (Louisville: Westminster John Knox, 2011), 1:177–89, 194–210. Julius Boehmer lists

YHWH would put it at odds with its literary context at Sinai, in which YHWH's name is repeatedly invoked. The Levites were to pronounce his name in their blessings (Num 6:24–27). The people were to remember or mention his name (זכר; Exod 20:24) but not the names of other gods (זכר; Exod 23:13). Deuteronomy records a command to swear oaths by YHWH's name (שׁבע; Deut 6:13). These instructions are inconsistent with a wholesale prohibition of saying the name.[87]

False or Unauthorized Teaching

A related cluster of interpretations has received more attention in recent years. These also take the NC as an elliptical expression referring to speech, but suggest that a specific *kind* of speech is proscribed—namely, unauthorized or false teaching or prophecy that is nonetheless stamped with YHWH's name ("Thus says YHWH"). Again the specific aim of the command depends on the meaning of שׁוא. Some take it as "false" ("you shall not use the name to teach falsely") or "empty" ("you shall not use the name without authorization"). Any use of YHWH's name for selfish advantage could be included here, whether it involves deceit or pretense. Some take שׁוא to mean "maliciously," so the NC prohibits cursing or deceiving others.[88] Some associate שׁוא with magical practices and read the NC as an injunction against using YHWH's name in magic.[89]

2,000 examples of "reserve before the name of God" (ibid., 277 n. 2, citing *Die neutestamentliche Gottesscheu und die ersten drei Bitten des Vaterunsers* [Halle: Mühlmann, 1917]).

87. See Paton, "Exodus XX. 7," 202; Elßner, *Das Namensmißbrauch-Verbot*, 63; John H. Walton, "Interpreting the Bible as an Ancient Near Eastern Document," in *Israel: Ancient Kingdom or Late Invention*, ed. Daniel I. Block (Nashville: Broadman & Holman, 2008), 315. The Psalms are replete with exhortations to know YHWH's name (Ps 91:14), call on the name (Ps 63:5[4]; 105:1; 116:4), declare the name (Ps 22:23[22]), cause his name to be remembered (Ps 45:1 [17]), bless the name (Ps 100:4; 145:1), sing to his name (Ps 66:2; 68:5[4]), and praise and exalt the name (Ps 7:18[17]; 34:4[3]; 54:8[6]; 96:2; 113:1; 148:5).

In addition, people of faith deliberately used the name by including YHWH theophorically in personal names. Biblical texts testify that Yahwistic theophoric names were common in Israel from the monarchic period forward. These echoes of the name "YHWH" suggest that its pronunciation was not considered taboo, even in the exilic and post exilic periods. Some names that exemplify this are אדניהו ("YHWH is my lord," 1 Kgs 1:8), יהושפט ("YHWH has judged," 1 Kgs 22:41; 2 Chr 17:1), and נחמיה ("YHWH has comforted," Neh 1:1). Note that Moses renamed Hoshea (הוֹשֵׁעַ = "he saves"; Num 13:8) Joshua (יְהוֹשֻׁעַ = "YHWH saves") in light of the exodus. A "Yahwizing" impulse is also seen in the adapted form יהוסף in Ps 81:6: the author/scribe of this Psalm has put a Yahwistic prefix on a historically non-Yahwistic name (יוסף). For further analysis of the geographical provenance and historical attestation of Israelite theophoric names, see Jeaneane D. Fowler, *Theophoric Personal Names in Ancient Hebrew: A Comparative Study*, JSOTSup 49 (Sheffield: JSOT, 1988), esp. pp. 365–66; Jeffrey H. Tigay, "Israelite Religion: The Onomastic and Epigraphic Evidence," in *Ancient Israelite Religion: Essays in Honor of Frank Moore Cross*, ed. Patrick D. Miller Jr., Paul D. Hanson, and S. Dean McBride (Philadelphia: Fortress, 1987), 157–94.

88. For an interpretation including all three senses of שׁוא ("selfishly, maliciously or foolishly"), see Wright, *Old Testament Ethics*, 262.

89. Representatives of each view are identified below.

Houtman reads the NC as prohibiting anything said in YHWH's name that YHWH does not support. He agrees that לא תשא is elliptical, referring to speech, but he sees no reason to limit this to "swearing an oath" and insists that "in vain" is a weak rendering of לשוא. Instead, לשוא relates both to the manner in which something is done and to the purpose for which it is done: someone, consciously, while invoking YHWH's name, makes a statement that is not supported, cannot be supported by YHWH's authority. The impression is created that YHWH stands behind what is affirmed, while in reality such is not the case. So one's fellow citizens are misled and harmed, if not directly, at least indirectly. Because, when the truth is violated and one can no longer depend on fellow citizens, the moral fiber holding society together unravels.[90]

He applies this command to court cases, prayer, prophetic teaching in YHWH's name, and worship.[91]

Other interpreters include "spiritual abuse" as a violation of this command. For example, based on a supposed malicious sense to שוא, Harrelson restates the command, "Do not use the power of religion to harm others."[92] The NC would then relate most directly to those in positions of leadership. If one assumes the Decalogue is directed only toward landowners, this application may be warranted.[93]

Some early Christian interpretations of the NC are difficult to categorize, but they seem to belong here under "false teaching." A few church Fathers read the NC Christologically. For them, "taking the LORD's name in vain" meant refusing to acknowledge the divinity of Jesus. This view arose from a typological interpretation of the Decalogue where the commands were divided into groups of three and seven, corresponding respectively to the two greatest commands. Augustine explains, "Just as the three

90. Houtman, *Exodus*, 3:36.

91. Ibid., 36–37.

92. Harrelson, *The Ten Commandments and Human Rights*, 194. For further discussion, see below, p. 29. Aside from magic and cursing, Harrelson (ibid., 64) includes spiritual abuse and false teaching as potential misuses of the name. Cf. Duane Christensen, *Deuteronomy 1:1–21:9*, 2nd ed., WBC 6A (Nashville: Thomas Nelson, 2001), 114. Martin Luther (*A Simple Way to Pray,* in *Devotional Writings II,* ed. Gustav K. Wiencke, trans. Carl J. Schindler, *LW* 43 [Philadelphia: Fortress, 1968], 195, emphasis mine) saw the Roman Catholic Church as the prime culprit in the violation of this aspect of the NC. In a sample prayer modeled on the Lord's prayer, he said,

> Destroy and root out the abominations, idolatry, and heresy of the Turk, the pope, and all false teachers and fanatics who wrongly *use thy name* and in scandalous ways *take it in vain* and horribly blaspheme it. They insistently boast that they teach the word and the laws of the church, though they really use the devil's deceit and trickery in thy name to wretchedly seduce many poor souls throughout the world, even killing and shedding much innocent blood, and in such persecution they believe that they render thee a divine service.

93. Aquinas rejected "false teaching" as a viable interpretation for this very reason. If the NC prohibits false teaching, only leaders are liable rather than all Israelites. See Aquinas, *ST* 1–2.100.5 ad 3. This section is reprinted in Brown, *The Ten Commandments*, 54. I expand on the addressees of the Decalogue in ch. 4.

first belong to the love of God, so the seven others are assigned to love of neighbor."[94] The number three is then taken to represent the Trinity, with one command pertaining to each member. The NC corresponds to Christ, therefore warning us "against thinking of the Son of God as creature."[95] Tertullian also interpreted the NC Christologically.[96] Much later, Luther accused Jews of breaking this command by not acknowledging the deity of Jesus.[97] His name must not be associated with anything less than his true identity. Since the denigration of Christ is heresy, failure to acknowledge his deity counts as false teaching. A more recent proponent of this notion is Ephraim Radner, who says that the execution of Christ was the ultimate "envainment" of the name.[98]

Magic

Another view, which has become increasingly popular over the past century, associates the NC with magic. The view is at least as old as the Protestant Reformation,[99] but it was revived in the mid-20th century by Mowinckel.[100] He assumed a Hegelian model of religious development where later expressions developed from earlier "primitive psychology."[101] Mowinckel saw in Israel's primitive history evidence for speech against one's neighbor intended to bring misfortune. This kind of magic or cursing depends on an etymological association of שׁוא with the Arabic root *sâʾa*. Since the Arabic means "to be bad or evil," the hypothetical Hebrew cognate would also have evil connotations. Mowinckel justified this association by citing occurrences of שׁוא in parallelism with other malicious words in the Hebrew Bible.[102] He did not deny the sense of "emptiness" for שׁוא, or "lie," but insisted that they share the same core sense of "troublemaker" and

94. Augustine, *Sermons II (20–50) on the Old Testament*, ed. John E Rotelle, trans. Edmund Hill, WSA 3/2 (Brooklyn, NY: New City, 1990), 33.2; 155.

95. Ibid., 33.3; 155; cf. Wilhelm Geerlings, "The Decalogue in Augustine's Theology," in *The Decalogue in Jewish and Christian Tradition*, ed. Henning Graf Reventlow and Yair Hoffman, LHB/OTS 509 (New York: T&T Clark, 2011), Sermon 8, 115.

96. Tertullian, *Against Praxeas* 7, trans. Ernest Evans (London: Constable, 1948), 138; see also *ANF* 3.7.602 (trans. Holmes).

97. Luther, *On the Jews and Their Lies*, in *The Christian in Society IV*, ed. Franklin Sherman, trans. Martin H. Bertram, *LW* 47 (Philadelphia: Fortress, 1971), 286.

98. Ephraim Radner, "Taking the Lord's Name in Vain," in *I Am the Lord Your God: Christian Reflections on the Ten Commandments*, ed. Carl E. Braaten and Christopher R. Seitz (Grand Rapids: Eerdmans, 2005), 88.

99. See Calvin, *Institutes* 2.8.22 [LCC 20:389]; Henning Graf Reventlow, "The Ten Commandments in Luther's Catechisms," in *The Decalogue in Jewish and Christian Tradition*, ed. Henning Graf Reventlow and Yair Hoffman, LHBOTS 509 (New York: T&T Clark, 2011), 141; Albrecht Peters, *Ten Commandments*, trans. Holger K. Sonntag, Commentary on Luther's Catechisms (St. Louis: Concordia, 2009), 150.

100. Mowinckel, *Psalmenstudien I*, 50–58; followed by Gerhard von Rad, *Deuteronomy: A Commentary*, trans. Dorothea Barton, OTL (Philadelphia: Westminster, 1966), 57.

101. Mowinckel, *Psalmenstudien I*, 50, AT.

102. He cites Isa 59:4; Hos 12:12; Zech 10:2; Ps 41:7; and Job 11:11. While these are

would have been closely associated in the ancient mind. For Mowinckel, this trouble would have involved magic spells.[103] As modern scholars have become more aware of the pervasiveness of magical practices in the ancient world, this reading has gained adherents.[104]

Anthony Phillips also defended the "magic" interpretation.[105] Phillips' discussion of the Decalogue centered on its role in Israel's covenant with YHWH. Breach of any of these commands constituted criminal behavior that put the entire society at risk because the covenant was violated.[106] Phillips recognized that שוא usually connotes a general worthlessness but insisted that since the other commands of the Decalogue are specific, this one must be specific as well. He rejected the idea that it could refer to blasphemy or false oaths, because a command against either would have been unnecessary.[107] Instead Phillips followed Mowinckel and others in seeing the NC as a prohibition of magical practices, since it invoked the divine name.[108] In particular, he read the NC as an injunction against cursing one's neighbor.[109]

Van den Branden advocates a magical reading because it avoids the substantial overlap with the command against false witness. If the first two commands regulate proper worship (one God, no idols) then a prohibition

negative contexts, to define a word based on its parallels is fundamentally flawed. שוא need not mean "malicious" in any of these cases.

103. Mowinckel, *Psalmenstudien I*, 56–57. His prime example is Isa 5:18, where he relies on Ezek 13:17–21 to supply a magical sense for "cords," but the pairing of בחבלי השוא with וכעבות העגלה ("cart ropes") makes this interpretation dubious. Klopfenstein (*Die Lüge*, 315–16) rejects Mowinckel's equation of שוא with magical practices, but he follows Mowinckel's interpretation of the NC. He posits a range of interpretations for שוא, from *empty* to *lying* to *evil*. Context determines which sense pertains in a given case (ibid., 317–20). However, for Klopfenstein (ibid., 119–20) even lying would have involved malicious action against the other.

104. Based on its occurrence in Isa 1:13 parallel to תועבה ("abomination"), Harrelson (*The Ten Commandments and Human Rights*, 63) translated שוא here as "destructive" or "offensive." However, it could just as easily mean "meaningless" or "worthless." See chapter 3 for discussion.

105. Anthony Phillips, *Ancient Israel's Criminal Law: A New Approach to the Decalogue* (New York: Schocken, 1970). Cf. Harrelson, *The Ten Commandments and Human Rights*, 61–66; Branden, "Le Décalogue," 110–12; Martin Noth, *Exodus: A Commentary*, trans. J. S. Bowden, OTL (Philadelphia: Westminster, 1962), 163; von Rad, *Deuteronomy*, 57; Kessler, "Die literarische, historische und theologische Problematik des Dekalogs," 9; Christensen, *Deut 1:1–21:9*, 114; Eugene H. Merrill, *Deuteronomy*, NAC (Nashville: Broadman & Holman, 1994), 149.

106. Phillips, *Ancient Israel's Criminal Law*, 154.

107. Phillips (ibid., 55) argues that blasphemy is not the subject of Lev 24 but rather an example of private cursing during a fight "with the evident aim of gaining control over the adversary through magical force," therefore violating the NC. For a similar argument against the oath-taking interpretation, see Brichto, *The Problem of "Curse,"* 59–63. Phillips' omission of Lev 19:12 in his discussion casts doubt on his reasoning.

108. Phillips, *Ancient Israel's Criminal Law*, 54.

109. Cf. *b. Tem.* 3a–b.

of magical practices within the cult makes sense.[110] Although van den Branden supports his reading by appealing to ANE magic texts, these do not offer specific parallels to the NC. For example, he cites Vandier, who says that knowledge of both human and divine names is the secret of the magician's power.[111] While names of the gods played a role in magic in the ancient world, the idea that the NC addresses this issue has yet to be established.

While the magical use of the name may fit well with the ANE environment, the argument to limit the NC to magic stands on thin lexical foundations. If magic or false teaching is in view, then the formulation of the NC with such generic terminology is strange. Sorcery could have involved many practices, only some of which would have involved the divine name.[112] Furthermore, as shown above, the use of the name in magic is only one of many possible uses of the name, and contextual clues are lacking to indicate that magic is in view (e.g., כשף; חבר). The "deliberately broad wording" of the NC suggests that we should not rule out other practices associated with the divine name.[113] Lexically speaking, we cannot *limit* the NC to magic, though it may well violate this command.[114]

Manfred Görg suggested that the magical misinterpretation arose from a wrong assumption about the etymology of שׁוא. Rather than tracing it to *nšʾ* 2, a root meaning "to be deceived,"[115] Görg noted an overlooked Egyptian cognate, *šwi*, "to be empty." He found this cognate to be a suitable basis both for the Egyptian noun *šw*, "void," and the Hebrew שׁוא.[116] However, like other critics of the magical view, he did not dismiss it entirely, suggesting specific applications of the NC to magic are appropriate.[117] He suspected that early Greek and Latin translations of the NC used a legitimate form of

110. Ironically, van den Branden ("Le Décalogue," 110–12) also allows that שׁוא could refer to idols, resulting in almost complete overlap with the previous command.

111. Jacques Vandier, *La Religion Égyptienne*, Les anciennes Religions orientales 1 (Paris: Presses Univeritaires de France, 1944), 199; Édouard Dhorme, *Les Religions de Babylonie et d'Assyrie*, Les anciennes Religions orientales 2 (Paris: Presses Univeritaires de France, 1949); both cited by Branden, "Le Décalogue," 110 n. 44–45, AT.

112. As argued by Meir Bar-Ilan, "'They shall put my name upon the people of Israel,'" *HUCA* 60 (1989): 27 n. 30.

113. Graupner, "Tora für die Völker," 64, AT.

114. Schmidt, *Die Zehn Gebote*, 83. Those who are unconvinced by the magical interpretation include Brevard S. Childs, *The Book of Exodus: A Critical, Theological Commentary*, OTL (Philadelphia: Westminster, 1974), 411; Huffmon, "The Fundamental Code Illustrated," 207 n. 10.

115. As Elßner (*Das Namensmißbrauch-Verbot*, 46) does. Relying on Sawyer, Gesenius-Buhl, and Klopfenstein, he associates שׁוא with Arabic, Ethiopic, Northwest Semitic, and Hamitic cognates that range in meaning from "empty" to "evil."

116. Manfred Görg, "Missbrauch des Gottesnamens," *BN* 16 (1981): 16–17. Although Görg credits Gesenius-Buhl for this overlooked cognate, I was unable to locate a note to that effect in any of the editions I consulted (including 1834, 1876, 1899).

117. Ibid., 17.

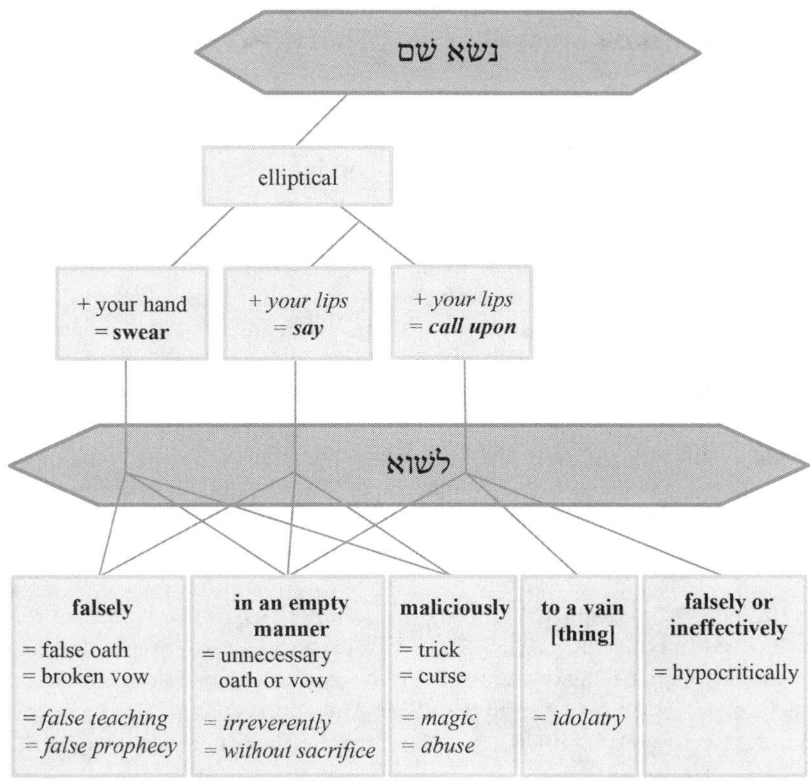

Figure 5. Elliptical interpretations of the Name Command, worship

"semantic specification."[118] All these elliptical readings take this potential for specification too far by limiting the application of the NC to speech.

You Shall Not Call on the Name

Before we test the possibility of a nonelliptical reading, other elliptical interpretations deserve mention. Several interpreters take the NC to mean "you shall not *call upon* the name." Some of these suppose it is elliptical ("lift the name *to your lips*"), while others read the phrase "lift up the name," as a metonymical idiom for calling on God in prayer. Still others understand שׁוא as a term for "idol," so the NC would prohibit idolatrous worship. Again, the range of senses for שׁוא allows for vastly different interpretations, from idolatry to improper sacrifice to hypocritical worship (fig. 5).

Idolatry

Those who interpret שׁוא as "idol" have ancient support. Seeking to protect God's name from association with idols, Tertullian (late 2nd–early

118. Ibid., 17 n. 14, AT.

3rd century) declared guilty those who refer to idols as "gods" because "the Law forbids us to call them gods and to apply this Name in vain [*in vano*]."[119] Clement of Alexandria (2nd century) announced that the NC warns not to "transfer His title to things created and vain [ἐπὶ τὰ γενητὰ καὶ μάταια], which human artificers have made."[120]

Two modern interpreters have argued for this view. In 1939, W. E. Staples argued on lexical grounds that the NC prohibits idolatry.[121] However, his lexical discussion is baffling. Citing Isa 5:26, Num 14:30, and Gen 19:21, Staples concluded that נשׂא meant "give."[122] How he arrived at this conclusion is unclear. He lists a series of euphemisms for "idol" in the Hebrew Bible, concluding that שׁוא "is used explicitly for an idol" in Jer 18:15 and Ps 24:4. He might be correct about Jer 18:15, but "idols" are not the only possible referent of שׁוא. Yʜᴡʜ laments, "For my people have forgotten me, they burn offerings לשׁוא, so they have fallen in their ways, the ancient paths."[123] The phrase could indicate that the Israelites were offering burnt sacrifices to "vain things" (idols), as Staples suggests, or "vainly" (ineffectively) to other gods. If the latter, Yʜᴡʜ laments the futility of their apostasy (see v. 12). While קטר לשׁוא likely refers to idolatrous practices in Jer 18:15, given the *piel* form of קטר, elsewhere in Jeremiah לשׁוא has nothing to do with idolatry. In fact, שׁוא indisputably means "idol" only twice in the Hebrew Bible, both times in construct with הבל.[124] In regard to Ps 24:4, Staples has simply assumed what he is trying to prove. No clear evidence here commends this interpretation over the alternatives. The verbs נשׂא and קטר cannot be equated. Without unambiguous support from either of these passages, Staples' case for the NC as a prohibition of idolatry is speculative.

But Staples is not the only modern advocate of this view. Calum Carmichael views Israelite laws as "the result of scribal art in formulating rules

119. Tertullian, *On Idolatry,* 10, 5–6, trans. J. H. Waszink and J. C. M. Van Winden, SVG 1 (New York: Brill, 1987), 41. Cf. 20, 3 (SVG 1:63) and *ANF* 3.10.67 and 3.3.636 (trans. S. Thelwall).

120. Clement of Alexandria, *Stromata* 6.16 (*ANF* 2:512, trans. A. Cleveland Coxe).

121. He admits that "an illegal purpose" could be in view, but finds that an injunction against idolatry fits better in the literary and historical context. On the Decalogue as a summary of 8th century BCE prophetic teaching, see W. E. Staples, "The Third Commandment," *JBL* 58 (1939): 325–26.

122. Ibid., 328.

123. Virtually all instances of קטר (*piel*) refer to idolatry, while קטר (*hiphil*) usually denotes the worship of Yʜᴡʜ (with a handful of exceptions: 1 Kgs 3:3; 11:8; 12:33; 13:1–2; 2 Kgs 16:13–15; Hos 2:15). A ל prefix consistently designates the party to whom the offering is directed—namely, other gods (e.g., Jer 1:16; 44:17). See *DCH* 7:243. For discussion, see Elßner, *Das Namensmißbrauch-Verbot*, 50, 53. On the other hand, לשׁוא often appears in Jeremiah with the adverbial sense "ineffectively" (see Jer 2:30; 4:30; 6:29; 46:11). If לשׁוא is adverbial here rather than substantive, idolatry is not precluded. It simply emphasizes that incense burned to other deities is ineffective.

124. Psalm 31:7; Jonah 2:9. In Jer 18:15, the *piel* form of קטר connotes idolatry. I discuss this in ch. 3.

about problems derived from a scrutiny of national traditions."[125] In *The Origins of Biblical Law*, he extends that thesis to the משפטים , among which he includes the Decalogue. He reads the NC as a deliberately formulated response to the golden calf incident. Aaron supposedly "lifted up YHWH's name" to the calf idol by referring to it as YHWH (Exod 32:4–5).[126] His eventual punishment was death (Num 20:24). The Israelites were warned not to repeat his error.[127] However, this connection also relies on the dubious interpretation of לשוא as "to an idol." Not only are the lexical arguments in favor of idolatry unconvincing, but it also seems redundant to have two injunctions against idolatry side-by-side in the Decalogue's seminal list of commands.[128] The previous command (Exod 20:4–6) categorically prohibits the worship of idols.

Empty-Handed Worship

Lewis Paton creatively suggested that the NC refers to "worship without sacrifice." Like Staples and Carmichael, he supposed that the phrase "lift up the name of YHWH" meant to call upon him in worship. By comparing the NC with other passages where נשא indicates speech, he concluded that it must refer to crying out loudly.[129] But for Paton the adverbial use of שוא indicates the worshiper is *empty-handed*.[130] By comparing the Decalogue with other law collections in the Hebrew Bible, he claimed to have discerned a structural pattern common to each collection where laws relating to idolatry are followed by laws about sacrifice, and then Sabbath.[131] Based on that

125. Calum M. Carmichael, *The Origins of Biblical Law: The Decalogues and the Book of the Covenant* (Ithaca, NY: Cornell University Press, 1992), 1.

126. The text does not explicitly say that Aaron "lifted YHWH's name" to the calf, but the correlation is implicit. After fashioning the image, the people announced, "This is your God, O Israel, who brought you up from the land of Egypt." Aaron responded by building an altar and proclaiming a "festival for YHWH" (חג ליהוה), complete with burnt offerings (עלה) and fellowship offerings (שלם). Apparently he felt the golden calf was compatible with YHWH worship.

127. Carmichael, *Origins of Biblical Law*, 33–34. Louis Hartman ("God, Names of," *EJ* 7:675) supports this view, arguing that the NC is "more likely" about idolatry than the common alternatives, "false swearing," or the pronunciation of God's name.

128. Also noted by Phillips, *Ancient Israel's Criminal Law*, 54.

129. Paton, "Exodus XX. 7," 205. However, נשא does not appear independently in any of the passages he cites. He admits that נשא only refers to loud and expressive speech when accompanied by another word like "weeping," "lamentation," or "prayer." In only two biblical passages could נשא possibly mean "utter": Exod 23:1 and Ps 15:3. Paton argues that both of these refer to *receiving* a false report or reproach. He rightly points out that if the NC targeted such a "false report" it would belong in the second half of the Decalogue rather than the first, where the focus is Godward.

130. He insists that the preposition ל attached to שוא indicates either time, result, or direction, never purpose (ibid., 208). Contra Ronald Williams, *Hebrew Syntax: An Outline*, 2nd ed. (Toronto: University of Toronto Press, 1976), §277; Christo H. J. van der Merwe, Jackie A. Naudé, and Jan H. Kroeze, *A Biblical Hebrew Reference Grammar*, Biblical Languages: Hebrew 3 (New York: Sheffield, 2002), §39.11.II; Joüon §168c; *IBHS* §11.2.10d.

131. Paton, "Exodus XX. 7," 209.

pattern, since the NC follows a prohibition of images, it should concern sacrifice. Paton assumed that in ancient Israelite religion to call upon YHWH necessitated an animal sacrifice.[132] His only evidence is Exod 34:20b, which reads, "And they shall not be seen before me empty-handed [ריקם]."[133] However, this verse lacks any connection to the NC. Though perhaps every trip to the tabernacle included a sacrifice, we have no indication that the NC is cultic or that נשׂא שׁם should be limited to temple worship. Furthermore, it is doubtful that every prayer required sacrifice. In the Psalms as well as biblical narratives, people often called upon God without mention of a sacrifice.[134]

Paton rightly complained that others interpret נשׂא too specifically when they read it as "taking oaths," and שׁוא when they connect it to "magical practices," but his proposal is equally narrow. Like others, Paton overlooked the closer parallel with the high priestly garments in Exod 28. Furthermore, his so-called structural pattern is questionable.[135] Paton over-generalizes his lexical and structural conclusions to bolster his reading of the NC. While his view is hypothetically possible, it lacks direct support.[136]

Hypocritical Worship

The final elliptical view understands the NC as a prohibition of hypocritical worship. Like Paton's "worship without sacrifice," this view sees "lifting up the name of YHWH" as a reference to worship. However, unlike Paton, proponents of this interpretation do not read לשׁוא in a temporal and concrete sense as "empty-handed" but as an abstract adverb of *manner*, "hypocritically." Gordon McConville suggested that the phrase could refer to "false, manipulative" worship.[137] People who publicly call on YHWH with-

132. Ibid.

133. Ibid. The statement is also found in Exod 23:15.

134. See, e.g., Pss 31:17; 63:4; and 105:1. Narrative examples include Judg 15:18; 1 Chr 4:10; Lam 3:55; and Jdt 6:21.

135. True, Exod 34 instructs Israel regarding the worship of other gods (vv. 13–16), the making of idols (v. 17), and cultic celebrations (vv. 18–26), in that order. However, Lev 19 does not exhibit the neat pattern Paton suggests. As many have pointed out, the laws lack an obvious order. Instructions regarding parents and Sabbaths *precede* the command against idolatry (vv. 3–4), which is then followed by laws about sacrifices (vv. 5–8), and then instructions to care for the vulnerable in the community (vv. 9–10). Stealing, lying, and swearing follow that (vv. 11–12). So while Paton is right that sacrifices follow idolatry in Lev 19, no discernible progression precedes or follows this. In fact, Decalogic prohibitions are scrambled throughout the chapter, making it a strange source for a structural analogy. See John E. Hartley, *Leviticus*, WBC 4 (Dallas: Word, 1992), 308.

136. E.g., H. A. McNeile, *The Book of Exodus*, 3rd ed. (London: Methuen, 1931), 117–18.

137. J. G. McConville (*Deuteronomy*, AOTC [Downers Grove, IL: InterVarsity, 2002], 128) supposes the NC has to do with "the worship of other gods." For an application to prayer, see Peter Craigie, *The Book of Deuteronomy*, NICOT (London: Hodder & Stoughton, 1976), 156. Cf. James K Bruckner, *Exodus*, NIBCOT (Peabody, MA: Hendrickson, 2008), 184. At first Schüngel-Straumann (*Der Dekalog: Gottes Gebote?* SBS 67 [Stuttgart: KBW, 1973], 96–97) suggests that the NC prohibits ritualistic use of God's name in worship, but she later includes many other arenas in which the name might be misused, such as magic, false swearing, and unauthorized preaching.

out meaning it or only in order to get their own way lift up his name לשוא. While this interpretation avoids some of the problems with Paton's view, it reads נשא שם as an idiom for worship without clear justification for doing so.

King Alfred's civil law code based on the Decalogue, which dates between 890 and 940 CE, reads, "You (must) not call upon my name in vain because you (will) not be innocent in my presence if you call upon my name in vain" [AT].[138] This rendering comes closest to the nonelliptical interpretation that will be tested in the rest of this work. However, it still limits the application of the command to speech. Those who take YHWH's name *on their lips* are in danger of calling upon him *in vain* or *hypocritically*. This limitation to speech is not required by the context.

"All of the Above"

Before examining the nonelliptical interpretation, we must assess the view of a growing group of interpreters who allow the polyvalence of the NC to stand. They recognize that God's "name" was employed for a variety of purposes in Israel's religious and social life. One might "lift the name" in a variety of ways, for a variety of reasons. Above all, שוא is sufficiently vague to cast doubt on a narrow application. As Radner insists, "The prohibition against taking the Lord's name 'in vain' easily takes aim at the very center of *every act* we do and at its motivation in the human heart, even and especially as these motivations clothe themselves with religious goals."[139] Accordingly, Radner and many others avoid a single application, such as swearing falsely, worshiping idols, or using magic. Instead, they proscribe "all (or some combination) of the above."

For example, in his lengthy discussion of the NC, Patrick Miller sees oath taking as the primary issue. However, the ambiguous wording of the command compels him to extrapolate other misuses of the name: in worship, blessing, cursing, prayer, swearing, false prophecy, irreverence, and Christology.[140] His interpretation is broad enough to account for virtually any spoken misuse of the divine name.

Martin Luther cited the NC at least 21 times in his collected works. He applied it to a wide range of activities, including false oaths (*LW* 4:336; 13:218; 22:504), false teaching (10:462; 27:119; 43:195), prayer (4:361) and sacraments

138. Alfred's laws are preserved in two manuscripts, H: "*Ne minne naman ne cig þu on ydelnesse forðam þu ne byst unscyldig wið me gif þu on idelnesse (ge)cygst minne naman*"; and E: "*Ne minne noman ne cig ðu on idelnesse forðon þe ðu ne bist unscyldig wið me gif ðu on idelnesse cigst minne noman.*" See F. Liebermann, *Die Gesetze der Angelsachsen* (Halle: Scientia Aalen, 1960), 26–27. *Cig* is from *ciegan*, which means "to call, name, to call upon, invoke." My translation utilized John R. Clark Hall, ed., *A Concise Anglo-Saxon Dictionary for the Use of Students* (New York: Macmillan, 1894).

139. Radner, "Taking the Lord's Name in Vain," 80. See also Cassuto, *Exodus*, 243; Richard D. Nelson, *Deuteronomy: A Commentary*, OTL (Philadelphia: Westminster, 2002), 81; Houtman, *Exodus*, 3:36.

140. Miller, *The Ten Commandments*, 81–114.

(34:85; 36:300 f., 360; 40:292; 54:12), blasphemy (34:85), and the general behavior of those who call themselves Christians (29:58; 46:24, 33).[141]

While others provide similar lists of speech-acts covered by the NC, 17th-century Puritan theologian Thomas Watson's may be the most complete. According to Watson, the tongue is the prime offender, encompassing various modes of speech including irreverence, hypocrisy, profanity, false worship, unbelieving prayer, the use of Scripture by wicked people, oaths (either excessive, unnecessary, vile, or false), false authorization, unseemly speech, rash vows, speaking evil of God, and making promises one does not intend to keep.[142]

Although some insist the NC is ambiguous or broad enough to include a variety of potential locutions, others limit the *sense* to one meaning while extending the *implications* of the NC to a broader range of behaviors. According to John Durham, the NC "is couched in language deliberately chosen to permit a wide range of application, covering every dimension of the misuse of Yahweh's name."[143] Thomas Aquinas argued that although oath-taking is precisely prohibited, by extension "*every misuse of God's name is thereby prohibited.*"[144] Whereas Durham locates the breadth of meaning in the command itself, Aquinas encompassed a broader field only by extension.[145]

Thomas Elßner argues that ANE and biblical parallels adduced by most interpreters are unpersuasive because they needlessly constrict the scope of the NC.[146] For Elßner the NC is intentionally broad enough to prohibit a wide range of speech-related offenses by which the name of YHWH might be abused.[147] While his work is commendable, his conclusion ultimately

---

141. Luther (*LW* 47:286) even accused Jews of breaking this command by not acknowledging the deity of Jesus. Since his interpretation goes beyond speech, we will consider his views again under the nonelliptical reading of the NC below.

142. Thomas Watson, *The Ten Commandments*, rev. ed. (London: Banner of Truth, 1965), 85–91. The only interpretations he omits are magic, idolatry, unlawful pronunciation, and the failure to acknowledge Jesus' divinity.

143. Durham, *Exodus*, 288.

144. Aquinas, *ST* 2a2æ, 122.3.2, trans. T. C. O'Brien (Westminster: Eyre & Spottiswoode, 1972) 41:301, emphasis mine.

145. Coffin ("The Third Commandment," 188) advocated a broad interpretation by arguing for a diachronic shift in the meaning of שׁוא. Though he admits that שׁוא does not occur often enough to trace clear development, he nevertheless concludes that שׁוא was first malicious or false, connected particularly with oath taking. He attributes later reticence to pronounce YHWH's name to the shift in meaning for שׁוא to "profane" or "empty." Interestingly, though Coffin spent the bulk of his time on שׁוא, he never allowed for "idol" as a possible meaning. Coffin's overall thesis depended heavily on the evolutionary development of monotheism and its superiority over other ANE religions.

However, if we accept the nonelliptical reading of the NC, then no practical difference results from translating שׁוא as malicious, deceitful, false, or empty. Each indicates a form of hypocrisy.

146. Elßner (*Das Namensmißbrauch-Verbot*, 12–28) interacts almost exclusively with German scholars.

147. Ibid., 65, 84.

rests on the faulty assumption that the collocation with שֵׁם makes נשׂא an improper *verbum dicendi*, without explaining why the same phrase (נשׂא שֵׁם) in Exod 28:12, 29 does *not* involve speech.[148] Though he admits the lack of evidence in the Pentateuch or DH for the use of נשׂא as an improper *verbum dicendi*,[149] Elßner focuses his analysis of נשׂא on its occurrences in later "stereotyped phrases" involving speech (e.g., נשׂא קול, "raise a voice"; נשׂא משׁל, "proclaim an oracle"; נשׂא קינה, "raise a complaint"; etc.), concluding that the NC is a later exilic addition to the Decalogue.[150] He discusses a few phrases in which שֵׁם is not speech-related, such as חלל שֵׁם (Lev 18:21; 22:32) and טמא שֵׁם (Ezek 43:7, 8), where the name is defiled through actions rather than words, but neglects to consider how the NC might function similarly.[151] Instead, Elßner suggests the Decalogic context evoked a poetic mode of discourse that may be euphemistic for abuse of the name.[152] In the end, his work is helpful in countering some of the faulty interpretations of the NC, but Elßner fails to offer a robust alternative.[153]

The Name Command as a Nonelliptical Expression

The majority of interpreters assume that the NC prohibits some type of speech, perhaps because names are often *spoken* entities. However, as we shall see in ch. 3, "name" can denote one's fame or reputation, as well as (in certain idioms) a written or oral claim to ownership. A few interpreters have recognized this semantic breadth, though they have not always known how to justify their conclusion that the NC involves more than speech. Some have supposed that the NC is elliptical and its primary concern is oath taking, but its application may be extended to include other behavior.

Those who have attempted to read the NC nonelliptically focus on נשׂא and ask, "What might it mean to 'lift up' or 'bear' YHWH's name? And what

148. Ibid., 41. Elßner (ibid., 43–44, AT) claims that שֵׁם "in principle involves . . . pronunciation." However, three of his four examples of שֵׁם without a suffix do not involve a spoken name (Num 17:18[3]; 1 Kgs 1:47; 2 Kgs 14:27). His fourth example could involve speech, but not necessarily (2 Kgs 16:24). Ibid., 97–98.

149. Elßner, *Das Namensmißbrauch-Verbot*, 98. He also admits that, aside from Ps 16:4, "no further evidence [is] attested in the Old Testament of the syntagmatic relationship לא/בל נשׂא את שׁם/שׁמותם with the semantic import 'mention the name/names,'" p. 101, AT.

150. Ibid., 37–41, 276. Strangely, he misses several occasions where נשׂא indicates speech: 1 Kgs 8:31; 2 Kgs 9:25; 2 Chr 6:22; and Jer 9:17. On his view of the date of the NC, see ibid., 102, 151–52, 281–82.

151. Elßner, *Das Namensmißbrauch-Verbot*, 73–78.

152. Ibid., 85. Cf. Lev 24:11, 16; Job 1:5; 2:9. If Lev 24 illustrates a narrow application of the NC, as Elßner suggests, then why must Moses inquire of YHWH? His other examples are unpersuasive because ברך is inherently positive but is used in place of "curse." In the NC, נשׂא becomes pejorative with the addition of לשׁוא (ibid., 69).

153. His translation of the NC is odd: "You must not minimize the name of YHWH thy God, as if he were a vain [thing]." See Elßner, *Das Namensmißbrauch-Verbot*, 174. "Minimize" seems to have the opposite sense as נשׂא.

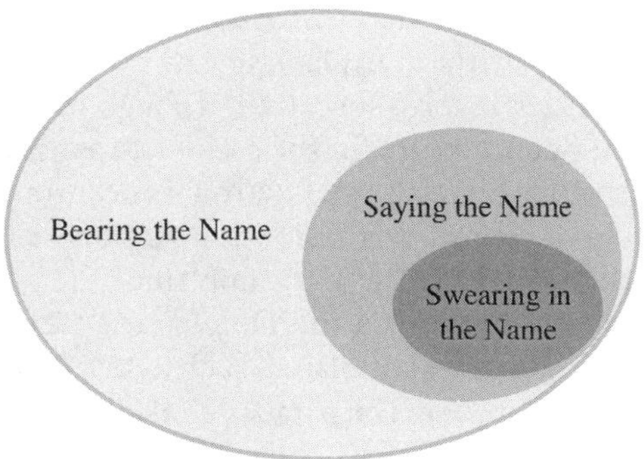

Figure 6. Broad application of the Name Command

would constitute bearing his name לשוא?" Name-bearing does not necessarily preclude other applications of the NC, since "bearing the name" could have implications for both words and actions. As fig. 6 shows, "bearing the name" is a broader, behavioral interpretation of the NC that includes speech-related interpretations within it. This interpretation reads the NC in light of the concept that YHWH's name was proclaimed over Israel (e.g., Num 6:27; Deut 28:10; 2 Chr 7:14) to indicate their elect status. Accordingly, they represented him by "bearing his name" among the nations. This non-elliptical, or "representational," interpretation reads the NC as an injunction against misrepresenting YHWH. Those who bear his name must not do so "in vain" (fig. 7)

Rabbinic Interpretation

In the Pesiqta Rabbati, a series of Jewish Scripture lessons for use on feast days,[154] the NC is clearly associated with swearing falsely.[155] However, here the rabbis seek to distinguish this command from its "apparent repetition" in Lev 19:12. They offer three additional interpretations: (1) false teaching/authority, (2) misrepresentation, and (3) superfluous oaths.[156] The second relates most directly to our concern here. The rabbis explain, "You are not to put on tefillin and wrap yourself in your prayer shawl, and then, disregarding the name of the Lord, go forth and commit transgressions."[157] Since the *tefillin*, or phylacteries, symbolize the name of God,[158] they should

154. Although William Braude (*Pesikta Rabbati: Discourses for Feasts, Fasts, and Special Sabbaths*, Yale Judaica 28 [New Haven, CT: Yale University Press, 1968], 2–5) argues that the *Pesiqta Rabbati* was written during the 7th century CE, an editorial note by Mordecai Margulies claims the section on the Decalogue dates to 3rd- or 4th-century CE Palestine.

155. Ibid., *Pesiq. Rab.* 27.4; 543.

156. 1: ibid., *Pesiq. Rab.* 22.4; 457. 2: ibid., *Pesiq. Rab.* 22.5; 458. 3: ibid., *Pesiq. Rab.* 22.6; 465.

157. Ibid., *Pesiq. Rab.* 22.5; 458.

158. The front of a head *teffilla* bears the letter ש, and the knot is traditionally tied in the shape of the letter ד, with the end of the strap representing the letter י. Taken together, these letters spell שדי (*shaddai*), or "Almighty." For the arm *teffila,* the strap is

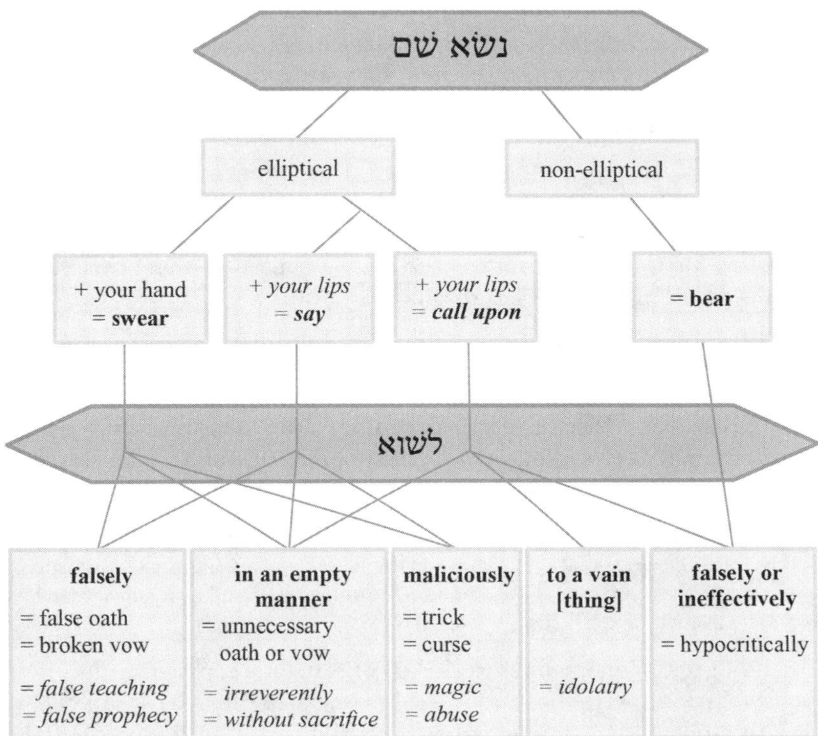

Figure 7. Nonelliptical interpretation of the Name Command

only be worn by one who is committed to obeying Torah. Similarly, the Babylonian Talmud linked Deut 28:10 to the *tefillin*: "And all the peoples of the earth shall see that the name of the Lord is called upon thee [שׁם הי נקרא עליך], and they shall be afraid of thee."[159] The Talmud also connects these four crimes: "vain oaths, false oaths, profanation of the Divine Name, and the desecration of the Sabbath." An editor's footnote reads, "Any unworthy action which reflects discredit upon Judaism—since Judaism is blamed for it—is regarded as profanation of the Divine Name."[160]

Elsewhere the rabbis decided that God no longer performed miracles in answer to their prayers because they did not uphold the sanctity of God's name with their very lives.[161] In the first Talmudic example (*b. Ber.* 6a), the NC was closely linked with the profaning of God's name. The second (*b. Šabb.* 33a) touched on the biblical idea that the people of God were responsible

wrapped in the shape of a *shin,* with knots in the shapes of ד and י. For this reason, the *teffilin* may not be worn by the impure. See Louis Isaac Rabinowitz, "Teffilin," *EJ* 19:578.

159. *B. Ber.* 6a; see Rabinowitz, "Teffilin," *EJ* 19:578.

160. *B. Šabb.* 33a (151 n. 12; cf. *ʾAbot* 5.9 and 4.4).

161. *B. Ber.* 20a.

for bringing honor to the name by the way they lived. This behavioral focus is also evident in *b. Pesaḥ.* 53b, where Hananiah, Mishael, and Azariah sanctified the name by going into the fiery furnace. A footnote reads, "This is one of the great principles of Judaism: a man must *by his actions* sanctify the Divine Name."[162] This principle expresses well the representational reading of the NC, and the connection between them is at least implied by the footnote on *b. Šabb.* 33a, cited above. Although Jewish interpreters have almost always read the NC as an injunction against false swearing, the wider biblical theme that the Israelites bore the name of YHWH and thus represent him to the nations was not forgotten.

Early Christian Interpretation

Some early Christian interpreters also connected God's name to his people's behavior.[163] Second Clement calls for repentance for hypocrisy, "so that the Name (τὸ ὄνομα) may not be blasphemed on our account" (2 Clem 13:1).[164] This blasphemy results from disobedience:

> For when the pagans hear from our mouths the oracles of God, they marvel at their beauty and greatness. But when they discover that our actions are not worthy of the words we speak, they turn from wonder to blasphemy, saying that it is a myth and a delusion. (2 Clem 13:3)

The author of this anonymous work did not explicitly connect the NC with a behavioral interpretation, but he freely associated the behavior of believers with God's name, or reputation.[165] Similarly, to the Philippians Polycarp wrote of "those who bear the name of the Lord hypocritically" (τῶν ἐν ὑποκρίσει φερόντων τὸ ὄνομα τοῦ κυρίου; Pol. *Phil.* 6:3b), and those "through whom the name of the Lord is blasphemed" (*per quem nomen domini blasphematur*; Pol. *Phil.* 10:3a).

The Shepherd of Hermas made the connection between the NC and believers' behavior more explicit. Toward the end of his writings, Hermas gave a series of parables that portrayed believers in Jesus as those who received (λαμβάνω; cf. LXX Exod 20:7)[166] his name in baptism, making them "bearers" of that name (*Herm. Sim.* 9.16.3; 93:3b–4a).[167] This privilege of having "the Name of the Son of God proclaimed over" them was available to

162. *B. Pesaḥ.* 53b (261 n. 5; trans. H. Freedman, emphasis mine).

163. For now, I will treat only extrabiblical Christian texts.

164. 2 Clement 13:2 cites LXX Isa 52:5 verbatim, which speaks of God's name being blasphemed among the nations. All citations from the Apostolic Fathers are taken from Michael Holmes, *The Apostolic Fathers: Greek Texts and English Translations*, 3rd ed. (Grand Rapids: Baker Academic, 2007).

165. On issues of authorship, see ibid., 132.

166. In ch. 4, there is a fuller discussion of the NC in the LXX.

167. On baptism as "sealing" with the name, see Carolyn Osiek, *The Shepherd of Hermas: A Commentary*, Hermeneia (Minneapolis: Fortress, 1999), 206, 235, 238. See esp. *Herm. Sim.* 9.16.3–7; 93:3–7.

people from all nations who heard and believed (*Herm. Sim.* 9.17.4; 94:4). However, some were later found unworthy because they "have the Name (ὄνομα μὲν ἔχουσιν), but are devoid of faith, and there is no fruit of truth in them" (*Herm. Sim.* 9.19.2; 96:2). Any shameful behavior after baptism profaned the name; Hermas insisted, "If you bear (φορῇς) the Name but do not bear his power, you will bear his Name *in vain* (εἰς μάτην ἔσῃ τὸ ὄνομα αὐτοῦ φορῶν)" (*Herm. Sim.* 9.13.2; 90:2, emphasis mine).[168] But those worthy of special honor were "those who suffered for the Name of the Son of God" (*Herm. Sim.* 9.28.2; 105:2). To them the angel said, "You who suffer for the sake of the Name ought to glorify God, because God has considered you worthy that you should bear (βαστάζω) this Name and that all your sins be healed" (*Herm. Sim.* 9.28.5; 105:5; cf. 1 Pet 4:14–16).[169] Hermas seemed to echo the NC deliberately with the rare phrase "in vain" (εἰς μάτην),[170] specifically connecting it with the notion of "bearing" (φορέω and βαστάζω) the name after "receiving" (λαμβάνω) it in baptism. The echoes are unmistakable, though Hermas disambiguated the notion of "carrying."

Hermas was not the only early interpreter to have understood the NC this way. In his restatement of the commands of the Decalogue, Clement of Alexandria deliberately expanded the NC by using two Greek words to represent the Hebrew נשׂא, which most often means to "lift up," "bear," or "carry." Evidently he recognized that λαμβάνω fails to capture unambiguously the idea that the name is *carried* by God's people. Of the NC he said, "Now the second word is declaring it is necessary not to receive (λαμβάνω) nor to carry (ἐπιφέρω) the great majesty of God, which is the Name . . . upon vain, created things."[171] By warning Christians not to confer the name of Yhwh on something made by humans, Clement's view aligns with the "idolatry" view of Staples and Carmichael discussed above. However, Clement did ***not*** read the NC elliptically; he did not interpret it strictly as speech; and he was not content with the LXX translation of נשׂא as λαμβάνω. Both Clement and Hermas took נשׂא in its most natural sense as "lift up" or "carry," while Hermas provides early evidence of the representational interpretation.

---

168. Cf. LXX Exod 20:7. The "power" corresponds mostly to the fruits of the Spirit—namely, faith, self-control, power, patience, sincerity, innocence, purity, cheerfulness, truth, understanding, harmony, and love. See *Herm. Sim.* 9.15.2; 92:2.

169. Osiek (*Shepherd of Hermas*, 251) notes that believers carried (φορέω) the name as their "long-term identity," while other characters in the vision bore heavy weight (βαστάζω). The switch to βαστάζω indicates that because of persecution the name "has become a burden that brings on suffering." Both verbs appear in *Herm. Sim.* 9.14.6; 91:6.

170. Cf. ἐπὶ ματαίω, LXX Exod 20:7. The word μάτην ("in vain"), identical to *Herm. Sim.* 9.13.2 (90:2), is found only twice in the New Testament in that form (Matt 15:9; Mark 7:7). It is the adverbial form of the adjective ματαίῳ occurring in LXX Exod 20:7 and Deut 5:11.

171. Clement of Alexandria, *Stromata* 6.16.137.3, in *Clemens Alexandrinus* 2, *Stromata Buch I–VI*, ed. Otto Stählin, GCS 15 (Leipzig: Hinrichs, 1906), 501, line 15, my translation, taking the last phrase as a hendiadys (cf. Eph 3:12, "bold access"). Online: http://books.google.com/books?id=n1wPAAAAYAAJ&printsec=frontcover&source=gbs_ge_summary_r&cad=0#v=onepage&q&f=false.

Medieval and Reformation Interpretation

The notion of baptism as the act of stamping or sealing believers with Jesus' name is also found in medieval exegesis of the NC. In a series of lectures given by St. Bonaventure in 1267, he attributed oath taking to the literal interpretation of the command, but he also explored the spiritual interpretation: "Listen, you who have been marked by the name Christian, a character has been imprinted on you by the power of the name of God, but later when you sin, you void the power of the sacrament."[172] He outlined three ways the sacrament could be violated: (1) by not believing in the first place, (2) by not being ready for the sacrament, and (3) by becoming apostate.[173] Thomas Aquinas took a similar view. Though he also referred to false oaths as the primary sense of the NC, he said that if someone returns to a life of sin after baptism, "God's name has been taken in vain."[174] These moves to interpret the NC more broadly exhibit the right instinct, but lack exegetical justification.

Martin Luther's ubiquitous use of the NC has already been mentioned. Here we need only to explain his extension of its application beyond speech to behavior. He clearly saw both Jews and Christians as bearing the name of God and linked the NC with the Lord's Prayer, "hallowed be your name" (Matt 6:9). If we pray for the sanctification of God's name, then we also must work so that we do not dishonor the name we bear.[175] For Luther, the implications were practical. In *The Christian in Society III*, Luther appealed to the peasants and urged them not to take up arms against their rulers because they "bear the name of God" by calling themselves Christians, and that name ought not to be taken in vain.[176] Similarly, his basis for condemnation of the Jews is that "they bore God's name," making their rejection of Jesus all the more serious.[177] Here Luther's thinking is clearly in line with the representational interpretation.

Interpreters from the Reformation to the Present

Puritan Thomas Watson (c. 1620–1686) included hypocrisy in his extensive list of violations of the NC, saying, "When we profess God's name, but

172. Bonaventure, *St. Bonaventure's Collations on the Ten Commandments*, trans. Paul J. Spaeth (St. Bonaventure, NY: Franciscan Institute, 1995), 56.

173. Ibid. These three roughly correspond to the possible senses of שׁוא: *false*, *empty*, and *malicious*. Kuntz (*Ten Commandments in History*, 36) writes that, according to 14th-century Englishman Richard Rolle, the NC is violated whenever Christians participate in the Eucharist unworthily.

174. Thomas Aquinas, *The Commandments of God: Conferences on the Two Precepts of Charity and the Ten Commandments*, trans. Laurence Shapcote (London: Burns, Oates & Washbourne, 1937), 37. Cf. Aquinas, *ST* 2a2æ, 122.3.2 (trans. O'Brien, 297–99), emphasis his.

175. *LW* 46:33.

176. "Admonition to Peace," *LW* 46:24. Here Luther specifically invokes the NC.

177. *LW* 47:286.

do not live answerably to it, we take it in vain."[178] Later Matthew Henry adopted virtually the same position: "We take God's name in vain . . . by hypocrisy, making a profession of God's name, but not living up to that profession. Those that name the name of Christ, but do not depart from iniquity, as that name binds them to do, name it in vain; their worship is vain (Matt 15:7–9), their oblations are vain (Isa 1:11, 13), their religion is vain (Jas 1:26)."[179] More recently John Stott insisted that we not limit the NC to speech:

> His holy name can be dragged in the mud by our careless use of language, and most of us would do well to revise our vocabulary from time to time. But to take God's name in vain is not just a matter of words—it's also about thoughts and deeds. Whenever our behavior is inconsistent with our belief, when what we do contradicts what we say, we take God's name in vain. To call God "Lord" and disobey him is to take his name in vain. To call God "Father" and be filled with anxiety and doubts is to deny his name. To take God's name in vain is to talk one way and act another.[180]

Writing to lay audiences, Stott, Henry, and Watson all insisted that the NC cannot be restricted to speech. Though they provided no exegetical basis for doing so, they effectively stepped beyond the elliptical interpretation into the realm of the nonelliptical, representational view.

R. Kendall Soulen arrives at this same conclusion about the NC by looking at the biblical theme of the name of God and how the people of God are to interact with his name. His argument is thematic rather than lexical.[181] For example, he associates the NC with the desecration of the name decried by Isaiah and Ezekiel, and says that it warns the Israelites not to do or say anything that detracts from God's integrity.[182]

Clear Advocates of the Nonelliptical Interpretation

In 1989, Jewish scholar Meir Bar-Ilan rejected the idea that the NC is "symbolic or metaphorical" in favor of what he called a "concrete" or "tangible" reading, similar to that employed by those who wear phylacteries as a concrete fulfillment of Deut 6:4–9.[183] In connection with the Priestly

178. Watson, *The Ten Commandments*, 85.

179. Matthew Henry, *Matthew Henry's Commentary on the Whole Bible* (Peabody, MA: Hendrickson, 1991), 284.

180. John R. W. Stott, *Basic Christianity* (Grand Rapids: Eerdmans, 2008), 81.

181. For R. Kendall Soulen ("The Blessing of God's Name," 47–61 in Roger Van Harn, ed., *The Ten Commandments for Jews, Christians, and Others* [Grand Rapids: Eerdmans, 2007], 49), oath taking is the natural concern of this command, but the language is sufficiently broad to include other applications.

182. Ibid., emphasis mine. Harrelson (*The Ten Commandments and Human Rights*, 66) does not argue exegetically for a representational interpretation of the NC, but his conclusion precisely expresses what the representational interpretation entails, saying that the nations should be able to find out what Yhwh is like by watching Israel.

183. Bar-Ilan, "They Shall Put My Name," 27. Cf. John Huehnergard and Harold Liebowitz, "The Biblical Prohibition against Tattooing," *VT* 63 (2013): 74.

Blessing of Num 6:24–27, Bar-Ilan posited the existence of an ancient ceremony whereby the priests actually wrote the name of YHWH on the bodies of those receiving the blessing. His lexical evidence for this is not convincing. He depended heavily on the double transmission of tradition (both oral and written).[184] He adduced as evidence the story of Cain, on whom YHWH "put a mark" (שׂים אות; Gen 4:15), and the vision of Ezekiel where the angel is told to "set a mark" on the foreheads of the righteous (תוה תו; Ezek 9:4).[185] On the basis of these and other passages, he says that the priests are literally to "put" (שׂים; "write") YHWH's name on the Israelites (Num 6:27).[186] Extrapolating from this, the NC warned those who "take up the name" (on their body) not to profane that name by failing to obey God's commands.[187] This interpretation avoids the anomalous translation of נשׂא as "utter" or "swear," and consequently the overlap with the command against false witness, and fits better with the immediate context in the Decalogue.[188]

However, Bar-Ilan stretched the evidence, claiming that "the writing of the name YHWH upon the body was very widespread in ancient times."[189] While we have some indication of such practices, most passages he cites are figurative, visionary, or susceptible to other interpretations. Furthermore, Bar-Ilan's interpretation seems to imply that only those who still bore the priestly writing legibly could actually violate the NC.

A few others have offered exegetical warrant for the representational view. In 1952, A. J. Wagner argued briefly that the current popular interpretation of Exod 20:7 did not do justice to the Hebrew. His discussion centered on the Hebrew word נשׂא, suggesting that it could mean "to bear or carry" the name of God—that is, to claim allegiance to him. The command warns God's people not to do so falsely. He supposed that this straightforward reading of the NC got off track very early and became associated with oath taking and later with profanity.[190] Wagner does not explain why; he simply raises the issue and calls for re-assessment.

Allan Harman marshalls lexical, contextual, and theological evidence for a representational reading, insisting that the LXX rendering of the NC does not lend itself readily to blasphemy, but fits more naturally with the idea of "receiving" the name (in order to bear it).[191] Furthermore, in no

---

184. Bar-Ilan, "They Shall Put My Name," 22.

185. Ibid., 23–24. Cf. Sandra Jacobs, "The Body Inscribed: A Priestly Initiative?" in *The Body in Biblical, Christian and Jewish Texts*, ed. Joan E. Taylor, LSTS 85 (London: Bloomsbury, 2014), 11–13.

186. Other passages he cites to illustrate bodily inscriptions include Isa 44:5; 49:15–17; Job 31:35; Song 8:6; and Hag 2:23.

187. Bar-Ilan, "They Shall Put My Name," 28.

188. Ibid., 27, 30.

189. Ibid., 24.

190. A. J. Wagner, "An Interpretation of Exodus 20:7," *Int* 6 (1952): 228–29; cited by Merrill, *Deuteronomy*, 149 n. 36, though Merrill does not fully appropriate Wagner's point.

191. Allan M. Harman, "The Interpretation of the Third Commandment," *RTR* 47 (1988): 1–7. Cf. Daniel I. Block, "Bearing the Name of the LORD with Honor: A Homily

other passage does נשא mean "to speak" without extra modifiers.[192] Harman also argues that "falsely" is an inadequate translation of the broader word שׁוא, which usually refers to "emptiness" or "worthlessness."[193] He contends that the closest parallel expression to נשא שׁם is Exod 28:12, 29, which describes Aaron's high priestly breastpiece.[194] Just as the high priest "bears the names" of the twelve tribes on his person and so represents them before YHWH, so Israel bears the divine name. Furthermore, the word שׁם ("name") is more than a spoken appellation. Most significant for the NC, several idioms that include שׁם involve affixing a name to a person, place, or object to indicate ownership.[195] Numbers 6:27 announces that in pronouncing the priestly blessing, YHWH's name was figuratively "placed" upon the Israelites. The idea that Israel belonged to YHWH and that his name had been "proclaimed over her" implied a responsibility to represent him well among the nations.[196]

Harman has much in common with Bar-Ilan, but offers a more satisfactory interpretation of the NC, insofar as he avoids the historical and exegetical tensions of Bar-Ilan's concrete interpretation. Harman's representational reading appears solid lexically, contextually, and theologically.

The present task is to assess the validity of the representational interpretation advanced by Harman, while providing more detailed substantiation. Only a full-length monograph can do justice to the complexity of the issues involved—contextual, historical, lexical, and theological. The weight of the history of interpretation may pull against the representational reading of the NC, but as a viable alternative it deserves full consideration. Chapter 3 offers a detailed lexical and historical analysis of the NC, followed by a careful look at the character of the Decalogue and its literary context in ch. 4. Then, with the help of cognitive linguistics, ch. 5 examines the theological import of the NC.

---

on the Second Command of the Decalogue (Exod 20:7; Deut 5:11)," *BSac* 168 (2011): 20–31; reprinted in Daniel I. Block, *How I Love Your Torah, O Lord! Studies in the Book of Deuteronomy* (Eugene, OR: Cascade, 2011), 61–72. Harman ("Interpretation of the Third Commandment," 4) contends that this reading supports the Decalogic structure of Deuteronomy, which he adopts for his later commentary. See Allan M. Harman, *Deuteronomy: The Commands of a Covenant God*, Focus on the Bible (Ross-shire, Scotland: Christian Focus, 2007), 78.

192. Ibid., 3.

193. Ibid., 1, 4–5.

194. Ibid., 4; cf. Block, "Bearing the Name," 63.

195. Harman, "Interpretation of the Third Commandment," 3. Cf. Block, "Bearing the Name," 63.

196. Harman, "Interpretation of the Third Commandment," 3–4. Cf. Block, "Bearing the Name," 64, 66.

Chapter 3

A Reexamination of the Name Command: Lexico-Historical Considerations

> The name of God, therefore, is freighted with all the power and holiness that is God's. The community that cannot make anything to represent God and cannot put anything in God's place is freely given the name of God as representation and manifestation of the reality of God. This is how God is known, in and through the name YHWH.
>
> —Patrick Miller, *The Ten Commandments*

Having explored the history of interpretation of the NC, this chapter engages its key lexemes with a view toward a constructive proposal. I begin with an exploration of the variety of meanings for the Hebrew word שֵׁם, both on its own and as part of idiomatic expressions. Following this, I will examine each of the other key words in turn, focusing on how each is used in the Hebrew Bible and the earliest translations. Chapter 5 will evaluate the motivation for the unusual phrase נשׂא שׁם in light of conceptual metaphor theory and explore the Sinai narratives for the most illuminating parallels.

First, a few comments are necessary about the narrative setting. Careful attention to Moses' multiple ascents and descents in the narrative of Exod 19 and 20 presents a literary framework in which Moses was with the people at the base of the mountain when YHWH spoke the Ten Words (see Exod 19:24–25; 20:21).[1] Between these bookends of descent and ascent, the Decalogue itself is portrayed as direct divine speech (20:1).

The NC is expressed in 2nd-person masculine singular form, signaling each individual Israelite's responsibility to obey. The recapitulation of the command is distinctive; the repetition of the salient admonition encloses a threat of punishment for the rebellious (כי לא ינקה יהוה את אשר־ישא את־שמו לשוא). A sanction such as this is unique to the first two commands of the Decalogue, binding them together and underscoring the seriousness of violation.[2] Like the NC, the previous command is grounded in YHWH's

---

1. The narrative structure of this section of Exodus is particularly challenging. See, e.g., Van Seters, "'Comparing Scripture with Scripture.'" Childs (*Book of Exodus*, 393–402) discusses the theological significance of the present setting.

2. Not only do these commands share a threat of punishment but the language employed in each command *together* echoes YHWH's self-description in Exod 34:6–7. For

character: "You shall not worship them [other gods, v. 3] or serve them, for I, YHWH, am a jealous God, attending to the iniquity of the fathers upon the children to the third and fourth [generation] of those who reject me" (Exod 20:6). God himself will punish offenders.

The direct object marker (את־שם־יהוה) makes clear that "name" is the object of the negated verb נשׂא and that the name in question is YHWH.[3] The addition of אלהיך underscores the covenantal relationship that forms the basis for this command. YHWH is not a random despotic deity demanding respect, but rather Israel's own God, the one who rescued her from Egypt (Exod 20:2).[4] Given the complexity of the investigation, we will first consider the word שׁם and the variety of idioms in which it is employed.

Exodus 20:7 // Deuteronomy 5:11

לא תשׂא את־שם־יהוה אלהיך	You shall not **bear** the **name** of YHWH, your God,
לשוא כי לא ינקה יהוה	**in vain**, for YHWH will not **acquit**
את אשר־ישׂא את־שמו לשוא	one who **bears his name in vain**.

שׁם

The designated object of נשׂא in the NC is את־שם־יהוה. Though the translation of שׁם as "name" is straightforward, its significance requires elucidation.[5] The linguistic and historical analysis that follows will explore

a detailed analysis of this allusion, as well as an argument that Exod 20:3–6 expresses a single command, making the NC the second command, see below, pp. 106 and 132–134.

3. Elßner (*Das Namensmißbrauch-Verbot*, 77) points out the tendency of premasoretic scribes to insert a Paseq, or vertical separator, between words that express opposites. See, e.g., Ezek 43:8b, where "name of YHWH" is separated from the governing verb טמא ("defile"). Building on this observation, we note that no Paseq appears in either version of the NC, suggesting that the verb נשׂא is not inherently derogatory. It is not the "bearing" that is problematic, but rather "bearing . . . in vain."

4. The phrase יהוה אלהיך, ubiquitous in Deuteronomy, is also at home in Exodus, appearing 8 times with the singular 2nd person pronominal suffix and 4 times with the plural. Elßner's analysis of this phrase is skewed by his failure to include the plural. He claims יהוה אלהיך is absent from Leviticus and Numbers, though the phrase יהוה אלהיכם appears 28 times. He states that יהוה אלהיך is a deuteronomic expression, but that in the NC one cannot separate יהוה from את־שם, a phrase he dates to the Postexilic Period, overruling the deuteronomic character of the overall expression. See ibid., 102–3, 277. But note, e.g., Exod 10:8 and Deut 4:29, where יהוה אלהיכם is introduced by the direct object marker ־את .

5. Translation of שׁם in the LXX (ὄνομα), Targums (שׁם) and other ancient versions (Syriac, *šm*; Latin, *nomen*) is likewise predictable. Johan Lust (*A Greek-English Lexicon of the Septuagint* [Stuttgart: Deutsche Bibelgesellschaft, 1992], 334) and T. Muraoka (*A Greek-English Lexicon of the Septuagint* [Walpole, MA: Peeters, 2009], 498–99), both define ὄνομα as "name, fame, reputation." Perhaps due to the influence of Greek philosophy, several lexicons embrace the old idea that a name contains a person's essence. See BDAG 712; L. Hartman, "ὄνομα," *EDNT* 2:519; Bietenhard, "ὄνομα," *TDNT* 5:243.

the ways that the Hebrew Bible speaks of the name of YHWH as well as the range of ways that names functioned in the ancient world. The inherent danger in such an enterprise is illegitimate totality transfer. However, the goal here is to develop sensitivity for the variety of שׁם–related idioms employed and possible meanings available to the biblical writer so that we may select the most appropriate and likely interpretation for the NC, given shared lexical, syntactic, and contextual factors.

The word שׁם appears 864 times in the Hebrew Bible,[6] with roughly 44 percent of these referring to YHWH.[7] Usually שׁם signals a simple appellation,[8] as in, "YHWH is his name" (יהוה שׁמו; Exod 15:3). As with human names, YHWH's proper name uniquely identified him.[9] God revealed his personal name, YHWH, to Moses (Exod 3:15), indicating how people were to identify and address him (Exod 3:15b; 20:24).[10] Since YHWH's name came to be associated with his acts on Israel's behalf, its connotations rested on a history of divine action rather than etymology.[11] When nations heard what

6. See *DCH* 8:422–31; Allen P. Ross, "שֵׁם," *NIDOTTE* 4:147–51; Reiterer, Ringgren, and Fabry, "שֵׁם," *TDOT* 15:128–176; A. S. van der Woude, "שֵׁם," *TLOT* 3:1348–67; cf. Hoftijzer and Jongeling, "šm$_1$," *DNWSI* 1155–59. The Akkadian cognate for שֵׁם, *šumu*, carries almost the same range of meaning: "name, fame, reputation, [a pronoun], offspring, item" (*CAD* Š/3 284–97; cf. *AHw* 3:1274–75). As in Hebrew, Akkadian names can be bestowed, honored, profaned, praised, invoked, erased, made known, or forgotten. See Hayim ben Yosef Tawil, *An Akkadian Lexical Companion for Biblical Hebrew: Etymological-Semantic and Idiomatic Equivalents with Supplement on Biblical Aramaic* (Jersey City, NJ: Ktav, 2009), 404–7.

7. By my count, YHWH's שׁם is mentioned 379 times, not counting the angelic/theophanic appearances in Gen 32:30 and Judg 13.

8. I am using "appellation" as defined in Webster (p. 68): "a name or title that describes or identifies a person or thing; designation."

9. A previous generation conceived of the name as capturing the "essence" of a person. See above, p. 47 n. 5. Today scholars are more cautious about making this equation, but many emphasize names' ritual or magical power. See Denise M. Doxey, "Names," *OEAE* 2:490. Knowledge of someone's name was thought to give access or even control over them. See also Dozeman, *Exodus*, 486; Schüngel-Straumann, *Der Dekalog*, 94; Vandier, *La Religion Égyptienne*, 199.

10. In contrast, YHWH promised to cut off the worship of other gods so that their names would no longer be remembered (Hos 2:19[17]; Zech 13:2, both זכר *niphal*). Without cultic attention, the gods themselves would be forgotten. The Israelites were not to הזכיר the names of other gods in any way, either through speaking them aloud (Exod 23:13) or by swearing by them, serving them, or bowing down to them (Josh 23:7). The expressions זכר שׁם (*qal* or *niphal*) and הזכיר שׁם (*hiphil*) have to do with "remembering" a name or "causing him to be remembered." *HALOT* 1:270; Martin Rose, "Name of God," *ABD* 4:1002. In the Hebrew Bible, people often expressed a desire to know the name of God or his messengers (Gen 39:29; Exod 3:13, 15; 6:3; Judg 13:6, 17–18; Ps 9:11; Isa 64:1; cf. Test. Levi 5:5). In the ANE knowing a god's name was a mark of privilege, with attendant responsibilities to treat it carefully. See the "Legend of Isis and the Name of Re," trans. Robert K. Ritner, *COS* 1.22:33–34.

11. Walther Zimmerli, *I Am Yahweh* (Atlanta: John Knox, 1982), 81–82. Cf. Austin

YHWH had done for the Israelites, they concluded that he was committed to Israel as a people (Josh 9:9; cf. 1 Kgs 8:41–43; cf. 1QM 11, 14).

Name can also refer metonymically to YHWH (e.g., Ps 18:50[49]), or to his fame, reputation (e.g., Exod 9:16), or authority (Exod 5:23).[12] In rare poetic passages the name almost takes on a hypostatic quality, but even here שם may be read as metonymic for YHWH himself (e.g., Isa 30:27; Deut 28:58b).[13]

שם *as a Declaration of Possession*

נקרא שם על

A standard naming formula used throughout biblical literature is קרא שם, with the *qal* form of קרא followed by שם as the object in apposition to the given name ("to call a name *x*"; e.g., Exod 2:10; 17:7).[14] More important for this project is a variation of this standard formula: the ***niphal*** of קרא with שם as the subject followed by the preposition על attached to a pronominal

D. Surls, *Making Sense of the Divine Name in the Book of Exodus: From Etymology to Literary Onomastics*, BBRSup 17 (Winona Lake, IN: Eisenbrauns, 2017).

12. The metonymic use of שם for a person applies exclusively to YHWH in the Hebrew Bible. His name was loved (Ps 5:12; cf. 11QPs[a] 19, 12), praised (1 Chr 16:35; Ps 7:18), serenaded (2 Sam 22:50; Ps 9:3), blessed (Job 1:21; Ps 96:2), glorified (1 Chr 16:29; Isa 24:15; cf.1QS[b] 4, 28), thanked (Ps 44:9; 122:4), sought (Ps 83:17), feared (Deut 28:58; Neh 1:11; Ps 61:6; Isa 59:19), honored (Ps 86:9, 12), exalted (Ps 34:3; Mic 5:3; 1QM 14, 4), trusted (Ps 20:8; Isa 50:10), thought about (Mal 3:16), waited for (Ps 52:11) and called on (Gen 4:26; 1 Kgs 18:24; etc., 25 times total). Offerings (Isa 60:9) and incense (Mal 1:11) were presented to his name. The nations gathered to it (Jer 3:17) and someday even they would call on the name of YHWH (Zeph 3:9). The name was a refuge (Zeph 3:12) or strong tower (Prov 18:10; cf. 1QSb 5, 28), and a protection for the righteous (Ps 20:2; 91:14; 124:8). According to van der Woude ("שֵׁם," *TLOT* 3:1365), שם sometimes functioned as a personal pronoun.

Fame, reputation: See also 2 Sam 7:23, 26; 1 Chr 17:21; Neh 9:10; Ps 106:8; Isa 63:12, 14; Jer 32:20; Dan 9:15. For שם as metonymy for human fame, reputation, or memory, see Reiterer, "שֵׁם," *TDOT* 15:146–47.

Authority: To act in YHWH's name (בשם־יהוה) was to represent him and carry out his will. This idiom also applies to human delegations (e.g., 1 Sam 25:5; 1 Kgs 21:8; Esth 3:12, 8:8, 10).

13. Cf. Ps 75:2; 4 Esdr 7:60. So also Sandra L. Richter, *The Deuteronomistic History and the Name Theology:* lĕšakkēn šĕmô šām *in the Bible and the Ancient Near East*, BZAW 318 (Berlin: de Gruyter, 2002), 11; van der Woude, "שֵׁם," *TLOT* 3:1363. In Isa 30:27, שם may be a later anti-anthropomorphic addition. See *HALOT* 2:1551.

14. This formula is ubiquitous in Genesis (57 times) but appears frequently in other OT books as well, with a special concentration in Isa 58–62, showing the diachronic persistence of the formula. Cf. Hossfeld and Kindl, "קָרָא: VII. Naming," *TDOT* 13:126). Most instances involve a birth or naming a place to remember an event there. In one case, someone assigned a name to YHWH using this expression; Hagar called YHWH אל ראי ("the God who sees"; Gen 16:13). קרא שם once means "remember" (Ruth 4:14). Another version of this formula, more common with corporate naming, lacks שם and introduces the object with ל. Occasionally, both שם and ל appear for emphasis. For example, Gen 2:20; Isa 62:2; 65:15; Ruth 4:17. For discussion, see *DCH* 7:296; Hossfeld and Kindl, "קָרָא: VII. Naming," *TDOT* 13:126, 130.

suffix. To distinguish between these phrases, I will include the prefixed נ when referring to the standard (*qal*) naming formula. נקרא שם על appears 21 times in the Hebrew Bible.[15] Careful consideration of military and legal contexts will clarify what the idiom means when YHWH's name is the subject. In the first example, Joab attempted to motivate King David to resume military leadership when the latter was preoccupied with family affairs:

2 Samuel 12:28

ועתה אסף את־יתר העם	Now gather the remainder of the people
וחנה על־העיר ולכדה	and encamp against the city and capture it,
פן־אלכד אני את־העיר	lest I capture the city myself
ונקרא שמי עליה	and **my name is proclaimed over it.**

David's abdication of leadership left open the possibility that Joab, his army commander, would receive credit for a victory. Joab's statement was ambiguous about *who* would declare his name. By giving the king fair warning, he could not be charged with sedition. Perhaps he planned to do so himself, thereby claiming the captured city of Rabbah as his own.[16] Or perhaps he simply anticipated that others would recognize him as the conquering hero, making his name famous in Rabbah. Either way, David would miss out on an opportunity to secure his own political power.

Isaiah 4:1 applied the same idiom to a legal marriage arrangement:

15. Twice a similar phrase (קרא + בשם) is used with the same import, resulting in 23 total appearances. See Isa 43:7; 48:1; cf. 63:19. Although קרא בשם (*qal*) normally means "call *on* the name," these two cases use the *niphal* form, resulting in the reflexive meaning "called *by* the name." While קרא שם (*qal*) is more common in early texts, קרא שם על (*niphal*) predominates during and after the exile. See Hossfeld and Kindl, "קָרָא: VII. Naming," *TDOT* 13:126–27. Reiterer ("שֵׁם," *TDOT* 15:146–47) fails to list נקרא שם על separately from other expressions involving קרא. He also blurs the distinction between YHWH calling people by name and calling them by *his* name (ibid., 155). The former indicates appointment to a task while the latter indicates a claim to ownership. For discussion of נקרא שם על, see Hossfeld and Lamberty-Zielinski, "קָרָא: VIII. Property Law," *TDOT* 13:131; Louis Jonker, "קרא," *NIDOTTE* 3:973; *HALOT* 2:1130; Richter, *DH and Name Theology*, 84; Roland de Vaux, "Le lieu que Yahvé a choisi pour y établir son nom," in *Das ferne und nahe Wort: Festschrift L. Rost*, ed. Fritz Maass (Berlin: Alfred Töpelmann, 1967), 219–28; van der Woude, "שֵׁם," *TLOT* 3:1363; Johannes Goldenstein, *Das Gebet der Gottesknechte: Jesaja 63,7—64,11 im Jesajabuch* (Neukirchen-Vluyn: Neukirchener Verlag, 2001), 105; Wolfgang Lau, *Schriftgelehrte Prophetie in Jes 56–66: eine Untersuchung zu den literarischen Bezügen in den letzten elf Kapiteln des Jesajabuches* (Berlin: de Gruyter, 1994), 300.

16. Joab's warning makes sense as an oral claim to ownership and need not imply a stone inscription (2 Sam 12:28). Jair's naming of a captured city after himself (Havvoth-jair) uses nearly the same expression; though *qal* rather than *niphal* (ויקרא אתם על־שמו; Deut 3:14). Psalm 49:12[11] employs a variation, perhaps inspired by phonological parallelism (קראו בשמותם עלי אדמות). Isaiah 48:2 employs the idiom in reverse. There the Israelites "call themselves after the holy city" (מעיר הקדש נקראו). For other examples of cities named after people, see Gen 4:17 (Enoch → Enoch); Gen 24:10 (Nahor → Aram-naharaim, or the city of Nahor); Josh 19:47 (Dan → Dan); Josh 21:11 (Arba → Kiriath-arba); and 1 Kgs 16:24 (Shemer → Samaria); cf. 2 Sam 18:18 (Absalom's monument).

Table 2.* נקרא שם על *in the Hebrew Bible

נקרא שם על		Deut	Sam	Kgs	Isa	Jer	Dan	Amos	Chr	
secular use			×		×					2
Name of YHWH	ark		×						//×	2
	temple			×		××××××			//×	8
	city					×	××			3
	people of Israel	×			×	×	×		×	5
	person					×				1
	nations							×		1
		1	2	1	2	9	3	1	3	22

Isaiah 4:1

והחזיקו שבע נשים באיש אחד For seven women will seize one man
ביום ההוא לאמר in that day, saying,
לחמנו נאכל ושמלתנו נלבש "We will eat our own food and wear our own clothes,
רק יקרא שמך עלינו only **let your name be proclaimed over us.**
אסף חרפתנו Take away our reproach!"

Here, the prophet spoke of a coming day of judgment for Judah in which so many men would fall in battle that a leadership vacuum would result (3:6–7, 12, 25). In that day, widows would greatly outnumber the available men and would band together and beg to be taken under the legal and social protection of a husband by having him claim them as his own.[17] In this way they could avoid public disgrace. The women would not give up their own personal names in exchange for a man's name; instead, they would take on his name as a designation of a proper marital relationship (most likely using the formula "*x*, wife of *y*"), reflecting his claim on them and their security in him.[18] Here the oral nature of this claim is obvious.

In light of these examples involving human names, we may consider contexts in which the idiom נקרא שם על involves YHWH's name (table 2). The phrase is only associated with a handful of entities: the ark (2 Sam 6:2 // 1 Chr 13:6); the temple (1 Kgs 8:43 // 2 Chr 6:33; Jer 7:10, 11, 14, 30; 32:34; 34:15); Jerusalem (Jer 25:29; Dan 9:18–19); the Israelites (Deut 28:10; 2 Chr 7:14; Isa 63:19; Jer 14:9; Dan 9:19; cf. cf. 4Q504 1 II, 12); Jeremiah (Jer 15:16); and, on

17. Hossfeld and Lamberty-Zielinski, "קָרָא: VIII. Property Law," *TDOT* 13:131.

18. For example, 2 Sam 11:3: "Is this not Bathsheba, the daughter of Eliam, the wife of Uriah the Hittite?" In keeping with the conventions of a patriarchal society, Bathsheba was identified in relation to male authority. Cf. Gen 24:51; Judg 4:17; 2 Kgs 22:14. Tobit 3:8 may provide another legal example, though in Greek. According to Codex Sinaiticus a woman was married to seven husbands without "being named by one of them" (without taking their names; καὶ ἑνὸς αὐτῶν οὐκ ὠνομάσθης). In most other MSS ὠνομάσθης reads ὠνάσθης, "to gain benefit from." See *Tobit*, Septuaginta: Vetus Testamentum Graecum 8/5 (Göttingen: Vandenhoeck & Ruprecht, 1983), 82.

one unusual occasion, the nations (Amos 9:12). While some have suggested the phrase שׁם יהוה נקרא על means Yhwh's name is *read* upon these entities, implying a physical inscription,[19] the entire phrase שׁם יהוה נקרא על appears to be lexicalized as a recognition of ownership.[20] The declaration of a name *over* (על) something constitutes an oral claim reminiscent of a physical inscription or branding, as the following examples demonstrate.

We will explore each category to which this phrase was applied in the order listed in table 2, beginning with the ark.

2 Samuel 6:2

ויקם וילך דוד	And David got up and went
וכל־העם אשר אתו	and all the people who were with him
מבעלי יהודה	from Baʿalah of Judah
להעלות משם את ארון האלהים	to bring up from there the ark of God
אשר־נקרא שם	**over which a name is proclaimed** –
שם יהוה צבאות	the name of Yhwh of armies
ישב הכרבים עליו	enthroned on the cherubim.

1 Chronicles 13:6

ויעל דויד וכל־ישראל בעלתה	And David and all Israel went up to Baʿalah,
אל־קרית יערים אשר ליהודה	to Kiriath Jearim, which belongs to Judah,
להעלות משם את ארון האלהים	to bring up from there the ark of God,
יהוה יושב הכרובים	(of) Yhwh enthroned on the cherubim,
אשר־נקרא שם	which is **called a name**.

The subtle differences between these parallel texts cannot mask their basic similarity; they describe the same event. In 2 Sam 6:2, שׁם lacks the pronominal suffix we might expect, but its definiteness is signaled by the

19. See Meir Bar-Ilan, "Magic Seals upon the Body among Jews in the First Centuries CE (Hebrew)," *Tarbiz* 57 (1987): 41; idem, "They Shall Put My Name"; Jacobs, "The Body Inscribed," 12. Cf. Daniel I. Block, "No Other Gods: Bearing the Name of Yhwh in a Polytheistic World," in *The Gospel according to Moses: Theological and Ethical Reflections on the Book of Deuteronomy* (Eugene, OR: Cascade, 2012), 246.

20. I prefer the translation "proclaimed over" to "read upon." Though קרא can mean "read" in the *qal* (e.g., Deut 17:19 and 31:11, which refers to public proclamation of written texts), only twice does the *niphal* of קרא clearly mean "read" (Esth 6:1; Neh 13:1; *HALOT* 2:1131). Neither matches the grammar of נקרא שׁם על. In both cases a document is read aloud to someone, which explains the passive *niphal*. Still, given the relative rarity of *niphal* קרא we might posit a correspondence between *niphal* and *qal*, in which case a variety of other syntactical correspondences might be expected. In the *qal*, the object of קרא (i.e., that which is being "read") is marked in one of four ways: (1) the direct object marker את (Deut 31:11; 2 Kgs 5:7; 22:16; 23:2 = 2 Chr 34:30; Jer 29:29; 36:6, 10; 51:63), (2) a pronominal suffix (2 Kgs 19:14; 22:8, 10; Jer 36:15, 21), (3) the preposition ב (Deut 17:19; Jer 36:13, 14?; Hab 2:2; Neh 8:3, 8, 18; 9:3; 2 Chr 34:18), or (4) no marker at all (Exod 24:7; Josh 8:35; Isa 34:16; Jer 6:8). Isaiah 34:16 belongs in the final category because the compound preposition מעל technically marks the object of the verb דרשׁ ("consult"; *DCH* 2:474), rather than קרא. The ב-prefix may indicate an emphasis on reading only a selection from a particular document.

appositional phrase "the name of Yhwh of armies, enthroned on the cherubim." This may explain why Chronicles employs שׁם without any suffix and lacks the prepositional phrase עליו, resulting in a unique, shortened expression (נקרא שׁם).[21] Since עליו was already separated from נקרא שׁם, the latter is all that remained of the original idiom after the Chronicler shifted Samuel's appositional phrase forward. Even so, נקרא שׁם clearly refers to the name Yhwh.[22]

These are the only cases where the ark was associated with Yhwh's name. The occasion was significant; as the most treasured object of the tabernacle, housed in its inner sanctum, the ark was thought to be the footstool of Yhwh's throne and guarantee of his presence. Its 20-year absence from the tabernacle jeopardized Yhwh's presence among his people (see 1 Sam 4:3, 21). Powerful signs accompanied its sojourn in Philistine territory, implying that it remained an object of Yhwh's attention (1 Sam 5:1–6:21). David brought it back to his city, ostensibly in hopes of securing Yhwh's blessing on his reign as king (see 1 Sam 6:12). When the ark returned, the narrator commented that David was "settled" in his palace, having "rest" on all sides (2 Sam 7:1).

The temple was also attributed to Yhwh using the idiom נקרא שׁם על. A few examples will suffice:

1 Kings 8:43 // 2 Chronicles 6:33[23]

אתה תשמע השמים מכון שׁבתך	Now may you hear in heaven your dwelling place
ועשׂית ככל אשׁר־יקרא אליך הנכרי	and do according to all the foreigner calls to you
למען ידעון כל־עמי הארץ את־שׁמך	so all the peoples of the earth will know your **name**,
ליראה אתך כעמך ישׂראל	to fear you as your people Israel [do],
ולדעת כי־שׁמך נקרא	and to know that **your name is proclaimed**
על־הבית הזה אשׁר בניתי	**over** this house that I built.

In a prayer punctuated with references to the name, Solomon used the phrase שׁמך נקרא על־הבית to reiterate that the temple he built for Yhwh was the legitimate cult site.[24] He hoped that even foreigners who prayed to Yhwh at his temple would discover this, and in so doing would come

21. Other parts of 1 Chr 13:6 are laconic: וילך, ויקם, and צבאות are all missing.

22. But we have no evidence that Yhwh's name was inscribed on the ark. Given the precise detail of the tabernacle instructions, the absence of a directive to inscribe the ark with Yhwh's name makes such an inscription unlikely (Exod 25:10–22). This idiom must then denote oral ascription.

23. These parallel passages are nearly identical, particularly with reference to our key phrase.

24. The Apocrypha make similar statements. The temple was built in his name (Sir 47:13), in a place sanctified for his name (3 Macc 2:9), and was said to have his name proclaimed over it (τὸν οἶκον οὗ ἐπεκλήθη τὸ ὄνομά σου ἐπ' αὐτῷ, Bar 2:26; 1 Macc 7:37). Cf. 1 Esd 4:63: "The temple where his name is named upon it" (τὸ ἱερόν οὗ ὠνομάσθη τὸ ὄνομα αὐτοῦ ἐπ' αὐτῷ). This expression likely indicates an oral declaration of ownership: "This temple is Yhwh's."

to know Yhwh's name. That is, they would know that Yhwh, and not another god, was Israel's deity, and that Solomon's temple was the authorized place of worship.[25] Answered prayers would confirm Yhwh's authorization of this place. Note that שׁם is being used in two distinct ways here, first to identify Yhwh (metonymy) and then in our key idiom to denote his possession of the temple. The activation of both senses in the same text is a brilliant play on words that provides rhetorical continuity to Solomon's prayer.

As table 2 shows, the phrase נקרא שׁם על was a favorite of Jeremiah's. He drew on two deuteronomic ideas—that Yhwh claimed the central sanctuary as his own and that he claimed the people of Israel as his own—both using the same idiom. By extension, he could apply נקרא שׁם על to the city of Jerusalem because it housed the temple, and to himself as a faithful Israelite.[26] Here is a prime example:

Jeremiah 7:9–12 (cf. 7:14, 30)

הגנב רצח ונאף	Will you steal, murder, and commit adultery
והשׁבע לשׁקר וקטר לבעל	and swear falsely and sacrifice to Baʿal
והלך אחרי אלהים אחרים	and walk after other gods
אשׁר לא־ידעתם	whom you have not known,
ובאתם ועמדתם לפני בבית הזה	and then come and stand before this house
אשׁר נקרא־שׁמי עליו	**over which my name is proclaimed**
ואמרתם נצלנו	and say "We are delivered!" —
למען עשׂות את כל־התועבות האלה	so that you may do all these abominable things?
המערת פרצים היה הבית הזה	Is this house—**over which my name is pro-**
אשׁר־נקרא־שׁמי עליו בעיניכם	**claimed**—a robbers' hideout in your eyes?
גם אנכי הנה ראיתי נאם־יהוה	Look, I myself have seen it," declares Yhwh.
סכי לכו־נא אל־מקומי אשׁר בשׁילו	"For go now to the place which is in Shiloh
אשׁר שׁכנתי שׁמי שׁם בראשׁונה	where I placed my name at first,
וראו את אשׁר־עשׂיתי לו	and see what I have done to it
מפני רעת עמי ישׂראל	in the face of my people Israel's wickedness."

Jeremiah 7:9–12 is an important passage for at least three reasons. First, it draws attention to the link between obedience to covenant principles, highlighting five of those outlined in the Decalogue, and the official cult site, which belongs to Yhwh. An immoral lifestyle was incompatible with worship of Yhwh.[27] Second, it describes the general state of moral degra-

25. Appealing to Jer 7:4, Block ("No Other Gods," 253 n. 63) speculates that the temple might have had an inscription on the foundation or above the door declaring it to be היכל יהוה, declaring to all the name of the divine resident. However, the narrative lacks detailed building instructions to confirm this (1 Chr 28:11–19).

26. See also Jer 25:29; cf. Ezek 48:35. Note Hossfeld and Lamberty-Zielinski, "קָרָא: VIII. Property Law," *TDOT* 13:131. William Holladay (*Jeremiah 1: A Commentary on the Book of the Prophet Jeremiah Chapters 1–25*, Hermeneia [Minneapolis: Fortress, 1986], 458–59) avers that Jeremiah's application of the idiom to himself evokes marriage imagery (cf. Isa 4:1). Because he was celibate for the sake of his ministry (16:2), Jeremiah's "joy" (שׂשׂון) and "delight" (שׂמחה) in Yhwh could be compared to a bridal couple's (see Jer 7:34 and 16:9). Cf. Jack R. Lundbom, *Jeremiah 1–20*, AB 21A (New York: Doubleday, 1999), 744.

27. On the Decalogic echoes in Jer 7:9–10, see discussion on pp. 21–22.

dation into which Israel had fallen. While the holiness of YHWH's temple should have deterred immoral behavior, instead the Israelites relied on the temple in their midst to guarantee their immunity to punishment, treating it as a robber's hideout. Their disregard for YHWH's "place" would result in the forfeiture of their own security in the land.[28] Third, and most importantly for this project, Jeremiah 7 demonstrates the lexical overlap between the two idioms, נקרא שם על and לשכן שמו שם. Shiloh was identified as the first cult site where YHWH "placed his name," and the temple in Jerusalem as the replacement site "over which his name was proclaimed." "Placing the name" was perceived as the conceptual equivalent to an oral declaration of ownership.[29] This equation will become significant for the discussion that follows.

Jeremiah 32:34

וישימו שקוציהם	But they set up their detestable things
בבית אשר־נקרא־שמי עליו	in the house **over which my name is proclaimed**
לטמאו	to defile it.

YHWH's claim was exclusive; the declaration of his name over his "house" entailed the rejection of all other gods and their images.[30] For the Israelites to introduce idols into the temple defiled it, violating YHWH's sovereign right.

Jeremiah 34:15–16a

ותשבו אתם היום	But you yourselves returned recently
ותעשו את־הישר בעיני	and you did the right thing in my eyes
לקרא דרור איש לרעהו	by each man emancipating his neighbor,
ותכרתו ברית לפני	and you made a covenant before me
בבית אשר־נקרא שמי עליו	in the house **over which my name is proclaimed.**
ותשבו ותחללו את־שמי	Yet you turned and profaned my name
ותשבו איש את־עבדו	by each man bringing back his slave,
ואיש את־שפחתו	and each man his maidservant

In contrast to Jer 32:34, occasionally Israel did what was right within the temple walls. Here, they covenanted before YHWH to release Israelite slaves. However, their behavior outside the temple profaned YHWH's name because it violated their sworn commitment by reinstituting slavery. Thus, the name of YHWH was made a witness to falsehood. This example demonstrates that the first idiom (נקרא שם על) was not completely lexicalized so that the use of "name" was merely coincidental. The second phrase (חלל

28. Richter, *DH and Name Theology*, 91–93.

29. This conclusion is corroborated by Jer 44:26, where נקרא is used for the *oral* invocation of YHWH's name in an oath. Similarly, in Ps 49:12 the *qal* of קרא + על indicates that people had claimed land as their own (בשמותם; "by their names"). Here the syntax of our idiom is taken over by the *qal* expression to indicate an oral claim.

30. The word שקוצים was invariably associated with idolatry (cf. Deut 29:16; 1 Kgs 11:5).

את־שם) was evoked precisely because "name" links it with the first, providing another potent word play, though two distinct meanings of שׁם are employed. The first phrase underscores YHWH's rightful *possession* of the temple while the second emphasizes the damage done to his *reputation*. The shared lexeme שׁם is sufficiently multivalent to be harnassed for divergent purposes while providing rhetorical continuity to the prophet's message.

Jeremiah 25:29

כי הנה	"For look,
בעיר אשר נקרא־שמי עליה	on the city **over which my name is proclaimed,**
אנכי מחל להרע	I am beginning to bring calamity.
ואתם הנקה תנקו	As for you, will you possibly avoid punishment?
לא תנקו	You will not go unpunished,
כי חרב אני קרא	because I am summoning a sword
על־כל־ישבי הארץ	against all the inhabitants of the land/earth,"
נאם יהוה צבאות	declares YHWH of armies.

In Jer 25:29, the city of Jerusalem was the object claimed by YHWH as his own. Jeremiah spoke to the kings of all the nations surrounding Jerusalem (25:18–26), warning them of YHWH's impending judgment. The consequences of Israel's sin would extend beyond the temple to the entire city. If his claim on Jerusalem did not preclude its severe punishment, how much more would the nations suffer his wrath? That which belonged to YHWH was only protected if he continued to be honored there.[31] Note the echo of Exod 20:7 as well—those occupying the city claimed by YHWH will "not go unpunished."

Deuteronomy 28:9–10

יקימך יהוה לו לעם קדוש	YHWH will establish you as his own holy people
כאשר נשבע־לך	just as he swore to you
כי תשמר את־מצות יהוה אלהיך	if you keep the commands of YHWH your God
והלכת בדרכיו	and walk in his ways
וראו כל־עמי הארץ	And all the peoples of the earth will see
כי שם יהוה נקרא עליך	that **the name YHWH was proclaimed over you**,
ויראו ממך	and they will be afraid of you.

Now we have come full circle to the only occurrence of the phrase נקרא שׁם על in the Pentateuch, in the heart of the covenant blessings (Deut 28:10). Here a whole group of people—rather than a single object or an individual—was said to belong to YHWH. Just as Joab was on the verge of being known as the conqueror of a city (2 Sam 12:28), so YHWH would be known as the one to whom Israel owed her existence as a nation. The *hiphil* of קום underscores his role as prime actor; *YHWH* was responsible for Israel's status as a holy people. Under the right conditions, YHWH's claim on Israel would

31. On YHWH's "choosing" Jerusalem, see 1 Kgs 11:13, 32, 36; 14:21; 21:7; 23:27; 2 Chr 6:6; 12:13; 33:7; Zech 1:17; 2:16; 3:2. For another example, see discussion of Daniel on p. 59 below.

inspire fear among the nations (cf. v. 7).[32] However, these lavish blessings depended on Israel's obedience to covenant stipulations (vv. 1–2, 9b, 13b, 14). Here, the concept of YHWH's reputation is not specifically expressed using a "name" idiom. Instead, one almost has the sense that YHWH's brand on Israel is legible; the peoples "see" it (i.e., YHWH's name) and are afraid.[33] Later in this chapter, covenantal breach was depicted as a failure to "fear this honored and fearsome name" (ליראה את־השם הנכבד והנורא הזה; 28:58)—that is, YHWH himself—and would result in an avalanche of curses. Belonging to YHWH required the Israelites to honor his "name." Again, this shared lexeme (שׁם) provided a convenient homiletical connection for the distinct concepts of name as metonymy and as a sign of possession.

Four other passages join Deuteronomy in applying the idiom נקרא שׁם על to the people of Israel.[34]

Isaiah 63:19a

היינו מעולם לא־משלת בם	We have become those over whom you have not ruled,
לא־נקרא שמך עליהם	those **over whom your name has not been proclaimed**.

Isaiah 63:19 is controversial because its laconic style creates ambiguity. A few translations and commentators follow the Targums, reading it as a *contrast* between Israel and the nations: while *Israel* belongs to YHWH, *others* do not.[35] A much larger group follows the LXX, perceiving it as a *comparison* between Israel and the nations. She has become *just like* those who do not belong to YHWH.[36] The wider context of the lament, which depicts Israel's downward slide, favors the latter interpretation.[37] The prophet chose

32. While normal syntax is verb-subject-object (VSO), here שׁם יהוה appears before the verb for emphasis. It is either a noun construct ("name of YHWH") or epexegetical ("name, YHWH").

33. At the same time, Deut 28:10 makes especially clear נקרא שׁם על that cannot be translated "the name is *read* upon." The nations' recognition of Israel's status before YHWH did not depend on the legibility of a forehead inscription, but on the quality of covenant obedience. This passage would present a strange mixed metaphor if the nations were to "see" that YHWH's name is "read" on Israel. Usually (though not always) when קרא indicates reading, the emphasis falls on aural proclamation (e.g., Neh 8:8).

34. Baruch and Maccabees also apply the translated idiom to Israel (τὸ ὄνομά σου ἐπεκλήθη ἐπὶ Ισραηλ, Bar 2:15; 2 Macc 8:15).

35. See KJV; NIV; Bruce Chilton, trans., *The Isaiah Targum*, ArBib 11 (Collegeville, MN: Liturgical Press, 2005), 122; Edward J. Young, *The Book of Isaiah*, NICOT (Grand Rapids: Eerdmans, 1974), 3:489.

36. See LXX; Vulg.; NRSV; NASB; Peter Höffken, *Das Buch Jesaja: Kapitel 40–66*, Neuer Stuttgarter Kommentar Altes Testament 18 (Stuttgart: Katholisches Bibelwerk, 1998), 234; Lau, *Schriftgelehrte Prophetie in Jes 56–66*, 299–300; Goldenstein, *Das Gebet der Gottesknechte*, 104); Joseph Blenkinsopp, *Isaiah 56–66*, AB 19B (New York: Doubleday, 2003), 253; Shalom M. Paul, *Isaiah 40–66*: Translation and Commentary, ECC (Grand Rapids: Eerdmans, 2012), 579.

37. For an extended discussion of the context, see Torsten Uhlig, *The Theme of Hardening in the Book of Isaiah*, FAT 2/39 (Tübingen: Mohr Siebeck, 2009), 294–314. On the

to depict this moral turpitude by comparing Israel with those who did not and never had borne YHWH's name. Israel's elect status had been all but reversed.[38] A request for a theophany reminiscent of Sinai follows, by which YHWH might once again adopt Israel for himself as a people. Readoption would hardly make sense if Israel's status had not degenerated.[39] On the basis of YHWH's fresh appearance, his name would be made known to his enemies (Isa 63:19b–64:1[2]). YHWH's identity or reputation and his possession of Israel are again rhetorically linked via שׁם.

Jeremiah and Daniel both appealed to YHWH's reputation in their prayers:

Jeremiah 14:7a, 9

אם־עונינו ענו בנו	"Though our sins testify against us,
יהוה עשׂה למען שׁמך	YHWH, act **for the sake of your name**."
למה תהיה כאישׁ נדהם	"Why are you like a man astonished,
כגבור לא־יוכל להושׁיע	like a warrior not able to save?
ואתה בקרבנו יהוה	Yet you are in our midst, YHWH,
ושׁמך עלינו נקרא	and **your name over us is proclaimed**.
אל־תנחנו	Do not lay us aside!"

Jeremiah appealed for God to act on Israel's behalf for the sake of his own name (14:7a). The syntax of נקרא שׁם על is doubly marked by bringing both the subject (שׁמך) and prepositional phrase (עלינו) before the verb, stressing the bond put into effect by YHWH's claim on Israel. Although she belonged to YHWH, Israel was languishing. YHWH's reputation was at stake; therefore his response was critical. The distinct concepts of possession and reputation are again rhetorically linked by the lexeme שׁם.

Daniel 9:18–19

הטה אלהי אזנך ושׁמע	"Incline, O my God, your ear and hear.
פקחה עיניך וראה שׁממתינו	Open your eyes and see our desolations
והעיר אשׁר־נקרא שׁמך עליה	and the city **over which your name is proclaimed**,
כי לא על־צדקתינו	for not because of our righteousness

tendency of LXX Isaiah to allow context to influence the translation, see Ronald Troxel, *LXX-Isaiah as Translation and Interpretation: The Strategies of the Translator of the Septuagint of Isaiah* (Boston: Brill, 2008), 134.

The syntax also favors the comparative interpretation. The lack of אשׁר or כי emphasizes the severed ties between YHWH and Israel. While the predicative use of an unmarked relative clause is common in Arabic, it is uncommon in Hebrew. *IBHS* (p. 338) gives two examples: Jer 2:8 reads, "They followed [*those who*] cannot help (ואחרי לא־יועלו הלכו)," while Isa 65:1 says, "I was sought by [*those who*] had not asked (נדרשׁתי ללוא שׁאלו); I was found by [*those who*] did not seek me (נמצאתי ללא בקשׁני)." Cf. Joüon 157a, 158d.

38. The shocking theme of YHWH as enemy of his own people appears frequently. For example, Isa 31:2–4; 50:11; Jer 21:4–6; Ezek 5:5–17; Hos 6:1; 13:1; Lam 2:5; 3:10–11.

39. See Irmtraud Fischer, *Wo ist Jahwe?: Das Volksklagelied Jes 63,7—64,11 als Ausdruck des Ringens um eine gebrochene Beziehung* (Stuttgart: Katholisches Bibelwerk, 1989), 57.

אנחנו מפילים תחנונינו לפניך	do we cause our supplications to fall before you,
כי על־רחמיך הרבים	but because of your great compassion.
אדני שמעה אדני סלחה	Lord, hear. Lord, forgive.
אדני הקשיבה ועשה אל־תאחר	Lord give attention and act. Do not delay.
למענך אלהי כי־שמך נקרא	For your sake, God, for **your name is proclaimed**
על־עירך ועל־עמך	**over your city and over your people**."

Daniel applied the idiom both to the city of Jerusalem and to the people of Israel. He also alluded to the priestly blessing, asking YHWH to "let his face shine" on them again, thereby reaffirming that they belonged to him (v. 17; cf. Num 6:23–27).[40] Like Jeremiah, Daniel entreated YHWH to have compassion for his own sake (למען אדני; v. 17).[41] In this case שם does not occur, demonstrating that the association of the concepts of possession and reputation does not depend on a single lexeme, but is rather conceptual. In v. 19, שמך appears in front of the verb to underscore the importance of YHWH as owner. The pronominal suffixes on both city and people reinforce YHWH's ownership. Because he was associated with both entities, it was in his own interest to restore them, in spite of their sin (9:5–11).[42] The desolation of Jerusalem reflected negatively on YHWH's sovereignty.

2 Chronicles 7:14[43]

ויכנעו עמי	And if my people humble themselves,
אשר נקרא־שמי עליהם	**over whom my name is proclaimed,**
ויתפללו	and pray,
ויבקשו פני	and seek my face,
וישבו מדרכיהם הרעים	and turn from their wicked ways,
ואני אשמע מן־השמים	then I myself will hear from heaven,
ואסלח לחטאתם	and I will forgive their sin,
וארפא את־ארצם	and I will heal their land.

40. See also John Goldingay, *Daniel*, WBC 30 (Nashville: Thomas Nelson, 1996), 254–55.

41. Like Daniel, Baruch's prayer recalled how God had "made himself a name" by bringing Israel out of Egypt (Bar 2:11), after which Israel sinned and was scattered among the nations. He prayed, "Hear, Lord, our prayer and our supplication and *deliver us for your sake* and give us grace before those who carried us into exile, *in order that all the earth may know that you are the Lord our God because your name is proclaimed over Israel and over his descendants*" (Bar 2:14–15, emphasis mine; cf. 3:5–8; Sir 36:17; Pr Azar 1:10–11; 20–22; 2 Macc 1:27). Baruch combines language from Dan 9 with echoes of Jeremiah and Deuteronomy. See David deSilva, *Introducing the Apocrypha: Message, Context, and Significance* (Grand Rapids: Baker Academic, 2002), 203.

42. The psalmists often appealed to YHWH to act on their behalf for the sake of his name (למען שמו). They pled for forgiveness (Ps 25:11; 79:9), guidance (Ps 31:4[3]), intervention (Ps 109:21), and preservation (143:11) because of his reputation.

43. On the text-critical issues created by the absence of this statement in the parallel 1 Kings text, see H. G. M. Williamson, *1 and 2 Chronicles*, NCBC (Grand Rapids: Eerdmans, 1982), 225; Ralph W. Klein, *2 Chronicles: A Commentary*, Hermeneia (Minneapolis: Fortress, 2012), 110; Sara Japhet, *I and II Chronicles: A Commentary*, OTL (Louisville: Westminster John Knox, 1993), 614.

In spite of covenant unfaithfulness on Israel's part, in the midst of God's judgment, he promised restoration if they repented. This possibility was rooted in the fact that YHWH's name had been proclaimed over them. They were *his* people. The Chronicler also assured Israel of his presence among them by saying that his "eyes" and "heart" would always be at the temple (v. 16). Although he promised to "hear from heaven," his was not a distant claim to ownership, but implied his attentive presence. Verse 16 connects the concepts of election and name, saying, "I have chosen (בחרתי) and consecrated this temple *so that* my name may be there forever (להיות־שמי שם עד־עולם, emphasis mine)."[44] Thus, in concert with 1 Kgs 9:3, the Chronicler identified three aspects of YHWH's disposition toward the Israelites in v. 16: his name (claim to ownership), his eyes (attentive presence), and his heart (consistent will to forgive).[45]

Amos 9:12

למען יירשו את־שארית אדום	"For they will possess the remnant of Edom
וכל־הגוים	and all the nations
<u>אשר־נקרא שמי עליהם</u>	**over whom my name is proclaimed**,"
נאם־יהוה עשה זאת	declares YHWH, who does this.

A final example of the idiom נקרא שם על breaks with the pattern seen thus far. Amos 9:12 shockingly suggests that YHWH had claimed some from among the Gentiles as his own, applying to the nations (הגוים) the otherwise nationalistic epithet, "over whom my name is proclaimed."[46] This notion was so scandalous to Jews of antiquity that the Targum rearranged the sentence to make Israel the subject.[47] New Testament apostles appealed to this passage as the clearest proof that Gentiles might join the people of God

44. For an overview of other Hebrew terms used to express the concept of election, see Horst Dietrich Preuss, *Old Testament Theology*, trans. Leo G. Perdue, OTL (Louisville: Westminster John Knox, 1995), 1:31–33. I follow Preuss (ibid., 1:37) in defining "election" in relation to YHWH's historical acts on Israel's behalf rather than as a "supratemporal or primeval divine decree." Through the mighty acts of YHWH in Egypt and in the exodus YHWH demonstrated his election of Israel (Deut 4:37–38).

45. *His eyes*: YHWH's attention did not guarantee immunity; he responded as he "saw" fit (e.g., cf. 1 Chr 19:13; 21:7; 2 Chr 16:9). Subsequent kings were judged according to whether they did "what was right" or "what was evil in the eyes of YHWH" (e.g., 2 Chr 20:32; 21:6; 22:4; 24:2). *His heart*: The Chronicler often described loyal commitment or will with reference to לב. For example, 1 Chr 12:39; 17:9; 28:9; 29:9; 2 Chr 6:14; 30:12.

46. The ambiguity of the Hebrew allowed diverse interpretations. The MT reads, "that they may possess the remnant of Edom and all the nations over whom my name is proclaimed" (למען יירשו את־שארית אדום וכל־הגוים אשר־נקרא שמי עליהם). This statement could imply military domination; ירש appears in military contexts and the *hiphil* means "dispossess" (e.g., Deut 2:12, 21–24; Judg 1:19). However, in Amos 9:12 the object of possession is people ("the remnant of Edom") rather than territory, even though the verb is *qal*. For land possession, see Gen 15:7; 28:4; Num 15:13; Deut 1:8.

47. Cf. Kevin Cathcart and Robert Gordon, *The Targum of the Minor Prophets*, ArBib 14 (Wilmington, DE: Michael Glazier, 1989), 96 n. 38. For discussion, see Christopher

apart from conversion to Judaism (Acts 15:15–18). If YHWH had proclaimed his name over them, as evidenced by their faith in him, they were automatically part of the believing community, without a need for circumcision.

The preceding survey of passages where the idiom נקרא שם על refers to the name of YHWH is consistent with its appearances in 2 Sam 12:28 and Isa 4:1. Rather than simple "naming" or renaming, the idiom נקרא שם על denotes a claim of ownership put into effect by oral declaration.[48] The proclamation that Israel belonged to YHWH need not imply a written inscription or brand on Israel that could actually be "read."[49] By the exilic and post-exilic periods, נקרא שם על became a standard way to refer to Israel's covenantal status. Even when applied to inert objects such as the temple, the focus was on the covenant relationship implied by YHWH's official residence among the Israelites. Its recurrent association with YHWH's identity and reputation is not surprising given the potential for rhetorical exploitation of the frequently shared lexeme שׁם and the natural overlap between these concepts.

קרא בשם *and* קרא על־שם

A cluster of expressions similar to נקרא שם על involve the adoption of a legal heir. The syntax is slightly different, owing to different circumstances, but the concept is related: a person's name is legally attached to someone else. Here the preposition על or ב is attached directly to שׁם as the object, rather than subject, of קרא (*niphal*). As with the previous idiom, the following examples include both human and divine applications. The first examples are from Jacob's blessing of Joseph's sons, Ephraim and Manasseh:

Genesis 48:5–6

ועתה שני־בניך הנולדים לך	Now your two sons who were born to you
בארץ מצרים עד־באי אליך מצרימה	in the land of Egypt before I came to you to Egypt
לי־הם אפרים ומנשה	are mine—Ephraim and Manasseh—
כראובן ושמעון יהיו־לי	just as Reuben and Simeon are mine.
ומולדתך אשר־הולדת אחריהם	But your children who are born after them
לך יהיו	will be yours,
על שם אחיהם	**according to the name of their brothers**
יקראו בנחלתם	**they will be named** in their inheritance.

Here Jacob orally claimed his grandsons, Ephraim and Manasseh, as his own sons in regard to inheritance and land distribution. However, their future siblings (yet unborn) would not share this generational promotion;

Wright, *The Mission of God: Unlocking the Bible's Grand Narrative* (Downers Grove, IL: IVP Academic, 2006), 495–97.

48. Cf. *HALOT* 2:1130: "an expression of ownership and control." See also Lau, *Schriftgelehrte Prophetie in Jes 56–66*, 299–300; Michael Hundley, "To Be or Not To Be: A Reexamination of Name Language in Deuteronomy and the Deuteronomistic History," *VT* 59 (2009): 533–55; Walter Kaiser, "שֵׁם," *TWOT* 2:934.

49. Contra Bar-Ilan, "Magic Seals," 41; idem, "They shall put my name"; Jacobs, "The Body Inscribed," 12.

instead, they would inherit from their older brothers.[50] As a result, Ephraim and Manasseh became eligible to receive Jacob's blessing before he died:

Genesis 48:16b

ויקרא בהם שמי	**And may my name be named on them**
ושם אבתי אברהם ויצחק	**and the name of my fathers, Abraham and Isaac,**
וידגו לרב בקרב הארץ	and may they multiply in the midst of the earth.

The blessing includes a variation of the idiom נקרא שם על. Here instead of על we find a ב-prefix, which can also mean "on" (see Ps 101:6; Isa 66:20).[51] The covenant blessings of Abraham, Isaac, and Jacob became theirs because of this legal "adoption," that they might multiply greatly. The jussive force of Jacob's blessing implied his desire that these boys continue to be known as his even after his death.

Among the returnees to Judah after the exile was a priest who had taken the family name of his wife's ancestor, Barzillai. It utilizes the same syntax as Gen 48:6.

Ezra 2:61 (// Nehemiah 7:63)

ומבני הכהנים	And from the sons of the priests,
בני חביה בני הקוץ בני ברזלי	the sons of Habaiah, sons of Hakkoz, sons of Barzillai
אשר לקח מבנות ברזלי הגלעדי	(who took from the sons of Barzillai the Gileadite a
אשה ויקרא על־שמם	wife, and **was called by their name**).

A matriarchal lineage is found nowhere else in the Hebrew Bible.[52] The post-exilic Barzillai may have been motivated by the inheritance and favor available through his wife's family. The ancestral Barzillai was a wealthy man, both loyal and generous to King David, and therefore a recipient of royal favor.[53] However, the consequent loss of the second Barzillai's priestly ancestry resulted in his exclusion from priestly privileges (Ezra 2:62 // Neh 7:64).[54]

In these examples, ancestry was legally altered by a change in family name, expressed with the idiom קרא על־שם (*niphal*). A related example involving YHWH's name is found in the book of Isaiah:

---

50. Their promotion is either alongside or in place of their uncles, Reuben and Simeon. For discussion, see Kenneth Mathews, *Genesis 11:27–50:26*, NAC (Nashville: B&H, 2005), 874–80; Gordon J. Wenham, *Genesis 16–50*, WBC (Dallas: Word, 1994), 453–65; E. A. Speiser, *Genesis*, AB 1 (New York: Doubleday, 1964), 357.

51. *DCH* 2:82; *HALOT* 1:104.

52. Joseph Blenkinsopp (*Ezra–Nehemiah*, OTL [Louisville: Westminster John Knox, 1998], 92) calls the situation "quite exceptional." Cf. F. Charles Fensham, *The Books of Ezra and Nehemiah*, NICOT (Grand Rapids: Eerdmans, 1982), 56.

53. See 2 Sam 17:27–29; 19:31–39; 1 Kgs 2:7. Cf. 1 Esdr 5:38.

54. So Williamson, *1 and 2 Chronicles*, 37. Since priestly records were lost, consultation of the Urim and Thummim was necessary to discern YHWH's will on how to proceed (Ezra 2:63 // Neh 7:65). The purity of the priesthood and therefore the well-being of the entire nation was at stake. Cf. Lev 22:12, which excluded a priest's daughter from eating priestly food if she married outside the tribe.

Isaiah 43:7

כל הנקרא בשמי **Everyone called by my name,**
ולכבודי בראתיו and for my glory whom I created,
יצרתיו אף־עשיתיו whom I formed, even whom I made.

Note that the verb קרא is again *niphal*, indicating that these were people over whom YHWH's name had been proclaimed. They were identified as belonging to him, created especially to bring YHWH glory.[55]

Though the syntax varies, the expressions listed here participate in the same conceptual world as נקרא־שם על, a world where tangible property and legitimate social relations were often governed by oral claims.[56]

להיות שמו שם, לשום שמו שם, *and* לשכן שמו שם

In addition to the above expressions (נקרא שם על, קרא על־שם, and קרא בשם), which express a claim to ownership, another cluster of related idioms function similarly: להיות שמו שם, לשום שמו שם, לשכן שמו שם.[57] With these, YHWH explicitly claimed ownership of two entities, the same entities "over which his name was proclaimed": the place of worship and the people of Israel. However, prior to the "placing" of YHWH's name in the land, he called for the removal of other names.

That ANE rulers were concerned about this prospect is evident from the standard closing statement on stone monuments that calls down curses on anyone who removes the ruler's name.[58] While the Hebrew expressions

55. For discussion, see John Oswalt, *The Book of Isaiah: Chapters 40–66*, NICOT (Grand Rapids: Eerdmans, 1998), 142.

56. By "conceptual world," I suggest not an ontological reality for שם but rather a mental association or structure of thought triggered by the key word שם and the shared subject matter of these idioms. Though we cannot reduce an idiom to the sum of its parts, research demonstrates that even unrecognized conceptual metaphors related to "highly conventional metaphorical expressions" trigger associations that shape the way we think and talk. See Zoltán Kövecses, *Metaphor: A Practical Introduction*, 2nd ed. (Oxford: Oxford University Press, 2010), 40–42. Even if these Hebrew idioms do not point to a practice involving an inscribed name, the activation of a shared source domain (CLAIMING OWNERSHIP BY INSCRIBING A NAME) naturally evokes name-related metaphorical mappings, whether conscious or not. I discuss conceptual metaphor theory more in ch. 5.

57. The phrases לשכן שמו שם and לשום שמו שם may have lexicalized in part due to the pleasing alliteration of ש and מ. For a discussion of phonological influence in lexicalization, see Ian Wilson, "Merely a Container? The Ark in Deuteronomy," in *Temple and Worship in Biblical Israel*, ed. John Day (New York: T&T Clark, 2007), 23.

58. One Neo-Assyrian example ("Saba'a Stela," trans. K. Lawson Younger, in *COS* 2.114E:274) reads,

> A later prince who takes this stela from its place; whoever covers (it) with dirt or puts (it) in a Taboo House, or erases the name of the king, my lord, and my name, and writes his own name; may Aššur, the father of the gods, curse him and destroy his seed (and) his name from the land.

For other examples from various locations and times in the ANE, see *COS* 2.32 (Phoenicia), 2.91 (lines 119–51; Old Akkadian), 2.111 (lines 118–57; Late Old Babylonian from

that involve cutting off, wiping out, or removing a name almost always refer to the death of descendants so that a person's memory dies out, in two places the physical removal of an inscribed stone may be implied.[59] Both Deut 7:24 and 12:3 employ the expression אבד את־שם:

Deuteronomy 7:24

ונתן מלכיהם בידך	And he will give their kings into your hand
והאבדת את־שמם	**and you will destroy their names**
מתחת השמים	from under the heavens.
לא־יתיצב איש בפניך	No one will be able to stand before you
עד השמדך אתם	until you have exterminated them.

Since other physical objects were to be destroyed—images to be burned, altars broken, and sacred stones (מצבת) smashed (vv. 5, 25)—destroying the kings' names could include destroying or effacing physical monuments that bore their names, representing their claim to sovereignty over the territory. At the very least, Israel's destruction of kings in the land of Canaan was to be so comprehensive that the names of those rulers would be forgotten.

Deuteronomy 12:3

ונתצתם את־מזבחתם	And you shall tear down their altars,
ושברתם את־מצבתם	and shatter their sacred pillars
ואשריהם תשרפון באש	and their asherah poles you shall burn with fire
ופסילי אלהיהם תגדעון	and the images of their gods you shall cut to pieces
ואבדתם את־שמם	**and you shall destroy their names**
מן־המקום ההוא	from that place.

Here divine, rather than royal, names are in view. As in Deut 7:24, to destroy their names could indicate the extent of destruction (they will no longer be remembered) or it could involve effacing or obliterating physical

Mari), 2.114A (lines 11b–19; Neo-Assyrian). See also *KAI* 2:37–38, text 26A, iii.13–iv.1; *COS* 1.113:416, colophon; Annick Payne, *Iron Age Hieroglyphic Luwian Inscriptions*, SBLWAW 29 (Atlanta: SBL, 2012), 71–72, 2.3.5 Karkamiš A11b+c, §19–25; ibid., 83–84, 2.3.9; Karkamiš A6, §1–7, 27–31; ibid., 93–94, 2.4.3 Tell Ahmar 6, §1–2, §8–9; §29; LH xlix 18–80, in M. Roth, *Law Collections from Mesopotamia and Asia Minor*, SBLWAW 6 (Atlanta: Scholars Press, 1995), 136–37. Cf. Richter, *DH and Name Theology*, 155, 184–203; Sandra L. Richter, "The Place of the Name in Deuteronomy," *VT* 57 (2007): 344–46.

Though this attitude toward effacement was common to all ANE cultures, it did not deter everyone. In Egypt, Akhenaten boldly removed the name of the god Amun from every monument, replacing it with the name of Aten. This act was tantamount to claiming that Amun had never existed. See Assmann, *The Search for God in Ancient Egypt*, 199. In a similar power play centuries later in Mesopotamia, Esarhaddon inscribed his own name and the name of Aššur on cult images of other peoples. See Nathaniel B. Levtow, *Images of Others: Iconic Politics in Ancient Israel*, BJSUCSD 11 (Winona Lake, IN: Eisenbrauns, 2008), 166–67.

59. For example, אבד את־שם: Ps 41:6[5]; מחה את־שם: Deut 9:14; 25:6; 29:19; 2 Kgs 14:27; Ps 9:6[5]; 109:13; cf. Exod 17:14 (the object is זכר rather than שם); Deut 25:19; Judg 21:17; כרת שם: Ruth 4:10; Isa 14:22; שמד את־שם: 1 Sam 24:22; Isa 48:19; cf. 2 Sam 14:17. For a different matter, see Hos 2:19 (סור את־שם), where the names of false gods were "removed" from Israel's vocabulary.

cult inscriptions.[60] The author contrasts this destruction with YHWH's own selection of a proper cult site (v. 5), saying that he will "establish his name" there. If a physical inscription was intended, then Israel was called upon to destroy the names of the Canaanite gods by smashing the altars and sacred stones on which they were engraved (12:3) in order to clear the way for YHWH's own inscribed name (12:5).[61] The Israelite craftsmen who built the tabernacle were nowhere instructed to write, embroider, or engrave YHWH's name, except on the high priest's medallion, so it is not clear whether such an inscription was made.[62] Nevertheless, whether oral or written, the transfer of sovereignty to YHWH is implied.

Now we return to the three virtually synonymous idioms introduced above. The first of these, לשכן שמו שם, appears primarily in Deuteronomy, referring six times as a "sentence appellative" to the place YHWH would choose as a central cult site (Deut 12:11; 14:23; 16:2, 6, 11; 26:2).[63] The implications are spelled out in part in Deut 26:1–2:

Deuteronomy 26:1–2

והיה כי־תבוא אל־הארץ	And when you have come into the land
אשר יהוה אלהיך נתן לך נחלה	that YHWH your God is giving you as a possession
וירשתה וישבת בה	and you possess it and you are dwelling in it,
ולקחת מראשית	then take some of the firstfruits
כל־פרי האדמה	of all the fruit of the ground
אשר תביא מארצך	that you bring in from the land
אשר יהוה אלהיך נתן לך	that YHWH your God is giving you,
ושמת בטנא והלכת אל־המקום אשר	and put [it] in a basket and go to the place
יבחר יהוה אלהיך	where YHWH your God will choose
לשכן שמו שם	**to put his name there.**

"The place" (המקום) would be selected (בחר) by YHWH, and as a centralized cult site it would unite all the Israelites in their new land. Significant acts of worship were to take place in this authorized location, requiring regular travel as soon as military tasks were accomplished and the territory was firmly in their grasp (ירש; 26:1).[64]

60. Cf. Num 33:52 (שמד); 2 Kgs 10:26–28.

61. So Richter, "The Place of the Name in Deuteronomy," 345–46; idem, *DH and Name Theology*, 209–10; idem, "Placing the Name, Pushing the Paradigm: A Decade with the Deuteronomistic Name Formula," in *Deuteronomy in the Pentateuch, Hexateuch, and the Deuteronomistic History*, ed. Konrad Schmid and Raymond F. Person Jr., 64–78 (Tübingen: Mohr Siebeck, 2012), 71 n. 29.

62. This absence of stone inscription may indicate an early desire for a centralized sanctuary. If the "place" where YHWH put his name was the high priest's forehead, then the only legitimate cult site would be wherever he served. But see Block, "No Other Gods," 253 n. 63.

63. For a helpful explanation, see ibid., 252–55. The idiom also appears in Deut 12:11; 14:23; 16:2, 6, 11; 26:2; cf. Ezra 6:12; Neh 1:9; Jer 7:12; 11QT 45, 12; 47, 4; 53, 9–10; 56, 5.

64. Aside from bringing firstfruits, the Israelites were to celebrate Passover there (Deut 16:2–6) and the Festival of Weeks (Deut 12:10–11), as well as bring any burnt offerings, sacrifices, tithes, and special gifts (Deut 12:11; 14:23).

Nehemiah 1:9 applies the phrase לשכן שמו שם to the temple in Jerusalem, while in Jeremiah YHWH applies it to the tabernacle at Shiloh, calling it "my place where . . . I placed my name at first" (Jer 7:12).[65] Proponents of so-called name theology point most often to this phrase as evidence for their view that YHWH's hypostatic name took up residence in the temple *instead of* his own personal presence.[66] They claim that later biblical authors realized YHWH could not be fully present because of his transcendence, and so they spoke of him putting his name there instead as a token. As many argue, this thesis is problematic on several levels, though we must chiefly reckon here with its failure to account for the borrowed idiom (and later with its abuse of metaphor).[67]

Sandra Richter reevaluated name theology by means of comparative Semitic study of the idiom, לשכן שמו שם (traditionally translated, "to cause his name to dwell there"; e.g., KJV). After exploring this phrase in cognate languages, Richter concluded that the idiom was borrowed from the Akkadian (*šuma šakānu*) monumental tradition where it designated ownership of a place through an *inscribed* name.[68] That the idiom was known in Canaan is clear from EA 287:60–63, which reads, "Look, the king has established his name [*ša-ka-an* MU-*šu*] in the land of Jerusalem forever and he simply cannot abandon it, viz. the city state of Jerusalem."[69] This public declaration implied the king's responsibility to care for what he owned. A city under

65. Jeremiah 7:12 is the only example in the latter prophets of any of these three idioms.

66. Notable proponents of Name Theology include Gerhard von Rad, *Studies in Deuteronomy*, trans. David Stalker (Chicago: Regnery, 1953), 38–39; Moshe Weinfeld, *Deuteronomy and the Deuteronomic School* (Oxford: Oxford University Press, 1972), 193, 197; Tryggve N. D. Mettinger, *The Dethronement of Sabaoth: Studies in the Shem and Kabod Theologies*, trans. Frederick H. Cryer, ConBOT 18 (Lund: Gleerup, 1982), 78–79; F. Dumermuth, "Zur deuteronomischen Kulttheologie und ihren Voraussetzungen," *ZAW* 70 (1958): 59–98.

67. Several scholars have argued persuasively against this notion. Gordon McConville ("God's 'Name' and God's 'Glory,'" *TynBul* 30 [1979]: 149–63) pointed out that "name" and "glory" were alternative ways of speaking about God's presence; in ordinary settings, Israel worshiped God's "name," while during a theophany his "glory" was on display. More recently, Peter Vogt (*Deuteronomic Theology and the Significance of Torah: A Reappraisal* [Winona Lake, IN: Eisenbrauns, 2006], 192–97) demonstrated that the focus of Deut 12 on YHWH's "name" (e.g., v. 5) corresponds to its rejection of the "names" of other gods (v. 3). The point is not the nature of his presence, but his exclusive sovereignty.

68. Richter, *DH and Name Theology*, 7. On the lexicography of the phrase *šuma šakānu* with examples relating to boundary stelas, see *CAD* 17:293.

69. Anson F. Rainey, *The El-Amarna Correspondence* (Leiden: Brill, 2015), 1:1113. Note that MU is the logographic reading for *šumu*, or "name." S. Dean McBride (*The Deuteronomic Name Theology* [Ph.D. diss., Harvard University, 1969], 117) says of EA 287:60–63 that "name . . . implies sovereign presence and authority which the Egyptian ruler has obligated himself to maintain." Cf. Richard S. Hess, "Hebrew Psalms and Amarna Correspondence from Jerusalem," *ZAW* 101 (1989): 253.

siege or region in chaos reflected negatively on the king's military strength. The presence of numerous victory stelae in the Levant with the inscribed names of conquering kings reinforces the connection between this phrase and the monumental tradition.[70] Richter suggests that Biblical Hebrew borrowed this idiom to refer to claims of ownership with or without an actual inscription.[71] As she insists, if the biblical idiom denotes a claim to sovereignty, attempts to interpret the phrase as a reference to YHWH's hypostatic name (vis à vis his actual presence) are illegitimate.[72] YHWH's "name" was not an alternative to his active presence.[73] Rather, as part of these idioms, his name identified him as the rightful owner.

---

70. A monumental image of Hadad-Yithʿi at Tell Fakhariyeh contains both the Akkadian and Aramaic phrases side-by-side, reinforcing the conclusion that western Semitic borrowed the idiom from Akkadian. See Richter, *DH and Name Theology*, 202–3. For English translation, see *COS* 2.34. For further discussion of the Aramean context, see K. Lawson Younger Jr. *A Political History of the Arameans: From Their Origins to the End of their Polities* (Atlanta: SBL, 2016), 242–69. On the complex ritual significance of boundary monuments, see Ann Shafer, "Assyrian Royal Monuments on the Periphery: Ritual and the Making of Imperial Space," in *Ancient Near Eastern Art in Context: Studies in Honor of Irene J. Winter by Her Students*, ed. Jack Cheng and Marian H. Feldman, CHANE 26 (Leiden: Brill, 2007), 133–159.

71. Roland de Vaux ("Le Lieu que Yahvé a choisi") concluded that the same expressions denoted YHWH's ownership but he neglected their Akkadian provenance.

72. McConville ("God's 'Name' and God's 'Glory,'" 162–63) suggested that Deuteronomy established YHWH's priority over against potential rivals. Accordingly, "name" was a more appropriate descriptor than "glory," which is associated with God's theophanic presence. Because other gods were false, they had no glory comparable to YHWH's. Those who see a sharp distinction between glory and name often associate the ark with YHWH's presence or glory (see Deut 10:8). McConville (ibid., 149–52) drew on 2 Sam 6:62 as counter evidence; there, the ark itself was said to have had the name proclaimed over it. Like Richter, he preferred to understand the name as a legal expression of ownership compatible with "glory" theology. For a recent argument linking the ark with divine presence, see Wilson, "Merely a Container?"

Other opponents of this form of "name theology" include Wilson, *Out of the Midst of the Fire*, SBLDS 151 (Atlanta: Scholars Press, 1995); Vogt, *Deuteronomic Theology*, 113–59; Rendtorff, *The Canonical Hebrew Bible*, 594; Raymond Dillard and Tremper Longman, *An Introduction to the Old Testament* (Grand Rapids: Zondervan, 1994), 103; Soulen, *The Divine Name(s) and the Holy Trinity*, 154; John Goldingay, *Isaiah*, NIBCOT (Peabody, MA: Hendrickson, 2001), 117, 173–74; van der Woude, "שֵׁם," *TLOT* 3:1360–62; Reiterer, "שֵׁם," *TDOT* 15:156; Bietenhard, "ὄνομα," *TDNT*, 5:256, but see p. 258. Eichrodt (*Theology of the Old Testament*, 41–42, 44) suggested that "name theology" emerged only in later Judaism. That is, YHWH's name became a guarantee of his presence and power without restricting his sovereignty. Cf. Jer 7:4.

73. Moreover, we need not assume that the concept of ownership espoused by this idiom precludes "presence." Later passages, such as 2 Chr 20:9, preclude absolute separation: "If evil comes upon us, sword, judgment, or pestilence, or famine, we will stand before this house *and before you* (ולפניך) because your name is on this house (כי שמך בבית הזה), and we will cry out to you in our distress and you will hear and you will save" (emphasis mine). Here, the personal presence of YHWH is guaranteed at the temple precisely *because*

The second idiom, לשׂום שׁמו שׁם, is collocated with an abbreviated form of לשׁכן שׁמו שׁם in Deut 12:5, referring to the central worship site.

Deuteronomy 12:5

כי אם־אל־המקום	But to the place
אשׁר־יבחר יהוה אלהיכם	where YHWH your God will choose
מכל־שׁבטיכם	from among your tribes
לשׂום את־שׁמו שׁם לשׁכנו	**to put his name there, to place it,**
תדרשׁו ובאת שׁמה	you shall seek, and there you shall come

Richter contends that the now redundant לשׁכנו is the result of a scribal gloss (לשׂום שׁמו שׁם) of the unfamiliar Akkadian (*šuma šakānu* // לשׁכן שׁמו שׁם) that eventually made it into the text itself.[74] While it was meant to clarify the meaning of subsequent uses of the obscure phrase throughout the chapter, the inclusion of both phrases side-by-side ultimately proved confusing.[75]

The full phrase לשׂום שׁמו שׁם appears twice more in Deuteronomy (12:21; 14:24), acknowledging that the journey to the chosen place of worship may be far for some Israelites. The Samaritan Pentateuch employs לשׁכן שׁמו שׁם instead in both cases, and the LXX renders לשׂום as ἐπικαλέω, the word normally used to translate לשׁכן. These examples further corroborate Richter's contention that the two phrases were interchangeable at some time in Israel's history.[76] In Kings and Chronicles, לשׂום שׁמו שׁם appears frequently to indicate that YHWH had indeed "placed" his name as he promised—not only on the temple (1 Kgs 9:3; 2 Chr 6:20; 33:7), but also on the city of Jerusalem in which the temple was built (1 Kgs 11:36; 2 Kgs 21:4, 7; 2 Chr 12:13; 33:7).[77]

---

he has claimed it as his own. This is also evident in Deut 12, where name-placing idioms are most prominent. Verse 7 indicates that worship done in the place where YHWH will "put his name" (לשׂום שׁמו שׁם; 12:5) would be carried out "before YHWH" (לפני יהוה). Wilson (*Out of the Midst of the Fire*, 204–5) rightly concludes that Deut 12–26 does not emphasize divine transcendence and that YHWH was portrayed as immediately present at the central worship site, the "place of the name." Cf. Vogt, *Deuteronomic Theology*, 113–59. Anne Knafl ("Forms of God, Forming God: A Typology of Divine Anthropomorphism in the Pentateuch" [Ph.D. diss., University of Chicago, 2011], 117–31, 264–74) builds on Wilson's and Richter's work to criticize "name theology" by focusing on the phrase לפני יהוה in Deuteronomy. Knafl demonstrates that Deuteronomy shows no evidence of correcting traditional beliefs about YHWH's presence at the cult site. Instead, it allows the idea of YHWH's presence to coexist with the borrowed Akkadian idiom (*šuma šakānu* // לשׁכן שׁמו שׁם) denoting sovereignty. Cf. idem, "Deuteronomy, Name Theology and Divine Location" (paper presented at the Annual Meeting of the SBL, Atlanta, November 2010).

74. Richter (*DH and Name Theology*, 46–48) follows Tov (*Textual Criticism of the Hebrew Bible*, 2nd rev. ed. [Minneapolis: Fortress, 2001], 42) in repointing לְשִׁכְנוֹ, an otherwise unattested noun, to read לְשַׁכְּנוֹ, an infinitive construct of שָׁכַן with a 3ms suffix.

75. Richter, *DH and Name Theology*, 63, 217.

76. Ibid., 45. According to the Göttingen LXX and BHQ Deuteronomy, both texts are stable.

77. YHWH also claimed Shiloh by placing his name there (Jer 7:12). Three times, this expression was an alternate naming or name-change formula for people (Abimelech, Jdg 8:31; Jacob/Israel, 2 Kgs 17:34; and Abraham, Neh 9:7).

These were the same entities "over which his name was proclaimed" (נקרא שם על), offering independent support for Richter's conclusion that "placing the name" was equivalent to a legal claim of ownership.[78]

The third idiom, להיות שמו שם, is a "periphrastic reflex" of the previous idioms, first appearing in Solomon's dedicatory speech. Significantly, the Chronicler used it in place of לשׂום שמו שם (cf. 1 Kgs 9:3 // 2 Chr 7:16; 2 Kgs 21:4 // 2 Chr 33:4). Substitution also works in the other direction, showing that the phrases were interchangeable (cf. 1 Kgs 8:29 // 2 Chr 6:20).[79] While לשכן שמו שם and לשׂום שמו שם emphasize the act of claiming ownership, להיות שמו שם highlights the resulting state of belonging to YHWH. 1 Kings 23:27 is worth citing in full:

1 Kings 23:27

ויאמר יהוה	And YHWH said,
גם את־יהודה אסיר מעל פני	"Even Judah I will remove from my presence,
כאשר הסרתי את־ישׂראל	just as I removed Israel,
ומאסתי את־העיר הזאת	and I will reject this city
אשר־בחרתי את־ירושׁלם	that I had chosen—Jerusalem—
ואת־הבית אשר אמרתי	and the house, of which I said,
יהיה שמי שם	'**My name will be there**.'"

This bleak passage indicates the impermanency of covenant benefits. Judah faced removal from the land and rejection of the elect place, precipitated by the sins of King Manasseh (v. 26). Here election (בחר) is again associated with YHWH's placing of his name (יהיה שמי שם) and the privilege of being in his presence (מעל פני). The collocation of election language with all three of these name idioms is hardly coincidental. Of the roughly 90 texts in the Hebrew Bible where YHWH chose (בחר) someone or something, at least 24 are directly connected with Richter's key name idioms (לשכן שמו שם, לשׂום שמו שם, and להיות שמו שם), with 17 more instances referring to "the place" using a shorthand expression (e.g., המקום אשר יבחר; Josh 9:27), bringing the total count to almost half.[80] The election of the place for a central sanctuary was a prime concern of the biblical history, and the standard

78. Richter (*DH and Name Theology*, 205) situates the Akkadian phrase and its Hebrew cognate in a military context, emphasizing that YHWH "captured this new territory" and "claimed it as his own." Cf. G. J. Wenham, "Deuteronomy and the Central Sanctuary," *TynBul* 22 (1971): 114. The purpose of the ceremony envisioned in Deut 27 was to signal YHWH's (and Israel's) claim to Canaan in fulfillment of his covenant promises to the ancestors at the site where those promises were made (Gen 12:7; cf. Josh 24:1). Whether or not Mt. Ebal represented the first of a series of sites that were marked as "the place" that YHWH would claim is debated. For an affirmative interpretation, see Richter, "The Place of the Name in Deuteronomy"; for a more cautious view, see Daniel I. Block, "'What Do These Stones Mean?' The Riddle of Deuteronomy 27," *JETS* 56 (2013): 17–41.

79. Richter, *DH and Name Theology*, 48–51. See also 2 Kgs 23:27; 2 Chr 6:5–6.

80. By my count. Other shorthand expressions include מקום שם־יהוה ("the place of the name of YHWH"; Isa 18:7) and בית לשמי, designating the temple as "a house for my name." The latter appears at least 35 times in Samuel, Kings, and Chronicles (e.g., 2 Sam 7:13; 1 Kgs 8:16–20; 1 Chr 22:7–10), indicating YHWH's ownership of the sanctuary and his

means of expressing this involved a name-idiom. Beyond this collocation, YHWH's other elect entities included priest (10 times), king (19 times), and the whole nation of Israel (14 times).[81] Note the correspondence between two of the main entities YHWH "chose" (בחר)—place and people—and the primary name-idioms (לשׂום שׁמו שׁם and נקרא שׁם על). Significantly, a variation of לשׂום שׁמו שׁם was applied to the nation of Israel via the priestly blessing,[82] providing a lexical bridge for the associated concepts of election expressed by the idioms לשׂום שׁמו שׁם and נקרא שׁם על:

Numbers 6:24–27

דבר אל־אהרן ואל־בניו לאמר	"Speak to Aaron and to his sons, saying,
כה תברכו את־בני ישׂראל	'Thus you are to bless the Israelites;
אמור להם	say to them,

attentive presence there. Malachi 1:11 expands the notion of "the place" by speaking of a day in which incense would be offered to YHWH's name "in every place" (בכל־מקום).

81. The word בחר is rare in the Sinai narratives, appearing only in disputes over Aaron's leadership; twice he is confirmed as the "chosen" priest (Num 16:5, 7; 17:20). However, election language proliferates in Deuteronomy. Cf. Preuss, *OT Theology*, 1:27–28. The DH employs deuteronomic language, eager to identify the chosen *king* and the chosen *place* and affirming *Levites* as the legitimate temple functionaries. YHWH "chose" both the people of Israel (e.g., Deut 4:37; 14:2; Isa 14:1; Ezek 20:5) and a central place of worship (city/temple, Deut 12 *passim*, 1 Kgs 8:16, 44, 48; 2 Chr 12:13; Zech 1:17). In addition, YHWH "chose" Abram (Neh 9:7), the king (Deut 17:15; 1 Sam 10:24; David, 1 Chr 28:4; Ps 89:20–21[19–20]; Solomon, 1 Chr 28:5–6, 10; Zerubbabel, Hag 2:23), the priests/Levites (Deut 18:5; 21:5; 1 Chr 15:2; Ps 105:26), Isaiah's "servant" (Isa 43:10; 49:7), and the land of Israel (Ps 47:5[4]).

82. The discovery of 7th–6th-century BCE silver amulets inscribed with this blessing at Ketef Hinnom suggests its apotropaic quality was taken seriously. See Jacob Milgrom, *Numbers [Ba-midbar]*, JPS Torah Commentary (Philadelphia: Jewish Publication Society, 1990), 52. Recent reevaluation of the amulets increases the likelihood of an apotropaic function; the last line apparently calls YHWH the "rebuker of [E]vil." So Lewis, "ʿAthtartu's Incantations," 211. Cf. Richard S. Hess, *Israelite Religions: An Archaeological and Biblical Survey* (Grand Rapids: Baker Academic, 2007), 279–80. The amulets may also represent a concrete application of the command to "place the name" on Israel. So Aaron Demsky and Meir Bar-Ilan, "Writing in Ancient Israel and Early Judaism," in Martin Mulder, ed., *Mikra: Text, Translation, Reading and Interpretation of the Hebrew Bible in Ancient Judaism and Early Christianity* (Peabody, MA: Hendrickson, 2004), 17; Jacobs, "The Body Inscribed," 11–13.

For a helpful discussion of the priestly blessing and later allusions to it, see Fishbane, *Biblical Interpretation*, 329–34. For detailed exegesis and discussion of text critical issues, see P. A. H. de Boer, "Numbers 6:27," *VT* 32 (1982): 1–13. However, de Boer (ibid., 13) does not follow the lead of the evidence he cites for the meaning of the phrase ושׂמו את־שׁמי על. While his examples indicate a symbolic naming or name change (Abram to Abraham, Gen 17:5 and Neh 9:7; Abimelech, Judg 8:31; Jacob to Israel, 2 Kgs 17:34; Daniel and friends to Babylonian names, Dan 1:7), de Boer emends the consonantal text to propose this reading: "And when they shall name me The Most High of the Israelites, I, on my part, will bless them." Baruch Levine (*Numbers 1–20*, AB 4A [New Haven, CT: Yale University Press, 1993], 228) also downplays the significance of YHWH's name here, seeing it as a simple invocation.

יברכך יהוה וישמרך	"May YHWH bless you and protect you.
יאר יהוה פניו אליך ויחנך	May YHWH smile at you and be gracious.
ישׂא יהוה פניו אליך וישׂם לך שׁלום	May YHWH show you favor and grant you peace."'
ושׂמו את־שׁמי על־בני ישׂראל	So **they shall set my name on the Israelites,**
ואני אברכם	and I myself will bless them."

The blessing in YHWH's name was the vehicle for "placing that name upon" his chosen people. Only the chosen priests were to pronounce it, and the blessing was directed not toward humanity as a whole but to the Israelites in particular. The unique Hebrew idiom by which YHWH characterized this blessing (ושׂמו את־שׁמי על), in conjunction with a triple repetition of his name, suggested a transformation of status. Israel was thereby claimed as YHWH's own and positioned to receive his grace, protection, favor, and peace.[83]

The association of YHWH's name with his chosen people seems analogous to his choosing a central site for worship. Both involve election for a particular purpose.[84] And for both that election is expressed by "placing the name" upon the chosen entity. As pointed out above, Jer 7:9–12 correlates the expressions נקרא שׁם על and לשׂום שׁמו שׁם, applying both to the cult site, and demonstrating that "to call a name over" and "to place the name" accomplish the same thing: YHWH has claimed ownership.[85] As I will argue in chapter 5, branding is the most appropriate and fruitful conceptual background by which we can make sense of the otherwise strange expression in the NC: נשׂא שׁם. A people who have had YHWH's name proclaimed over them in an act of oral branding must not subsequently bear that holy name "in vain."

The Use of Names in Seals and Branding

As discussed above, monumental inscription (or reinscription) was one means of declaring ownership. Names were also affixed to objects by means of seals and to people by means of branding or tattoos. All three practices shed light on the current project.

According to the archaeological record, the use of seals in Israel was widespread.[86] Unlike other ancient civilizations where seals were primarily or even exclusively pictoral, seals in Israel during the 7th–6th centuries

83. See NJPS. The rabbis discussed how linking YHWH's name with Israel motivated his discipline, so that his name might not be profaned. See *Num. Rab.* 5.6 on Num 4:18; H. Freedman and Maurice Simon, eds., *Midrash Rabbah*, 3rd ed. (New York: Soncino, 1983), 5:148–50. Deuteronomy 28:8–11 reiterates the connection between name and blessing, while Ps 67:1–2 elaborates the missional implications.

84. On election, see above, p. 101 n. 46.

85. Bar-Ilan ("Magic Seals," 41; "They shall put my name") argued that priests literally wrote YHWH's name on Israelite foreheads. But Num 6:27 need not require a physical inscription. Instead, it could indicate an oral claim to ownership, as with נקרא שׁם על.

86. Keel and Uehlinger (*Gods, Goddesses, and Images of God in Ancient Israel*, 10, 405) count over 8,500 seals or seal impressions found in Israel, with examples spanning her entire history. Magness-Gardiner ("Seals," *OEANE* 4:510) observes that the largest

BCE usually bore inscriptions.[87] A primary function of these seals was to indicate ownership, especially between 1000 and 500 BCE.[88] As is widely known, the vast majority of seals feature the *lamed inscriptionis*, or personal name prefixed with a *lamed*, indicating possession.[89] For example, one typical Hebrew seal reads *lḥnn bn ḥlqyhw hkhn*, or "Belonging to Ḥanan, son of Ḥilqiyāhu, the priest."[90] A seal such as this would have been used to stamp physical property or important documents, functioning as a signature.[91] Another function was to authenticate merchandise, letters, or other documents.[92] Seals inscribed with the king's name were sometimes given to those with delegated authority (e.g., Gen 41:42; Esth 3:12, 19; 8:2, 8, 10; Dan 6:18).[93] Other seals were held by administrative officers and bore their own names. Still others belonged to individual citizens.

Most seals were owned and wielded by humans,[94] but some bore a divine name. Only a few such seals have been discovered, and it is unclear whether

concentration dates to the Early Bronze period, well before the Patriarchs. These were used for decorating pottery, rather than for commerce.

87. Hundreds of inscribed Israelite seals and seal-impressions have been unearthed. See Graham Davies, "Some Uses of Writing in Ancient Israel in the Light of Recently Published Inscriptions," in *Writing and Ancient Near Eastern Society: Papers in Honour of Alan R. Millard*, LHBOTS 426 (New York: T&T Clark, 2005), 155–74. For transcriptions of Hebrew and other inscribed seals, see "Seals and Seal Impressions," trans. Jeffrey H. Tigay and Alan R. Millard, *COS* 2.70–79:197–204. Cf. Alan Millard, "Owners and Users of Hebrew Seals," *Eretz Israel* 26 (1999): 131; idem, "The Corpus of West Semitic Stamp Seals: Review Article," *IEJ* 51 (2001): 81. The prohibition of images in Israel's worship may have contributed to the aniconic nature of Israel's seals. One of the covenant curses directly pertains to the work of an engraver, warning that any skilled craftsman who fashions idols shall be cursed (Deut 27:15). The worship of Yhwh did not capture everyone's allegiance in ancient Israel, as both the Bible and the material culture attest (see Keel and Uehlinger, *Gods, Goddesses, and Images of God in Ancient Israel*), but perhaps the skill of engraving was so specialized that a greater control was possible over production.

88. Millard, "Owners and Users of Hebrew Seals," 129.

89. A brief perusal of *AHI* (esp. 1:396–416; 2:172–86) confirms the ubiquity of this practice. Cf. Hestrin and Dayagi-Mendeles, *Inscribed Seals*, 9.

90. See Nahman Avigad and Benjamin Sass, *Corpus of West Semitic Stamp Seals*, 2nd ed. (Jerusalem: Israel Academy of Sciences and Humanities, 1997), 59–60, no. 28; *AHI* 1:100.734; *COS* 2.79:204.

91. Similarly, more than 1,000 stamped jar handles unearthed in Israel bear the inscription *lmlk*, or "belonging to the king." Much discussion surrounds the function of these jars. Most likely, they reflect King Hezekiah's preparations for Sennacherib's invasion. For details, see Andrew G. Vaughn, *Theology, History, and Archaeology in the Chronicler's Account of Hezekiah*, ABS 4 (Atlanta: SBL, 1999); Nadav Na'aman, "Hezekiah's Fortified Cities and the 'LMLK' Stamps," *BASOR* 261 (1986): 5–21; *COS* 2.77:202. For color photographs, see Philip J. King and Lawrence E. Stager, *Life in Biblical Israel*, LAI (Louisville: Westminster John Knox, 2001), 312–13.

92. Hestrin and Dayagi-Mendeles, *Inscribed Seals*, 7.

93. A. R. Millard, "Königssiegel," *RlA* 6:140. Note the geographic and chronological spread of these examples.

94. For a discussion of kings' seals, see A. R. Millard, "Königssiegel," in *RlA* 6:135–40.

they were votive seals or were actually used to make impressions.[95] Several were attributed to the god Aššur, but they do not appear to have been used in the temple. Collon suggests they were used to seal official documents in the City Hall.[96] A cone-shaped Edomite seal dating from the late seventh to the early sixth century bears this inscription: "belonging to Qosa," the principal Edomite deity, using the *lamed inscriptionis*.[97] This phrase may indicate that the bearer was devoted to Qosa's service and acted as his representative. Similarly, a seal of Moabite provenance bears the name "Kemosh."[98] Either of these may be abbreviated theophoric names, as Hestrin and Dayagi-Mendeles suggest, but they could also be complete. Divine seals are also mentioned in Hittite prayers and diplomatic texts.[99] For this project it is important to note that a single seal, inscribed with someone's name, could be used to make impressions on a variety of objects for various purposes, functioning as a virtual signature. Each impression would then display the name of the seal-owner. In rare cases, that owner could be the deity.[100]

In addition to stone inscriptions and stamp seals that claimed ownership, names were affixed to living property by means of branding. Human branding was widespread in the ancient world.[101] Owners branded their slaves to indicate ownership as early as 2000 BCE, and people were sometimes

95. The number of Mesopotamian seals depicting deities increased during the Akkadian dynasty. See Magness-Gardiner, "Seals," *OEANE* 4:511. The uncertainty is noted by R. Opificius, "Gottessiegel," *RlA* 3:577–79.

96. Dominique Collon, *First Impressions: Cylinder Seals in the Ancient Near East* (Chicago: University of Chicago Press, 1988), 131. Opificius ("Gottessiegel," *RlA* 3:577–79) discussed not only the Aššur seals but also two belonging to Ea, which Wiseman felt were proper "Gottessiegel." Inscribed clay tablets held in the British Museum mention both seals. See ibid., 580. Cf. John 6:27. Other seals belonging to deities were apparently not intended to make impressions because their inscriptions are not carved in reverse. Some may have been intended as jewelry for the statue. See ibid., 578. Others would have been placed before the god as votive offerings. However, according to Collon (*First Impressions*, 131), seals carved only with the name of a god were not votive but rather personal divine seals.

97. Philip J. King, *Jeremiah: An Archaeological Companion* (Louisville: Westminster John Knox, 1993), 62. Some suppose that Qos is an abbreviation for a personal name; e.g., the Edomite king named Qawsgabri (*COS* 2.73:201).

98. Hestrin and Dayagi-Mendeles, *Inscribed Seals*, 144; cf. 17 (Moabite seal of Kemoshʿam [son of] Komoshʾel the scribe).

99. Singer, *Hittite Prayers*, 25, no. 2 (CTH 389.2), §6; Gary M. Beckman and Harold A. Hoffner, *Hittite Diplomatic Texts*, SBLWAW 7 (Atlanta: Scholars Press, 1999), 123, 18C §28.

100. In an interesting use of metaphor, 4 Esdras speaks of Israel as having been sealed (4 Esdr 2:38; 10:23). 4 Esdras 2:16 also declares that God will recognize his name in the elect and raise them from the dead. Perhaps he has in mind a seal impression. In Codex Sinaiticus, Tob 11:14 reads, "May his great name be upon us" (γένοιτο τὸ ὄνομα τὸ μέγα αὐτοῦ ἐφ' ἡμᾶς). The phrase is lacking in other MSS. See Hanhart, *Septuaginta: Tobit*, 151.

101. See, e.g., *KAI* 2:283, text 233, line 12; Muhammad A. Dandamaev, *Slavery in Babylonia: From Nabopolassar to Alexander the Great (626–331 B.C.)*, ed. M. A. Powell and D. B. Weisberg, trans. V. A. Powell (DeKalb: Northern Illinois University Press, 1984), 229–34.

branded or tattooed with "the name or symbol of the deity" to show their dedication to temple service or a desire for divine protection.[102] This mark was usually on the back of the hand or wrist but could also be on the head, ears, or face.[103] Ishtar's symbol was a star, whereas Marduk and Nabu were represented by a spade and a stylus, respectively.[104]

No concrete evidence confirms the branding of slaves in ancient Israel.[105] However, several texts allude positively to the idea of a brand or tattoo as a symbol of dedication to God and/or divine protection.[106] In Gen 4:15, "YHWH put a mark on Cain (וישׂם יהוה לקין אות) so that anyone finding him would not smite him." The content of the mark or sign and method of affixation are unknown, but the apotropaic function is evident.[107] In the book of Isaiah the prophet speaks of a future day in which God's Spirit would renew his people and many would claim allegiance to him:

Isaiah 44:5

זה יאמר ליהוה אני	This one will say "I am YHWH's!"
וזה יקרא בשם־יעקב	and that one will be called by name, "Jacob."

102. See ibid., 488–89; A. Guillaume, "Is 44:5 in the Light of the Elephantine Papyri," *ExpTim* 32 (1920): 377–78. Further examples of slaves whose hands were branded with their owner's names are listed in *CAD* Š/3 287, 292. On the distinction between personal and temple slaves, see Mathew Stolper, "Inscribed in Egyptian," in *Studies in Persian History: Essays in Memory of David M. Lewis*, ed. Maria Brosius and Amélie Kuhrt, Achaemenid History 11 (Leiden: Nederlands Instituut voor het Nabije Oosten, 1998), 135.

103. For a discussion of various methods of branding or tattooing, see Nili S. Fox, "Marked for Servitude: Mesopotamia and the Bible," in *A Common Cultural Heritage: Studies on Mesopotamia and the Biblical World in Honor of Barry L. Eichler*, ed. Grant Frame et al. (Bethesda, MD: CDL, 2011), 268; Joachim Oelsner, Bruce Wells, and Cornelia Wunsch, "Neo-Babylonian Period," in *A History of Ancient Near Eastern Law*, ed. Raymond Westbrook (Leiden: Brill, 2003), 2:927, 932; Dandamaev, *Slavery in Babylonia*, 229–34, 488–89; Guillaume, "Is 44:5," 377–78. For a helpful summary of the functions of human branding, see Sandra Jacobs, *The Body as Property: Physical Disfigurement in Biblical Law*, LHBOTS 582 (London: Bloomsbury, 2014), 205–11.

104. Dandamaev, *Slavery in Babylonia*, 488–89.

105. Ear-piercing rather than branding signalled voluntary lifetime service (Exod 21:5-6). The Jewish branding of foreign slaves is known from the Neo-Babylonian and Persian periods. For examples, see Jacobs, "The Body Inscribed," 7. However, Jacobs' logic falters in her discussion of texts from the Sinai narratives, where she assumes Israel's leaders were physically marked (והמה בכתבים; Num 11:24–26; ibid., 12–13). It is more natural to assume that Moses' gathering of the elders involved an invitation list. If the priestly blessing was accompanied by a physical mark, then *all* Israelites would have been marked, neutralizing the elders' uniqueness. Jacobs' alternate interpretation, where the document is a "divine ledger" (cf. Exod 32:32–33), is equally flawed because it would also have included all covenant members, not just the leaders.

106. See Fox, "Marked for Servitude," 276.

107. The expression שׂים אות corresponds to the Akkadian *šamâtu*, used to describe the branding of temple slaves. See Raymond Philip Dougherty, *The Shirkûtu of Babylonian Deities*, YOS 5–2 (New Haven, CT: Yale University Press, 1923), 85; Jacobs, *The Body as Property*, 213–14.

וזה יכתב ידו ליהוה	**This one will write on his hand, "Belonging to YHWH"**
ובשם ישׂראל יכנה	And by the name 'Israel' he will be called an honorary name.

Eager to belong to YHWH, they would brand themselves both orally and physically with YHWH's name.[108] Note that both claims use the designation from the high priestly medallion: ליהוה. Whether or not this vision was literally enacted, it communicates a renewed desire to belong to YHWH and the sealing of that allegiance through a physical brand or tattoo.[109]

The most elaborate biblical text involving a tattoo is found in Ezekiel:

Ezekiel 9:3a–4

ויקרא אל־האיש הלבש הבדים	And he called to the man wearing linen
אשׁר קסת הספר במתניו	who had a writing kit at his side,
ויאמר יהוה אלו	and YHWH said to him,
עבר בתוך העיר	"Pass through the midst of the city
בתוך ירושלם	through the midst of Jerusalem
והתוית תו על־מצחות	**And mark with a mark** on the foreheads
האנשים הנאנחים והנאנקים	of the men who sigh and groan
על כל־התועבות	over all the abominations
הנעשׂות בתוכה	that are being done in its midst."

In Ezekiel's vision a scribe with an inkpot or writing case (קסת הספר)[110] was to physically "mark with a mark on the foreheads" all those distressed by the sin of Jerusalem (9:4). This mark signaled their fidelity to YHWH.

108. Reading יקרא and יכנה as passive verbs with Symmachus (for יקרא) and the Syriac, Tgs., and Vulg. (for יכנה). This shift simply involves a change in vocalization. The final verb is lacking in most LXX manuscripts. Karen Jobes and Moisés Silva (*Invitation to the Septuagint* [Grand Rapids: Baker Academic, 2005], 133) prefer the Alexandrian reading: "And another one will write, I am God's." But the Hebrew Vorlage likely contained the Tetragrammaton. The Isaiah Tg. softened the Hebrew to read "I am *of the fearers of* YHWH," but both phrases retained the Tetragrammaton. See Chilton, *Isaiah Targum*, 87.

Scholars debate whether this refers to Jews or Gentiles. Some rabbis used Isa 44:5 to show parity between God's love for Gentile proselytes and for Israel. For example, *Num. Rab.* 8.2 on Num 8:6. Indeed, the verb כנה designates an *honorary* title or name (*DCH* 4:434–35). Cf. 2 Esdr 1:22–24, where God threatened to give his name to other nations because Israel had blasphemed it. Cf. Guillaume, "Is 44:5," 378. Alternatively, Block ("The View from the Top: The Holy Spirit in the Prophets," in *Presence, Power, and Promise: The Role of the Spirit of God in the Old Testament*, ed. David G. Firth and Paul D. Wegner, 202–6. [Downers Grove, IL: IVP Academic, 2011]) sees the pouring out of the Spirit as a sign of covenant renewal for Israel, whereby he again claims them as his own. Cf. Isa 32:15; Joel 3:1–2[2:28–29]; Ezek 39:29; Zech 12:10. See also Oswalt, *Isaiah 40–66*, 168.

109. Another Isaianic text describes God tattooing himself to show his commitment to Israel: "See, on the palms I have inscribed you (חקתיך); your walls are before me continually" (49:16).

110. The word קסת, a loanword from the Egyptian (*gšti*), refers to a "writing kit" with a niche for a pen and recessed areas for ink. For a description, see G. R. Driver, *Semitic Writing: From Pictograph to Alphabet*, 3rd ed. (London: Oxford University Press, 1976), 86–87; cf. Daniel I. Block, *The Book of Ezekiel: Chapters 1–24* (Grand Rapids: Eerdmans, 2005), 305; Walther Zimmerli, *Ezekiel 1*, trans. Ronald E. Clements, Hermeneia (Philadelphia: Fortress, 1979), 224; *DCH* 7:272.

Here תו could refer to the last letter of the Hebrew alphabet. In paleo-Hebrew תו was written as ✗ and used to denote "possession or affiliation," especially to a divine being.[111] Alternatively, the תו could denote someone's personal signature or identifying mark. For example, after Job made his case for innocence, he certified its authenticity by declaring,

Job 31:35

מי יתן־לי שׁמע לי	Who will give me a hearing?
הן־תוי שׁדי יענני	Look—**my signature**;[112] may Shaddai answer me
וספר כתב איש ריבי	and my adversary write an indictment!

Likewise, in Ezekiel the mark on the foreheads of the righteous may have been YHWH's signature, denoting that they belonged to him and thereby came under his protection (cf. Isa 44:5).[113] While Ezekiel does not explicitly state that the content of the mark is YHWH's *name*, it is possible, given the ancient practice of tattooing temple slaves with the name of the deity, the use of תו to mean signature in Job, and the echoes of this passage in Rev 14:1, where the mark of the divine name is explicit.

In addition to physical branding, the notion of oral "branding" is also attested in the ANE; more to the point, calling a name over someone is explicitly compared to a brand. A royal inscription from Tiglath-pileser I (1114–1076 BCE) claimed that Shamash appointed him as ruler, and that his people were subjects of the god Enlil, "whose name was proclaimed over the princes."[114] Apparently, this statement claimed ownership as well as suzerainty, and offers a close parallel with Israel as those "over whom YHWH's name was proclaimed" and who were expected to serve him loyally. In an Akkadian text the god Gibil names things, and thereby decrees their fate. One line reads, "Whatever is called by a name, you brand."[115] Here the con-

111. *HALOT* 2:1693. For extensive ANE evidence of forehead pendants inscribed with a תו, see Othmar Keel, "Zeichen der Verbundenheit: Zur Vorgeschichte und Bedeutung der Forderungen von Deuteronomium 6,8 f. und Par.," in *Mélanges Dominique Barthélemy: Études Bibliques Offertes A L'Occasion de son 60 Anniversaire*, OBO 38 (Göttingen: Vandenhoeck & Ruprecht, 1981), 194–212.

112. Another possibility is that תו indicates Job's "desire" (תוה; otherwise unattested), in which case the verse would read "Look, my desire is that Shaddai would answer me." See *DCH* 8:597, 599; Driver, *Semitic Writing*, 206–7. *HALOT* 2:1694 rejects this suggestion in favor of Fohrer's view that Job's תו is analogous to the fingernail impressions on Babylonian clay tablets. See Georg Fohrer, *Das Buch Hiob*, KAT 16 (Gütersloh: Mohn, 1963), 443. Fohrer (*Ezechiel*, HAT 13 [Tübingen: Mohr Siebeck, 1955], 54) compares this mark to the branding of slaves, resulting in an identification that someone belongs to YHWH and enjoys his protection. Jacobs (*The Body as Property*, 203) translates it "[my] *tav* of Shaddai," which she understands apotropaically. If she is correct, Job appeals to God's signature on him as grounds for divine deliverance.

113. Block, *Ezekiel 1–24*, 307.

114. The Akkadian reads: "*ša si-qir-šu* UGU *ma-li-ki*.MEŠ *né-bu-ú*." See A. Kirk Grayson, "Tiglath-pileser 1:A.O.87," RIMA 2/13, lines 1.33–35.

115. Reiner, *Šurpu*, 53, line 14.

cept of oral branding is explicit, though it probably refers to the branding of an entity with its own name rather than the deity's.

Dishonor of YHWH's שׁם

Clearly, the NC prohibits mistreatment of YHWH's name. While נשׂא is not inherently negative, as we shall see below, to נשׂא שׁם לשׁוא is a crime worthy of punishment. Now I will examine expressions involving שׁם where the governing verb is unambiguously negative to see whether any patterns emerge regarding the mistreatment of YHWH's name. At least seven such negative verbs are attested: חלל, בזה, טמא, נקב, קלל, תפשׂ, and נאץ. The most common is חלל.

חלל את־שׁם

The word חלל is a verbal homonym with four or five apparently unrelated meanings.[116] Here the meaning is "to profane, or make profane use of [the name]"; the collocation with שׁם occurs 14 times in biblical literature. Leviticus 19:12, already discussed above (p. 16), explicitly connects the profanation of YHWH's name with false swearing by his name (cf. *CD* XV 2, 3). Similarly Jeremiah 34:15–16 (see above, pp. 54–56), describes the violation of a covenant made at the temple. The repossession of released slaves profaned YHWH's name because the covenant had been made at his house (the "place of the name"), and likely *in* his name. These examples involve failure to honor his spoken name. However, a variety of other behaviors, none involving speech, also profaned his name, suggesting that in these cases "name" is used metonymically for YHWH's reputation.[117]

Leviticus 20:2b–3 (cf. 18:21)

איש איש מבני ישׂראל	Any one of the Israelites
ומן־הגר הגר בישׂראל	or from the foreigners sojourning in Israel
אשר יתן מזרעו למלך מות יומת	who gives of his offspring to Molech shall surely die;
עם הארץ ירגמהו באבן	the people of the land shall stone him with stones.
ואני אתן את־פני באיש ההוא	And I will set my face against that man
והכרתי אתו מקרב עמו	and cut him off from the midst of my people
כי מזרעו נתן למלך	because from his offspring he gave to Molech
למען טמא את־מקדשי	**so** defiling my sanctuary
ולחלל את־שׁם קדשׁי	**and profaning my holy name**

Leviticus 18:21 and 20:3 both indicate that child sacrifice profaned YHWH's name, but the syntax is least ambiguous in the latter, with למען linking the abominable action and its result: sanctuary and name were profaned. The defilement of both sanctuary and name naturally related because the

116. חלל 1 = "to profane"; 2 = "to begin"; 3 = "to be pierced"; 4 = "to play the flute"; 5 = "to tremble." *DCH* 3:234–36.

117. For an exploration of all 19 instances of the phrase חלל שׁם, see Jacob Milgrom, "The Desecration of YHWH's Name: Its Parameters and Significance," in *Birkat Shalom: Studies in the Bible, Ancient Near Eastern Literature, and Postbiblical Judaism Presented to Shalom M. Paul on the Occasion of His Seventieth Birthday*, ed. Chaim Cohen et al. (Winona Lake, IN: Eisenbrauns, 2008), 1:69–81.

sanctuary was the "place where YHWH put his name." Given YHWH's absolute claim on Israel's worship, the worship of other gods (here Molech) violated his sovereignty and the pagan practices associated with this apostasy clouded YHWH's reputation.

Leviticus 21:1, 5–6 (cf. 22:2, 32)

ויאמר יהוה אל־משה	And YHWH said to Moses,
אמר אל־הכהנים בני אהרן	Speak to the priests, the sons of Aaron,
ואמרת אלהם	and say to them,
לנפש לא־יטמא בעמיו	'For a corpse do not defile yourself among his people.'
לא־יקרחו קרחה בראשם	. . . They are not to shave a bald spot on their head
ופאת זקנם לא יגלחו	and the corners of their beards they are not to cut
ובבשׂרם לא ישׂרטו שׂרטת	and on their flesh they are not to cut an incision
קדשים יהיו לאלהיהם	Holy, they are, to their God,
ולא יחללו שם אלהיהם	**so they shall not profane the name of their God**
כי את־אשי יהוה	because with the offering by fire to YHWH
לחם אלהיהם הם מקריבם	the bread of their God they bring near
והיו קדש	and they are holy.

Purity laws for priests included restrictions on their marriages and funerary involvement. Contact with dead bodies, traditional mourning practices, and even movement outside the sanctuary area were limited, to maintain personal purity and thereby preserve the holiness of their sacrifices.[118] Leviticus 22:2 likewise instructs priests to "treat with awe" (נזר, *niphal*) the sanctuary offerings, "so they do not profane my holy name" (ולא יחללו את־שם קדשי). To safeguard these offerings, a variety of practices are proscribed, such as eating sacred offerings while unclean or offering them to one outside the priestly family (22:3–16). More broadly, *every* Israelite was to ensure that offerings were free of defects and were offered in an acceptable way (22:17–30). The instruction was repeated for the benefit of the entire community:

Leviticus 22:32

ולא תחללו את־שם קדשי	Do not **profane my holy name,**
ונקדשתי בתוך בני ישׂראל	that I may be sanctified in the midst of the Israelites
אני יהוה מקדשכם	I am YHWH who sanctifies you.

The holiness of the entire nation (notice the plural verb תחללו and plural pronominal suffix on מקדשכם) required them to interface with YHWH in a carefully prescribed manner so that the name (YHWH's reputation) would not be profaned.

Ezekiel 20:39

ואתם בית־ישׂראל	As for you, house of Israel,
כה־אמר אדני יהוה	this is what the Lord YHWH says:
איש גלוליו לכו עבדו	Go, each one serve his filthy idols.

118. Jacobs ("The Body Inscribed," 4–6, 8, 14–15) associates bodily incisions with tattoos (Lev 19:28) but suggests the latter is not a mourning rite. Rather, since pagan temple servants were branded, any tattoo on a Levite would contradict their dedication to YHWH. Cf. Huehnergard and Liebowitz, "The Biblical Prohibition against Tattooing," 69, 77.

ואחר אם־אינכם שׁמעים אלי	And later, if you fail to listen to me—
ואת־שם קדשי לא תחללו־עוד	**but my holy name you shall no longer profane**
במתנותיכם ובגלוליכם	with your gifts and your filthy idols.

Here, Israel's sin was idolatry.[119] In this passage, a sarcastic encouragement to continue in their abominable behavior is followed by a half-expressed threat[120] and then a promise to supersede their punishment with his grace. The uncleanness of their worship profaned Yhwh's reputation.

Although profanation of the name was usually a feature of *cultic* violations (as the examples above demonstrate), Amos extended profanation of the name to a variety of *moral* infractions.[121]

Amos 2:6–8

כה אמר יהוה	Thus says Yhwh,
על־שלשה פשעי ישראל	"For three transgressions of Israel,
ועל־ארבעה לא אשיבנו	even for four I will not relent.
על־מכרם בכסף צדיק	For they sold the innocent for silver,
ואביון בעבור נעלים	the needy for a hidden bribe.[122]
השאפים על־עפר־ארץ	They trample upon the dust of the earth
בראש דלים	on the heads of the poor,
ודרך ענוים יטו	and thrust aside the path of the oppressed,
ואיש ואביו ילכו אל־הנערה	and a man and his father go to the same maiden
למען חלל את־שם קדשי	**with the result that my holy name is profaned,**
ועל־בגדים חבלים	and upon pledged garments
יטו אצל כל־מזבח	they thrust [themselves] down beside every altar
ויין ענושים ישתו בית אלהיהם	and they drink levied wine in the house of their god!"

The grammar requires that these indictments against Israel function together, each describing another aspect of the social injustice characteristic of Israelite society. In each line another constituent is placed before the verb, linking it to the preceding statement so that the whole list becomes a single portrait of a people plagued by social injustice (cf. Amos 8:4–6). Economic oppression and callous treatment of the poor went hand in hand with sexual impropriety,[123] abusing the vulnerable by taking the bodies of

119. The Hebrew גִּלּוּלִים is likely derived from the consonants of גלל, which means "to roll," with the vowels of שִׁקֻּצִים (cf. Ezek 5:11; Nah 3:6, "detestable thing, filth"), and by extension here connotes "dung pellets." This is one of Ezekiel's favorite derogatory words to refer to idols, appearing 39 times in the book. "Filthy idols" attempts to convey the sense of the word as well as its referent. For discussion, see Block, *Ezekiel 1–24*, 226. Joüon (§177e) notes that asyndetic constructions are common with joint imperatives.

120. This passage probably contains the apodosis of a maledictory curse lacking its protasis. See Joüon §165a. As such, it could be translated, "And later, you will certainly listen to me, and my holy name you shall no longer profane." The persistence of Israel's spiritual adultery is so unthinkable that Ezekiel cannot express it.

121. Cf. Shalom M. Paul, *Amos: A Commentary on the Book of Amos*, Hermeneia (Minneapolis: Fortress, 1991), 83.

122. For a detailed linguistic argument that נעלים is not the dual of the noun נעל, "sandal," but rather a conjugated form of the verb עלם, "to hide," see ibid., 78.

123. While the expression הלך אל is not used elsewhere to describe sexual activity,

young women, the garments of debtors, and the resources of the powerless at will in order to facilitate pagan practices.[124] Older and younger generations collaborated in this blatant sin.

This egregious behavior resulted in exile, but even then YHWH's "name" continued to be profaned. Ezekiel wrote from the vantage point of the exile:

Ezekiel 36:20

ויבוא אל־הגוים אשר־באו שם	And when they came to the nations where they went,
ויחללו את־שם קדשי	**they profaned my holy name**
באמר להם	by having it said of them,
עם־יהוה אלה	"These are the people of YHWH,
ומארצו יצאו	but they came out of his land."

The immediate context reinforces that Israel was responsible for profaning YHWH's name through blatant covenant violations involving bloodshed and idolatry (v. 18, 31). Because of the close association between YHWH and Israel, their disastrous fate (exile) damaged his reputation. The NLT captures well the import of this verse: "These are the people of the LORD, but he couldn't keep them safe in his own land!" Yet the nations' assessment of Israel's situation was inaccurate. Rather than proof of YHWH's impotence, the exile was the consequence of Israel's covenant unfaithfulness. As v. 17 explains, "When the house of Israel was dwelling in their own land, they defiled it by their ways and by their deeds" (cf. v. 19). Ultimately, God's people deserved expulsion; exile was among the covenant curses for failure to obey (cf. Lev 26:14–15, 33; Deut 28:15, 36–37, 64). Israel's fate reflected negatively on YHWH because it appeared to other nations that YHWH was either incompetent or had intentionally reneged on his covenant promises.

In summary, Israel profaned YHWH's name (חלל את־שם) through a variety of objectionable behaviors. On the one hand, cultic infractions were naturally name-profaning because they were carried out in direct violation of cultic regulations at the "place of the name." These infractions included child sacrifice (Lev 18:21; 20:3), failure to follow proper protocol for sacred offerings (Lev 21:6; 22:2, 32), broken agreements sworn in the temple (Jer 34:15–16), and idolatrous worship (Ezek 20:39). On the other hand, the social injustice outlined by Amos (2:7) and the exile itself (Ezek 36:20–21) profaned YHWH's name because his reputation was staked on their obedience. Their behavior was unseemly for those belonging to him, and their fate created the impression that YHWH had failed to protect his people.[125]

Paul (ibid., 82) argues that it does here, noting cognate phrases in Akkadian (*ana alāku*) and Aramaic (אזל על) where both imply intercourse.

124. Paul (ibid.) offers a detailed argument against any cultic connotations of the sexual act, citing the lack of "sexual overtones" in v. 8 and the absence of cultic vocabulary in v. 7. However, the pairing of "going in" (v. 7) and "stretching out" (v. 8) could imply as much. I have translated יטו as "thrust [themselves] down" in order to highlight the parallel use of יטו in v. 7. Minimally, lying down by the altar is portrayed as another violation of social justice, as the echo of יטו underscores.

125. Cf. 4 Esdr 10:22; Jdt 5:20–21; Sir 36:22; 2 Macc 1:27. John Evans ("An Inner-Biblical

Other Negative Expressions

Other expressions where a negative verb is paired with YHWH's name as an object exhibit a similar range of implicated behavior. As in the examples from Leviticus above, the priests despised (בזה) his name by disregarding YHWH's instructions regarding the sacrificial system.[126]

Malachi 1:6–7

בן יכבד אב ועבד אדניו	A son honors his father and a servant his master.
ואם־אב אני איה כבודי	Then if I am a father, where is my honor?
ואם־אדונים אני איה מוראי	and if I am a master, where is my respect?
אמר יהוה צבאות לכם	says YHWH of armies to you,
הכהנים בוזי שמי	priests who **despise my name**.
ואמרתם במה בזינו את־שמך	But you say, 'How have **we despised your name**?'
מגישים על־מזבחי לחם מגאל	By approaching my altar with desecrated bread.
ואמרתם במה גאלנוך	Yet you ask 'How have we desecrated you?"
באמרכם שלחן יהוה נבזה הוא	By saying the table of YHWH is **despised**.

Malachi 1:6–7 is explicit about the manner in which YHWH's name was mistreated. Here the priests were at fault for offering defiled food on YHWH's altar (blind, lame, or diseased animals; v. 8), and verbally treating the sacrificial system with contempt.[127] These actions resulted in a loss of blessing (Mal 2:2). To fail to honor God properly by giving him the best animals was equivalent to desecrating the name itself. Note the metonymic use of שם for YHWH. Dishonor and disrespect were unworthy of him.[128]

Ezekiel 43:7–8 is equally explicit about the causes for defilement of YHWH's name. There the people defiled YHWH's name (טמא את־שם) through spiritual-political prostitution (זנות; trying to attract favors from other nations; cf. Ezek 23) and by disregarding sacred space, crowding it with other buildings and littering it with the apparatus of a royal funerary cult (בפגרי מלכיהם במותם).[129] These indictments do not concern their *words*, as one

Interpretation and Intertextual Reading of Ezekiel's Recognition Formulae with the Book of Exodus" [Th.D. diss., University of Stellenbosch, 2006], 292) also recognizes both dimensions of the desecration of YHWH's name.

126. See Milgrom, "Desecration of YHWH's Name," 75.

127. For further discussion, see ibid.

128. However, Malachi spoke of a future, righteous remnant who would commit to be YHWH's covenant people (Mal 2:5; 3:16). God promised to spare this remnant from judgment and adopt them as his treasured possession (סגלה), just as he did at Sinai (Mal 3:17–20[3:17–4:2]). This new remnant would bring honor to his name among the nations by living righteously and serving faithfully. Their designation as the סגלה represents a significant development in OT theology. Elsewhere, the term is applied to the entire nation to indicate their elect status in contrast to the nations (e.g., Exod 19:5–6). Here only a subgroup of faithful Israelites will receive the honored title. For discussion, see Pieter Verhoef, *The Books of Haggai and Malachi*, NICOT (Grand Rapids: Eerdmans, 1987), 322.

129. It is not clear whether stelae were set up in the temple precinct in honor of dead kings, in which case פגר refers to "lifeless masses," or whether royalty were buried on or near temple grounds, in which case פגר means "corpses." For discussion, see Block, *Ezekiel 25–48*, 582–86; cf. Jacob Milgrom, *Leviticus 23–27*, AB 3B (New York: Doubleday,

might expect with the defilement of a name, but rather their abominable *actions* (בתועבותם אשר עשׂו), which tarnish YHWH's reputation.

Another expression can involve speech. An Israelite of mixed descent cursed (נקב/קלל) YHWH's name and received the death penalty:

Leviticus 24:11a, 15–16

ויקב בן־האשה הישׂראלית	And the son of the Israelite woman **designated**
את־השם ויקלל	**the name and disparaged [it]**
ויביאו אתו אל־משה . . .	and they brought him to Moses . . .
איש איש כי־יקלל אלהיו	Anyone who **disparages his God**
ונשׂא חטאו	will bear his sin
ונקב שם־יהוה מות יומת	**One who designates YHWH's name** shall certainly die;
רגום ירגמו־בו כל־העדה	Let all the witnesses certainly stone him
כגר כאזרח	—whether foreigner or full citizen—
בנקבו־שם יומת	**on account of his designating the name** he shall die.

The collocation נקב שם often indicates someone expressly designated by name for a task,[130] but that meaning makes little sense here. However, for at least two reasons we need not suppose a different root (such as קבב) to explain the negative use of נקב in Lev 24. נקב usually means either "bore through," "establish," or "denote."[131] A negative instantiation of the third meaning is operative here. First, the Akkadian cognate, *naqabu*, is undoubtedly negative ("to deflower, rape").[132] Second, v. 16 clearly employs the *qal* active participle of נקב, making its reappearance in v. 11 more probable. Most likely נקב is euphemistic for open disparagement of YHWH (cf. Job 2:9), since the unambiguously negative קלל is never paired directly with "YHWH" in the Hebrew Bible (though note LXX 1 Sam 3:13). This may also explain the narrator's avoidance of the name "YHWH" in his statement of the offense (vv. 11, 16). The meaning of נקב שם in the present context is clarified in v. 15, which announces the oracular judgment based on this case: anyone who "disparages his God" (כי־יקלל אלהיו) is guilty.

Elßner avers that the need for divine revelation regarding this case suggests that it lacks precedent; therefore, Lev 24 cannot relate to the NC.[133] However, the question at hand is whether the otherwise clear prohibition against cursing God (קלל; Exod 22:27) applied to someone of mixed descent.[134] Ultimately, the man's parentage did not excuse him from the death penalty (see Lev 24:22; cf. Lev 20:9). Yet it was not to be imposed merely because he

2001), 2317; idem in conversation with Daniel I. Block, *Ezekiel's Hope: A Commentary on Ezekiel 38–48*, (Eugene, OR: Cascade, 2012), 110–11.

130. With a ב prefix—Num 1:17; 1 Chr 12:32[31]; 16:41; 2 Chr 28:15; 31:19; Ezra 8:20; cf. Isa 62:2.

131. *HALOT* 1:718–19.

132. Ibid. Cf. perhaps also Job 3:8; Prov 11:26.

133. Elßner, *Das Namensmißbrauch-Verbot*, 79–80.

134. For discussion, see Jonathan Vroom, "Recasting *Mišpāṭîm*: Legal Innovation in Leviticus 24:10–23," *JBL* 131 (2012): 27–44. Alternatively, Richard Averbeck suggested (in personal conversation) that the need for clarification arose because the exact penalty had not yet been specified.

pronounced the name, something encouraged elsewhere (e.g., Deut 6:13), but because the man *disparaged* it. Note that the man did not curse his human antagonist *in* the name or *by* the name (cf. 1 Sam 17:43). Rather he abused the name directly and verbally (Lev 24:15; cf. Exod 22:27).[135] This same phrase, קלל אלהים, appears in 1 Sam 3:11–14 with reference to the sons of Eli, who mishandled their sacred roles as YHWH's priests.[136] Thus, קלל השם describes an inappropriate utterance in Lev 24:11 (cf., v. 15) and קלל אלהים a series of actions unbefitting YHWH's priests in 1 Sam 3:13.

Proverbs 30:9 contains the only collocation of תפשׂ with שׁם. Normally, תפשׂ means "to seize, capture, or handle," but here it means "to handle disrespectfully, profane."[137]

Proverbs 30:8–9

שׁוא ודבר־כזב הרחק ממני	Emptiness and words of falsehood keep far from me;
ראשׁ ועשׁר אל־תתן־לי	poverty or riches do not give me.
הטריפני לחם חקי	Let me devour my portion of bread.
פן אשׂבע וכחשׁתי	Lest I am satiated and deny
ואמרתי מי יהוה	by saying, "Who is YHWH?"
ופן־אורשׁ וגנבתי	Or lest I become impoverished and steal,
ותפשׂתי שׁם אלהי	**thus profaning the name of my God.**

The sage asked God to supply his daily needs, not too much and not too little, so that his speech and actions would be pure. If satiated, he might deny YHWH. If impoverished, he might resort to stealing.[138] Either course

135. Contra Brichto (*The Problem of "Curse,"* 150), who argues that the context of this passage as well as the parallel expression in 1 Sam 3:11–14 suggest that the man's mistreatment of another human was "an act of *qillel ʾelōhīm*." Cf. Lev 19:14. For further discussion of Lev 24, see Milgrom, *Leviticus 23–27*, 2107–8; Gordon J. Wenham, *The Book of Leviticus*, NICOT (Grand Rapids: Eerdmans, 1979), 311; Fishbane, *Biblical Interpretation*, 101; John Hartley, *Leviticus*, 404, 408–9; Gary Alan Long, "נקב," *NIDOTTE* 3:149–50; Brichto, *The Problem of "Curse,"* 143–50, 200–202.

136. See also 1 Sam 2:27–36. This reading of 1 Sam 3:13 follows the LXX θεόν rather than the MT's מקללים להם. The MT may reflect a scribal emendation to mitigate the idea that YHWH failed to punish immediately one who cursed him or to avoid saying "cursing God." This verse is listed along with 10 other instances of scribal "euphemism" in the *Mekhilta*. For discussion, see Tov, *Textual Criticism of the Hebrew Bible*, 65–67; Ralph W. Klein, *1 Samuel*, WBC (Nashville: Thomas Nelson, 1983), 30. Alternatively, the loss of the א could have been accidental, since we might expect the scribes to change "curse" to "bless" rather than "God" to "themselves." So M. A. Zipor, "Some Notes on the Origin of the Tradition of the Eighteen *tiqqûnê sôperîm*," *VT* 44 (1994): 91–92.

137. *DCH* 8:668. On the shared ethical context of חלל and תפשׂ, see Rick Byargeon, "Echoes of Wisdom in the Lord's Prayer (Matt 6:9–13)," *JETS* 41 (1998): 363.

138. Michael V. Fox (*Proverbs 10–31*, AB 18B [New Haven, CT: Yale University Press, 2009], 859) connects the name and stealing because a thief tends to lie under oath. Also, Milgrom (*Leviticus 1–16*, 336) argues that an oath is necessary for the claimant to prove ownership in cases where the thief is unknown or denies wrongdoing. For a more nuanced reading, see Averbeck, "אָשָׁם," *NIDOTTE* 1:560. However, the concept of name-bearing provides an alternative explanation. Stealing is immoral, and any immorality performed by those who bear YHWH's name damages his reputation. While stealing directly

of action—one involving speech and one entailing behavior—would profane Yhwh's name.

The last expression to consider is נאץ שם. Yhwh's enemies treated his name irreverently (נאץ) by oppressing his people and destroying his sanctuary.

Psalm 74:10, 18 [piel]

עד־מתי אלהים יחרף צר How long, God, will the adversary revile (you)?
ינאץ אויב שמך לנצח . . . The enemy **treats your name irreverently** without end. . . .
זכר־זאת אויב חרף יהוה Remember this: enemies revile Yhwh.
ועם נבל נאצו שמך And foolish people **treat your name irreverently**.

Psalm 74 calls Yhwh to remember his covenant with Israel for twin reasons (vv. 2, 20). First, his enemies have profaned (חלל) the "dwelling place of your name" (משכן־שמך; v. 7; cf. v. 3),[139] leaving Yhwh open to mockery. Yhwh's reputation was at stake because the official cult sites had been decimated (v. 8). Second, Yhwh's people were afflicted and vulnerable (vv. 19–21). Yhwh's name and his people are not explicitly linked in this Psalm, but the connection is implied. The reviling of the name involved the destruction of both the temple and the "people of your inheritance" (v. 2).

Isaiah 52:5b [hithpolel]

כי־לקח עמי חנם "For my people are taken away undeservedly.
משליו יהילילו נאם־יהוה Those ruling them howl," declares Yhwh.
ותמיד כל־היום שמי מנאץ "Constantly, all day, **my name is treated irreverently**."

Israel's exile brought abuse on Yhwh. He seemed either powerless or unwilling to rescue those who claimed to belong to him. Through the prophet, he assured his people that they would again experience his salvation (v. 10). For our purposes, the important feature in this passage is the connection between the exile and the mistreatment of Yhwh's name.[140] This instance appears to be verbal; Yhwh's name was spoken irreverently to cast him in a negative light. However, it retains conceptual links with Ezek 36:20, where "name" may be metonymic for Yhwh or his reputation rather than referring to a spoken appellation; in both cases Israel's devastation reflected negatively on Yhwh because of the intimate association between them.[141]

Similarly, the reputation of gods in the ANE was bound up with the fate of the lands and people with whom they were identified.[142] ANE gods were obligated to protect their possessions. A Hittite text notes that the Sun-goddess of Arinna chose Hatti for herself as her own land.[143]

precedes profanation and therefore is closely associated with it, the syntactical symmetry in the four lines of v. 9 links the denial "Who is Yhwh?" with profanation of the name.

139. The phrase משכן־שמך appears to be a reflex of the idiom לשכן שמו שם.

140. See also Jer 14:21.

141. See also Milgrom, "Desecration of Yhwh's Name," 78.

142. Hundley, "To Be or Not To Be," 545. Ran Zadok ("Names and Naming," *OEANE* 4:93) suggested that theophoric names might evoke the protection of a god, but it is impossible to be certain.

143. Singer, *Hittite Prayers*, 97, no. 21 (CTH 383), §1.

Her ownership explains why a supplicant could pray, "All the surrounding lands have begun to attack Hatti. Let this become a further reason for vengeance for the Sun-goddess of Arinna. Goddess, *do not degrade your own name*!"[144] In this case, a military defeat would spell defamation for the sun-goddess.[145] Around the 15th century BCE, an Akkadian scribe spoke of Ishtar's exalted name and then prayed for her to alleviate his suffering, "May your very great forgiveness be with me! May those who see me in the street magnify your name."[146] Ishtar's reputation was associated with her treatment of a devotee. If that man prospered, Ishtar would be glorified by observers.

This exploration of the mistreatment of YHWH's name sheds light on the current study. YHWH's name (sometimes metonymic for YHWH himself or his reputation) was disparaged both inside and outside the cultic apparatus, through violations involving a range of both words and actions. Especially significant is the association between Israel's behavior, Israel's fate, and YHWH's reputation. When Israel acted badly, YHWH was brought into disrepute. When Israel suffered devastation, YHWH was mocked. Perhaps the expression נשׂא שם לשוא participates in this field of discourse wherein the close association between YHWH and Israel put YHWH's "name" at risk because of Israel's covenant unfaithfulness.

Sanctification of YHWH's שׁם

Twice the Hebrew Bible speaks of the sanctification of YHWH's name, once explicitly contrasting this to the profanation of his name among the nations. In theory, his name would be sanctified when his people honored him again.[147] Isaiah announced on YHWH's behalf, "They will sanctify my name (יקדישו שמי); They will sanctify the Holy One of Jacob" (Isa 29:23b). The empty worship (v. 13) and crooked behavior (vv. 15, 20–21) of God's people would be purified by a fresh work of God among them and their children (v. 23a). His *reputation* would be restored by Israel's proper worship. They would begin treating him as he deserved.

According to Ezekiel, since this behavior was not forthcoming, YHWH would take matters into his own hands. Contrary to Israel's beliefs, the

---

144. Ibid., 51, no. 8 (CTH 376A), §4, emphasis mine.

145. The "Treaty between Shattiwaza of Mittanni and Suppiluliuma I of Hatti" (Beckman and Hoffner, *HDT*, 53–54, 6B, §11) outlined the benefits for humans:

> Thus says Prince Shattiwaza and indeed also the Hurrian: If we observe this treaty and oath of His Majesty, Suppiluliuma, Great King, King of Hatti, Hero, Beloved of the Storm-god, the gods whose names we have invoked shall go with us, exalt us, protect us, and be good to us.

146. Anna Elise Zernecke, "A Shuilla: Ishtar 2, 'The Great Ishtar Prayer,'" in Lenzi, *Akkadian Prayers and Hymns*, 284, lines 100–101. See also *ANET* 2:385, lines 100–101.

147. On both occasions, sanctification of the name is a future promise rather than a present reality. The link between personal holiness and sanctification of the name is implicit in the psalmist's prayer: "Lead me in right paths for your name's sake" (Ps 23:3).

"present theological crisis" that YHWH was determined to resolve was not the exile per se but rather the resulting desecration of his name.[148]

Ezekiel 36:22–23

לכן אמר לבית־ישׂראל	Therefore, say to the house of Israel,
כה אמר אדני יהוה	'Thus says the Lord YHWH:
לא למענכם אני עשׂה בית ישׂראל	Not for your sake am I acting, house of Israel,
כי אם־לשׁם־קדשׁי	but rather **for my holy name**,
אשׁר חללתם בגוים	which you profaned among the nations
אשׁר־באתם שׁם	where you went.
וקדשׁתי את־שׁמי הגדול	**For I will sanctify my great name**
המחלל בגוים	that was profaned among the nations,
אשׁר חללתם בתוכם	which you profaned in their midst.
וידעו הגוים כי־אני יהוה	And the nations will know that I am YHWH,
נאם אדני יהוה	declares the Lord YHWH
בהקדשׁי בכם לעיניהם	**when I am sanctified by you** before their eyes.

Here, the sanctification of YHWH's name and the sanctification of YHWH are one and the same, confirming that "name" is used metonymically for YHWH.[149] The verses that follow unveil YHWH's drastic plan to sanctify his own name by cleansing Israel from sin, giving her a heart transplant, bestowing the Spirit, and renewing the covenant, resulting in the fruitfulness of the land, the restoration of Israel's cities, and the installation of a Davidic shepherd (36:24–37; cf. 39:25–29). Divine action is paramount. However, the dishonor to YHWH would not be fully resolved until the Israelites themselves took YHWH's decrees seriously, resulting in the sanctification of YHWH's reputation in the sight of the nations (36:27). Ultimately, the nations would realize that the exile was not due to YHWH's impotence or his betrayal but rather Israel's rebellion (39:23–24). Israel's repentance and covenant restoration would demonstrate YHWH's true identity to the nations (Ezek 36:23, 28, 31). Thus, the sanctification of YHWH's name would require dramatic action on God's part resulting in Israel's appropriate response.

Summary of Findings on שׁם

In sum, the phrase "name of YHWH" appears in a variety of senses in the Hebrew Bible—as a linguistic unit that refers directly to YHWH through metonymy, as a metonymic reference to his fame, reputation, or authority, and in various idioms that indicate his claim to ownership. Several facts should

148. Block, *Ezekiel 25–48*, 351–52. Verses 23b–38 are lacking in P967, on which, see Johan Lust, "Textual Criticism of the Old and New Testaments: Stepbrothers?" in *New Testament Textual Criticism and Exegesis: Festschrift J. Delobel*, ed. A. Denaux, BETL 161 (Leuven: Leuven University Press, 2002), 28–30; Ashley S. Crane, *Israel's Restoration: A Textual-Comparative Exploration of Ezekiel 36–39*, VTSup 122 (Leiden: Brill, 2008), 230–44. However, since proto-MT fragments of Ezekiel from Masada and Qumran predate P967 by over 200 years, it is likely that both editions of Ezekiel coexisted for some time. See Hector Patmore, "The Shorter and Longer Texts of Ezekiel: The Implications of the Manuscript Finds from Masada and Qumran," *JSOT* 32 (2007): 231–42.

149. It is also further evidence against "name theology."

be very clear by now. First, "name" is not limited to a spoken appellation. Second, the proliferation of texts regarding the "place of the name" and the people "called by his name," as well as their juxtaposition in key texts involving the priestly ministry indicates that Israel's identity as a people is bound up with YHWH's claim on them, and thereby with his "name." Third, the range of behaviors by which God's people do damage to his reputation suggests that the warning of the NC against the abuse of YHWH's name ought to be considered with reference to these broader concerns.

נשׂא

Of the critical words in the NC, נשׂא is arguably the most crucial to define. Given its broad range of meaning and almost limitless idiomatic combinations, it is not surprising to find it the locus of most discussion on this verse. The word נשׂא appears 658 times in the Hebrew Bible, with wide distribution across the canon. The most common meaning of נשׂא is "to lift up" or "to carry."[150] In the Hebrew Bible, a variety of objects were carried or transported, such as the components of the tabernacle (Exod 25:14) or offerings (Deut 14:24).[151] Less often, נשׂא means "to take" (to steal or take as plunder [Num 16:15]). Occasionally, it has the sense of "wear" [an ephod] (1 Sam 2:28; 14:3; 22:18).[152] The word נשׂא was also the verb of choice for bearing intangible objects: a blessing (Ps 24:5), a curse (1 Kgs 8:31, in some MSS), honor (Zech 6:13), slander (Ps 15:3), anger (Mic 7:9), reproach (Ps 69:8; Jer 15:15), a false report (Exod 23:1), iniquity or sin (Lev 5:1; 19:17), and knowledge (Job 36:3).[153]

Certain forms of speech regularly appear as a direct object of נשׂא: weeping (Gen 21:16), a loud cry (Num 14:1), an oracle (2 Kgs 9:25), a lamentation (Jer 7:29), a משׁל (or "discourse"; Job 27:1), and sometimes a prayer (2 Kgs 19:4). "To lift up a voice" is to call out loudly (Judg 9:7). In poetic texts, נשׂא occasionally indicates the act of speaking without a direct object, though the transitive nature of נשׂא would seem to require one (Isa 3:7; 42:2, 11).

150. For specific studies of the term, see *DCH* 5:758–70; *HALOT* 1:724–27; Victor Hamilton, "נשׂא," *NIDOTTE* 3:160–63; Stoltz, "נשׂא," *TLOT* 2:769–74; Fabry, "נָשָׂא," *TDOT* 10:24–40; cf. Jacob Hoftijzer and K. Jongeling, "nšʾ$_1$," *DNWSI* 760–63.

151. Other objects that were "carried" include children (Gen 21:18; 2 Kgs 4:36–37), corpses (Judg 16:31; Amos 6:10), a standard (Jer 4:6; 50:2), tribute (2 Sam 8:2, 6; Ps 96:8), building materials (1 Kgs 15:22), and wood (Lam 5:13). Aside from the NC and not counting idiomatic expressions such as "lift up the eyes," נשׂא means "lift up" or "carry" at least 60 times in the Pentateuch. See the appendix of this volume.

152. Though the usual word for "wearing" is לבשׁ (e.g., Deut 22:11). Propp (*Exodus 19–40*, 432) suggests that נשׂא may have described "wearing" the ephod because it was "suspended from the shoulders."

153. Similarly, the word נשׂא is used figuratively in the sense of "enduring" or emotionally "bearing" a burden (Exod 18:22; Num 11:12–17; Deut 1:9; Isa 1:14). Even the land "bore up" under the people (Gen 13:6; 36:7; cf. Prov 20:31). As in English, trees "bore" fruit (Joel 2:22; Hag 2:19). Ironically, Israel physically "carried" her idols (Amos 5:26), but YHWH "carried" his people (Exod 19:4; Deut 1:31; Isa 40:11; 46:3–4; 63:9).

However, in each case the context offers clear indicators that נשׂא refers to a speech-act (see underlined lexemes below). The terse constraints of poetry result in an elliptical expression. However, in no case does נשׂא function as a *verbum dicendi* without contextual clues.[154]

Isaiah 3:7

ישׂא ביום ההוא לאמר	**He will lift up** in that day, saying,
לא־אהיה חבשׁ	"I will not be the one who binds [wounds].
ובביתי אין לחם ואין שׂמלה	In my house there is no bread and no coat.
לא תשׂימני קצין עם׃	Do not set me as ruler of the people."

Isaiah 42:2

לא יצעק ולא ישׂא	He will not cry out nor will **he lift up**;
ולא־ישמיע בחוץ קולו׃	his voice will not be heard in the streets.

Isaiah 42:11

ישׂאו מדבר ועריו	Let the wilderness and its cities **lift up**
חצרים תשב קדר	—the villages where Kedar dwells—
ירנו ישבי סלע	Let the people dwelling in Selah cry aloud
מראשׁ הרים יצוחו׃	from the mountaintops let them shout.

A wide range of other idioms involving נשׂא are attested in the Hebrew Bible (table 3).[155] Here, I group similar idioms for ease of comparison.

In addition to all these idioms, נשׂא is frequently collocated with עון to denote bearing sin or the forgiveness of sin (66 times total).[156] The former draws on the broader metaphorical concept of sin as a burden.[157] Those

154. Contra Elßner (*Das Namensmißbrauch-Verbot*, 43–44). See above, p. 37 n. 140.

155. I define *idiom* as a phrase whose meaning is more than the sum of its parts. Here, I follow Arthur Gibson (*Biblical Semantic Logic: A Preliminary Analysis* [London: Sheffield Academic, 2001], 111), though he overstates the case by insisting that an idiom must be "completely ossified." On the potential for reactivation of common metaphors, see Andrea Weiss, *Figurative Language in Biblical Prose Narrative: Metaphor in the Book of Samuel*, VTSup 107 (Leiden: Brill, 2006), 193.

156. Baruch Schwartz ("Term or Metaphor: Biblical *nōśē ʿăwōn/pešaʿ/ḥeṭ*," *Tarbiz* 63 [1994]: 150) claimed that נשׂא עון was a figurative expression for sin's effect on an individual and the community. Rather than posit two distinct meanings for the idiom נשׂא עון, as others had done, one meaning "to bear punishment" and the other "to forgive," Schwartz insisted that the meaning of נשׂא עון depended on its subject, that it could mean either "to bear sin" or "to bear *away* sin," and that guilt rather than punishment was in view. See ibid., 168, 170; Baruch J. Schwartz, "The Bearing of Sin in Priestly Literature," in *Pomegrantes and Golden Bells*, ed. D. Wright, D. N. Freedman, and A. Hurwitz (Winona Lake, IN: Eisenbrauns, 1995), 10; contra Jacob Milgrom in conversation with Daniel I. Block, *Ezekiel's Hope*, 150.

Drawing on Schwartz's work, Gary Anderson (*Sin: A History* [New Haven, CT: Yale University Press, 2009], 27–28) traces the metaphorical concepts that describe sin and its removal. Early in Israel's history, sin was perceived as a burden to be carried, and forgiveness lifted that burden. But with the increased use of Aramaic, this metaphor was eclipsed by another: sin as a debt to be repaid. The Targums render the Hebrew נשׂא עון with the Aramaic קבל חוב ("to assume a debt"). For example, Lev 5:1. Anderson (ibid., 4, 19) follows Schwartz in seeing a unity of sense between the two dimensions of the phrase נשׂא עון.

157. Chapter 5 offers a fuller introduction to metaphorical concepts.

Table 3. Idioms Involving **נשׂא**

"To lift the hand" (נשׂא יד)	to strike	Ps 10:12
	to fight against	2 Sam 18:28; 20:21
	to signal	Isa 49:22
	to pray	Ps 28:2; 63:5; Lam 2:19
	to swear	Exod 6:8; Num 14:30; Ezek 20:5–6
	to see	Gen 24:63
"To lift the eyes" (נשׂא עיני)[158]	to show respect	2 Chr 32:23
	to show favor/ favoritism	Lev 19:15; 2 Kgs 3:14
"To lift a head" (נשׂא ראשׁ)	to restore to office	Gen 40:13
	to kill by beheading	Gen 40:19
	to register in a military list	Num 4:22
	to be encouraged	Job 10:15
"To lift one's own head" (נשׂא ראשׁ)	to face someone	2 Sam 2:22; Job 11:15; 22:26
Of Yhwh: "to lift his face" (נשׂא פנה)	to show favor	Num 6:26; cf. Deut 10:17
"To lift one's own face" (נשׂא פנה)	to arrogate oneself	1 Kgs 1:5; cf. 2 Kgs 14:10
"To lift someone else's face" (נשׂא פנה)	to accept	Gen 32:21[20]; cf. Gen 4:7
"To lift oneself" (מתנשׂא)	to desire something	Exod 35:21, 26; 36:2; Deut 24:15; Prov 19:18
"To lift one's heart/soul" to Yhwh (נשׂא נפשׁ/לב)	to flee to Yhwh for protection[159]	Ps 25:1; 86:4; 143:8
"To lift [someone else's] soul" (נשׂא נפשׁ)	to kill that person	i.e., "to take a life"; 2 Sam 14:14
"To lift [Yhwh's] soul" (נשׂא נפשׁ)	to represent [Yhwh]	Ps 24:4 (see below)
"To lift up (i.e., take) a woman" (נשׂא אשׁה)	to marry a woman	Judg 21:23
"To lift up a kingdom" (נשׂא ממלכה)	to exalt or establish a kingdom	2 Sam 5:12; 1 Chr 14:2

who sinned were weighed down with iniquity until it was forgiven. The expression "to bear sin" (נשׂא עון) is common in the cultic contexts of Exodus,

158. A unique idiom found 4× only in Esther is "to lift up grace in someone's eyes" (נשׂאת חן בעיני; = to find favor; e.g., Esth 2:15).

159. Michael Barré ("Mesopotamian Light on the Idiom *nāśāʾ nepeš*," *CBQ* 52 [1990]: 46–54) argued on the basis of Sumerian and Akkadian parallels that when Yhwh was the object of נפשׁ אל נשׂא, the correct translation is "to flee for protection to (Yahweh), to seek refuge in (Yahweh)."

Leviticus, Numbers, and Ezekiel. In the Day of Atonement ritual described in Lev 16, the sins of the community were placed on the head of a goat, which "bore" (נשׂא) the sin into the desert, far from the community.[160] However, noncultic passages manifest a lexicalized version of נשׂא meaning "forgive" (e.g., Gen 50:17; Ps 32:1; Hos 1:6; cf. CD 3_{18}).[161] By "lexicalized," I mean that in these passages the underlying metaphorical concept of sin as a burden is all but lost and נשׂא functions as a "fixed" or "frozen" idiom that mean "forgiveness."[162] As I discuss below, the presence of both an active metaphorical concept and a lexicalized expression in Biblical Hebrew involving נשׂא will prove illuminating for this project.

In addition to these data from the Hebrew Bible, the Akkadian cognate, *našû*, exhibits almost the same semantic range as the Hebrew נשׂא. Not only did it usually mean "to lift" or "to carry," but it was also employed similarly with regard to punishment, meaning both "to bear [a punishment]" and "to remove [evil]."[163] A precise lexical parallel to the phrase נשׂא שׁם ("lift up the name") is not yet attested in Akkadian.[164] However, *našû* can mean "to take, accept, receive [something from . . . someone]." It can also mean "to wear [clothing, a crown]" or "to bear [. . . a brand]," or "to wear or carry [a symbol],"[165] a notion to which I will return.

---

160. The goat bore the sins of the community, not of the priesthood, whose sins were absolved through blood rites prior to the goat ritual. See Baruch A. Levine, *Leviticus*, JPS Torah Commentary (Philadelphia: Jewish Publication Society, 1989), 106–7. The full range of the people's sins was included (את־כל־עונת בני ישׂראל ואת־כל־פשעיהם לכל־חטאתם: Lev 16:21). See Hartley, *Leviticus*, 241.

161. Joseph Lam (*Patterns of Sin in the Hebrew Bible: Metaphor, Culture, and the Making of a Religious Concept* [New York: Oxford University Press, 2016], 58–65) rejects the idea that the meaning of נשׂא in the idiom נשׂא עון depends on its subject, arguing on source-critical grounds that נשׂא עון refers to bearing sin when used in priestly literature but is lexicalized elsewhere as "forgive." To substantiate his claim for lexicalization, Lam lists examples where נשׂא means "forgive" without contextual clues regarding burden-bearing and where the object or recipient is preceded by a ל-prefix. He argues cogently that the ל signals syntactic conflation of נשׂא with סלח, whose object normally takes a ל prefix. Since the lexicalization of נשׂא created a "near-synonym" of סלח, it began to behave syntactically in the same way; ibid., 38–39; cf. Preuss, *OT Theology*, 178; Fabry, "נָשָׂא," 36. Lam then lists passages lacking the phrase נשׂא עון, where sin is perceived as a weight, showing that the concept of sin as a burden was independent of this metaphor. See also Joseph Lam, review of Gary A. Anderson, *Sin: A History*, *RBL* [http://www.bookreviews.org] (2010).

162. This metaphorical concept of sin as a burden was revived when Ezekiel illustrated the bearing of iniquity with a physical sign act (Ezek 4:4–5; 14:10). Block (*Ezekiel 1–24*, 176–80) argues convincingly that Ezekiel's "bearing of iniquity" was not expiatory but rather a retrospective dramatization of Israel's 390 years of sin for which they must suffer punishment. Contra G. A. Cooke, *A Critical and Exegetical Commentary on the Book of Ezekiel*, ICC (Edinburgh: T&T Clark, 1951), 52–53.

163. Lam (*Patterns of Sin*, 58) notes Akk. *našû* never precisely means to "forgive" sin.

164. Tawil, *Akkadian Lexical Companion*, 249–50.

165. *CAD* lists two examples for "bearing a brand," both of which include the Akkadian *šindu* ("brand") and *šumu* ("name"). By itself *našû* did not mean "to bear a brand," but it could mean this as part of a longer expression (*CAD* N/2 80, 86).

With this general survey of נשׂא in mind, it remains to consider the meaning of the expression נשׂא שׁם. Aside from the NC, only three passages speak of lifting or bearing *a name* (Exod 28:12, 29; Ps 16:4).[166] We have already discussed Ps 16:4 in ch. 2. A brief review will suffice here.

Psalm 16:4

ירבו עצבותם אחר מהרו	They multiply their pains, exchange other [gods],[16]
בל־אסיך נסכיהם מדם	I will not pour out their drink offerings of blood,[17]
ובל־אשׂא את־שׁמותם על־שׂפתי	nor will I **lift up their names upon my lips**.

The psalmist claims that YHWH is his only Lord (v. 2), and that he would have nothing to do with those who followed other {gods} (v. 4a). He refuses to participate in their cultic rituals (v. 4b), and will not even "lift their names" upon his lips (ובל־אשׂא את־שׁמותם על־שׂפתי; v. 4c). By mentioning "lips," the psalmist narrows the phrase to specify that a speech act is in view. Not only did he reject the very thought of participating in idolatrous cults, but he also refused even to pronounce the names of other gods. If Ps 16:4 employs the same expression as the NC, its concretization of the metaphorical concept underscores a contrast: those who "bear" YHWH's name may not "bear" the names of other gods, even on their lips.

Given their proximity to the Decalogue, Exod 28:12 and 29 are crucial to this discussion. The neglect of these priestly passages in discussions of the NC is puzzling. They share with the NC the verb נשׂא followed by the direct object marker את and the noun שׁם. Not only is this the closest lexical match to the NC, but the shared context of the Sinai Narratives of Exodus makes them an obvious choice for potential parallels. In terms of narrative analysis, these are geographical and chronological co-texts with the NC and therefore deserve close examination.

Exodus 28:12

ושׂמת את־שׁתי האבנים	And you are to put the two stones
על כתפת האפד	upon the shoulders of the ephod,
אבני זכרן לבני ישׂראל	stones of remembrance for the sons of Israel,
ונשׂא אהרן את־שׁמותם	and Aaron shall **bear their names**
לפני יהוה על־שׁתי כתפיו	before YHWH upon his two shoulders
לזכרן:	for a memorial.

Exodus 28:29

ונשׂא אהרן את־שׁמות בני־ישׂראל	So Aaron shall **bear the names** of the sons of Israel
בחשׁן המשׁפט על־לבו	on the breastpiece of decision upon his heart

166. Several words semantically related to נשׂא are paired with שׁם. The name YHWH is exalted (רום: Ps 34:4[3]; Neh 9:5; שׂגב: Ps 148:13) and majestic (i.e., lifted up; גאון: Mic 5:3). Each of these examples implies the lifting up or exalting of the name. נשׂא also appears in parallel to רום on several occasions (Num 24:7; Isa 13:2; 33:10; 38:23[//2 Kgs 19:22]; 49:22; Hab 3:10; Prov 30:13). However, נשׂא never clearly means "exalt" in the *qal*; all the possible cases are intransitive (i.e., reflexive) and uncertain (Hos 13:1; Ps 89:23; 139:20), making it unlikely that the NC bears the meaning "You shall not *exalt* the name of YHWH your God in vain." See *DCH* 5:768.

Table 4. Translation Overlap of* נשׂא *and λαμβάνω

נשׂא	→	99 Greek words
	157×	
36 Hebrew words	→	λαμβάνω

בבאו אל־הקדשׁ when he enters into the holy [place]
לזכרן לפני־יהוה תמיד: as a memorial before YHWH regularly.

In ch. 5, I will reflect more on the practical and theological significance of Exod 28:12, 29, but for now note that in these texts נשׂא שׁם is not an idiom or figurative expression; the high priest literally and physically "bore" or "wore" the names of the Israelite tribes engraved on the precious stones on his shoulders and breastpiece.[167] He carried them as he did his duties "before YHWH." As long as the high priest performed his duties in the holy place, YHWH would be reminded of his covenant commitment to his people. Though the expression נשׂא שׁם is not repeated there, the high priest also wore the inscribed name of YHWH with the *lamed inscriptionis* on his forehead medallion. The medallion signaled his responsibility for guilt related to cultic service so the people could be acceptable to YHWH (Exod 28:36–38).[168]

With this general understanding of נשׂא, we turn to the NC. Chapter 2 pointed out the problems with reading this command elliptically. Obviously, נשׂא *could* occur in idiomatic expressions of oath taking ("to lift a hand") or speech ("to lift to the lips" or "to lift one's voice"). However, in the case of the NC, the former possibility is grammatically unlikely, because the specified direct object of נשׂא is the "name" (את־שׁם־יהוה), not hand. The NC also lacks the requisite contextual clues to indicate that speech is in view (e.g., "to say," "cry out," "voice," or "lips"). If the expression is not elliptical, then the basic meaning of "bear" or perhaps even "wear" should be considered. Analogous to Aaron's bearing the names of the tribes and the name of YHWH on his person, Israel bore YHWH's name. Aaron's "bearing the names"

167. The significance of this article of clothing is reflected by the amount of textual space devoted to it, more than any other priestly garment. See Hamilton, *Exodus*, 486. זכרון ("remembrance") appears twice in Exod 28:12; both the high priest and YHWH are reminded of the Israelites—the high priest as representative and YHWH as benefactor. See Sarna, *Exodus*, 179, 183. According to Philip Jenson (*Graded Holiness: A Key to the Priestly Conception of the World*, JSOTSup 106 [Sheffield: Sheffield Academic, 1992], 128), the inscribed stones reminded YHWH to intervene on Israel's behalf. The inscriptions on the high priestly garments (forehead, shoulders, and breastpiece) may be analogous to the command for Israelites to write the torah on their foreheads, arms, and hearts (Exod 13:9, 16; Deut 6:6–8). See Propp, *Exodus 19–40*, 524.

168. Hamilton (*Exodus*, 492) mistakenly suggests that נשׂא עון means "remove iniquity" in v. 38, but "bear responsibility" in v. 43. Instead, both indicate that Aaron "bore iniquity" for sanctuary-related infractions, while his prescribed offerings later absolve him of guilt (e.g., Lev 16:11–14). Propp (*Exodus 19–40*, 448–50) argues that Aaron bore all of Israel's transgressions, which he yearly transferred to the scapegoat.

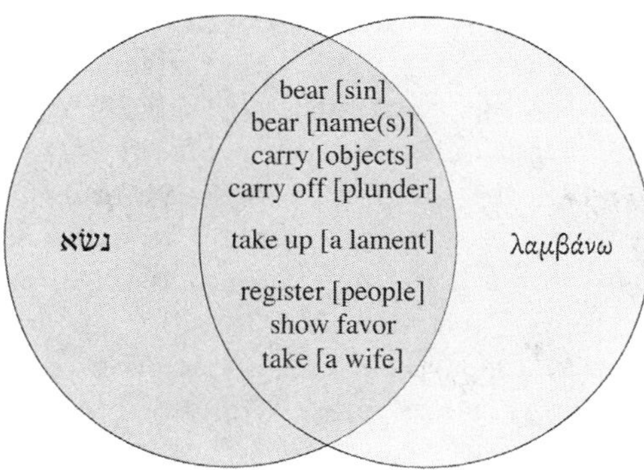

Figure 8. Semantic overlap of נשא and λαμβάνω

was not idiomatic. He physically carried them on the ephod. For Israel the name of YHWH was not physically legible, but had been proclaimed over them in an act of oral branding (Num 6:27). Like the placing of his name on the central sanctuary, this proclamation indicated they belonged to him. The NC warned them not to "bear" the name יהוה אלהיך in vain. The inclusion of the epithet אלהיך ("your God") reinforced the covenant relationship on the basis of which this command was given. They were not to bear the name of their covenant God in vain.

LXX

We have considered the meaning of נשׂא in its other instances in the Hebrew Bible as well as its Akkadian cognate *našû*, finding that in both languages the basic meaning was "to bear" or "carry," with a wide range of possible idiomatic uses. Ancient Bible translations show how the earliest interpreters of the NC understood this word. The Old Greek translations invariably render נשׂא in Exod 20:7 and Deut 5:11 with forms of λαμβάνω.[169] For the NC, the texts of both the MT and the LXX are stable, suggesting that נשׂא appears in the Vorlage of the LXX. However, λαμβάνω was by no means the only option available to translators. In other contexts, the LXX used no fewer than 99 different Greek words to translate נשׂא (*qal*).[170] Like נשׂא, λαμβάνω exhibits a broad semantic range—it was used to translate 36 different Hebrew words.[171] Of these, the most common is לקח ("to take"). However, λαμβάνω renders 157 נשׂא times (table 4 and appendix). With words

169. "Old Greek translations" refers to the MSS represented in the Göttingen Septuagint, including Aquila, Symmachus, and Theodotion, collectively known for our purposes as the LXX. On these passages, see Wevers, *Septuaginta: Exodus*, 241; John William Wevers, ed., *Deuteronomium*, Septuaginta: Vetus Testamentum Graecum 3/2 (Göttingen: Vandenhoeck & Ruprecht, 1977), 111; and Fridericus Field, *Origenis Hexaplorum* (Hildesheim: Olms, 1964), 1:115, 281.

170. T. Muraoka, *A Greek-Hebrew/Aramaic Two-Way Index to the Septuagint* (Walpole, MA: Peeters, 2010), 283.

171. HRCS 2:847.

as flexible as נשא and λαμβάνω, we will do well to determine the extent of overlap between the meanings of these two words and the other conditions under which λαμβάνω was used to translate נשא (fig. 8, p. 93).[172]

Both Lust and Muraoka define λαμβάνω primarily as "to take," or "to take hold of."[173] Most of the other possible definitions for λαμβάνω involve acquisition (to procure, to fetch, to seize, to capture, to take in marriage, to pick up, to choose), but it can also mean "to pronounce or utter," "to carry," "to overpower," "to consider," "to undertake," "to take away," and "to remove."[174] As a translation of נשא, λαμβάνω can mean "take up (a taunt/lament)" (Ezek 19:1; Hab 2:6), "take away (a dead body)" (Amos 6:10), or "pick up (a child)" (Gen 21:18; 31:17; e.g., to place [on a camel]), "to take up" (Gen 27:3; Josh 4:8 ["pick up"]), "register (people)" (Exod 30:12; Num 3:40),[175] "show favor" (Mal 1:9; 2:9; Jer 52:31),[176] and "take away" or "carry off" (in the sense of seizing or stealing something; Num 16:15; 2 Kgs 5:21; Isa 8:4). Occasionally, it denotes "getting" or "receiving" (Ps 24:5 [LXX 23:5]; 82:2 [LXX 81:2]; Ecc 5:18; Hab 1:3; Zech 6:13). It can even mean "to accept" (1 Chr 21:24), "to carry" (Num 11:12; 1 Chr 15:15; 2 Chr 5:4), or "to bring" (Deut 12:26), and is consistently used in Leviticus and Numbers for "*bearing* (sin/reproach/insults)."[177] Most significantly, in addition to its appearance in both versions of the NC, λαμβάνω appears in Exod 28:29 [LXX 23] for Aaron's *bearing* the names of the tribes.[178]

While the idea of "taking" predominates, as mentioned above, "receiving" is attested in the Psalms and Minor Prophets. This latter sense is also present in classical Greek for both literal and figurative expressions. In two examples from Plato, λαμβάνω was combined with ὄνομα to mean "called by (a) name" ("take/receive/come to be known by a name").[179] By the time of the NT, "receive" was its primary sense, especially in "theologically significant"

---

172. For a table including all 157 passages where λαμβάνω translates נשא, see the appendix.

173. Muraoka, *Greek-English Lexicon*, 423–24; Lust, *Greek-English Lexicon*, 276.

174. For pronunciation or utterance, Muraoka (*Greek-English Lexicon*, 424) lists the NC as well as passages that talk about "lifting up a dirge" or "taking up insults." However, he marked this section with an asterisk, indicating uncertainty. Similarly, Lust (*Greek-English Lexicon*, 276) mentions Mic 2:4, where the word refers to "taking up a taunt."

175. Or, "lift the head" (MT; cf. Num 4:2, 22; 26:2; 31:26, 49). According to Delling ("λαμβάνω," *TDNT* 4:6), λαβὲ (τὸ κεφάλαιον) is one of several Hebraisms in the LXX that does not correspond to wider Greek usage.

176. Lit., "lift the face" (MT); "receive the face" (LXX).

177. Leviticus 5:1, 17; 7:18; 16:22; 17:16; 19:8, 17; 22:9; 24:15; Num 5:31; 9:13; 14:34; 18:1, 22, 23, 32; 30:16.

178. See the appendix, pp. 182–186. This analysis is based on HRCS.

179. Plato, *The Statesman,* 305d (LCL, Plato, vol. 8, 175, trans. H. N. Fowler, emphasis mine): "quite properly *called by* special *names*" (κατὰ τὴν ἰδιότητα τῶν πράξεων τοὔνομα δικαίως εἴληφεν ἴδιον, emphasis mine). Crasis occurred here with the definite article and ὄνομα. Cf. Plato, *Symposium,* 173d (LCL, Plato, vol. 3, trans. W. R. M. Lamb, 84–85.

Table 5. MT and Targum Onqelos (Exod 20:7)[180]

MT	לא <u>תשׂא</u> את־שם־יהוה אלהיך לשוא
OT	לא <u>תימי</u> בשמא דיוי אלהך למגנא
MT	כי לא ינקה יהוה את אשר־<u>ישׂא</u> את־שמו <u>לשוא</u>:
OT	ארי לא יזכי יוי ית <u>דיימי</u> בשמיה <u>לשקרא</u>:

contexts, such as receiving glory, honor, the Spirit, grace, etc.[181] Revelation contrasts the worshipers of the beast, who "receive [or bear] the mark of his name" (τις λαμβάνει τὸ χάραγμα τοῦ ὀνόματος αὐτοῦ; Rev 14:11), with servants of God who bear his seal on their foreheads (Rev 3:12; 7:2–3; 14:1).

In sum, while "receive" is a relatively rare meaning of λαμβάνω in the LXX, it is sometimes appropriate for passages where it translates נשׂא.[182] Its attestation in classical and later Greek means we cannot rule out the sense of "receive" with respect to the NC. Plato used it to refer to the "naming" process.[183] However, even more prominent in the LXX is the sense of "carry" or "bear," especially in the Pentateuch (and again in Ezekiel) which often speaks of bearing sin. Ultimately we cannot know whether the translators of the LXX saw the name of God as something Israel received or something she carried/bore (or both), but either sense fits the interpretation advocated here. λαμβάνω never refers to taking an oath in any corpus,[184] and only concerns an utterance when other clear contextual clues are present (e.g., "take up a lament").[185] The prevailing tendency of the LXX to translate נשׂא as λαμβάνω for carrying objects, carrying off plunder, bearing sin, and Aaron's bearing the names suggests that the LXX NC would have conveyed this sense for ancient readers.

Aramaic Targums

The Targumic translations of both versions of the NC exhibit typical characteristics. As demonstrated below, in most cases a fairly literal

180. Critical text according to Alexander Sperber, ed., *The Bible in Aramaic Based on Old Manuscripts and Printed Texts*, vol. 1: *The Pentateuch according to Targum Onkelos* (Leiden: Brill, 1959), 122. Aside from morphological differences, the same text is presented by A. Berliner, ed., *Targum Onkelos* (Berlin: Gorzelanczyk, 1884), 82.

181. Delling, "λαμβάνω," *TDNT* 4:5–6; cf. A. Kretzer, "λαμβάνω," *EDNT* 2:336. As noted in ch. 2, Hermas speaks of baptism as "receiving" the name (εἰ μὴ λάβοι τὸ ὄνομα τὸ ἅγιον αὐτοῦ; *Herm. Sim.* 9.12.4; 89.4, cf. 8), alluding to the NC (*Herm. Sim.* 9.13.2; 90:2). Cf. BDAG 583–85; Osiek, *Shepherd of Hermas*, 235, 238.

182. Delling, "λαμβάνω," 4:6.

183. See n. 175, above.

184. In two cases, a minor textual emendation (from נשׁא to נשׂא) would result in someone "taking up an imprecation" (1 Kgs 8:31; 2 Chr 6:22), but the context makes clear that curses are in view. λαμβάνω was apparently not used for oath taking in Classical Greek.

185. Elßner (*Das Namensmißbrauch-Verbot*, 6) agrees that λαμβάνω is not a *verbum dicendi*, but its semantic range includes "lifting" or "bearing."

Table 6. MT and Targum Neofiti (Exodus 20:7)[186]

לא תשׂא את־שם־יהוה אלהיך לשוא	MT
עמי בני ישראל לא יסב גבר מנכון ית שמה דייי אלהיה על־מגן	NT
כי לא ינקה יהוה את אשר־ישׂא את־שמו לשוא:	MT
ארום לא מזכי ייי ביום דינא רבא ית מן די יסב שמה דייי אלהיה על־מגן :	NT

translation of the Hebrew was supplemented with additional material. Sometimes a single word—usually נשׂא or שׁוא—was replaced. This is not surprising, since these two words carry the most freight semantically in this verse and are subject to such a wide range of interpretations.

Targum Onqelos (ca. 50–150 CE), the oldest and least expansive of the Targums, reads ימי ("to say, swear") for נשׂא and שׁקר ("false") for the second occurrence of שׁוא in Exod 20:7 (table 5, p. 95).[187] These substitutions disambiguate the verse considerably by narrowing its field of reference to false and unnecessary swearing.[188] The translation fits the characterization of Onqelos given by Flesher and Chilton, who observe that though Onqelos typically contains no expansions, it tends not to give the most literal rendering of the Hebrew.[189] Clearly the translator understood Exod 20:7 as an injunction against false swearing·

The next oldest are the Palestinian Targums (ca. 200–300 CE), including both Neofiti and the so-called Fragmentary Targums. Neofiti's "painstakingly literal translation" preserves the ambiguity of the original Hebrew, and supplements it just as it does elsewhere (table 6).[190] Rather than using a verb for "swearing," Neofiti employs the more precise נסב ("to lift up, take, carry, or bear") in Exod 20:7.[191] The most significant addition is "on the great day of judgment," which explains why immediate punishment is not evident for violations of the NC.

186. Critical text according to Alejandro Díez Macho, trans., *Neophyti 1: Targum Palestinense MS de la Biblioteca Vaticana, Tomo II: Éxodo*, Textos y Estudios Consejo de Redacción 8 (Madrid: Consejo Superior de Investigaciones Científicas, 1970), 129. Tg. Neofiti on Deuteronomy is almost identical, except for "man" (אנשׁ), the transposition of the particle ית from line 1 to 2, and the replacement of "his God" (אלהיה) in line 2 with "holy" (קדישה). See Alejandro Díez Macho, trans., *Neophyti 1: Targum Palestinense MS de la Biblioteca Vaticana, Tomo V: Deuteronomio*, Textos y Estudios 11 (Madrid: Consejo Superior de Investigaciones Científicas, 1978), 59.

187. Interestingly, the first instance of שׁוא in this verse is rendered מגן, which means "for nothing, in vain," while the second is שׁקר ("lie, falsehood"). M. Sokoloff, *A Dictionary of Jewish Palestinian Aramaic of the Byzantine Period*, Dictionaries of Talmud, Midrash and Targum 2 (Ramat-Gan: Bar Ilan University Press, 1990), 291, 565. Cf. Jastrow 580, 729.

188. So also Elßner, *Das Namensmißbrauch-Verbot*, 8.

189. Paul Flesher and Bruce Chilton, *The Targums: A Critical Introduction* (Waco, TX: Baylor University Press, 2011), 83.

190. Flesher and Chilton, *The Targums*, 75.

191. Jastrow 915. Sokoloff (*Dictionary of Jewish Palestinian Aramaic*, 352–53) lists "to take, to remove, to receive, to marry, or to buy."

Table 7. MT and Pseudo-Jonathan (Exod 20:7)[192]

לא <u>תשׂא</u> את־שם־ יהוה אלהיך לשוא	MT
עמי בני ישראל לא <u>ישתבע</u> חד מנכון בשום מימריה דייי אלקכון[193] על מגן	PJ
כי לא ינקה יהוה את אשר־<u>ישׂא</u> את־שמו לשוא:	MT
ארום לא מזכי ייי ביום דינא רבא ית כל מאן ד<u>משתבע</u> בשמיה על מגן:	PJ

The Fragment Targums are more expansive, as one might expect, since they anthologize Targumic readings that diverge from the Hebrew Bible. In spite of the variety of extant expansions, these fragments seem to "share a tradition of common translation," as Flesher and Chilton suggest.[194] However, they differ from Neofiti by reading "swear" (either שׁבע, ימי, or both) for נשׂא and by providing justification for the command.[195]

The latest of the Targums, known as Pseudo-Jonathan (ca. 300–400 CE), includes elements of both Targumic streams in its translation of Exod 20:7, as it typically does elsewhere (table 7).[196] First, Pseudo-Jonathan retains the interpretive specification of swearing found in Onqelos and the Fragment Targums. Second, Pseudo-Jonathan incorporates Neofiti's additions ("My children, people of Israel" and the reference to "the great day of judgment"). Its avoidance of anthropomorphism is more pronounced than other Targums; *memra* separates name and YHWH.[197]

A final text that must be considered is the Samaritan Targum to the Pentateuch (ST). For the NC, the Samaritan Pentateuch (SP) reflects MT exactly (table 8, p. 98).[198] However, since the ST shows no evidence of influence from other Targumic traditions in either direction, it offers an independent witness to the meaning of the NC.[199] As elsewhere in the ST, here we find a "highly literal" translation of the Hebrew, without expansion or transposition.[200] The only substitution is the demonstrative pronoun הלא

192. Critical text according to David Rieder, ed., *Pseudo-Jonathan: Targum Jonathan Ben Uziel on the Pentateuch* (Jerusalem: Salomon's Press, 1974), 112.

193. אקלא was an alternate form of אֱלוֹהַּ (Jastrow, 73).

194. Flesher and Chilton, *The Targums*, 81.

195. Critical text according to Michael L. Klein, *The Fragment-Targums of the Pentateuch according to their Extant Sources*, AnBib (Rome: Pontifical Biblical Institute, 1980), 76:2:84; Michael L. Klein, *Genizah Manuscripts of Palestinian Targum to the Pentateuch* (Cincinnati: Hebrew Union College Press, 1986), 1:267, 277.

196. Flesher and Chilton, *The Targums*, 88.

197. Implying that to speak YHWH's name would be presumptuous, but to refer to the "name of the *word* of YHWH" was acceptable, as long as one did not do it in vain.

198. Critical text according to Abraham Tal and Moshe Florentin, eds., *The Pentateuch: The Samaritan Version and the Masoretic Version* (Tel Aviv: Haim Rubin Tel Aviv University Press, 2010), 254–55, 538–39.

199. See Flesher and Chilton, *The Targums*, 126.

200. See ibid., 347. Abraham Tal ("The Samaritan Targum of the Pentateuch," in *Mikra: Text, Translation, Reading and Interpretation of the Hebrew Bible in Ancient Judaism and Early Christianity*, ed. Martin Mulder [Peabody, MA: Hendrickson, 2004], 201) suggests

Table 8. MT and Samaritan Targum (Exod 20:7)[201]

לא תשא את־שם־יהוה אלהיך לשוא	MT
לא תסבל ית שם יהוה אלהך למגן	ST
כי לא ינקה יהוה את אשר־ישא את־שמו לשוא:	MT
הלא לא יזכי יהוה ית דיסבל ית שמה למגן:	ST

("this one") for the conjunction כי, creating a resumptive expression.[202] For נשא, the ST has the conceptual equivalent סבל ("to carry, bear, or support"), which in the Hebrew Bible always refers to a burden, or the act of bearing a burden.[203] The resulting translation is as follows: "You shall not bear the name of Yhwh your God in vain, [for] this one Yhwh will not acquit, [one] who bears his name in vain" [AT].

In sum, the Targums preserve at least two interpretive traditions for the NC. One, represented by Onqelos, the Fragment Targums, and PJ, construes the verse more narrowly as an injunction against false oaths. The other, preserved independently by Neofiti and the ST, retains the breadth of the MT and suggests (or at least allows for) the representational reading in which Yhwh's name must not be carried in vain.

Syriac Peshitta

The Syriac Peshitta (ca. 150 CE) draws on the first of these Jewish exegetical traditions by narrowing the reference of Exod 20:7 to oaths.[204] A

that the "'slavish' literalness" sometimes veils "subtle midrashic interpretations," indicating that the translators were more adept than some have thought.

201. The two extant MSS for the ST, J and A, are identical for Exod 20:7, except that A lacks the particle ית to represent the direct object marker preceding "one who bears" in line 2. Critical text according to Abraham Tal, *The Samaritan Targum of the Pentateuch: A Critical Edition*; part 1: *Genesis, Exodus*, Texts and Studies in the Hebrew Language and Related Subjects (Tel-Aviv: Tel-Aviv University Press, 1980), 4:302–3. MS J of Deut 5:11 is identical to J of Exod 20:7. See Abraham Tal, *The Samaritan Targum of the Pentateuch: A Critical Edition*; part 2: *Leviticus, Numeri, Deuteronomium*, Texts and Studies in the Hebrew Language and Related Subjects (Tel-Aviv: Tel-Aviv University Press, 1981), 5:321.

202. The word הלא is an "affirmative particle," according to Sokoloff (*Dictionary of Jewish Palestinian Aramaic*, 165). Jastrow (p. 352) takes הלא as a variant of הלה.

203. סבל appears 20× in the MT. Twice סבל appears where we might expect נשא, speaking of the "bearing of iniquity" (Isa 53:11; Lam 5:7). סבל is further associated with נשא in 1 Kgs 5:29 and Neh 4:11 (men who "carry burdens"; נשא סבל); and Isa 53:4 (where נשא parallels סבל). Occasionally, the LXX leaves סבל untranslated or subsumes it in an idiom (2 Chr 2:1; Isa 9:3; 10:27; 14:25; 46:4a, 7; 53:4). Three times סבל is translated ἄρσις (1 Kgs 5:29; 11:28; Ps 81:7 [LXX 80:7]), and once νωτοφόρων ("one who carries on the back"; 2 Chr 2:17). Cf. 2 Kgs 8:9, where ἄρσις translates משא ("load" or "burden"). In Isa 46:4, Yhwh twice "carries" Israel, using the verbal form of סבל. The second of these is translated by ἀναλαμβάνω, providing another possible analogy with the NC, where נשא becomes λαμβάνω.

204. While the exact time and location of the Syriac translation is debated, Jewish exegetical influence on the Peshitta Pentateuch is widely recognized. Here, as elsewhere in the Pentateuch, the LXX shows no influence, and the reading matches *Tg. Onq.* See

Table 9. Latin Vulgate of the NC[205]

Exodus 20:7	*Deuteronomy 5:11*
non **adsumes** nomen Domini Dei tui **in vanum** **nec enim habebit insontem Dominus eum** qui adsumpserit nomen **Domini Dei sui** **frustra**	non **usurpabis** nomen Domini Dei tui **frustra** **quia non erit inpunitus** qui **super re vana** nomen **eius** adsumpserit

literal translation is as follows: "You shall not swear by the name of the Lord your God in falsehood" [*lʾ ymy bšm dy mry ʾlh bdglw*].[206] This reading obviously interprets the Hebrew נשׂא שׁם as an idiom meaning to "take an oath" (Syr. *ymʾ*), not surprising given the flexibility used by Syriac translators.[207]

Latin Vulgate

The NC provides an interesting exemplar of Jerome's translation method in the Latin Vulgate. The pentateuchal books were among the last that Jerome translated, and so exhibit a freer style than his earlier work. Therefore, we should not be too surprised by the differences between his translations of Exod 20:7 and Deut 5:11.[208] His free rendering employs different Latin words for נשׂא, שׁוא, and נקה (table 9). In fact, stylistic variety is evident even within a single passage; Exod 20:7 and Deut 5:11 each contain two different Latin expressions for שׁוא.[209] While Jerome followed the Old Latin in the first half of Exod 20:7, he reworked the rest of the verse.[210]

Peter B. Dirksen, "The Old Testament Peshitta," in *Mikra: Text, Translation, Reading and Interpretation of the Hebrew Bible in Ancient Judaism and Early Christianity*, ed. Martin Mulder (Peabody, MA: Hendrickson, 2004), 260, 277, 279, 284.

205. Critical text according to Robertus Weber and Roger Gryson, eds., *Biblia Sacra: Iuxta Vulgatum Versionem*, 5th ed. (Stuttgart: Deutsche Bibelgesellschaft, 2007). The Douay Rheims of 1609 is identical (except *qui* became *gui*; Swift Edgar, ed., *The Vulgate Bible*, vol. 1: *The Pentateuch, Douay Rheims Translation*, Dumbarton Oaks Medieval Library (Cambridge, MA: Harvard University Press, 2010), 380–81, 904–5.

206. Translation from the critical text: *The Old Testament in Syriac according to the Peshitta Version*, (Leiden: Brill, 1977), 1:163.

207. See Dirksen, "The Old Testament Peshitta," 259. For this meaning of *ymʾ*, see J. Payne Smith, ed., *A Compendious Syriac Dictionary* (Winona Lake, IN: Eisenbrauns, 1998), 193.

208. The latter half of the NC is quite different; only 3 of the 13 words from Exod 20:7b recur in Deut 5:11b, and these in a different order.

209. Both *vanus* and *frustra* can mean either "empty" or "false." *Frustra* appears second in Exod 20:7 and first in Deut 5:11, while *vanus* occupies the other place. On Jerome's preference for stylistic variety, see Michael Graves, "Vulgate," in *Textual History of the Bible*, ed. Emanuel Tov and Armin Lange (Leiden: Brill, 2016), 1A:278–89.

210. The Old Latin of Exod 20:7 reads "*non assumes nomen Dei tui in vanum : non enim mundabit eum Dominus qui sumit nomen ejus in vanum*." See Pierre Sabatier, *Bibliorum Sacrorum latinæ versiones antiquæ seu Vetus Italica* (Regis Typographum & Bibliopolam, 1743). Old Latin lacks Deut 5:11.

The Exodus version preserves the breadth of the MT ("You shall not assume[211] the name of the Lord your God in vain"), while the version in Deuteronomy comes closer to an oral interpretation of the command ("You shall not employ[212] the name of the Lord your God for nothing"). In spite of these differences, *assumo* reappears in Deut 5:11b, linking the meanings more tightly. In the end, both of Jerome's versions of the NC allow for a representational interpretation. Indeed, they convey this possibility more clearly than any modern-day English translations.

Summary of Findings on נשׂא

This study of נשׂא, including its idiomatic uses, its Akkadian cognate (*našû*), its collocation with שׁם, and its rendering in the earliest translations (LXX [λαμβάνω], the Samaritan Targum, Neofiti, and the Latin Vulgate), suggests the meaning "to bear" or "carry," or possibly "receive." Only in Targum Pseudo-Jonathan, Onqelos, the Fragment Targums, and the Peshitta was נשׂא שׁם clearly taken as an idiom meaning "to swear." The idea that a name could be borne is plausible, given the similar meaning of cognate words in Aramaic, Akkadian, Greek, and Latin. In the Hebrew Bible, נשׂא never refers to oath taking, and never refers to speech without explicit contextual cues.

שׁוא

The word שׁוא appears 53 times in the Hebrew Bible, including 36 times as an unprefixed noun,[213] and once as a proper name (1 Chr 2:49).[214] It is most common in the latter prophets, Job, and Psalms. Though שׁוא is technically a substantive, when prefixed with a *lamed* preposition it can have an adverbial sense.[215]

---

211. Pliny the Younger (61–114 CE; *Letters,* 4.15.3 [Bibliotheca Teubneriana, Schuster, 1952]) wrote of a good citizen who "assumed the name of his grandfather" (*avi quoque nomen assumpsit*) in spite of their differences. Accessed with Perseus 6/7/13. Elßner (*Das Namensmißbrauch-Verbot*, 10) translates *adsumes* as *heranziehen* ("use"), *hinzunehmen* ("accept"), or *zu Hilfe nehmen* ("utilize").

212. That is, vocally. So Elßner, *Das Namensmißbrauch-Verbot*, 10. Cicero (106–43 BCE; *In Verrum* 5.162 [Peterson, Oxford Classical Texts, 1917]) wrote of a man being beaten who made repeated entreaties to his Roman citizenship ("he *employed* [*usurpo*] the name [of his] city"; *sed cumimploraret saepius usurparetque nomen civitatis*). Accessed on Perseus, June 7, 2013: Cicero. M. Tvlli Ciceronis Orationes: Divinatio in Q. Caecilivm. In C. Verrem Recognovit brevique adnotatione critica instruxit Gvlielmvs Peterson Rector Vniversitatis MacGillianae. William Peterson. Oxford. e Typographeo Clarendoniano. 1917. Scriptorum Classicorum Bibliotheca Oxoniensis.

213. This total includes instances where it appears in construct or is linked with a direct object marker, but without a prefix.

214. If a verbal form of שׁוא exists, it may mean deception or the exaction of tribute. Linguists are unsure of the proper root of the form יַשִּׁא in Ps 89:23 or יַשִּׁי in Ps 55:16, so either might be irrelevant to this study. See *HALOT* 2:1424–25. For a few interpretive options, see deClaissé-Walford, Jacobson, and Tanner, *Psalms*, 677; Mitchell Dahood, *Psalms II: 51–100*, AB (Garden City, NY: Doubleday, 1968), 317.

215. On the adverbial sense of the *lamed* prefix, see *IBHS* §11.2.10d (e.g., 1 Kgs 5:5;

The meaning of the unprefixed noun ranges from "emptiness" or "ineffectiveness," to "falseness,"[216] concepts that are not mutually exclusive. In the context of interpersonal, legal disputes, שׁוא describes a testimony with no grounding in reality (Exod 23:1; Deut 5:20; Isa 59c:4; Ps 35:17).[217] Six times שׁוא appears in construct with דבר to indicate unreliable speech (Isa 59:4; Ezek 13:8; Ps 12:3; 41:7; 144:8, 11).[218] The word is often found in parallel with speech-related terms that mean "falsehood" or outright "deception" (Ezek 13:7; Ps 24:4; 144:8, 11; Prov 30:8; Job 31:5). However, many instances have nothing to do with speaking. For example, Job lamented "months of emptiness" (ירחי־שׁוא; 7:3), while Isaiah castigated the Israelites for bringing "futile offerings" (מנחת־שׁוא; 1:13).[219] Two passages refer to men who are characterized by שׁוא (מתי־שׁוא; Job 11:11; Ps 26:4).

The word שׁוא often means futile, useless, or empty (Job 7:3; 15:31; 35:13; Ps 89:48; 60:13 [11]; 108:13 [12]; Jer 46:11). Lamentations and Ezekiel are concerned with so-called visions or prophecies that are not based on true revelation. These fabricated prophecies are therefore "false" or "empty" (Lam 2:14; Ezek 12:24; 13:7, 9, 23; 21:28–29; 22:28; Zech 10:2), even when made in YHWH's name (Ezek 13:6; 22:28).

Twice שׁוא refers to an idol, both times in construct with הבל (Ps 31:7[6]; Jonah 2:9). The collocation with הבל may reflect the notion that an idol is

Gen 30:30; 2 Sam 18:5; Isa 8:6). *HALOT* 1:509 lists several examples, all from the Pentateuch, of adverbial expressions where *lamed* is prefixed to a noun (e.g., Gen 33:14; Exod 24:10). A clear example of an adverbial *lamed* is found in Lev 25:18, where the Israelites are encouraged to carry out faithfully God's commands, "so that you may dwell upon the land securely (לבטח)." Curiously, *DCH* includes no comparable category. Perhaps the adverbial sense is carried primarily by semantics rather than syntax.

216. *Emptiness*: Job 7:3; 15:31; 35:13 (perhaps ineffective here); Ps 119:37 (worthless); Isa 30:28 (worthlessness; i.e., chaff); Hos 10:4; 12:12 (worthless). *Ineffectiveness*: Ps 60:13[11]; 89:48[47]; 108:13[12]; 127:1–2; Isa 1:13; Mal 3:14. Shepherd ("שׁוא," *NIDOTTE* 4:53–55) sees "ineffectiveness and falseness" as the most basic senses of the word. *Falseness*: Usually related to speech: Exod 23:1; Deut 5:20; Job 11:11; 31:5; Ps 12:3; 26:4; 41:7; 144:8, 11; Prov 30:8; Isa 59:4. In Ezekiel שׁוא refers to false visions or oracles—visions YHWH has not given and oracles he has not spoken: Ezek 12:24; 13:6–9; 13:23; 21:28; 21:34; 22:28. Cf. Lam 2:14.

217. Elßner (*Das Namensmißbrauch-Verbot*, 48) argues the NC is not strictly legal because of the (theological) prohibition of foreign gods in the immediate context.

218. Markl (*Der Dekalog als Verfassung des Gottesvolkes*, 112) suggests that שׁוא always connotes a particular use of language (e.g., dishonesty, falsehood, futility). He cites Isa 59:4; Hos 10:4; Zech 10:2; Ps 41:7; 144:8, 11; and Prov 30:8. However, his examples all contain contextual clues that require speech. In Ezek 13:8, שׁוא was "spoken": "Because you have spoken emptiness [דברכם שׁוא] and envisioned lies." Psalm 12:3[2] (שׁוא ידברו) explicitly mentions speech as well.

219. Elßner (*Das Namensmißbrauch-Verbot*, 49) explains, "Since the inner attitude of the sacrifice does not match the outer actions, YHWH rejects this sacrifice. Therefore, these offerings are ultimately without effect." See also Isa 5:18; 30:28; Mal 3:14; Ps 60:13; 108:13; 127:1–2; Mal 3:14. The division between thinking, speaking, and doing is artificial. When שׁוא refers to lying, it implies "far more than theoretical disagreement, but also practical harmfulness" (Klopfenstein, *Die Lüge*, 319, AT).

only a "breath of emptiness" or a "wasted breath."[220] Dahood claimed extensive evidence for "idol" as part of the semantic range of שׁוא.[221] However, nowhere does nominal שׁוא indisputably mean idol without הבל.[222] Every example listed in *DCH* under שׁוא as "idol" or "image" is followed by a parenthetical note suggesting another possible meaning. For example, Ps 119:37, "Turn my eyes from seeing שׁוא," could be translated "vanity" or "worthlessness" rather than "idol." The "men of שׁוא" in Psalm 26:4 could be "dishonest men" rather than "men who worship idols."[223] This possibility should caution us against reading שׁוא as idol without additional contextual support.

Mowinckel suggested that שׁוא means "evil knitted by magic" because expressions for devious activity sometimes occur in parallel with שׁוא, and because possible Arabic and Ethiopic cognates carry malicious overtones.[224] His prime example was Isa 5:18, where חבלים supposedly corresponds to knotted cords used for magic in the ANE.[225] Admittedly, when שׁוא appears in parallel with negative words such as falsehood, deceit, dishonesty, violence, worthlessness, and iniquity, it connotes duplicity.[226] However, to insist on a magical nuance is excessive. For Mowinckel's thesis to stand, inextricable linkage between deception and devious magic spells is required, but this connection is lacking in all the passages he cites.[227] Furthermore,

220. The word חבל is paired with לא־אל ("non-gods") in Deut 32:21. See Reiterer, "שׁוא," *TDOT* 14:458. So also Elßner (ibid., 52–53), who concludes that by itself שׁוא means ineffective or worthless.

221. Dahood, *Psalms I*, 151. Hamilton ("שׁוא," *TWOT* 2:908) argues that because idols are "unsubstantial" and "unreal," idolatry is an appropriate translation in Ps 24:4. See also Shepherd, "שׁוא," *NIDOTTE* 4:53–55.

222. So Reiterer ("שׁוא," *TDOT* 14:450, 459), who suggests that שׁוא *describes* the foreign gods rather than designating an "idol." This could also be the case in Jer 18:15; while the collocation of שׁוא with *piel* קטר makes idolatry likely, the phrase לשׁוא could be translated, "to what is worthless." In other words, שׁוא could designate the idols in a derogatory way rather than directly identifying them. In Job 31:5, שׁוא could easily mean "falsehood" rather than "idol" (ibid., 14:452; contra Dahood, *Psalms I*, 151).

223. *DCH* 8:271. Other examples given are Sir 15:7, Ps 24:4, and Job 31:5, all of which could mean "falsehood."

224. Mowinckel, *Psalmenstudien I*, 50–57, esp. p. 52, AT. See above, p. 13 n. 20. Though Mowinckel's work is dated, it continues to be cited as the definitive work on the meaning of שׁוא. In Ps 35:17, מִשֹּׁאֵיהֶם is usually translated with this malicious sense ("ravages," NRSV, NIV; "attacks," NET, NJPS), but the context allows for a meaning in keeping with other uses of שׁוא. Verse 20 speaks of deception or false accusations.

225. Ibid., 51, AT.

226. For specifics, see *DCH* 8:271.

227. Mowinckel, *Psalmenstudien I*, 56–57. While some accept Mowinckel's argument (e.g., *HALOT* 2:1425–26), others are unconvinced. See Shepherd, "שׁוא," *NIDOTTE* 4:54; Reiterer, "שׁוא," *TDOT* 14:447–60. Schüngel-Straumann (*Der Dekalog*, 97) finds Mowinckel's argument plausible, but includes magic among other misuses of Yhwh's name, such as empty worship, false swearing, or unauthorized preaching, even though each

his proposed etymologies cannot bear the weight of his interpretation; whatever its etymology, ultimately the sense of שׁוא must be determined by its context.[228]

Klopfenstein suggested a range of meanings for שׁוא, from "evil" to "emptiness," with "lies" and "deceit" between those extremes. In legal texts the focus is on lying, while in prophetic texts the context determines whether שׁוא leans toward "evil" or merely "empty."[229] However, Klopfenstein's discussion is as circular as Mowinckel's. He assumes the sense of a word can be wholly determined by parallel words in poetic texts.[230]

The word שׁוא appears with a *lamed* prefix in both versions of the NC (Exod 20:7; Deut 5:11), twice in the Psalms (Ps 24:4; 139:20), and five times in Jeremiah (2:30; 4:30; 6:29; 18:15; 46:11). This *lamed*-construction results in a prepositional phrase with an adverbial sense, specifying the *manner* in which something is done. The instances of this syntactical construction in Jeremiah are less ambiguous than Psalms, and therefore more helpful in discerning the semantic range of לשׁוא. Their subject matter also compares favorably with the NC. Jeremiah 2:30 (cf. 6:29) describes the ineffectiveness of Yhwh's discipline: "In vain [לשׁוא] I have struck your sons; they accepted no chastening." It has not had its desired effect. Similarly, Jer 4:30 describes the futility of Israel's pandering to other lovers: "In vain [לשׁוא] you make yourself beautiful; lovers despise you." After Yhwh has judged the Egyptians, their remedies are said to be לשׁוא (Jer 46:11). Here as elsewhere, the

---

requires a different nuance for שׁוא. Philologically speaking, her view is indefensible. Though Klopfenstein (*Die Lüge*, 315) agrees with Mowinckel's etymology, he finds many of his specific claims unconvincing.

228. On the overemphasis on etymology in modern lexicons, see James Barr, *Comparative Philology and the Text of the Old Testament* (Oxford: Clarendon, 1968), 115; Lothar Kopf, "Das arabische Wörterbuch als Hilfsmittel für die hebräische Lexikographie," *VT* 6:3 (1956): 286–302.

229. Klopfenstein, *Die Lüge*, 317. Cf. Reiterer, "שׁוא," *TDOT* 14:452.

230. For example, Klopfenstein (*Die Lüge*, 315–16) cites Job 11:11 and Ps 26:4 as evidence that שׁוא means "magic" because of the parallels, "men of emptiness" and "pretenders." Since magic is hidden and these men are evil, Klopfenstein concludes they must be practicing magic. Similarly, Ps 41:7 refers to "magical mischief" simply because שׁוא and "mischief" appear together. However, parallelism cannot guarantee the semantic equivalence of paired words. See Barr, *Comparative Philology*, 278–79.

Sawyer ("שׁוא," *TLOT* 3:1310–12) rejects both extremes of Klopfenstein's spectrum ("evil" or "empty"), preferring a more generic connotation of "deceit" or "falseness." So also Frank-Lothar Hossfeld, *Der Dekalog: Seine späten Fassungen, die originale Komposition und seine Vorstufen* (Göttingen: Vandenhoeck & Ruprecht, 1982), 77; Childs, *Book of Exodus*, 411; Schmidt, *Die Zehn Gebote*, 83. Görg ("Missbrauch des Gottesnamens," 17) associates שׁוא with the Egyptian *šwi*, "to be empty," which corresponds well with the meaning of שׁוא in many biblical passages and rules out a magical interpretation. Still, although we lack clear evidence that שׁוא means "magic" in the NC, magical practices would also be inappropriate for those who proportedly bear Yhwh's name. Cf. Sawyer, "שׁוא," *TLOT* 3:1311; Schmidt, *Die Zehn Gebote*, 83.

sense of לשוא seems to be "ineffective" or "for naught."[231] An idolatrous, malicious, or magical sense for לשוא does not work in these passages. The two psalms that collocate נשׂא and לשוא are difficult to interpret and will be discussed in an excursus at the end of this chapter. Neither the NC nor these enigmatic psalms offer contextual support for idolatry or magic.[232] On this basis, we can conclude that in the NC YHWH warns his people not to bear his name "ineffectively" or "falsely" (hypocritically).[233] This interpretation comports well with occurrences of שוא in Exod 23:1 and Deut 5:20, which describe a report or testimony that has no basis in reality. Israel's representation of YHWH must not be duplicitous or empty.

LXX

The LXX always reads the prefixed form לשׁוא as ἐπὶ ματαίῳ. The range of meaning for μάταιος (an adjective) corresponds closely with שוא, including empty, false or deceptive, and ineffective.[234] Like שׁוא, μάταιος can refer to idols ("vain things," plural), since idols are without substance (see Lev 17:7; Ezek 8:10; Jonah 2:9; 2 Chr 11:15), but only when other contextual indicators of idolatry are present.[235]

Other Ancient Translations

The Targums usually translate לשוא as על־מגן or למגן, which means "for nothing," or "in vain."[236] However, in Targum Onqelos לשקרא ("falsely") appears in place of the second לשׁוא. Similarly, the Syriac *bglwtʾ* explicitly

231. Usually translated "in vain." So also Elßner, *Das Namensmißbrauch-Verbot*, 49–50, who notes that לשוא is fronted for emphasis. On Jer 18:15, see above, p. 33.

232. Reiterer ("שׁוא," *TDOT* 14:450) agrees that the context offers no support for reading לשוא as idolatry. Based on parallelism, van Gemeren ("Psalms," *EBC* 5:260) suggests that Ps 24:4 condemns dishonesty, rather than idolatry.

233. Although שוא can mean "false," it only describes false oaths once: Hos 10:4 condemns אלות שׁוא ("false/empty oaths"), covenants that are all talk and no commitment. References to false oaths typically involve שקר (Exod 20:16; Lev 5:22; Zech 8:17; cf. Ps 144:8). For example, Joseph A. Fitzmyer, *The Aramaic Inscriptions of Sefire*, Biblica et Orientalia 19 (Rome: Pontifical Biblical Institute, 1967), 99, 3 14b–17.

234. Muraoka (*Greek-English Lexicon*, 443) defines μάταιος as "meaningless, worthless, lacking in substance, counterfeit, false, irreverent, and frivolous." Lust (*Greek-English Lexicon*, 291) also includes "vain." On deception, see Bauernfeind, "μάταιος," *TDNT* 4:519–24. Klopfenstein (*Die Lüge*, 320) criticized the LXX μάταιος for שׁוא because it prejudiced later generations to interpret it as "vain" rather than "lying." However, both connotations are possible for μάταιος.

235. See Lust, *Greek-English Lexicon*, 291. μάταιος often has this sense, suggesting a later development whereby "vain things" became a frozen designation for idols. LSJ (p. 1084) identifies three classical senses for μάταιος: (1) "*vain, empty, idle*"; (2) "*rash, irreverent, profane*"; and (3) "*idly, without ground*" (used adverbially). Idols do not appear on their list.

236. Sokoloff, *Dictionary of Jewish Palestinian Aramaic*, 291. Jeremiah 4:30, 6:29, 18:15, and 46:11 have לא להנאה ("without benefit") instead.

means "in falsehood,"[237] emphasizing the deception involved in breaking the command.[238] As mentioned above, the Vulgate uses two Latin expressions for שׁוא, probably for stylistic reasons. Both Latin words (*vanus* and *frustra*) can mean either "empty" or "false." *Frustra* appears second in Exod 20:7 and first in Deut 5:11, while *vanus* occupies the other place. Either term captures the Hebrew sense reasonably well.[239]

In short, from ancient times interpreters recognized the basic sense of לשׁוא as "false, empty, or ineffective." Some emphasized the deceptive aspect of breaking the command, while others employed a more general word to indicate ineffectiveness or emptiness. None of these translations specified a magical, a malicious, or an idolatrous sense for שׁוא. Lacking other contextual clues, these meanings are unlikely. For Israel to bear YHWH's name לשׁוא was to bear it ineffectively or falsely—that is, as those who claimed to belong to him but whose conduct was inconsistent with this claim. A claim to covenantal membership without faithfulness to covenant stipulations was "empty."

נקה

Although נקה relates to the absolution of guilt, it is not a cultic word. It never appears in discussions of guilt and/or cleansing from sin in Leviticus, Ezekiel, or Chronicles, where we might expect it.[240] Rather, נקה involves moral innocence or blamelessness in a legal setting. The one set of occurrences that could be considered "ritualistic" retains this moral/legal tone (Num 5:19, 28, 31); a woman not guilty of adultery could prove her innocence by undergoing an ordeal. If she was found guilty, her husband was declared innocent (נקה) but she must "bear her sin" (תשׂא את־עונה; Num 5:31). The verb occurs in both *piel* and *niphal* stems; while the latter describes the state of exemption, the *piel* involves a declaration or denial of such an exemption.

The verb נקה (44 times) and its related adjective נקי (43 times) can refer to freedom or exemption from the consequences of an oath (Gen 24:8, 41; cf. Josh 2:17–20).[241] But the range of offenses that will or will not be exempt from punishment is broader than this. The adjective describes freedom from obligation to warfare or work (Num 32:22; Deut 24:5; cf. 1 Kgs 15:22) or freedom from punishment for theft or ownership of an ox who gored someone to death (Gen 44:10; Exod 21:28). More than half the adjectival uses can be translated "innocent," either innocent in general, or "innocent blood" in

237. Smith, *A Compendious Syriac Dictionary*, 83.

238. *Syriac Peshitta*, 163.

239. So also Elßner, *Das Namensmißbrauch-Verbot*, 9.

240. Of its 44 occurrences in the Hebrew Bible, 25 are *niphal* and 18 are *piel*, with only one *qal*. For studies of the word, see Van Leeuwen, "נקה," *TLOT* 2:764; Warmuth, "נָקָה," *TDOT* 9:553–63; J. P. J. Olivier, "נקה," *NIDOTTE* 3:152–54; Hoftijzer and Jongeling, "nqy_1," *DNWSI* 757.

241. So Propp, *Exodus 19–40*, 174.

reference to one unjustly killed.[242] "Innocent" is a prominent meaning in the DH, latter prophets, and wisdom, but is absent in the first four books of the Pentateuch.[243]

In Proverbs, a range of guilty behavior "will not be rendered innocent" (לא ינקה), including adultery (6:29), evil (11:21), pride (16:5), false witness (19:5, 9), greed (28:20), and gloating over someone else's misfortune (17:5).[244] In Jeremiah 25:29, YHWH announced his coming wrath to the nations, telling them, "I am beginning to work disaster on the city over which my name is proclaimed (נקרא־שמי עליה), so shall *you* be rendered completely innocent (הנקה תנקו)? You will not be declared innocent (לא תנקו) because I am calling for a sword against all the inhabitants of the earth." If the punishment for sin extends even to those who belong to YHWH and bear his name, then the nations will certainly not be exempt.[245]

Most significantly, YHWH revealed himself as one "who bears iniquity and transgression and sin" (נשׂא עון ופשע וחטאה), but nevertheless "does not render [the guilty] innocent" (ונקה לא ינקה פקד; Exod 34:7; table 10).[246] This statement clearly alludes to the first two commands of the Decalogue, binding them together. As the first command also states (Exod 20:5b–6), YHWH is one who פקד עון אבת על־בנים על־שׁלשים ועל־רבעים and displays חסד לאלפים. Furthermore, reference to YHWH bearing (נשׂא) iniquity and his refusal to "render [the guilty] innocent" (לא ינקה) echo the language of the NC.[247] According to the NC, the failure to bear (נשׂא) YHWH's name rightly precludes a declaration of innocence (לא ינקה).[248] On its own the shared language between the NC and Exod 34:6–7 would not be enough to establish an allusion, but the verbatim repetition of material from the first command makes the other allusion more plausible. The point of connection is YHWH's characteristic refusal to overlook sin.

Israel's bearing of YHWH's name did not merely indicate that they belonged to him. The NC stipulates that this name bearing was not passive,

---

242. *Innocent*: The occurrences in Job fall in this category: Job 4:7; 9:23; 17:8; 22:19; 22:30; 27:17. Also Exod 23:7; Pss 2:8; 15:5; 24:4; 94:21; Prov 1:11. *Unjustly killed*: Deuteronomy 19:10, 13; 21:8–9; 27:25; 1 Sam 19:5; 2 Kgs 21:16; 24:4; Ps 106:38; Prov 6:17; Isa 59:7; Jer 2:34; 7:6; 19:4; 22:3; 22:17; 26:15; Joel 4:19; Jonah 1:14.

243. Other examples include Jdg 15:3; Ps 19:14; Jer 2:35; and Joel 4:21.

244. As Warmuth ("נָקָה," *TDOT* 9:555) also notes, in Proverbs "the verb is always negated; the punishment is never named but is certain to be inflicted."

245. Other declarations of Israel's lack of exemption from punishment include Jer 30:11 and 46:28. Cf. Edom (Jer 49:12); Egypt and Edom (Joel 4:21); one who harms YHWH's anointed (1 Sam 26:9); Shimei (1 Kgs 2:9); Job (of himself, Job 9:28; 10:14).

246. Cf. Num 14:18; Nah 1:3. Whether נשׂא עון means "to bear sin" or "to forgive sin" here is unclear. Lam (*Patterns of Sin*, 32) opts for "forgiver of iniquity" because the context of Num 14:18, where Exod 34:6–7 is echoed, appeals for forgiveness.

247. Fishbane supposes that the dependence goes in the other way—the Decalogue reuses Exod 34:6–7 for its motivation clauses (*Biblical Interpretation*, 344–45).

248. Houtman (*Exodus*, 3:37) suggests a play on words in the NC with לא ינקה and the divine epithet אל קנא in Exod 20:5. However, these phrases seem too distant.

Table 10. Exodus 34:6–7 and the Decalogue

Exod 20:5b–7 // Deut 5:9b–11	*Exod 34:6–7*
כי אנכי יהוה אלהיך	יהוה יהוה
אל קנא פקד עון אבת	אל רחום וחנון
על־בנים	ארך אפים ורב־חסד ואמת
על־שלשים ועל־רבעים לשנאי	נצר חסד לאלפים
ועשה חסד לאלפים	נשא עון ופשע וחטאה
לאהבי ולשמרי מצותי	ונקה לא ינקה
לא תשא את־שם־יהוה אלהיך לשוא	פקד עון אבות
כי לא ינקה יהוה	על־בנים ועל־בני בנים
את אשר־ישא את־שמו לשוא	על־שלשים ועל־רבעים
Because I, YHWH, your God,	YHWH, YHWH,
am a jealous God,	a God compassionate and gracious,
who visits the iniquity of the fathers	slow to anger and great in covenant
upon the sons	faithfulness and truth,
until the third and fourth	who guards covenant faithfulness
[generations]	for thousands,
of those who hate me,	who bears iniquity and transgression
but who demonstrates	and sin,
covenant faithfulness	yet who certainly does not render
for thousands of those who love me	[the guilty] innocent,
and who keep my commands.	who visits the iniquity of the fathers
You shall not bear the name of YHWH,	upon the sons and the son's sons,
your God, in vain,	upon the third and fourth
for YHWH will not render innocent	[generations].
one who bears his name in vain.	

but active; it was not to be done ineffectively. Therefore, YHWH's claim on his people required a response consonant with his character; failure to do so would incur punishment. An allusion to the NC in Exod 34:6–7, where YHWH's character is most fully expressed, should come as no surprise.

LXX

In Exod 20:7, the Septuagint renders נקה with καθαρίζω, which normally means "to cleanse," but can also indicate moral purity or freedom from the guilt or defilement of sin.[249] The sense differs slightly from Hebrew because legal connotations are absent. Instead, καθαρίζω emphasizes the stain of sin that must be subsequently washed away. Elsewhere, καθαρίζω and its derivatives translate נקה to express a range of moral behavior for which cleansing was needed, including hidden faults or presumptuous sins (Ps

249. This range of meaning is attested from classical Greek to NT times. Lust (*Greek-English Lexicon*, 218) identifies the following meanings for καθαρίζω: "to purify, cleanse, purge, purify, acquit." Muraoka (*Greek-English Lexicon*, 348) places more emphasis on the ritual or moral aspects of the cleansing. See also LSJ 850; BDAG 488–89; Joseph Henry Thayer, trans., *Greek-English Lexicon of the New Testament*, 4th ed. (Edinburgh: T&T Clark, 1901), 312.

19:13–14 [LXX 18:12–13]), unfulfilled oaths (Gen 24:8), and guilt in general (Exod 34:6–7; Num 14:18; Jer 25:29 [LXX 32:29]).[250] A range of behaviors might also be associated with "bearing the name in vain," for which cleansing or release from guilt would be needed.

Other Ancient Translations

The Targums consistently rendered נקה as זכה ("to acquit, justify"),[251] which reflects the legal connotations of the word (over against the LXX's focus on moral purity). Similarly, the Syriac Peshitta uses *zkʾ*, which means "to hold or pronounce innocent, to acquit, justify, clear."[252] This translation corresponds well with the Hebrew and Aramaic. The Vulgate translates נקה two ways in the NC (table 9, p. 99). Exodus 20:7 reads *habebit insontem* ("regard as innocent"), while Deut 5:11 reads *erit inpunitus* ("be unpunished"). Either is appropriate.

The motivation clause of the NC indicates the seriousness with which YHWH expected his people to take this command. For covenant members who failed to bear YHWH's name appropriately, acquittal was precluded. In keeping with his character, when their actions betrayed covenantal unfaithfulness, YHWH threatened to declare them guilty.

Conclusion

Through this wide-ranging lexical and historical inquiry, I have argued that the NC is best read in light of the conventional language of ownership transfer in which YHWH declares his name over the Israelites to claim them as his own. The oral imprinting of his name on his people implied their duty to represent him well. The responsibility to bring honor to his name was serious, necessitating a severe penalty for failure. I therefore propose to translate the NC this way: "You shall not bear the name of YHWH, your God, in vain, for YHWH will not render innocent one who bears his name in vain." While the individual lexemes are sufficiently flexible to admit other interpretations, the representational reading of this passage is most satisfying, given the lack of contextual clues to support another reading, such as false oaths, magic, idolatry, or wrongful pronunciation of the name.

Excursus: Psalm 24:4 and Psalm 139:20 in Light of the Name Command

Outside the NC, נשׂא and לשוא are collocated only in Ps 24:4 and 139:20. Because these passages are often cited as evidence that the NC prohibits

250. The Hebrew text of these passages is stable (regarding נקה). Based on the Göttingen LXX (where available, and Ralph's for Genesis and Jeremiah), the Greek translations are stable as well (variants in Exod 34:6–7 and Num 14:18 are other forms of καθαρίζω).

251. Sokoloff, *Dictionary of Jewish Palestinian Aramaic*, 177. Similarly, *HALOT* 2:1864 defines זכה as "to be clean," "to be innocent," or (in the *pael*) "to acquit."

252. Smith, *A Compendious Syriac Dictionary*, 115.

false swearing, they demand closer consideration.[253] The LXX translations of Exod 20:7; Deut 5:11; and Ps 24:4 exhibit remarkable overlap, employing the rare phrase ἐπὶ ματαίῳ for לשׁוא (which appears nowhere else in the LXX), λαμβάνω for נשׂא, and καθαρίσῃ for נקה/נקי. This suggests that the Greek translator of Ps 24:4 recognized a correspondence with the NC.

Psalm 24:3–4

מי־יעלה בהר־יהוה	Who may ascend the mountain of Yhwh
ומי־יקום במקום קדשׁו:	And who may stand in his holy place?
נקי כפים ובר־לבב	One with innocent hands and a pure heart,
אשׁר לא־נשׂא לשׁוא נפשׁי	Who does **not represent** me **in vain**
ולא נשׁבע למרמה:	And does not swear deceitfully.

Having discussed Ps 24:4 in ch. 2, what remains is to explain how it might be read in concert with a representational reading of the NC. Psalm 24 is liturgical in nature, concerned with qualifications for ascending "Yhwh's hill" and standing in "his holy place"—that is, the sanctuary complex (24:3). In contrast to the typical ANE requirement of *ritual* purity for worship, here the psalmist envisions a whole generation *morally* pure enough to stand in God's presence (24:4–6).[254]

My proposed translation of Ps 24:4 accepts the MT's first-person ending on נפשׁ, with Yhwh as the understood speaker.[255] The abrupt change in voice fits the dialogical nature of this liturgical psalm; the questions of worshipers in v. 3 are answered by Yhwh himself in vv. 4–5. Yhwh's presence is presupposed by the direct address in v. 6b.[256] Just as "name" can

253. A few who recognize the apparent link between Ps 24:4 and the NC use the psalm to clarify the NC on the basis of parallelism. William Brown ("'Here Comes the Sun!': The Metaphorical Theology of Psalms 15–24," in *The Composition of the Book of Psalms*, ed. Erich Zenger, BETL 238 [Leuven: Peeters, 2010], 263) makes no explicit connection between them, but his interpretation of Ps 24:4 presupposes that the NC concerns oaths. McCann ("Psalms," 773) notes the allusion but does not advocate a representational reading. To my knowledge no one arguing for a representational reading of the NC has attempted to explain how this might affect the interpretation of Ps 24:4.

254. For further discussion, see deClaissé-Walford, Jacobson, and Tanner, *Psalms*, 250.

255. One Jewish interpreter supposes that the psalmist speaks on Yhwh's behalf (Feuer, *Sēfer Tehillîm*, 298). If the 3rd-person ending for נפשׁ of other manuscripts is accepted (נפשׁו), the sense of Ps 24:4 changes considerably, but without precluding my interpretation. The link to the NC would be severed and the verse would then read "who does not lift up his [own] soul in vain," which could indicate hypocritical worship as opposed to confident trust in Yhwh (cf. Ps 25:1). In keeping with the idiom "lift up one's soul" (cf. Hos 4:8), the parallel line would further illustrate the hypocrisy of the supplicants. Both their worship and their oaths in Yhwh's name are insincere.

256. Another change in person occurs in v. 6. First, the psalmist speaks of God in third person, and then switches to second person: "Such is the generation seeking *him*, who seek *your* face, [namely] Jacob." The apparent awkwardness in English creates a brilliant balancing effect in Hebrew poetry. Berlin (*Dynamics of Biblical Parallelism*, 40) discusses contrast in person under morphologic parallelism. Cf. Kugel, *Idea of Biblical Poetry*, 22); Nicholas Lunn, *Word-Order Variation in Biblical Hebrew Poetry: Differentiating Pragmatics and Poetics* (Waynesboro, GA: Paternoster, 2006), 15–16.

represent a person metonymically,[257] it is not uncommon for YHWH to refer to himself with נפשי ("my *nephesh*, person"), especially in poetic passages.[258] Accordingly, נפשי can be taken as an intensive personal pronoun ("me").[259] The righteous supplicant is one who does not bear or "represent" him "in vain."[260] The last two lines of the verse summarize two dimensions of misrepresentation. The righteous do not misrepresent YHWH either by blameworthy actions (cf. "innocent of hands"), or by swearing falsely, which would indicate duplicity (cf. "pure of heart").[261] The context thus reflects a range of activity that is broader than oath taking. Other interpretations of Ps 24:4 are possible, but here I have attempted to show how one might read the psalm as an echo of the NC.

Psalm 139:19–20

אם־תקטל אלוה רשע	O that you would slay the wicked, O God;
ואנשי דמים סורו מני:	And men of bloodshed depart from me
אשר <u>יאמרך</u> למזמה	Who <u>speak</u> of you deviously,
<u>נשׂא לשוא</u> עריך:	Your adversaries **lift up in vain**

This text is notoriously difficult. First, the singular consonantal form of נשׂא is problematic because the subject of this clause is plural.[262] One way to resolve the lack of agreement is by recognizing that subject-verb disagreement is not uncommon in Hebrew poetry as a feature of poetic balancing.[263] Another option, preferred by most commentators, takes the Masoretic pointing of נָשֻׂא as an unconventional form of the active נָשְׂאוּ,

257. As discussed above. See Reiterer, "שֵׁם," *TDOT* 15:136.

258. Contra Elßner, *Das Namensmißbrauch-Verbot*, 109. YHWH refers to himself with נפשי at least 14 times (Lev 26:11, 30; 1 Sam 2:35 [with prefix]; Isa 1:14; 42:1; Jer 5:9, 29; 6:8; 9:8; 12:7; 15:1; 32:41; Ezek 23:18 [twice]). In the examples from Leviticus, Isaiah, and Ezekiel, נפשי could easily be replaced with the first-person pronoun, "I." In Jer 15:1, נפשי seems to refer to YHWH himself. Other authors refer to YHWH's נפש in 3rd person (Judg 10:16; Ps 11:5; Prov 6:16; Jer 51:14 [with prefix]; and Amos 6:8 [with prefix]). In every case, a 3rd-person pronoun could replace נפש.

259. The word נפשי is especially common in poetry as a heightened, rhetorical way of referring to the self. Westermann ("נֶפֶשׁ," *TLOT* 2:757) calls it "the intensely purposive 'I.'" Cf. B. K. Waltke, "נֶפֶשׁ," *TWOT* 2:589.

260. As explained below, p. 144, נשׂא connotes physical carrying rather than lifting in exaltation. In metaphorical contexts such as this it draws on the concept LIFE AS A JOURNEY, where pious actions are expressed as forward movement in public view.

261. Perhaps line 4 echoes the NC, while line 5 evokes the command against false witness (Exod 20:16). If so, both actions ("innocent hands") and motivations ("pure heart/mind") of the righteous must be consistent with what God requires, so the righteous do not misrepresent YHWH ("who does not bear my soul in vain") or fellow Israelites ("who does not swear deceitfully").

262. This assumes that עָרֶיךָ is the subject rather than object of the verb. If taken as the object ("who lift in vain עריך"), the translation "your cities" would make the most sense, functioning metonymically for the people of Israel as a whole, who are misrepresented (i.e., slandered) by YHWH's enemies.

263. See Berlin, *Dynamics of Biblical Parallelism*, 40.

meaning "they lift up."[264] A third option, building on the second, is to read the verb as reflexive along with the NRSV: "who lift themselves up against you for evil."[265] However, if the verb carries a reflexive sense here, it would be a unique instance, and therefore less likely.[266]

The last word of the verse is even more puzzling. The MT's עָרֶיךָ could be an Aramaism meaning "your adversaries" (from עָר; cf. 1 Sam 28:16), or it could be vocalized as "your cities" (from עִיר; cf. Ezek 35:9).[267] The Targums read it as the former (בעלי־דבבך), while the LXX reads the latter (τὰς πόλεις σου).[268] Neither is an obvious fit with the context, but the first ("your adversaries") seems most likely for at least three reasons. First, the psalm as a whole includes other rare words, perhaps borrowed from Aramaic.[269] Second, the psalmist clearly identifies these people as Yhwh's enemies in v. 22. Third, the infrequency of the Aramaic עָר explains the LXX misreading, as well as the variant עֵדֶיךָ.[270] It also accounts for its proper translation in the Targums, for whose translators Aramaic would have posed no difficulty (*Tg.* Ps 139:20).[271]

---

264. The u-class vowel indicates a 3rd-person plural subject, rather than a passive or reflexive verb. See Leslie C. Allen, *Psalms 101–150*, WBC 21 (Waco, TX: Word, 1983), 253 n. 20b. This solution also pertains to the previous line, where the singular verb יאמרך, is given plural vowels (יֹאמְרֻךָ).

265. This translation requires other interpretive decisions, including a malicious sense for שׁוא, already dismissed above, and a conjectural emendation from עָרֶיךָ to עָלֶיךָ ("against you").

266. According to Reiterer ("שׁוא," *TDOT* 14:457), נשׂא is never reflexive, with the possible exception of Nah 1:5, "the earth heaves." In other cases where נשׂא means "to fight against," the object is "hand" ("to lift the hand against"; 2 Sam 18:28; 20:21). *DCH* (5:768) lists Ps 139:20 as the only potential passive of נשׂא, suggesting the "name" of Yhwh is the implied subject (= "it is uttered in vain [by] your adversaries").

267. With characteristic creativity, Mitchell Dahood (*Psalms III: 101–50*, AB [Garden City, NY: Doubleday, 1970], 284, 297) revocalizes עָרֶיךָ as *ʿārīk* ("array"), and redivides the previous line. He interprets this verse as concerning idolatry: "Because they gaze upon every figurine, raise their eyes to vanities arrayed."

268. *BHS* cites numerous manuscripts that read עֵדֶיךָ ("your witnesses," cf. Job 10:17; or "your onset"). See Reiterer, "שׁוא," *TDOT* 14:457; G. R. Driver, "Notes on the Psalms II: 73–150," *JTS* 44 (1943): 22. As mentioned above, others propose an emendation to עָלֶיךָ ("against you"; cf. Ezek 29:3). See Hermann Gunkel, *Die Psalmen: übersetzt und erklärt*, 4th ed., HKAT (Göttingen: Vandenhoeck & Ruprecht, 1926), 592, cited by Allen (*Psalms 101–150*, 253 n. 20c), who suggests that עָדֶיךָ could mean "your enemies." Cf. Dan 4:16.

269. Potential Aramaisms include "intention" (רע; vv. 2, 17), "recline" (רבע; v. 3), "word" (מלה; v. 4), "go up" (סלק; v. 8), and "foe" (ער; v. 20). See John Goldingay, *Psalms 90–150*, BCOT (Grand Rapids: Baker Academic, 2008), 628.

270. Elßner (*Das Namensmißbrauch-Verbot*, 57) considers an emendation to שׁמך ("your name" // Exod 20:7), but favors עדיך ("witnesses"), suggesting a parallel to Ps 24:4.

271. A different word appears in the Targums (בעלי־דבבך), perhaps because ער was already antiquated. The resulting translation is highly interpretive; both cola have to do with oaths. For an English translation, see Stec, *Targum of Psalms*, 234. Scribes often confused *resh* (ר) and *dalet* (ד). For example, MT Isa 33:8 ("cities") and 1QIsa[a] ("witnesses").

If this assessment is correct, the verse reads, "who speak of you deviously, your adversaries lift up in vain,"[272] which allows for more than one interpretive option. The expression is probably elliptical, since the verb lacks an object. It could mean either "your adversaries lift up (their voices) in vain," or "your adversaries lift up (a report against you) in vain," or "your adversaries lift up (your name) in vain." The elliptical expressions in Isa 3:7; 42:2, 11, where נשׂא (without an object) refers to speaking, favor the first. As in Ps 139:20, the context in Isaiah suggests speech.[273] Here the enemies of YHWH are explicitly speaking (אמר). The psalmist may have envisioned the enemies of YHWH railing against God to no avail.

Alternatively, the verse could echo Exod 23:1, where the Israelites are told not to "bear an empty report" (לא תשׂא שׁמע שׁוא) or act as "a malicious witness" (עד חמס). Both passages concern the wicked (רשׁע; Ps 139:19). However, in this case, YHWH's adversaries (his own people?) bear false witness against him rather than each other.

A third possibility is that Ps 139:20 alludes to the NC, leaving out "your name" due to the constraints of Hebrew poetry. The presence of the relatively rare לשׁוא supports this possibility; לשׁוא appears with נשׂא only in Ps 139:20; 24:4; and the NC. If my interpretation of the NC is correct and if Ps 139:20 alludes to it, the latter suggests that YHWH's own people, who bear his name, have borne it in vain, and so have become his adversaries.[274] The psalmist declared that these "men of blood" who plot against YHWH "have become my enemies" (לאויבים היו לי; 139:22). "Your adversaries" could then be a satirical title for unfaithful Israelites, the apostate compatriots of the psalmist.[275]

None of these interpretations is certain. Given the lexical similarities with the NC, my intention is to show how one *might* read this passage. Each reading of Ps 139:20 proposed here suggests that certain "men of blood" have become YHWH's enemies and are either speaking against, bearing false witness against, or misrepresenting YHWH.

See Emanuel Tov, *Textual Criticism of the Hebrew Bible*, 3rd rev. ed. (Minneapolis: Fortress, 2012), 329.

272. If the LXX τὰς πόλεις σου correctly translates עָרֶ֫יךָ, the meaning could be "your cities bear {your name} in vain," in which case the cities (synecdoche for the Israelites) misrepresent YHWH. The context describes these cities as YHWH's enemies, filled with violent men.

273. Contra Elßner, *Das Namensmißbrauch-Verbot*, 278. Unless יֹאמְרֻךָ in line 1 is emended to יַמְרֻךָ, which reflects a *hiphil* form of מָרָה, "to rebel" (cf. Ps 78:40).

274. Cf. Isa 63:19 NRSV and Deut 32:41, both of which suggest that Israel has become YHWH's enemy by breaking the covenant.

275. So Goldingay (*Psalms 90–150*, 637), for whom Ps 139 describes those who associate YHWH with emptiness and are therefore covenantally unfaithful.

Chapter 4

A Reexamination of the Name Command in the Context of the Decalogue

> Context always provides a narrowing of choices, even if it can only rarely allow for a complete elimination of ambiguity.
>
> —David H. Aaron, *Biblical Ambiguities: Metaphor, Semantics, and Divine Imagery*

A proper understanding of the NC depends on a correct assessment of its literary and historical contexts. The NC does not appear independently; it is one of ten "words" (דברים) in a closed series, known by its Greek title as the Decalogue. But what exactly *is* the Decalogue? And what role does it play in Israel's account of her history?[1] How we answer these questions will have significant bearing on how we read the NC. The first section of this chapter will assess the genre and purpose of the Decalogue in light of its broader historical contexts. The second section will examine its literary contexts—the book of Exodus, the Sinai narratives, and the book of Deuteronomy—considering how the Decalogue relates to the other Torah regulations as well as how it is internally structured. Not only does the context of the Decalogue shape the way we read it, but the Decalogue also shapes our reading of the rest of Israel's regulations. Attention to both directions of influence facilitates a more accurate assessment of the NC.

The Character of the Decalogue

The Decalogue as Law

The so-called Ten Commandments are arguably the most famous of all "laws" in human history. But the Decalogue is *not* law in the modern sense. Recent explorations of the function of laws in the ANE offer fresh perspective on ancient law, refining the distinctions between apodictic and casuistic laws, between laws and commandments, and between ceremonial and judicial laws.[2] While the Ten Words are framed as commands, the

1. For discussion, see p. 5 n. 12.

2. *Apodictic and casuistic laws*: Albrecht Alt (*Essays on Old Testament History and Religion*, trans. R. A. Wilson [Garden City, NY: Doubleday, 1967], 101–71) classified the Ten

rest of Israel's regulations cannot be neatly divided into one category or another.

Westbrook argues that ANE law codes belonged to the scientific enterprise, whose lists were not exhaustive or binding but generated a "formalized wisdom" that creatively covered a wide range of legal issues.[3] In contrast to modern legal citation, where the exact wording of a statute carries authority, ancient laws guided people in making wise judgments by treating sample cases, often from the periphery of ethical norms (e.g., Lev 24).

Michael LeFebvre argues that Israelite "law" fits this paradigm. He shows how even the Book of the Covenant, the Bible's oldest "law code," shows no evidence of having been used as "*the basis for* court decisions."[4] Instead, biblical legal material assisted judges by giving them perspective as they deliberated.[5] LeFebvre proposes that the *legislative* use of "law codes"

Words form critically as apodictic (as opposed to casuistic) law, categorical pronouncements unique to Israel that arose from a cultic setting. However, his sharp distinction between these has been deemed inadequate as archaeologists have since identified "apodictic" laws from other ANE cultures. See Samuel Greengus, "Law, Biblical and ANE Law," *ABD* 4:245.

Laws and commandments: Claus Westermann (*Elements of Old Testament Theology* [Atlanta: John Knox, 1982], 177–78) distinguished between "commandments" and "laws," suggesting that the former derive from an authoritative figure and the latter from a powerful institution. On the direct composition of laws rather than an origin in oral tradition, see Lohfink, "Kennt das Alte Testament einen Unterschied von 'Gebot' und 'Gesetz'? Zur bibeltheologischen Einstufung des Dekalogs," *JBTh* 4 (1989): 70–72; Moshe Greenberg, "Some Postulates of Biblical Criminal Law," in *A Song of Power and the Power of Song: Essays on the Book of Deuteronomy*, ed. Duane Christensen, SBTS 3 (Winona Lake, IN: Eisenbrauns, 1993), 288–89.

Ceremonial and judicial laws: Bernard Jackson ("The Ceremonial and the Judicial: Biblical Law as Sign and Symbol," *JSOT* 30 [1984]: 25–50) suggests that ceremonial and judicial laws had different audiences, the former exclusively Israelites, and the latter universal. However, the Decalogue lacks judicial features but is clearly directed at the Israelites as those redeemed from slavery to be YHWH's covenant people.

Some argue that the Sabbath Command is cultic, but it lacks cultic features (no temple/tabernacle, priest, sacrifice or ritual), and apparently antedates the cult (Exod 16:22–30). For discussion see Daniel I. Block, *Deuteronomy*, NIVAC (Grand Rapids: Zondervan, 2012), 165. For Edward L. Greenstein ("The Rhetoric of the Ten Commandments," in *The Decalogue in Jewish and Christian Tradition*, ed. Henning Graf Reventlow and Yair Hoffman, LHBOTS 509 [New York: T&T Clark, 2011], 11), the whole Decalogue is "quasi-cultic" because cultic regulations tend to be formulated apodictically. He points to analogous ritual texts from Ugarit.

3. Raymond Westbrook, "The Character of Ancient Near Eastern Law," 1–90 in *A History of Ancient Near Eastern Law*, 1:17, 20, 87.

4. Michael LeFebvre, *Collections, Codes, and Torah: The Re-characterization of Israel's Written Law*, LHBOTS 451 (New York: T&T Clark, 2006), 36, emphasis his. See Dale Patrick, "Law in the OT," *NIDB* 3:603; George E. Mendenhall, *Law and Covenant in Israel and the Ancient Near East* (Pittsburgh: Presbyterian Board of Colportage, 1955), 9.

5. This assessment need not preclude the divine origin of such decisions.

arose in the Hellenistic era.[6] Before then, "law collections" functioned as "descriptions of Yahwistic ideals," offering guidance to the Israelites and later wisdom for the king.[7]

In spite of demonstrable similarities between biblical and ANE regulations,[8] differences remain. Though many biblical instructions were common among ancient societies (e.g., murder, false witness, and adultery were forbidden elsewhere), the combination of these civil injunctions with instructions of a religious or cultic nature was unprecedented.[9] A simple perusal of Lev 19 will show the degree to which these domains are freely mixed in the Hebrew Bible. The biblical vision of ethics touches on every area of life; all is under YHWH's sovereignty. This realization should caution us against reading the NC either as a legal stipulation or as strictly civil, moral, or cultic in nature.[10]

---

6. Here he disagrees with Westbrook, who dates the rise of legislative use to the time of Ezra and Nehemiah. See LeFebvre, *Collections, Codes, and Torah*, 259.

7. Ibid., 259, 261, 90–95. LeFebvre provides extensive support to show Torah regulations as divine guidance rather than civil legislation. His conclusion justifies Eichrodt's characterization of Israelite law as a flexible, developing corpus adapted to real life situations. See Eichrodt, *Theology of the Old Testament*, 70–74. Cf. W. J. Dumbrell, *Covenant and Creation: A Theology of Old Testament Covenants* (Eugene, OR: Wipf & Stock, 2009), 91–92. This conclusion may mitigate claims that various biblical laws are contradictory. If Israel's regulations were intended to adapt to new settings, one would expect significant changes given Israel's transition from semi-nomadic to agrarian. Hittite laws provide an analog to Israel's rewritten law. See Kenneth A. Kitchen and Paul J. N. Lawrence, *Treaty, Law and Covenant in the Ancient Near East* (Wiesbaden: Harrassowitz, 2012), 3:248. One need not suppose a lengthy diachronic development of law in order to benefit from LeFebvre's work. The salient point of his thesis is the nonlegislative function of law in ancient Israel. Though laws were adapted over time, and additions were likely, LeFebvre presents no compelling reason to remove the core of Israel's regulations from the narratives that present them as divinely revealed at Sinai.

8. Because of the potential for confusing ANE "law" with modern law, whenever possible I will refrain from using designations such as "law codes," "law collections," or "laws" in favor of "regulations," "instructions," or "constitutional documents." These terms preserve the sense of regulatory function without requiring a legislative application.

9. Eichrodt, *Theology of the Old Testament*, 76–77. Cf. J. David Pleins, *The Social Visions of the Hebrew Bible* (Louisville: Westminster John Knox, 2001), 44.

10. So Wright, *Old Testament Ethics*, 288–89; Daniel I. Block, "The Grace of Torah: The Mosaic Prescription for Life (Deut 4:1–8; 6:20–25)," in *How I Love Your Torah, O LORD! Studies in the Book of Deuteronomy* (Eugene, OR: Cascade, 2011), 3–4. However, these categories may still be valuable for discerning the ongoing validity of a given regulation for faith communities today. For Christians, every regulation teaches about God and therefore can shape the life of faith. Some regulations have undergone more radical transformation than others in Christ. For a helpful discussion, see Sandra L. Richter, *The Epic of Eden: A Christian Entry into the Old Testament* (Downers Grove, IL: IVP Academic, 2008), 225–29. Kathryn Greene-McCreight ("Restless until We Rest in God: The Fourth Commandment as Test Case in Christian 'Plain Sense' Interpretation," 223–36 in *The Ten Commandments*, 228) traces this approach to ancient Christian exegesis.

The Decalogue as Divine Guidance

Rather than civil legislation, the Hebrew Bible preserves collections of divine pronouncements intended to guide Israel's life and worship. A closer look at the Decalogue confirms this conclusion. Most commands lack sanctions (e.g., murder, adultery, stealing), and many are too vague to enforce.[11] How does one determine whether parents have been properly honored or whether someone coveted his or her neighbor's property? However, as divine guidance the Decalogue is not merely suggestive. It prescribes how people must live if they are to please God, but does not legislate that behavior by giving specific penalties for disobedience. It creates a worldview by sketching the outer boundaries of righteous behavior within which the Israelites were to live and flourish.

However, unlike ANE judicial material, the Decalogue is embedded in a narrative.[12] Even where biblical regulations compare favorably with their ANE counterparts, the narrative context casts them in a different light. While most other forms of law operate as a "social control system," biblical regulations create and maintain a community based on shared covenantal values.[13] This observation is especially pertinent to the Decalogue, which is situated in not just one, but two significant contexts—the narrative account of the sojourn at Sinai and Moses' farewell address on the plains of Moab. These narratives further clarify the way the Decalogue should be heard—not as civil legislation, and not as divine guidance in an abstract or

11. Raymond Westbrook and Bruce Wells, *Everyday Law in Biblical Israel: An Introduction* (Louisville: Westminster John Knox, 2009), 13. In spite of this obvious deficiency, scholars continue to construe them legislatively. On the unenforceability of the Decalogue, see also Weinfeld, "The Decalogue: Its Significance, Uniqueness, and Place in Israel's Tradition," 15–16; Pleins, *Social Visions*, 47; J. W. Marshall, "Decalogue," *DOTP* 175; Block, "The Decalogue in the Hebrew Scriptures," 5.

12. Calum Carmichael (*The Ten Commandments* [Oxford: Oxford Centre for Postgraduate Hebrew Studies, 1983]) takes this narrative context seriously, arguing that the Decalogue recapitulates or responds to key events in history where Israel broke God's commands. For him, the initial Decalogic commands are a response to Aaron's sin with the golden calf ("other gods" and "idols" to whom his "name" has been raised for a "day of celebration") and the sin of Adam and Eve. Carmichael's original thesis pertained to Deut 12–26, but later he included the Book of the Covenant. See *The Laws of Deuteronomy* (Ithaca, NY: Cornell University Press, 1974); idem, *Origins of Biblical Law*. See also Assnat Bartor, *Reading Law as Narrative: A Study in the Casuistic Laws of the Pentateuch*, AIL 5 (Atlanta: SBL, 2010). In his own way, Knight (*Law, Power, and Justice*, 26) also emphasizes the literary nature of OT laws, insisting that a correspondence between written law and legal practice cannot be determined.

13. George E. Mendenhall, "The Conflict between Value Systems and Social Control," in *Unity and Diversity: Essays in the History, Literature and Religion of the Ancient Near East*, ed. H. Goedicke and J. J. M. Roberts (Baltimore: Johns Hopkins University Press, 1975), 169. For a summary of differences between covenant and law, see Walton, *Ancient Near Eastern Thought*, 299–301; Daniel I. Block, *The Gospel according to Moses: Theological and Ethical Reflections on the Book of Deuteronomy* (Eugene, OR: Cascade, 2012), 90–91.

a universal sense, but as divine guidance for a particular people in a unique historical situation.

The Decalogue as Treaty or Covenant

The covenant framework for the Decalogue is well recognized, and the correspondences between 2nd-millennium Hittite treaties and the Sinai covenant are well documented.[14] Like the Hittite suzerain-vassal treaties (1450–1200 BCE), the larger narrative of YHWH's covenant with Israel includes a preamble; a historical prologue; a list of stipulations (including apodictic commands); instructions for depositing the document in the temple; and a list of witnesses, curses, and blessings.[15]

Parallels with Hittite treaties go beyond form to include content and tone, which was more positive than later Assyrian counterparts. While the latter were designed to strike fear into the vassal,[16] Hittite kings portrayed

14. George Mendenhall, whose original work on covenants was republished as Mendenhall, *Law and Covenant*, continues to influence scholarship to this day. See, e.g., Wenham, "Law," *DTIB* 443; Clements, *Old Testament Theology*, 119; Kitchen and Lawrence, *Treaty, Law and Covenant*, 3:259.

15. Mendenhall, *Law and Covenant*, 32–34. The stone tablets themselves contain only a brief historical prologue, no clear section of blessings and curses (though Exod 20:5–6, 7b, and 12b provide hints), and no deposition or instructions for reading. The deposition appears in Exod 40:20. For discussion, see Daniel I. Block, "Reading the Decalogue Right to Left: The Ten Principles of Covenant Relationship in the Hebrew Bible," in *How I Love Your Torah, O LORD! Studies in the Book of Deuteronomy* (Eugene, OR: Cascade, 2011), 26–36. Because the form is not identical to a Hittite treaty, Schüngel-Straumann (*Der Dekalog*, 37–38) thinks of the biblical ברית as a mutual obligation rather than a covenant. Cf. Ernst Kutsch, *Verheissung und Gesetz: Untersuchungen zum sogenannten "Bund" im Alten Testament*, BZAW 131 (New York: de Gruyter, 1973); Walther Zimmerli, *Old Testament Theology in Outline*, trans. David E. Green (Edinburgh: T&T Clark, 1978), 49–50; Dale Patrick, *Old Testament Law* (Atlanta: John Knox, 1985), 224.

Since later (Neo-Assyrian) treaties contained neither prologue nor blessings, Mendenhall (*Law and Covenant*, 35) argued that the biblical record of YHWH's covenant must be as old as Hittite exemplars. Lack of contact between Israel and Hatti was no problem for his theory; since Hittite treaties are *international* in nature, he assumes they compare favorably with undiscovered treaties from other ANE cultures. Kitchen and Lawrence (*Treaty, Law and Covenant*, 2:268) demonstrate structural correspondences between the biblical and Hittite covenants. Later Assyrian treaties were deposited either in the royal archives (Simo Parpola, "International Law in the First Millennium," 2:1047–66 in *A History of Ancient Near Eastern Law*, 2:1059) or the inner sanctum of the temple (Jacob Lauinger, "Some Preliminary Thoughts on the Tablet Collection in Building XVI from Tell Tayinat," *JCSMS* 6 [2011] 11–12). Recently, Scott Morschauser ("Do Not Look to Egypt? On an Alternative to Joshua Berman's 'CTH 133 and the Hittite Provenance of Deuteronomy 13,'" [unpublished manuscript]) discussed potential parallels in Egypt from the same time period. Though his examples are not treaties per se, they depict loyalty oaths with similar expectations and punishments to those found in Deuteronomy.

16. Westbrook, "Character of ANE Law"; and Beckman, "International Law in the Second Millennium," in *A History of Ancient Near Eastern Law*, 1:84–85, 760, 763. The vassal was enjoined to remain loyal in his "love" for the King, swearing an oath of allegiance

themselves as benevolent and entered into covenants with willing vassals on whose behalf they had done favors.[17] In 13th-century letter, a Hittite emperor calls his vassal, the king of Ugarit, his "servant" and *sglt*, an Ugaritic term of endearment for a treasured vassal.[18] Similarly, in the Israelite covenant Yhwh refers to Israel as his "treasured possession" (סגלה, Exod 19:6).[19] Other treaty language in the Hebrew Bible is עבד ("servant"), בן ("son"), אח ("brother"), ידע ("know"), and שלום ("peace").[20] These terms of endearment strengthen the analogy with the older ANE Hittite treaties while distancing Israel's covenant from less-friendly Neo-Assyrian prototypes.

Like their neighbors, the Hittites made duplicate copies of a treaty, depositing one copy in the central sanctuary of each party's god.[21] Since Yhwh was the only deity involved and Israel was the only nation, both stone tablets were deposited in the ark of Yhwh in Israel's only tabernacle (Deut 4:13; 9:11; 10:5).[22] Yhwh thus simultaneously became the guarantor of his own faithfulness to the covenant as well as Israel's.[23]

---

that precluded alliances with other nations. While Assyrian treaties also enjoined the vassal to "love" the suzerain, loyalty and affection were not reciprocal. See Moshe Weinfeld, "Covenant Making in Anatolia and Mesopotamia," *JANES* 22 (1993): 135–37.

17. J. Berman, "CTH 133 and the Hittite Provenance of Deuteronomy 13," *JBL* 130 (2011): 37. Herbert B. Huffmon ("Contrasting Juridical Conceptions in Ancient Near Eastern Treaties and Covenants" [paper presented at the Annual Meeting of the SBL, Chicago, November 2012]) also insists that the biblical covenant is heir to Hittite rather than Neo-Assyrian attitudes. Assyrian kings did not even feign benevolence. See Weinfeld, "Covenant Making," 135–37.

18. *KTU* 2.39:7,12; noted by Daniel I. Block, "The Privilege of Calling: The Mosaic Paradigm for Missions (Deut 26:16–19)," in *How I Love Your Torah, O Lord! Studies in the Book of Deuteronomy* (Eugene, OR: Cascade, 2011), 152–53 n. 33. Harry Hoffner indicated in personal conversation (March 25, 2013) that no Hittite cognate to *sglt* or *sikiltu* has been discovered, but this text confirms that vassals were so conceived by the Hittite suzerain.

19. For a full discussion of this term, see John Davies, *Royal Priesthood: Literary and Intertextual Perspectives on an Image of Israel in Exodus* 19.6, JSOTSup 395 (New York: Continuum, 2004), 54–60. Cf. Moshe Greenberg, "Hebrew *sᵉgullā* : Akkadian *sikiltu*," *JAOS* 71 (1951): 172–74; Weinfeld, *Deuteronomy and the Deuteronomic School*, 226 n. 2; idem, *Deuteronomy 1–11*, 368.

20. McCarthy, *Treaty and Covenant*, 288–89. For a similar list, see Paul Kalluveettil, *Declaration and Covenant: A Comprehensive Review of Covenant Formulae from the Old Testament and the Ancient Near East*, AnBib 88 (Rome: Pontifical Biblical Institute, 1982).

21. Similar practices were likely followed with the so-called Vassal Treaties of Esarhaddon (VTE) or "Loyalty Oath Tablets." See Lauinger, "Some Preliminary Thoughts," 11; Huffmon, "Contrasting Juridical Conceptions." Vertical piercing of a tablet found at Tell Tayinat suggests it was on display upright in the temple sanctuary under the deity's watchful eye.

22. Meredith G. Kline, "The Two Tables of the Covenant," *WTJ* 22 (1960): 139; idem, *Treaty of the Great King*, 19; Block, "Reading the Decalogue Right to Left," 35.

23. Despite these similarities, striking differences in form and scope separate the biblical covenant from ANE analogues. Other Mesopotamian vassal treaties are accompanied by casuistic (rather than apodictic) laws. For discussion, see Greenstein,

While the Decalogue diverges from ANE treaties in significant ways, they have enough in common that Israel could refer to the ritual ark as "the ark of the treaty" (ארן העדת; Exod 25:22)[24] or "the ark of the covenant" (ארון ברית; Deut 10:8).[25] An ancient observer would readily have understood the tablets as delineating the loyal response of a vassal people (Israel) to the gracious acts of her suzerain (YHWH).[26] As Kitchen and Lawrence point out, the Bible does not preserve the formal covenant document itself but rather the "narrative *report*" of that covenant.[27] This observation accounts for its *formal* divergences from ANE patterns.

As for the *content*, Israel's election as YHWH's covenant people provides the necessary framework for understanding the peculiar blend of civil and religious regulations in the Decalogue.[28] The preamble to the Decalogue (Exod 20:2) demonstrates that YHWH's instructions were a gift to a people

"Rhetoric of the Ten Commandments," 9–10. Furthermore, the biblical list of stipulations is far longer and more developed than a typical treaty. See Greengus, "Law; Biblical and ANE Law," *ABD* 4:245. In addition, the divine-human relationship is unique. For discussion, see Shalom M. Paul, *Studies in the Book of the Covenant in the Light of Cuneiform and Biblical Law*, VTSup 18 (Leiden: Brill, 1970), 30–31; Carol L. Meyers, *Exodus*, New Cambridge Bible Commentary (New York: Cambridge University Press, 2005), 151; Weinfeld, "Covenant," *EJ* 5:253. Though no deity-nation treaty documents are extant from other ANE cultures, they may have conceived of a covenant between a deity and their king. Strikingly, a Phoenician inscription from Arslan Tash (7th century BCE) indicates that El and Asherah made a covenant with those responsible for the plaque. See Frank Moore Cross and Richard J. Saley, "Phoenician Incantations on a Plaque of the Seventh Century BCE from Arslan Tash in Upper Syria," in *Leaves from an Epigrapher's Notebook: Collected Papers in Hebrew and West Semitic Paleography and Epigraphy*, HSS 51 (Winona Lake, IN: Eisenbrauns, 2003), 267. Certain kings were called the "beloved" of a god. For example, Šuppiluliuma of Hatti was the "beloved of the Storm-god" (Kitchen and Lawrence, *Treaty, Law and Covenant*, 1:367, 391, 400–401), and Ramesses II of Egypt was "the beloved of Amen-Re" and other gods (ibid., 3:593). The citizens of Shechem may also have thought of themselves as bound by covenant with Baʿal ("Baʿal-Berith" in Judg 8:33 and 9:4). Alternatively, the title Baʿal-Berith could refer to Baʿal as witness to covenants between humans. For discussion, see M. J. Mulder, "Baal-Berith," *DDD* 143. In spite of these potential similarities, ANE suzerain-vassal treaties pertained to international politics rather than cult maintenance, and were enacted between a King and less powerful vassal. For discussion, see Paul, *Studies in the Book of the Covenant*, 38.

24. The word עדת (or its cognates) is a technical term for the treaty tablets in other ANE cultures. Cf. Exod 26:33–34; 30:6, 26; 39:35; 40:3, 5; Num 4:5; 7:89. See discussion below, p. 122.

25. Cf. Num 10:33; 14:44; Deut 31:9, 25, 26. See p. 122 n. 41.

26. See Block, "Reading the Decalogue Right to Left," 26–28, and discussion below on p. 119.

27. Kitchen and Lawrence, *Treaty, Law and Covenant*, 3:117, 124. While Deuteronomy includes treaty elements, most agree it is a collection of sermons. See also Vogt, *Deuteronomic Theology*, 26. McCarthy (*Treaty and Covenant*, 262–63) suggested that treaty *forms* were imposed centuries later on the ancient covenantal narratives. So also LeFebvre, *Collections, Codes, and Torah*, 51.

28. So Paul, *Studies in the Book of the Covenant*, 30–31.

freed from slavery, whose gratitude was to be expressed in obedience.[29] While other ANE treaties addressed international political relations, demanding political loyalty, most of Israel's stipulations concerned relationships within a single community and demanded religious loyalty. YHWH covenanted with only one nation,[30] so the stipulations pertaining to fellow-vassals were inter*personal* rather than inter*national* in nature.[31]

According to Shalom Paul, Israel's stipulations functioned constitutionally,[32] creating a new nation bound to be loyal to YHWH. Exodus 25:16 declares explicitly that the Decalogue is the core covenant document (העדת), declared by YHWH to the people and then transcribed and deposited in the ark as a permanent witness to the covenant (Exod 25:16, 21; 40:20).[33]

The Decalogue as a Portrait of a Covenant-Keeping Israelite

The Decalogue alone does not provide comprehensive coverage of civil or moral law in ancient Israel, and therefore should be read as a sampling to

29. So Terence E. Fretheim, *The Pentateuch*, ed. Gene M. Tucker, Interpreting Biblical Texts (Nashville, TN: Abingdon, 1996), 169. This aspect of the covenant is not unique to Israel. Cf. *Mekhilta Bahodesh* 5, on Exod 20:2 (cited by Stephen Westerholm, "Law in Early Judaism," *NIDB* 3:590); Mendenhall and Herion, "Covenant," *ABD* 1:1181, 1191; idem, *Law and Covenant*, 32; Wenham, "Law," *DTIB* 444; Patrick D. Miller, "Divine Command and Beyond: The Ethics of the Commandments," in *The Ten Commandments*; Roland de Vaux, "Review of 'Jahwes Eigentumsvolk: Eine Studie zur Traditionsgeschichte und Theologie des Erwählungsgedankens,'" *RB* 71 (1964): 117; Ferry, "Le Décalogue," 168; Eichrodt, *Theology of the Old Testament*, 57; Kline, "Two Tables," 144; Block, *Deuteronomy*, 172; idem, "Reading the Decalogue Right to Left," 30. According to Kitchen and Lawrence (*Treaty, Law and Covenant*, 3:255) the historical prologue of an ANE treaty typically motivated loyalty by emphasizing the "indebtedness" of one party to the other. Below, I discuss an argument that includes the preamble as part of the first word, or command.

30. Israel was not the only nation with whom YHWH dealt (see Deut 32:8), but the only one with which the relationship was regulated. The Israelite king was not law-giver or even mediator but a student of Torah who must embody its values paradigmatically (Deut 17:14–20). See Vogt, *Deuteronomic Theology*, 226. In contrast, other ANE cultures viewed the king as the primary source of legal wisdom. See Westbrook, "The Character of ANE Law," in *A History of Ancient Near Eastern Law*, 1:26.

31. Other covenant documents prohibit alliances with other nations (through marriage or otherwise), a prohibition at home in a suzerain-vassal treaty (Exod 34:12–16; Deut 7:1–6). See Gary Beckman, "International Law in the Second Millennium," in *A History of Ancient Near Eastern Law*, 1:756, 768. Any treaty with another king was regarded as treason. See Mendenhall and Herion, "Covenant," *ABD* 1:1180.

32. Paul, *Studies in the Book of the Covenant*, 31–32.

33. Vogt, *Deuteronomic Theology*, 158. Cf. Mendenhall and Herion, "Covenant," *ABD* 1:1183; Wright, *Old Testament Ethics*, 262; Dozeman, *Exodus*, 478; Martin Noth, *The Deuteronomistic History*, 2nd ed., JSOTSup 15 (Sheffield: Sheffield Academic, 1991), 92; Craigie, *Deuteronomy*, 149. Cassuto (*Exodus*, 238) says the Ten Words only *introduce* the covenant. For a more radical rejection of the Decalogue as covenant stipulations, see Schüngel-Straumann (*Der Dekalog*, 36), who argues that the covenant framework is a later imposition on the Sinai narrative. But if we assume that both Decalogue and covenant are later additions to Sinai, we are faced with the same conclusion—that the Decalogue constitutes the covenant stipulations in this (later) construal of the Sinai theophany.

illustrate the ethical framework for covenant life, rather than a summary.[34] The Decalogue sketched a portrait of the covenant-keeper as a paradigm or model for every member of the covenant community to emulate. Although this paradigmatic figure was described using male pronouns, by implication every woman and child was also included.[35] The Decalogue delineated the boundaries within which covenantal freedom must be exercised.[36] The commands concerned "ordinary life," rather than the specialized vocations of king, priests, or judges.[37] Every Israelite was responsible to obey.[38]

Though ultimately all are accountable to God for unethical conduct, only those YHWH has redeemed from bondage were expected to emulate the portrait presented in the Decalogue. The ethics embodied here flow from and are framed by the deliverance YHWH accomplished for his people (see Exod 20:2). While some commands may be similar to laws of surrounding nations, the narrative context makes these covenantal regulations,

---

34. See Waldemar Janzen, *Old Testament Ethics: A Paradigmatic Approach*, 1st ed. (Louisville: Westminster John Knox, 1994), 62, 92, 95.

35. The Decalogue may use male pronouns simply by default. For discussion, see Hess, Richard S., *The Old Testament: A Historical, Theological, and Critical Introduction* (Grand Rapids: Baker, 2016), 112. Alternatively, it may address male heads of Israelite households in particular, charging them to protect the rights of every other covenant member. Only a man could covet his "neighbor's wife," and only a head of household could ensure that everyone in it observed Sabbath rest. See Graupner, "Tora für die Völker," 92; Greenstein, "Rhetoric of the Ten Commandments," 3; Houtman, *Exodus*, 3:13. However, this need not preclude the application of the Decalogue to every Israelite. For example, Paul, *Studies in the Book of the Covenant*, 38; Childs, *Book of Exodus*, 400; Nielsen, *The Ten Commandments in New Perspective*, 137; Weinfeld, "The Decalogue: Its Significance, Uniqueness, and Place in Israel's Tradition," 10; Vogt, *Deuteronomic Theology*, 153–54.

Others characterize the Decalogue as a power play by landowners to protect their property and way of life. See David Clines, *Interested Parties: The Ideology of Writers and Readers of the Hebrew Bible*, JSOTSup 205 (Sheffield: Sheffield Academic, 1995), 34; cf. Douglas Knight, *Law, Power, and Justice*, 26; J. David Pleins, *Social Visions*, 60. These interpreters fail to acknowledge how the Decalogue *limits* the power and rights of those in control. As Walter Brueggemann (*Theology of the Old Testament: Testimony, Dispute, Advocacy* [Minneapolis: Fortress, 2005], 423–24) insists, Israel was to become "preoccupied with the well-being of the neighbor ... and prepared to exercise public power for the sake of the neighbor, even when that exercise of public power works against established interests." So also Joshua A. Berman, *Created Equal: How the Bible Broke with Ancient Political Thought* (New York: Oxford University Press, 2008); Peter T. Vogt, *Deuteronomic Theology*, 231; Block, "Reading the Decalogue Right to Left," 32; idem, "You Shall Not Covet," 138, 158.

36. Nelson, *Deuteronomy*, 78–79; Block, "Reading the Decalogue Right to Left," 36.

37. Nelson, *Deuteronomy*, 78. The general nature of the commands is the strongest evidence against reading the Decalogue as a power play on the part of Israel's leaders.

38. Paul, *Studies in the Book of the Covenant*, 38. Block (*Deuteronomy*, 399, 401) observes that even Deut 16:18–17:13, which concerns festival observance and administration of justice, is "not a manual for judges, kings, priests, and prophets, but an appeal to the people to be involved in the maintenance of righteousness."

addressing Israel as a covenant member. The NC, then, cannot be considered a universal prohibition; people outside the covenant do not bear his name. It is specifically applicable to his covenant people.[39]

The Decalogue and Israel's Other Constitutional Documents

The Decalogue was a key component of Israel's covenant, though the Ten Words themselves were rarely called a ברית (but see Deut 4:13).[40] The tablets were often referred to as the עדת (Exod 25:16, 21) or as לחת העדת ("tablets of the עדת"; Exod 32:15).[41] Rather than an *aural* "testimony," as the English implies, עדת points to a written legal "witness" or "testimony," referring to the king's coronation document or the "contractual obligations" of the Sinai covenant.[42] In the ancient Near East, the tablets on which a treaty was written were known as "*adê* tablets," and were deposited in the temple where the gods could be reminded of their duty to enforce them.[43] As for the Decalogue, the two tablets bore witness before YHWH to the covenant stipulations to which Israel had agreed and to which YHWH had committed himself. Because violation by any Israelite put the entire community at risk, the rest of Israel's regulations filled out the implications of the Decalogue for particular life situations to ensure that the community did not violate the divine will.[44]

---

39. On the tendency of the early church to read the Decalogue as universal law, divorced from its covenantal context, see Frédéric Chapot, "Réflexions antiques sur la structure du Décalogue: Entre appropriation et rationalisation," in *Le Décalogue au miroir des Pères*, ed. Rémi Gounelle and Jean-Marc Prieur, Cahiers de Biblia Patristica 9 (Strasbourg: Université Marc Bloch, 2008), 31. Some modern interpreters also make this mistake. E.g., Westermann, *Elements of Old Testament Theology*, 181.

40. Noted by Patrick D. Miller, "The Place of the Decalogue in the Old Testament and Its Law," *Int* 43 (1989): 234. In Gen 31:44, ברית and עד appear as a word pair. The Decalogue is referred to as "tablets of the covenant" (לוחת הברית) in Deut 9:9, 11, 15, and though Exodus typically calls it the "ark of the עדת," it is usually the "ark of the ברית" in Deuteronomy.

41. See also Exod 30:36; 40:20; and probably Deut 4:45 for עדת. For "tablets of the עדות," see Exod 31:18; 32:15; 34:29. The ark where the tablets were kept was regularly called the "ark of the עדות" (Exod 25:22; 26:34; 30:6; 39:35; 40:5; Num 4:5; 7:89; cf. Deut 31:26).

42. *HALOT* 1:790–91.

43. Kalluveettil (*Declaration and Covenant*, 31) identifies cognates for עדת in the Akkadian *adê* and the Aramaic *ʿdn/ʾdyʾ*. Cf. Jacob Lauinger, "Esarhaddon's Succession Treaty at Tell Tayinat: Text and Commentary," *JCS* 64 (2012) 87; Huffmon, "Contrasting Juridical Conceptions"; Simo Parpola and Kazuko Watanabe, *Neo-Assyrian Treaties and Loyalty Oaths*, SAA 2 (Helsinki: Helsinki University Press, 1988), xv.

44. See Mendenhall, *Law and Covenant*, 5, emphasis mine. See also Mendenhall and Herion, "Covenant," *ABD* 1:1183; Miller, "The Place of the Decalogue"; Fretheim, *The Pentateuch*, 156; Anthony Phillips, *Essays on Biblical Law*, JSOTSup 344 (New York: Sheffield Academic, 2002), 24; Gordon Wenham, "Law," *DTIB* 445; Roger Brooks, *The Spirit of the Ten Commandments: Shattering the Myth of Rabbinic Legalism* (San Francisco: Harper & Row, 1990), 30.

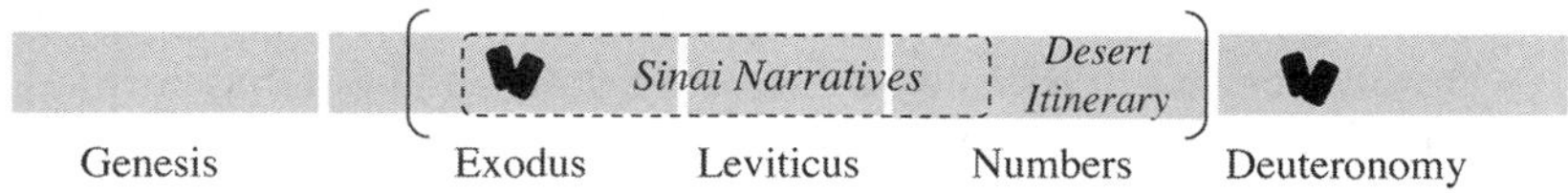

Figure 9. The narrative placement of the Decalogue

At the very least its current narrative position, preceding the Book of the Covenant as well as the Holiness Code and deuteronomic Torah, implies that these other constitutional documents derive from the former, enumerating the specific outworkings of the Decalogue in Israelite society.[45] These latter collections are still not "laws" in the modern, legislative sense, but would have informed individual and community behavior by specifying what covenantal obedience entailed for Israel. Exodus 18:13–16 suggests that many of these instructions would have arisen from disputes or other difficult cases brought to Moses for his deliberation, rooted in the divine decrees at Sinai (vv. 20–26).

Any exposition of the NC must take seriously the character of the Decalogue as a covenant document, intended to outline the behavior expected of Israel as YHWH's covenant partner. Furthermore, if the Decalogue is the source or foundation of Israel's Torah, we would expect variations of the NC to appear throughout the rest of the constitutional documents, fleshing out the portrait provided *in nuce* in Exod 20:7.

The Literary Context of the Decalogue

In order to appreciate fully the function of the Decalogue as a covenant document, its overall literary setting must be considered. The complex artistry of the Pentateuch provides several levels of narrative context (fig. 9).[46] Exodus and Deuteronomy each offer a distinct and coherent literary setting for the Decalogue (); a third setting is the "Sinai Narratives," spanning Exod 19:1 to Num 10:10. These narratives show thematic coherence and are clearly framed on either side by the desert itinerary.

The Book of Exodus as Context for the Decalogue

Exodus begins with the extraordinary multiplication of Jacob's descendants in Egypt, held together loosely by common ancestry. They are first

45. For a recent defense of the temporal priority of the Decalogue, see Kilchör, *Mosetora und Jahwetora*. Schwienhorst-Schönberger ("Das Verhältnis von Dekalog und Bundesbuch," 68, AT) feels that the Book of the Covenant croncretizes the Decalogue. Cf. Walter Moberly, "Exodus," *DTIB* 214. Likewise, many feel that the deuteronomic Torah is an exposition of the Decalogue. So Noth, *Deuteronomistic. History*, 92; Fretheim, *The Pentateuch*, 107. Cf. Mendenhall, *Law and Covenant*, 17; Wenham, "Law," *DTIB* 444. Whether Deuteronomy reflects a Decalogic structure will be considered below.

46. Overlapping structural patterns are evident, the product of a complex history of editorial work. The resulting layers accent different aspects of Israel's experience.

"sons of Israel . . . each man with his household" (בני ישראל . . . איש וביתו; Exod 1:1). By the end of the book this assembly of households has become a single house, referred to as "the whole house of Israel" (כל־בית־ישראל; Exod 40:38). Their national identity emerges in the narrative, with the Decalogue at the pinnacle. As a whole, Exodus highlights how Israel's experience of YHWH mirrored Moses'. He fled Egypt, encountered YHWH at a mountain in the wilderness, and was commissioned for service. Likewise, the Israelites fled Egypt, met YHWH at Sinai, became his people, and were commissioned for his service.[47]

From a social science perspective, Israel's desert journey provided ideal timing for YHWH's self-revelation and making the covenant. Unmoored from their former life of servitude in Egypt, the status of the Hebrews was uncertain. They had been set free, but by whom? And for what purpose? The shape of their new life was still indefinite. They had no place to call their own, and that lack of place, coupled with the scarcity of resources and the absence of community structures, left them vulnerable. Into this vacuum, YHWH spoke. There—far from home and routine, slavery and satiation—YHWH had their full attention. He revealed his name and nature and told them who they were and how they were to live. Their transformation from an amorphous mob of escapees to an organized camp of 12 tribes took place at the foot of Mt. Sinai. Their identity changed from Pharaoh's servants to treasured vassals of YHWH. The liminality of the desert facilitated this rite of passage. The unpredictability of these years required absolute allegiance to YHWH and his authorized representatives, relativizing individual ambitions. Sinai made them a covenanted people.[48]

Sinai stands at the center of this narrative, and Israel remained there throughout the book, having multiple encounters with YHWH in which he spoke audibly to Moses and manifested his glory (Exod 19–20, 24, 33–34, 40:34–35). At Sinai, he announced his intention to make them his own treasured possession from among the nations, a holy people and kingdom of priests (Exod 19:3–6). There, too, he revealed his will in the foundational covenant document (Exod 20:1–17). The NC belongs to this significant moment in Israel's history with YHWH, at the heart of the Exodus narrative at Sinai. The detailed and extensive tabernacle instructions that follow ensure the portability of YHWH's presence; given the proper abode, YHWH would continue to dwell in the center of the Israelite camp after the people left Sinai, and the stone tablets of the covenant ([illegible]) would have a permanent

47. For discussion, see Mark S. Smith, *The Pilgrimage Pattern in Exodus*, JSOTSup 239 (Sheffield: Sheffield Academic, 1997), 190–91.

48. On the liminality of the wilderness, see Robert L. Cohn, *The Shape of Sacred Space: Four Biblical Studies*, AAR Studies in Religion 23 (Chico, CA: Scholars Press, 1981); Ronald S. Hendel, "Sacrifice as a Cultural System: The Ritual Symbolism of Exodus 24,3–8," *ZAW* 101 (1989): 366–90. On the uniqueness of this deity-nation relationship, see Daniel I. Block, *The Gods of the Nations: Studies in Ancient Near Eastern National Theology*, 3rd ed. (Eugene, OR: Wipf & Stock, 2013), 61–74.

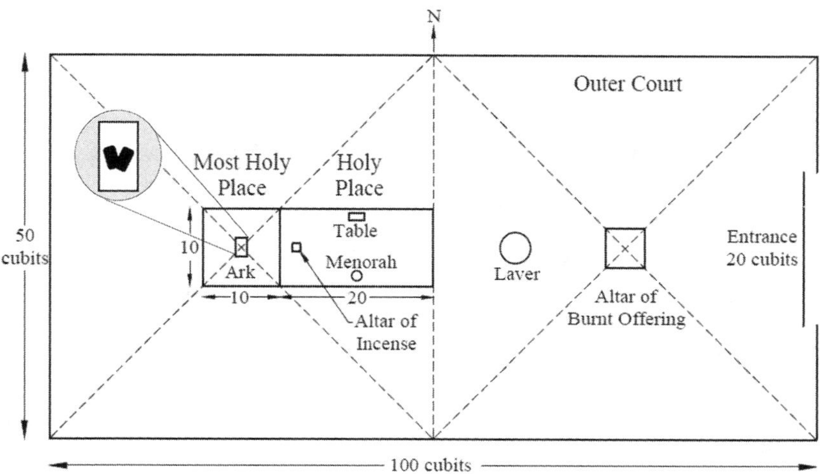

Figure 10. Geographic placement of the Decalogue

place in the epicenter of the inner sanctum (24:16; fig. 10).[49] The centrality of the Decalogue to the covenant relationship is apparent: given on Mount Sinai in the midst of a powerful theophany, the tablets were perpetually housed in the most sacred area of the tabernacle—a place filled with the glory of YHWH (Exod 40:35).

Several motifs in the narrative context of the Exodus Decalogue stand out. First, the Decalogue was given to a people freed from bondage. It prescribed how to respond to and live in that freedom. Second, it was given to a people specially chosen by YHWH. Their obedience to the Decalogue was not a prerequisite for their election as his people, but rather a response to God's grace. Third, the Decalogue functioned as a covenant document, formalizing their relationship with him, and declaring YHWH's expectations for the people he had chosen (cf. Exod 19:5–6). Fourth, though Israel broke the covenant within a matter of days, YHWH showed mercy by reaffirming his commitment to them, renewing the covenant, and providing a means for his presence to remain among them. The book of Exodus closes with the glory of God filling the completed tabernacle, assuring the portability of YHWH's presence (Exod 40:34–38; cf. Num 9:15–23).[50] The Sinaitic portion of Exodus is thereby framed by theophanies; it begins with the glory of God's presence on the mountain and the giving of the Decalogue, and ends with God's presence filling the tabernacle above the ark containing the Decalogue.

49. Diagram by Danny Imes. Adapted from Jacob Milgrom, *Leviticus 1–16*, AB 3 (New York: Doubleday, 1991), 135; and Daniel I. Block, *For the Glory of God: Recovering a Biblical Theology of Worship* (Grand Rapids: Baker Academic, 2014), 305

50. This retrospective summary that closes the book of Exodus assumes the fulfillment of instructions to consecrate the tabernacle and ordain the priests, which is not described in detail until Lev 8:10–13 (cf. Exod 40:16).

The Sinai Narratives as Context for the Decalogue

While the book of Exodus shows a unity of design, with a coherent beginning and end, the books of Leviticus and Numbers are obviously linked to it. Their narratives continue the story of Israel's desert sojourn, punctuated by instructions that clarify or supply what is lacking in the Covenant Code. Note the following links at the seams between books: Exodus closes with the glory of YHWH filling the tabernacle and Moses unable to enter (Exod 40:34–35); Leviticus begins with YHWH calling out to Moses from within the tent (Lev 1:1). Leviticus closes with the colophonic statement: "These are the commands YHWH gave Moses at Mount Sinai for the Israelites" (Lev 27:34); Numbers opens with YHWH again speaking to Moses—this time *inside* the tent at Sinai because provision has been made for atonement (Num 1:1; cf. Lev 9:23). At each seam the tabernacle is central, and the Israelites' location at Sinai is reiterated.

The literary bookend to Israel's arrival at Sinai (Exod 19:1–2) is found in Num 10:11–12, where the cloud lifted from the tabernacle and the Israelites set out from Sinai toward the land God promised them. All 59 chapters from Exod 19 to the first half of Num 10 take place at Sinai.[51] As such, we must also consider these narratives as a literary context for the NC.

Although Exodus closes with the tabernacle furnishings in place, no instructions have specified the maintenance of the cult. Leviticus supplies this lack, making provision for the forgiveness of sin and proper protocol for other sacrifices (Lev 1–7), the installation of the priesthood (Lev 8–9), and the purity of both priests and people (Lev 10–27). As such, it functioned as a manual for ongoing attention to the covenant relationship.[52] The final events at Sinai, recounted in Num 1–10, involved the registration and organization of the Israelites in preparation to leave the mountain and enter Canaan (Num 1:1–10:10).

The Sinai narratives are framed by Israel's desert travels. Although Num 33 suggests the full itinerary included at least 42 camp sites, the narrative account highlights only 6 stops on either side of Sinai, each marked by the appearance of the *wayyiqtol* ויסעו ("and they set out").[53] Further reinforcing

51. Leviticus contains no time or date stamp analogous to those that frame the Sinai narratives, but its contents are expressed as YHWH's speech to Moses (and sometimes Aaron) from the tent of meeting. Sinai is the setting of YHWH's instructions in Lev 7:38 (pertaining to the sacrifices in chs. 1–7); 25:1; 26:46; and 27:34. Narrative time comes to a halt in Leviticus, with the exception of the high priestly ordination (Lev 8–9), part of which happens "on the eighth day" (Lev 9:1), the sin of Nadab and Abihu (Lev 10), and the sin of the half-Israelite (Lev 24:10–23).

52. Note that these procedural texts follow the apostasy of Exod 32. Leviticus is YHWH's provision for the restoration of rebellious Israel, even anticipating future failures.

53. Leading to Sinai: Exod 12:37; 13:20; 15:22; 16:1; 17:1; 19:2. Leading away from Sinai: Num 10:12; 20:22; 21:4; 21:10; 21:11; 22:1. The handful of other locations specified lack the formulaic ויסעו ("and they set out"; Num 11:35; 12:16; 21:12–13). The verb נסע appears 17

this symmetry is the appearance of one travel-related imperative on either side of Sinai (Exod 14:2; Num 14:25), both of which mention the sea, and two instances of the *wayyiqtol* ויבאו ("and they entered") in conjunction with a stay on the journey (Exod 15:27; Num 20:1), bringing the total number of stops marked by *wayyiqtol* to 14, with the narrative block at Sinai in the center. Israel traversed 7 deserts (Sinai is the third) and is said to have "camped" 10 times.[54] This selective numeric artistry, reinforced grammatically, points to the central role of Sinai in Israel's sojourn.

In addition to this stylized itinerary, many stories recounted on either side of Sinai correspond to each other. Twice before Sinai and twice after, the Israelites complained they had no water (Exod 17:1–7; Num 20:2–11). On either side, Moses procured water from a rock (Exod 17:5–6; Num 20:11). On either side, the narrative describes the quail and manna God provided (Exod 16; Num 11). The angel of YHWH appeared in one incident on either side, both times protecting them from the evil designs of foreign kings (Exod 14:19–20; Num 22:21–35). The Israelites fought the Amalekites on either side (Exod 17:8–16; Num 14:39–45). The Israelites' response to the report of the scouts in Num 14 mirrors the response to Pharaoh's army before they crossed the sea (Exod 14:10–12)—they lament ever having left Egypt.[55] Immediately

times in the narrative if other conjugations are counted (Sinai is the seventh, followed by 10 more). For more discussion of this symmetry, see Cross, *Canaanite Myth and Hebrew Epic: Essays in the History of the Religion of Israel*, 308–16; Cohn, *The Shape of Sacred Space*, 18; Smith, *The Pilgrimage Pattern in Exodus*, 289.

54. Exodus 13:20; 15:27; 17:1; 19:2; Num 12:16; 21:10; 21:11; 21:12; 21:13; 22:1. The itineraries also mention "desert" 6x before the Sinai narratives (7 times, if Exod 13:18 is counted) and 7 times afterward, with a double mention directly on either side.

55. A close comparison reveals the further deterioration of the Israelites' mood. While in Exodus they wished to have stayed in Egypt *as slaves* rather than dying in the wilderness, in Numbers they wished to have *died* in Egypt or *died* in the wilderness rather than face the occupants of Canaan. While in Exodus they complained about Moses, in Numbers they complained about YHWH directly.

Exodus 14:11b, 12b	*Numbers 14:2b–3*
המבלי אין־קברים במצרים לקחתנו למות במדבר מה־זאת עשית לנו להוציאנו ממצרים: חדל ממנו ונעבדה את־מצרים . . . כי טוב לנו עבד את־מצרים ממתנו במדבר:	לו־מתנו בארץ מצרים או במדבר הזה לו־מתנו: ולמה יהוה מביא אתנו אל־הארץ הזאת לנפל 3 בחרב נשינו וטפנו יהיו לבז הלוא טוב לנו שוב מצרימה:
Weren't there enough graves in Egypt that you took us to die in the desert? What is this you have done to us— by bringing us out from Egypt? . . . Leave us alone so we can serve the Egyptians, for it is better for us to serve the Egyptians than for us to die in the desert.	"If only we had died in the land of Egypt, or in this desert if only we had died. For why has YHWH brought us to this land to fall by the sword? Our wives and small children will be booty! Is it not better for us to return to Egypt?"

preceding and following the Sinai narratives, Moses struggled under the burden of leadership (Exod 18:17–18; Num 11:10–15) and benefitted from the presence of a wise Midianite family member (Exod 18; Num 10:29–32) and elders who shared the load (Exod 18:24–26; Num 11:16–17). The lexical correspondence between these accounts is striking. In Num 11, Moses explicitly reused Jethro's language from Exod 18.[56] Other elements could be explored, but this list suffices to show the deliberate framing of the Sinai narratives in a way that sets them apart and highlights their significance.[57]

One significant narrative shift pertains to travels after Sinai. While both travel accounts describe the people's complaints and rebellion, after Sinai rebellion was punished (Num 11:1; 14:26–35).[58] Prior to Sinai, they learned to trust YHWH and Moses as his representative; after Sinai, their failure to trust merited punishment. Their covenant status, sealed at Sinai, inaugu-

56. In Exod 18, Moses' father-in-law Jethro expressed concern about Moses' workload, insisting, "the task (הדבר) is too heavy for you; you cannot do it alone," and recommending that Moses appoint elders to "bear the burden" of "all this people" (כל־העם הזה; Exod 18:23) with him so he would "be able to endure." After Sinai, when the pressure grew unbearable for Moses, he complained to YHWH, repeatedly using the phrase "all this people" (כל־העם הזה; Num 11:11, 12, 14) and employing Jethro's words to express the burden of responsibility. He concluded, "I am unable alone to carry all this people, for it is too heavy for me" (Num 11:14; cf. Deut 1:12), making explicit what was vague in Jethro's statement. While Jethro called the *task* [of judging] too heavy, Moses envisioned himself carrying the entire community through the desert; *they themselves* were too heavy to bear. Note the transposition and reuse of Jethro's language.

Exodus 18:18b	*Numbers 11:14*
כי־כבד ממך הדבר	לא־אוכל אנכי לבדי
	לשאת את־כל־העם הזה
לא־תוכל עשהו לבדך:	כי כבד ממני
For this thing is too heavy for you	I myself am unable alone
	To carry all this people
You are unable to do it alone	For it is too heavy for me

57. For example, before and after Sinai, God led Israel with the pillar of cloud, led her into battle, and revealed his glory. For further discussion of the "ring structure" around Sinai, see Smith, *The Pilgrimage Pattern in Exodus*, 285–90. Milgrom (*Numbers*, xviii) identified a larger chiasm spanning from Genesis to Joshua. The center of his chiasm is also Sinai, specifically Exod 33, where YHWH promised his presence would accompany the Israelites out of the wilderness. Cf. Jan Wagenaar, "Crossing the Sea of Reeds (Exod 13–14) and the Jordan (Josh 3–4): A Priestly Framework for the Wilderness Wandering," in *Studies in the Book of Exodus: Redaction, Reception, Interpretation*, ed. Marc Vervenne, BETL 126 (Leuven: Leuven University Press, 1996), 461–70.

58. For alternative accounts of Israel's murmuring, see G. W. Coats, *Rebellion in the Wilderness: The Murmuring Motif in the Wilderness Traditions of the Old Testament* (Nashville: Abingdon, 1968); W. Johnstone, "From the Sea to the Mountain: Exodus 15,22–19,2: A Case-Study in Editorial Techniques," in *Studies in the Book of Exodus: Redaction, Reception, Interpretation*, ed. M. Vervenne, BETL 126 (Leuven: Leuven University Press, 1996), 245–63.

rated a greater accountability.[59] The instructions that emanate from Sinai remake this people and reorder their way of life, making it possible for YHWH to dwell among them.

Deuteronomy as Context for the Decalogue

The deuteronomic Decalogue deserves separate treatment. As in Exodus, in Deuteronomy the Decalogue stands, together with a paraenetic call for faithfulness, at the head of Moses' instructions for Israel. The concentrated body of instructions that follow may be called the deuteronomic Torah (Deut 12–26). Though the form of the NC is identical in both versions, the new narrative context is significant. While the Exodus version was declared to a generation recently delivered from bondage in Egypt, the Deuteronomy Decalogue was ostensibly addressed to a new generation—those who were born or came of age during the wilderness wanderings—on the plains of Moab. Still, Moses spoke to them as if they had been at Sinai. This notion of "corporate continuity"[60] both implicated and assured this generation. "You rebelled," Moses told them (1:43), and yet "he declared to you his covenant, that is, he commanded you to do the Ten Words" (4:13).[61] For Moses, every generation of YHWH's covenant people was present at Sinai, witnessing YHWH's awesome presence and receiving his decrees. He went so far as to say "*with us* YHWH our God cut a covenant at Horeb. Not with our fathers did YHWH cut this covenant, but with us, those of us here today, all of us who are living" (5:2–3).[62] Moses' point was theological. With the exception of Joshua and Caleb, the previous generation had forfeited the benefit of covenant blessings by failing to obey YHWH. The covenant itself had not been abrogated, but its benefactions were reserved for a generation committed to walking in YHWH's ways.

The reiteration of the Ten Words assured this generation—and by extension every believing generation to come—that they were indeed YHWH's covenant people. Moses reinforced that connection by applying the covenant titles to them: "For you are a holy people (עם קדוש אתה ליהוה) belonging to YHWH your God. *You* YHWH your God has chosen out of all the peoples on the face of the earth to become his treasured people" (עם סגלה; Deut 7:6; cf. Exod 19:5–6). Like their parents at Sinai, they were elect. Therefore,

59. See also Milgrom, *Numbers*, xvi, 82.

60. Greg Beale used this term in a class lecture on the hermeneutical presuppositions of NT authors, but it is equally true of Moses at Moab. See also Jerry Hwang, *The Rhetoric of Remembrance: An Investigation of the "Fathers" in Deuteronomy*, Siphrut 8 (Winona Lake, IN: Eisenbrauns, 2012), 193.

61. For a brief discussion of this passage, see Block, *Deuteronomy*, 128 n. 13.

62. The indirect object עמנו is fronted for emphasis. Later, Moses provided the Israelites with a creedal-like statement that rehearsed this history. As they worshiped YHWH in the land, the Israelites were to confess that they had been enslaved in Egypt and that YHWH had delivered them (Deut 26:5–10; cf. 6:20–25, a creed that includes the Sinai regulations).

they were responsible for living by YHWH's covenant stipulations. Put another way, the rehearsal of the Decalogue in this new context to the next generation assured that it would continue to function programmatically for Israel's life with YHWH. As Moses formed the people's memory, their identity was thereby secured.

The Decalogue as Context for the Name Command

Scholars have suggested a variety of organizing structures for the Ten Words as well as ways in which the Decalogue provides a programmatic structure for the other constitutional documents, especially the deuteronomic Torah. A survey and evaluation of these various proposals will help determine whether structural considerations should influence how we read the NC. Keeping the NC in focus, this section will first explore the internal, microstructure of the Decalogue and then consider the possibility of its programmatic macrostructure.

Microstructure: Reading the NC in the Context of the Decalogue

The early church often failed to respect the narrative context of the Decalogue. Instead, it was extracted and used for catechesis, as a basic, universal ethic for training new Christians. Freed from its narrative context, the Decalogue (especially its second half) was deemed suitable for a Gentile audience.[63]

The primary hermeneutical lens for the early church's reading of the Decalogue was Jesus' statement in Matt 22:36–40 highlighting the two greatest commands: love for God and neighbor. Early interpreters assumed he must be summarizing the Ten Words.[64] Since by that time, the ANE covenant

---

63. Chapot, "Réflexions antiques sur la structure du Décalogue," 31. Cf. Martine Dulaey, "Le Décalogue, les tables de la Loi et la catéchèse," in *Décalogue au miroir des Pères* (Strasbourg: Université Marc Bloch, 2008), 49–63. Jews also used the Decalogue for catechesis. For example, the first-century CE Nash Papyrus contains a composite Hebrew text combining both versions of the Decalogue along with the *Shemaʿ*. See Tov, *Textual Criticism of the Hebrew Bible*, 118; F. C. Burkitt, "The Hebrew Papyrus of the Ten Commandments," *JQR* 15 (1903): 392–408; Stanley A. Cook, "A Pre-Massoretic Biblical Papyrus," *Proceedings of the Society of Biblical Archaeology* (1903): 34–57. A close relationship between the Decalogue and the *Shemaʿ* is maintained in the Talmud (*y. Ber.* 1:4), where Rabbi Levi claims that the Decalogue is contained within the *Shemaʿ*. Indeed, the *Shemaʿ* declares that YHWH alone is Israel's God, and exhorts the people to love him wholly (Deut 6:5–6), mirroring the first two commands of the Decalogue.

64. For earlier examples of this tendency, see Philo, *On the Decalogue*, LCL 7.12; Josephus, *Ant.* 3.5.4, 8. Sänger ("Tora für die Völker," 123) suggests the absence of NT quotations from the "first table" is due to the mixed church of Jews and Gentiles, which naturally made use of the growing tradition that used the "second table" for the basis of ethical reflection. Indeed, at first glance Rom 13:9–10 supports this view, because the text declares that four of the commands from the so-called "second tablet" are "summed up" in the command to love one's neighbor. However, this selection of commands is not

background of the Decalogue had been largely forgotten, interpreters did not realize that the two tablets would have been duplicates. They assumed that Jesus was substituting one command for each of the tablets, with those on the first tablet pertaining to love of God and those on the second to love of neighbor. The idea quickly caught on ("That'll preach!"), but just as interpreters disagreed over how to number the Ten Words, so they disagreed over how to divide them. Some imagined five on each tablet,[65] others supposed the first had four and the second six,[66] and still others suggested three on the first and seven on the second.[67] In any of these proposals, the NC belonged on the first tablet, highlighting one way believers are to show love for God—namely, by not misusing his name.

However, it is by no means clear where (or if) the commands ought to be divided. The Sabbath and Parents commands are not unambiguously vertical or horizontal. Obedience to each of the Ten Words expresses covenant loyalty to God ("love of God") and affects the neighbor. Even the first commands have interpersonal implications, since an Israelite who makes an image to worship puts the entire community at risk and denies the role of humanity as God's image.[68] Jesus did not explicitly divide the commands into two groups,[69] nor did he specify that he spoke only of the Decalogue.

exhaustive (as Paul added, "and any other command") and need not imply that *only* the Decalogue is in view.

65. Dulaey ("Le Décalogue," 50) lists Philo, Origen, Ireneaus, and Hilary as advocates. John Calvin (*Institutes of the Christian Religion*, ed. John T. McNeill, trans. Ford Lewis Battles, LCC [Philadelphia: Westminster, 1967], 20:2.8.12; 377–79) also mentions Josephus. For recent support, see Meyers, *Exodus*, 165; Sarna, *Exodus*, 108.

66. Ambrosiaster, *Commentaries on Galatians–Philemon*, trans. Gerald Lewis Bray, ACT (Downers Grove, IL: IVP Academic, 2009), 60; Calvin, *Institutes*, 20:2.8.12, 377–79. More recently, Mark E. Biddle, *Deuteronomy*, SHBC (Macon, GA: Smyth & Helwys, 2003), 106.

67. Augustine followed church tradition by viewing the structure typologically; the first three commands represented the Trinity and the last seven the days of creation. See Geerlings, "The Decalogue in Augustine's Theology," 117; Augustine, *Sermons II (20–50)*, 33.2; 155. He assumed that the Parents Command stood first on the second table on the basis of Eph 6:2, which calls it "the first command" (ibid., 33.4; 156). Rather, it is the first command *with a promise.*

68. So David W. Gill, *Doing Right: Practicing Ethical Principles* (Downers Grove, IL: IVP, 2004), 71. The most we can say in regard to content is that the commands proceed from divine to human affairs. So Greenberg, "Decalogue," *EJ* 5:525. As Sarna (*Exodus*, 108) points out, the Decalogue "opens with 'the Lord your God' and closes with 'your neighbor.'"

Other stylistic evidence is used to support a twofold division. Sarna (ibid.) notes that the first five are longer and contain the divine name, while the second five lack the divine name and are shorter. The first are unique to Israel, while the last are shared with other ANE cultures. Cf. Meyers, *Exodus*, 164. However, the final command is both long and unique to Israel, governing attitudes of the heart rather than enforceable behavior, and Sarna's enumeration is questionable on text-linguistic grounds. See below, p. 133.

69. Gill, *Doing Right*, 71.

His two greatest commands, taken together, embraced God's will for all human behavior.[70] Ultimately, we must reject these early misunderstandings of a two-tablet division. Given ANE treaty conventions, made more apparent with the discoveries at Tell Tayinat, the two tablets would have naturally contained duplicate copies of the entire list of commands.[71]

Complicating this picture is the fact that scholars disagree over how to number the commands.[72] That the Decalogue contains ten commands is affirmed in Exod 34:28, Deut 4:13, and 10:4. Differences in how to count them revolve around how to handle the first several and last two verses. While the constraints of the current project preclude an exhaustive analysis of other structural proposals, one option in particular is worth considering because of its implications for the NC.[73]

Lohfink and Otto suggested that the differences between versions of the Decalogue have to do with a subtle new structure imposed on Deuteronomy 5 that highlights the Sabbath Command (v. 12–15) as the "prin-

---

70. See also Kline, *Treaty of the Great King*, 25–26. Similarly, Zimmerli (*Old Testament Theology in Outline*, 133) rejects the division of the commands because the Decalogue is meant to address all of life. Even Calvin (*Institutes*, 20:2.8.11; 377), who divided the commands, saw an integral relationship between them.

71. The loyalty oath tablets found at Tell Tayinat are nearly identical to copies found elsewhere in Esarhaddon's realm. See Lauinger, "Some Preliminary Thoughts," 8. Since Israel's tablets were inscribed on both sides (Exod 32:15), half of the text naturally would have appeared on each side, but we have no reason to assume that the commands were thematically divided. On this, see Kline, "Two Tables," 139–42; Graupner, "Tora für die Völker," 75; Dillard and Longman, *Introduction to the OT*, 98.

72. For discussion, see Mordechai Breuer, "Dividing the Decalogue into Verses and Commandments," in *The Ten Commandments in History and Tradition*, ed. Ben-Zion Segal, trans. Gershon Levi (Jerusalem: Magnes, 1990), 291–330; Block, *How I Love Your Torah*, 56–60; DeRouchie, "Counting the Ten."

73. As is typical, some circularity is involved in establishing the structure. Structure can help interpret individual commands, but sometimes interpretation of those commands provides structural clues. For example, some proposed structures are based on a speech-related interpretation of the NC. Thomas Aquinas ("The Moral Precepts of the Old Law [1267–73]" in *The Ten Commandments*, 53) observes a progression from *actions* (no images), to *words* (NC), to *heart* (Sabbath). His association of Sabbath with heart is questionable, as is his limitation of the NC to words. Motyer (*The Message of Exodus*, 219) sees a chiasm with *thoughts* (worship YHWH, no images // no coveting), *words* (NC // false witness), and *deeds* (Sabbath // murder, adultery, theft), with family obligations in the center. His linking of worship with thoughts rather than actions betrays modern categories. Harrelson (*The Ten Commandments and Human Rights*, 40) arranges the commands topically in a four-part structure. Cf. Block, *For the Glory of God*, 86. T. Desmond Alexander (*From Paradise to the Promised Land: An Introduction to the Main Themes of the Pentateuch* [Grand Rapids: Baker, 1998], 85) relates the prohibition of images to "visual representations of God" and the NC to "verbal representations." He is right to see a relationship between images and the NC but not as a juxtaposition of sight and sound. More likely, YHWH forbids images because he has already provided a living image (cf. Gen 1:26–27) on whom his name is placed (cf. Num 6:27)—his covenant people.

cipal commandment."[74] According to Lohfink, this structure was created by replacing זכר with שׁמר, creating a "deuteronomic" inclusio with עשׂה at the end of the Sabbath Command, since שׁמר and עשׂה are often paired in deuteronomic literature.[75] Furthermore, the addition of "ox and donkey" (ושורך וחמרך) in the Sabbath Command forged a link with the last command, while the additional reference to "slavery in Egypt" (עבד ... בארץ מצרים) connected it with the first. The insertion of ו between each of the final commands linked them as a unit, resulting in an overall chiasm:[76]

1. Worship of YHWH	5:6–10	long	(מצרים)
2. Name of YHWH	11	short	
3. Sabbath	12–15	long	(ושורך וחמרך; מצרים)
4. Parents	16	short	
5. Moral commandments	17–21	long	(ושורך וחמרך)

Greenstein's observations about the coherence of Deut 5:6–10, the first unit, support the idea of taking them together as one command. He observes the following correspondences:

v. 6: A (motive)	I am YHWH your God
v. 7: B (prohibition)	You are not to have any other gods
v. 8: B′ (prohibition)	You are not to make yourself a carved-image
v. 9–10: A′ (motive)	I am YHWH your God[77]

However, Greenstein's chiasm can be improved. He rightly linked these verses, but he has not accounted for additional prohibitions in v. 9a that change the chiasm's emphasis.

v. 6: A (motive)	I am YHWH your God
v. 7: B (prohibition)	You are not to have any other *gods*
v. 8: C (central prohibition)	You are not to make a carved-image
v. 9a: B′ (prohibition)	You are not to bow down to or serve *them*
v. 9b–10: A′ (motive)	I am YHWH your God

74. Norbert Lohfink, *Theology of the Pentateuch: Themes of the Priestly Narrative and Deuteronomy*, trans. L. M. Maloney (Minneapolis, MN: Fortress, 1994), 260; Eckhart Otto, "Der Dekalog in den deuteronomistischen Redaktionen des Deuteronomiums," in *Die Zehn Worte: der Dekalog als Testfall der Pentateuchkritik*, ed. Michael Konkel, Christian Frevel, and Johannes Schnocks, QD 212 (Freiburg im Breisgau: Herder, 2005), 95–108.

75. Lohfink, *Theology of the Pentateuch*, 252–53. Weinfeld (*Deuteronomy and the Deuteronomic School*, 336, nos. 17, 17a, 17b) includes this word pair in his appendix of deuteronomic phraseology. See, e.g., Deut 4:16; 7:12.

76. Lohfink, *Theology of the Pentateuch*, 255–57. His outline follows, with Hebrew added. For Lohfink, the structure suits the exile, during which Sabbath synagogue services were central to Jewish religion (ibid., 262). However, an exilic date is not required to explain the Sabbath structure. "Rest" may be central because YHWH's land promise was nearing fulfillment. Furthermore, Sabbath-observance was the central sign of the covenant (Exod 31:12–17). Kilchör (*Mosetora und Jahwetora*, 330, 341) notes the "hinge" function of the Sabbath-related commands in Deuteronomy.

77. Greenstein, "Rhetoric of the Ten Commandments," 9. His analysis works with either version of the Decalogue.

This modified chiasm highlights the prohibition against carved images, and confirms that it is primarily concerned with images *of other gods*, not images of YHWH.[78] Since the worship of any other gods in the ANE would have included the use of physical representations of those deities, the command against images prevents apostasy. This interpretation accounts for the syntactical connection between להם ("to *them*"; 5:9a) and אלהים אחרים ("other *gods*"; 5:7), the only possible plural antecedent, and the mention of YHWH as קנא ("jealous"; 5:9).[79] It also fits with the discourse structure of the passage, providing some support for Lohfink's larger chiasm.[80]

This arrangement is significant because the NC becomes the second command of the Decalogue, immediately following the command for exclusive worship of YHWH. These two, regarding proper worship and proper representation, stand at the head of the covenant stipulations. The God who forbids making images points to his people as his legitimate representatives, a role they are not to take lightly. Read together, these first two commands reinforce the two dimensions of the covenant declaration, "I will be your God, and you will be my people."[81] Exodus 6:6–8 explicitly links the covenant formula with the exodus as a fulfillment of God's covenant with the Patriarchs:

> I am YHWH, and I will bring you out from under the compulsory labor of the Egyptians, and I will snatch you from their service, and I will redeem you with an outstretched arm and with great judgments. *And I will take you to myself as my own people, and I will be your God.* And you shall know that I am YHWH, your God, the one bringing you out from under the compulsory service of the Egyptians. And I will bring you to the land I swore with uplifted hand to give to Abraham, to Isaac, and to Jacob. I will give it to you as a possession. I am YHWH.[82]

Similarly, the Decalogue opens with a reminder of YHWH's having redeemed them from Egypt as he promised (Exod 20:2), and brought them

78. One might argue on the basis of Deut 4:15–28 that images of YHWH are also prohibited, but even there the concern seems to be other gods. YHWH is "jealous" (4:24) for Israel's complete devotion.

79. See Block, *How I Love Your Torah*, 59–60.

80. DeRouchie ("Counting the Ten") argues text-linguistically that vv. 6–10 constitute one command. My semantic chiasm corresponds to the discourse structure and therefore meets Smith's criterion for determining author-intended chiasms. See Craig Smith, "Criteria for Biblical Chiasms: Objective Means for Distinguishing Chiasms of Design from Accidental and False Chiasm" (Ph.D. diss., University of Bristol, 2009).

81. As Gentry and Wellum (*Kingdom through Covenant*, 344) recognize. The covenant formula is associated explicitly with redemption from Egypt (Exod 6:6–8; Jer 7:22–23; 11:1–5). It also points forward to what God will do in the restoration/new covenant (Jer 30:22; Ezek 36:27–28; cf. Hos 2:25[23]).

82. Emphasis mine. For discussion, see Daniel I. Block, "Covenance: A Whole Bible Perspective" (paper presented at the Annual Meeting of the ETS, Baltimore, MD, November, 2013), 13.

to himself rather than to a code of conduct (19:4). On this basis he declared they were to worship him exclusively (20:4–6) and live appropriately as those who belong to him (20:7). Exodus 6:3 highlights the significance of the revelation of his name. Knowing the significance of the name YHWH distinguishes the exodus generation and entails their responsibility not to squander this privilege (20:7).[83] From the foundation of this covenant relationship, outlined in the first two commands of the Decalogue, flow all the rest of the commands.[84] Ultimately, this covenantal footing fits with the Sabbath-centered focus because the Sabbath is also taken to be the sign (אות) of the covenant (see Exod 31:13; cf. Ezek 20:12–20). In sum, those who worship YHWH exclusively (no. 1) and live rightly as his people (no. 2) pattern the work week of their households after God's by resting on the seventh day (no. 3); they honor their parents (no. 4), and maintain the rights of their neighbor—rights to life (no. 5), marriage (no. 6), property (no. 7), and reputation (no. 8)—while maintaining the purity of their minds (nos. 9–10).

Macrostructure: Reading Deuteronomy as an Exposition of the Decalogue

Scholarly fascination with the structure of the Decalogue extends beyond its internal organization to its programmatic influence on other portions of the Hebrew Bible.[85] One popular proposal suggests that the deuteronomic Torah (Deut 12–26) is arranged in Decalogic order, so that each section of regulations corresponds to the next command of the Decalogue. The idea originated among modern scholars with W. Schultz, and a number of variations have been proposed.[86] Many remain unconvinced of the basic thesis, though the view seems to be gaining traction.[87] A full assessment is

---

83. See Surls, *Making Sense of the Divine Name*.

84. The combination of the traditional first two commands (no other gods, no images) requires that the last command (no coveting) be split (no lust, no coveting) to achieve a total of 10. The discourse features and syntax of the deuteronomic Decalogue make this division natural. See Block, *The Gospel according to Moses*, 169–73.

85. For example, David Noel Freedman (*The Nine Commandments: Uncovering the Pattern of Crime and Punishment in the Hebrew Bible* [New York: Doubleday, 2000]) argued that each book from Exodus to Kings portrays the serial breaking of the commands. In his scheme, the NC corresponds to Lev 24:10–23, where a man of mixed Israelite-Egyptian descent blasphemes the name and is put to death. Few have taken his imaginative proposal seriously. For a critique of Freedman's subjectivity, see Block, "Reading the Decalogue Right to Left," 47.

86. Nelson (*Deuteronomy*, 79) says Philo was the first to detect it.

87. McConville (*Deuteronomy*, 122) is intrigued but unconvinced. Nelson (*Deuteronomy*, 79) feels the thesis is weak with regard to the parents command. Tigay (*Deuteronomy*, 446–59, 534 n. 19) finds some decalogic links convincing, but not the overall structure. He proposes a different organizational scheme involving thematic and associative characteristics. Block (*Deuteronomy*, 301) feels the decalogic structure is "forced." On the other hand, in addition to those listed below, adherents include Gordon Wenham, "Law," *DTIB* 446; Pleins, *Social Visions*, 56.

Table 11. The Name Command in the Decalogic Structure of Deuteronomy[88]

Interpreter	*Section Corresponding to the NC*
W. Schultz (1859)	Deut 12–13 (ch. 14 unassigned)
S. Kaufman (1979)	Deut 13:1—14:27
G. Braulik (1993)	Deut 14:1–21
E. Otto (2002)	Deut 13:1—15:23
A. Harman (2007)	Deut 14:1–29
J. Walton (2012)	Deut 13 (ch. 14 unassigned)
B. Kilchör (2015)	Deut 14:1–21

beyond the scope of this project, but its implications for the NC are worth considering (table 11, p. 136).

As table 11 shows, each structural proposal links the NC with material between chs. 12 and 15 of Deuteronomy, with substantial overlap in chs. 13 and 14. However, most acknowledge that the Decalogic structure is weakest with regard to the NC. Braulik admits that ch. 14 relates only indirectly to the NC,[89] and rejects Kaufman's arrangement because the relationship of the NC with ch. 13 is "too remote."[90] Walton concedes that this relationship "hangs by a mere thread."[91] He sees a clear connection in the first part of ch. 13, where a prophet is presumably speaking falsehood in YHWH's name, but the correspondence breaks down with the ensuing examples of laypeople spreading apostasy, since they are not official spokespeople.[92] In his latest work, Walton labels ch. 14 as an appendix.[93]

Indeed, traditional ways of reading the NC do not fit well with the concerns of Deut 12–15. Oath taking, magic, and idolatry do not appear at all in

88. W. Schultz, *Das Deuteronomium*, Berlin: Gustav Schlawitz, 1859, iii–iv, 17–18; Braulik, "Sequence of Laws," 318–27; cf. Biddle, *Deuteronomy*, 103; Otto, *Theologische Ethik des Alten Testaments*, 101; Kilchör, *Mosetora und Jahwetora*, 96–107. John Walton ("The Decalogic Structure of the Deuteronomic Law," in *Interpreting Deuteronomy*, ed. David G. Firth and Philip S. Johnston [Nottingham: Apollos, 2012], 106) sees Deut 14 as a summary of the first three commands because no clear connection obtains between this chapter and any one command.

89. Braulik, "Sequence of Laws," 327.

90. Ibid., 321 n. 29. Kaiser (*Toward Old Testament Ethics*, 132) agrees with Kaufman's structure but feels the NC is "the most difficult to associate" with its corresponding section.

91. Walton, "Decalogic Structure," 99.

92. Ibid., 99–100. However, see 18:20, where prophets speak in the names of other gods. Walton (ibid., 100) calls these additional laws "tangential."

93. Walton's earlier article ("Deuteronomy: An Exposition of the Spirit of the Law," *GTJ* 8/2 [1987]: 221) included ch.14 under the NC, but his 2012 essay ("Decalogic Structure," 106) does not.

these chapters and seem unrelated. However, if the NC proscribes misrepresentation of YHWH by all who bear his name, the connection with Deut 12–14 is more obvious. Deuteronomy 12 speaks of the *place* where YHWH will put his name, the place to which Israel is called to come and worship. Deut 13 describes the consequences for enticing one's fellow Israelites to worship other gods. Because every Israelite bears YHWH's name, apostasy is treated with utmost seriousness, both for the one enticing and those who are led astray.[94]

Deuteronomy 14 turns out to be the most closely related to the NC, as Kilchör has argued.[95] The chapter begins with these words: "Sons you are, belonging to YHWH [ליהוה], your God. Do not cut yourselves and do not put baldness between your eyes [בין עיניכם] for the dead" (14:1). The locative phrase "between your eyes" is significant. YHWH had repeatedly enjoined the Israelites to fix his words as an emblem "between [their] eyes" as a reminder (Deut 11:18; cf. Exod 13:9, 16; Deut 6:8). Marking themselves for the dead would send competing messages. Furthermore, the high priest's forehead declared his consecration to YHWH with the same phrase [ליהוה]. Since the Israelites had been orally branded with YHWH's name by the high priest (Num 6:27), they were not to mark their bodies to show allegiance to anyone else.[96] Moses explained, "For you are a holy people, belonging to YHWH, your God. And you YHWH chose to become his own, to be a treasured people above all the peoples who are on the face of the earth" (14:2). Israel's identity was to be found in her election as YHWH's covenant partner.[97] That identity extended to every facet of life, even including diet. Deuteronomy 14:3–21 describes what Israel may and may not eat. Israel's prescribed diet was closely aligned with the sacrificial food laws.[98] They were "a holy people" before YHWH (14:21b), just as the high priest was "holy to YHWH" (Exod 28:36–38). Their holiness would be compromised by contact with the dead (14:1–2) or with unclean foods (14:3–21).[99] Through careful analysis of

94. Apostasy is treated again in Deut 17:1–13, but advocates of Decalogic structure suggest that the focus is either on proper implementation of the death penalty (// "Do not murder") or use of authority (// "Honor your father and mother"). For the latter, see Walton, "Decalogic Structure," 108.

95. Benjamin Kilchör (*Mosetora und Jahwetora*, 96, AT) says the connection is "not immediately apparent" but offers an intriguing proposal.

96. Jacobs, "The Body Inscribed," 14–16. Cf. Lev 21:5; Jer 16:6; 41:5; and 47:5, where laceration and head shaving are mourning rites. The Ugaritic "Baʿlu Myth" (trans. Dennis Pardee, *COS* 1.86:268) describes El's self-laceration as a mourning rite on Baʿal's death. Tigay (*Deuteronomy*, 136–37) suggests these extreme mourning rites were not appropriate for a consecrated people. Just as priests could not have bodily defects, so the Israelites, as a "quasi-priestly" people, must not injure themselves.

97. So also McConville, *Deuteronomy*, 248; cf. Lev 19:27–28.

98. See Block, *Deuteronomy*, 345.

99. On clean and unclean foods as symbolic of elect Israelites and nonelect foreigners, see Alexander, *From Paradise to the Promised Land*, 135. Cf. Lev 20:22–26. This

intertextual links, Kilchör demonstrates that Deut 14 recapitulates only those regulations from Lev 11 and 22 that desecrate YHWH's name because they pertain to the people who "bear his name" and not the foreigners living among them.[100] Then, in keeping with the humanitarian concerns of the book, YHWH reminds the Israelites that when they came to eat their tithes at "the place where he will place his name" (14:23) they must not overlook the powerless and poor among them (14:27–29), extending YHWH's blessing to others (14:29b). Each of these concerns amplifies the idea that Israel bore YHWH's name, and so must imitate him.[101]

This exposition alone is inadequate to establish the Decalogic structure of the deuteronomic Torah. While I remain unpersuaded regarding this larger structural thesis, my reassessment of the NC strengthens a weak part of the schema. Nowhere in Deut 12–15 are any laws on oath taking, magic, pronunciation of the name, or any of the other proposed interpretations of the NC, except false teaching (Deut 13:1–5). In fact, no laws on oath taking appear anywhere in the deuteronomic Torah (chs. 12–26), a surprising omission if that was the point of the NC, since other commands of the Decalogue are well-represented.[102] This observation reinforces doubts about traditional readings of the NC, particularly for advocates of Deuteronomy's Decalogic structure.

Even among those who reject the Decalogic structure of Deuteronomy, there is widespread agreement that the book unpacks the significance of the Decalogue by applying it to particular situations.[103] It is no surprise, then, that we find multiple instructions related to a representational reading of the NC (e.g., Deut 14:1–2; 18:6–7, 18–22; 21:5; 26:18–19), but no treatment of oath taking. The NC was intended to encompass a broad range of behaviors for those who bore YHWH's name among the nations. Israel was a

interpretation suits Deut 14, where Israel's holiness is explicitly mentioned as a preface to the food laws. Since YHWH's name marks Israel as the elect, the NC resonates here.

100. Kilchör, *Mosetora und Jahwetora*, 96–108.

101. Though Otto relates Deut 15 to the NC, it corresponds more closely to the Sabbath Command because it speaks of cancelling debts in the seventh year (cf. the seventh-day rest) and regulates treatment of household servants. Furthermore, firstborn animals are not to be put "to work" (Deut 15:19; cf. Sabbath rest).

102. The deuteronomic Torah bans magic (Deut 18:9–13), false prophecy (18:17–22), unfulfilled vows (23:21–23), and commercial dishonesty (25:13–16). Two earlier passages mention oaths (Deut 6:13; 10:20). However, if these are echoes of the NC, they do not appear where advocates of the decalogic structure of Deuteronomy expect them.

103. See, e.g., Tigay, *Deuteronomy*, 62; McConville, *Deuteronomy*, 120; Kaiser, *Toward Old Testament Ethics*, 81; Wenham, "Law," *DTIB* 445; Block, "You Shall Not Covet," 143; idem, "Deuteronomy," *DTIB* 170; Miller, "Ten Commandments," in *NIDB* 5:517; Dozeman, *Exodus*, 478; Pleins, *Social Visions*, 50, 60; Kline, "Two Tables," 140; Kline, *Treaty of the Great King*, 33. On the hermeneutical intent of the decalogic structure of Deuteronomy as "addressing the spirit of the law," see Walton, "Deuteronomy," 225; cf. Dillard and Longman, *Introduction to the OT*, 100–101.

holy people, and this status affected every aspect of her daily life, from diet and clothing to the treatment of servants and right worship.

Conclusion: The Decalogue and the Name Command

This chapter has explored the character and context of the Decalogue in order to properly situate the NC in its narrative environment. It has also briefly considered the relationship of the Decalogue to Israel's other constitutional documents. I have argued that the Decalogue did not function as civil legislation in ancient Israel; rather it offered divine guidance to YHWH's covenant people, intended to assure their freedom. Written in duplicate on stone tablets and placed in the ark, the Ten Words outlined what was expected of Israel as a vassal of her divine suzerain, who had graciously rescued her. These words painted a portrait of YHWH's covenant-keeping people, who were to worship YHWH alone and represent him before the nations by ordering their lives and relationships in accordance with his divine will.

The prominence of Sinai in Israel's faith tradition can hardly be overestimated. The Decalogue stands at the peak of the book of Exodus, divinely revealed in a dramatic theophany. The stone tablets occupied the most sacred place of the tabernacle, within the ark inside the holy of holies, symbolizing their centrality to the covenant, and likewise the centrality of the covenant to Israel's faith. Looking at the metanarrative of the Hexateuch, it is significant that the Decalogue was given to a people already redeemed but not yet possessing their inheritance. The liminality of the desert was the ideal place for the Hebrews to become the nation of Israel.

The worldview expressed in the Decalogue undergirds other Torah regulations, which flesh out specific behaviors that fall outside the boundaries of YHWH's will. These instructions revealed God's will for particular situations. They were obligatory, but neither inflexible nor impossible to keep (4:8; 30:11–13). In each new situation, YHWH guided his people in adapting the commands for a new context.

The representational reading of the NC suits this wider narrative context where election and covenant take center stage. It fits the Decalogic structure of Deuteronomy more naturally than others and accounts for the virtual absence of commands on oath taking in the deuteronomic Torah. Together with the first command, it reinforces the covenant formula, "I will be your God; you will be my people."

Chapter 5

Bearing YHWH's Name at Sinai

> Metaphors *teach*, and they do so by reorienting the reader's perception.
>
> —William P. Brown, "The Didactic Power of Metaphor"

Conceptual Metaphor in Biblical Literature

In addition to careful lexical and historical work, as well as analysis of literary context, an accurate understanding of the NC requires a consideration of its metaphoricity. Traditionally speaking, Exod 20:7 contains no metaphor, if the figure of speech is defined narrowly as "a declaration that one thing is (or represents) another" (THIS IS THAT).[1] However, if we attend to the implicit or conceptual metaphors that shape patterns of speech, new ways of thinking about the NC become possible.

A "conceptual metaphor" is an analogical word-picture that exists as a feature of thought, shaping how reality is perceived and, consequently, expressed in a variety of ways. Conceptual metaphors are implicit, rather than explicit, and therefore part of cognitive linguistics. In the words of George Lakoff and Mark Johnson, "Metaphors allow us to understand one domain of experience in terms of another."[2] They offer the example, TIME IS MONEY, a conceptual metaphor that influences a host of linguistic expressions, such as "You're *wasting* my time," "How do you *spend* your time?" and "That flat tire *cost* me an hour."[3] Whether or not we are conscious of them, conceptual metaphors shape speech and behavior. Contrary to the misconceptions of some, the search for conceptual metaphor is not based primarily on etymological concerns or the nature of the Hebrew language, nor on an attempt to psychoanalyze the author(s) or recover the ancient Hebrew mindset but

---

1. Bullinger, *Figures of Speech*, 735. For Bullinger only "distinct affirmation" counts as metaphor. He laments that "metaphorical" is used too loosely. This project follows the practice conventional among cognitive linguists of designating the source and target domains of a metaphor in small capital letters. A source domain is the concrete image employed to understand the more abstract target domain.

2. George Lakoff and Mark Johnson, *Metaphors We Live By* (Chicago: University of Chicago Press, 1980), 117.

3. See ibid., 7–8.

rather is rooted in patterns of actual language use whereby one concept is presented in terms of another.[4]

Metaphor theory is a burgeoning area of study for biblical scholars, many of whom are beginning to move beyond the classical Western notion of metaphor. Plato avoided metaphor, viewing it as inferior to Essence or Ideas,[5] while Aristotle allowed that an appropriate metaphor could be effective rhetorically.[6] The legacy of these classical Greek scholars, especially Plato, was a largely negative opinion of metaphor and an inattention to the cognitive processes that produce and recognize metaphor. However, more recently, biblical scholars have begun to draw on the insights of philosophical and cognitive linguists to help them understand and appreciate metaphor in the Bible. These scholars contend that metaphors are not merely stylistic or ornamental, but significantly shape our cognition.[7] A metaphor is more than the sum of its parts; it creates new worlds of possible meaning by triggering "networks of associations."[8]

Zoltán Kövecses offers an accessible yet methodologically rigorous introduction to metaphor, bringing those outside the field of cognitive linguistics up-to-date on the developments since Lakoff and Johnson's seminal work.[9] He demonstrates not only the intricate complexity of conceptual metaphors, but also their ubiquity in everyday communication. While poetry is known for its creative and unconventional metaphorical expressions, metaphor is an unavoidable part of the communicative process in ordinary conversations as well. Conceptual metaphors organize the way we all think about reality. These metaphors operate systemically and systematically, so that the potential motivations for a given expression may be reliably assessed.

---

4. Job Jindo ("Toward the Poetics of the Biblical Mind: Language, Culture, and Cognition," *VT* 59 [2009]: 222–43) explains, "Metaphors are 'mappings of structure' from one domain onto another. They thereby constitute a cognitive paradigm in light of which the language user organizes his or her complex knowledge of what is described metaphorically."

5. Bonnie Howe, *Because You Bear This Name: Conceptual Metaphor and the Moral Meaning of 1 Peter*, BIS 81 (Boston: Brill, 2006), 13–21.

6. On Aristotle's legacy, see Weiss, *Figurative Language*, 1–10. Howe (*Because You Bear This Name*, 11–27) recognizes some continuity between Aristotle and cognitive metaphor theory and blames Plato for negativity toward metaphor.

7. For many biblical scholars, *Metaphors We Live By* was a gateway to metaphor theory. However, some criticize Lakoff and Johnson for focusing almost exclusively on cognition at the expense of linguistic expressions. See Weiss, *Figurative Language*, 15–17.

8. Some metaphors draw on conventionalized language patterns or concepts, but others are innovative. See Alison Ruth Gray, "Psalm 18 in Words and Pictures: A Reading through Metaphor" (Ph.D. diss., Selwyn College, 2012), 18, 22; William P. Brown, "The Didactic Power of Metaphor in the Aphoristic Sayings of Proverbs," *JSOT* 29 (2004): 136; Lam, *Patterns of Sin*, 4.

9. Kövecses, *Metaphor*.

Table 12. Conceptual Metaphors in the Exodus Decalogue

20:2b	מארץ מצרים מבית עבדים	"from the land of Egypt, from the *house* of *slaves*"	A COUNTRY IS A DOMICILE; PART FOR WHOLE; MEMBER OF A CATEGORY FOR THE CATEGORY[10]
20:3	לֹא יהיה־לך אלהים אחרים על־פני	"you shall have no other gods *before me*"	RELATIONSHIP IS SPATIAL LOCATION;[11] PROXIMITY IS PRIORITY
20:4b	וכל־תמונה אשר בשמים ממעל	"or any likeness of what is *in the heavens above*"	REALM AS CONTAINER
20:5a	לא־תשתחוה להם	"you shall not *bow down* to them"	ACTION STANDS FOR DISPOSITION; PART FOR WHOLE
20:5b	פקד עון אבת על־בנים	"*attending to* the iniquity of the *fathers upon* the *sons*"	ACTION STANDS FOR DISPOSITION; SIN IS A BURDEN; MEMBER OF GROUP STANDS FOR WHOLE GROUP
20:5c	על־שלשים ועל־רבעים	"upon the *third* and upon the *fourth*"	NUMBER OF GENERATION STANDS FOR GENERATION (ellipsis)
20:5c 20:6a	לשׂנאי לאהבי	"those who *hate* me" "those who *love* me"	HATE STANDS FOR DEMONSTRATED COVENANT UNFAITHFULNESS; LOVE STANDS FOR DEMONSTRATED COVENANT FAITHFULNESS2[12]

Joseph Lam offers a biblical case study utilizing this broader definition of metaphor. For Lam, metaphors are rhetorical "vehicles" used to convey meaning in a particularly striking way.[13] Instead of isolating single words, Lam calls on interpreters to analyze a wider scope of metaphorical concepts together (as he has done with the sin-concept). When a constellation of figurative expressions is recognized, the underlying metaphorical concept may be identified and explored.[14]

Without this recognition of metaphoricity, something is irretrievably lost. The rhetorical contribution of a metaphor cannot be fully conveyed with non-metaphorical language because metaphors configure the way we

10. Slaves represented just one of many types of people living in Egypt during that period. But here, the entire society was conceived of as a "house of slaves."

11. This passage implies more than the physical arrangement of images in the Most Holy Place; YHWH's people were not even to consider any other rival gods.

12. These metonymical meanings for "love" and "hate" are a standardized part of the semantic range of these verbs in treaty contexts. See Weinfeld, *Deuteronomy and the Deuteronomic School*, 333.

13. Lam, *Patterns of Sin*, 6–8.

14. Ibid., 10–14, 210.

Table 12. Conceptual Metaphors in the Exodus Decalogue (cont.)

20:6a	לאלפים	"to *thousands*"	LARGE NUMBER STANDS FOR AN UNLIMITED AMOUNT; perhaps NUMBER OF GENERATION STANDS FOR GENERATION (ellipsis)
20:6b	ולשמרי מצותי	"to those who *keep my commands*"	AN UTTERANCE IS AN OBJECT; ATTENTIVE OBEDIENCE IS PHYSICALLY GUARDING AN OBJECT
20:8 (cf. v.11)	זכור את־יום השבת לקדשו	"remember the Sabbath day, by *consecrating it*"	TIME IS SPACE or TIME IS AN OBJECT
20:10	וגרך אשר בשעריך	"nor a foreigner who [is] *in your gates*"	PART FOR WHOLE; BOUNDARY STANDS FOR CONTAINED AREA; GATE STANDS FOR PROTECTION
20:11	את־השמים ואת־הארץ את־הים ואת־כל־אשר־בם	"the heavens and the earth, the sea *and all that is in them*"	SPACE IS A CONTAINER
20:12b	למען יארכון ימיך	"that your *days may be lengthened*"	LIFE IS A DAY or DAY STANDS FOR TIME; TIME IS DISTANCE; DISTANCE IS QUANTITY
20:13 (cf. v.14)	לא־תענה ברעך עד שקר	"you shall not respond to *your neighbor* (with) false testimony"	SOCIETY IS A NEIGHBORHOOD; PART FOR WHOLE; PERSON STANDS FOR AN ACCUSATION

think and act. An overly concrete reading of a metaphor dissolves the creative tension and distorts the meaning.[15]

Conceptual Metaphor at Sinai

Regulatory material is not the first place we would expect to find metaphor. But a careful perusal of the Decalogue and its literary context yields a host of metaphorical examples. Table 12 includes some of the clearest evidence, but other examples could no doubt be cited.[16]

15. Leo G. Perdue, *The Collapse of History: Reconstructing Old Testament Theology*, Overtures to Biblical Theology (Minneapolis, MN: Fortress, 1994), 204, 206; Weiss, *Figurative Language*, 219; Gray, *Psalm* 18 in Words and Pictures, 18; Brown, "The Didactic Power of Metaphor," 152; Carol A. Newsom, "A Maker of Metaphors: Ezekiel's Oracles against Tyre," in *"The Place Is Too Small for Us": The Israelite Prophets in Recent Scholarship*, ed. R. P. Gordon, SBTS 5 (Winona Lake, IN: Eisenbrauns, 1995), 192; Job Y. Jindo, *Biblical Metaphor Reconsidered: A Cognitive Approach to Poetic Prophecy in Jeremiah 1–24*, HSM 64 (Winona Lake, IN: Eisenbrauns, 2010), 32; Anderson, *Sin*, 4, 6, 13.

16. Many of the conceptual metaphors and metonymies mentioned below are discussed in Kövecses' *Metaphor: An Introduction* with English-language examples. Cognitive

Table 13. Conceptual Metaphor in the Name Command

Exod 20:7	לא תשא את־שם־יהוה אלהיך לשוא	"you shall not *bear the name* of YHWH, your God, in vain"	PLACING THE NAME IS CLAIMING OWNERSHIP; ELECTION IS BRANDING; OBEDIENCE IS A JOURNEY

Metaphor is common enough in instructional material; we need not doubt its presence in the NC on the basis of genre. Attention to conceptual metaphor reveals how pervasive it is in the surrounding chapters of Exodus as well. With this background in view, we now consider the NC itself (table 13).

I propose that the NC exhibits metonymy embedded in metaphor,[17] where NAME stands for YHWH'S CLAIM TO OWNERSHIP (declared at Sinai) and BEARING uses the metaphorical source domain of a JOURNEY to convey a charge to obedience. The Israelites are to conduct themselves as covenant members should in the sight of the nations. If merely "lifting" (raising or exalting) the name were intended, the Hebrew רום would have been more appropriate.[18] As it is, נשא usually implies forward movement, carrying something somewhere.[19] The command assumes that the NAME has been placed on the people, and that they therefore carry it. We will return to the JOURNEY concept below.

BRANDING is an appropriate source domain with which to describe this phenomenon for two reasons. First, the priestly blessing utilizes the language of physical branding to "put" (שׂים) YHWH's name on the Israelites (Num 6:27). In Gen 4:15, YHWH "put" (שׂים) a mark on Cain that others could see.[20] In addition, the Akkadian cognate to נשׂא, *našû*, was used to speak of "bearing" a brand.[21] While the cluster of idioms related to "placing the name" draws on the monumental tradition and usually evokes a stone inscription, "placing the name" on a person more naturally suggests a brand.

Second, the mapping of the conceptual domain BRANDING onto the conceptual domain ELECTION highlights a systematic set of associations (table 14), with implications for how Israel's election is conceived and expressed

linguists conventionally render conceptual metaphors using the formula A IS B or A AS B, and conceptual metonymy as A STANDS FOR B or A FOR B. These are not ontological statements but rather the explicit identification of source and target domains for an unstated but verifiably present metaphorical concept. The use of small capital letters signals this. On the degree to which conceptual metaphors are universal, see Kövecses, *Metaphor*, 195–213. Conceptual metaphors based on physiological experiences often happen across cultural boundaries.

17. For a general discussion of this phenomenon, see Kövecses, *Metaphor*, 187–88.

18. Note the exclusively vertical dimension of רום in *DCH* 7:441.

19. Unlike רום, נשׂא (*qal*) never connotes exaltation (*DCH* 5:758) but often describes forward movement (*DCH* 5:763–65). See also the appendix of this volume.

20. As noted by Bar-Ilan, "They Shall Put My Name," 24. Jacobs ("The Body Inscribed," 9–12) compares שׂים to its Akkadian cognate *šamātu*, which denoted the placing of a brand on a temple servant. See also Dougherty, *The Shirkûtu*, 78–91.

21. *CAD* N/2 80, 86.

Table 14. Conceptual Mapping of Election in Terms of Branding

Concrete Source: BRANDING	Abstract Target: ELECTION
the branded	Israel
the brander	YHWH (or his priests)
the act of branding	the priestly blessing
the brand	YHWH's Name
the social dynamic	the nations are aware
the result	possession / loyal service

in terms of selection, ownership, loyal service, protection, and even representation. Branded slaves bear the name of their owner (human or divine) so that their social status is permanently and publicly conspicuous.[22] Reading the NC in light of this conceptual metaphor with its associated inferences not only clarifies its meaning but also brings it into conversation with related texts, which together contribute to a biblical theology of election.

The origins of this conceptual metaphor lie in the ancient cultural practices of claiming ownership orally or by affixing one's name to something by sealing, inscription, or branding. The "perceived structural similarity" between these various methods of claiming ownership facilitated the application of terms from one domain (physical) to another (oral) and triggered a network of metaphorical extensions and entailments.[23]

A related entailment of the metaphorical expression *bear the name* is that YHWH's REPUTATION is at stake. This association is a natural result of two phenomena: (1) the potential for this association intrinsic to the concept of branding, especially with temple slaves, and (2) the idiomatic and/or metonymic use of NAME in both cases. While it would be illegitimate to suggest that every potential meaning of the lexeme שֵׁם is activated by any expression that contains שֵׁם, or that every instance of שֵׁם relates to these metaphors, we can argue that interrelated meanings of שֵׁם may simultaneously influence a choice of idiom, making it especially fitting for a particular context. Recent studies confirm "the comprehension of metaphorical expressions . . . *always* takes place with the simultaneous activation of source domains," even if the activation is subconscious.[24] In this case, since YHWH's NAME is the salient

22. The distinction between branding (burning with an iron implement) and tattooing (subcutaneous insertion of ink with needles) is difficult to discern in ancient literature. See Stolper, "Inscribed in Egyptian," 136 n. 12. Contra C. P. Jones, "Stigma: Tattooing and Branding in Graeco-Roman Antiquity," *JRS* 77 (1987): 139–55. For further discussion of human branding, see Jacobs, "The Body Inscribed," 6–8.

23. On this method, see Kövecses, *Metaphor*, 85. Kövecses (ibid., 325) explains that the "potential entailments" of a given source domain naturally arise from prevailing knowledge about that domain. See also Vyvyan Evans and Melanie Green, *Cognitive Linguistics: An Introduction* (Mahwah, NJ: Erlbaum, 2006), 173.

24. Kövecses, *Metaphor*, 41, emphasis mine.

Table 15. Evidence of the OBEDIENCE IS A JOURNEY Metaphor

Exod 18:20	והודעת להם את־הדרך ילכו בה	"and you shall cause them to know *the path in which they should walk*"[25]
Exod 23:2	לא־תהיה אחרי־רבים לרעת	"you shall not *follow* a multitude in wrongdoing"
Exod 32:8	סרו מהר מן־הדרך אשר צויתם	"they have quickly *turned aside from the path* that I commanded them [to take]"
Lev 20:23	ולא תלכו בחקת הגוי אשר־אני משלח מפניכם	"*you shall not walk* in the statutes of the nations which I am driving out before you"
Lev 26:3	אם־בחקתי תלכו ואת־מצותי תשמרו ועשיתם אתם	"If *you walk* in my statutes and keep my commands in order to do them"
Deut 4:3	כל־האיש אשר הלך אחרי בעל־פעור השמידו יהוה אלהיך מקרבך	"every man who *walked after* Baʿal-Peor YHWH your God destroyed from among you"
Deut 11:26	אם־לא תשמעו אל־מצות יהוה אלהיכם וסרתם מן־הדרך אשר אנכי מצוה אתכם היום ללכת אחרי אלהים אחרים	"if you do not listen to the commands of YHWH your God and *turn aside from the path* which I commanded you this day *to walk after* other gods"
Deut 17:20b	ולבלתי סור מן־המצוה ימין ושמאול	"nor *turn aside* from the commandment *right or left*"

feature of his claim to ownership of the Israelites, biblical authors naturally chose to speak of Israel's failure to obey YHWH as profaning his NAME (reputation), just as the failure to carry out cultic procedures properly would constitute profaning YHWH's NAME in the temple on which he had placed his NAME. Each of these is an extension of the core conceptual metaphor, activated in various contexts by distinct idioms or linguistic expressions.

To say ELECTION IS BRANDING is not to suggest that election actually involved physical branding (contra Bar-Ilan), nor that election was universally or consistently construed as branding. It also does not imply that the connection between these domains was ever explicit. Instead, ELECTION IS BRANDING expresses a concept underlying and giving rise to a number of other linguistic expressions with which we are now familiar: נקרא שם על, לשׂום שמו שם, למען שמו, חלל את־שם, and קדשׁ את־שם, among others.

While נשׂא שם is an unconventional way to activate an unusual metaphor, ELECTION IS BRANDING, the other key concept evoked, OBEDIENCE IS A JOURNEY, is more commonly expressed in a variety of ways. Throughout the Hebrew Bible, the concept of obedience to YHWH's commands is expressed using journey language. A few examples of this ubiquitous motif in the Pentateuch appear in table 15.

25. דרך usually refers to a "path" or "journey," e.g., Exod 3:18; 4:24; 13:17–18; Lev 26:22.

These selected texts illustrate the variety of expressions that manifest an underlying concept of OBEDIENCE TO YHWH AS A JOURNEY. Not only do words such as *path*, *walk*, and *turn aside* express this concept, but elsewhere the verb נשׂא is employed figuratively with reference to Israel's journey:

Numbers 11:12, 14 (cf. 17)

האנכי הריתי את כל־העם הזה	"Did I conceive this whole people?
אם־אנכי ילדתיהו	Did I give birth to them,
כי־תאמר אלי	that you should say to me,
שׂאהו בחיקך	'*Carry them in your arms!*'
כאשר ישׂא האמן את־הינק	—*just as one who is nursing* ***carries*** *an infant*—
על האדמה אשר נשבעת לאבתיו. . .	to the land you promised to their ancestors? . . .
לא־אוכל אנכי לבד לשׂאת	I am not able alone to ***carry***
את־כל־העם הזה	this whole people,
כי כבד ממני	for it is *too heavy* for me."

We could identify several other related metaphors, such as TO LEAD IS TO BEAR A BURDEN, TO LEAD IS TO PARENT, A LEADER IS A MOTHER, A NATION IS A PERSON, etc. However, here the main point is that נשׂא is used figuratively for bearing a burden, and that it is also the appropriate verb for something *carried* on a literal journey toward a destination. Just as a nursing mother carries an infant, so Moses "carries" Israel on their journey. For him, the burden is not physical, but rather the weight of leadership and decision making (cf. v. 17). This strengthens the feasibility of a metaphorical understanding of נשׂא in the NC as well as its appropriateness in light of the journey metaphor.

Motivation for the Metaphor

But why talk about election in these terms? Why connect ELECTION with the act of BRANDING or OBEDIENCE with a JOURNEY? Kövecses explains that a particular linguistic expression may be motivated by a variety of implicit concepts in combination with conventional knowledge about a subject.[26] We might express the potential influences in the following way:[27]

general conventional knowledge about the FUNCTION OF NAMES IN THE ANE
specific knowledge about the FUNCTION OF NAMES IN ISRAELITE CULTURE[28]
the metonymy NAME STANDS FOR REPUTATION
the metaphor PLACING THE NAME ON SOMETHING IS CLAIMING OWNERSHIP
(arising from the metonymy [INSCRIBED] NAME STANDS FOR OWNERSHIP)
the metaphor PROCLAIMING THE NAME OVER SOMEONE IS CLAIMING OWNERSHIP
(a subset of the generic metaphor CAUSATION IS PHYSICAL TRANSFER)
the metonymy NAME STANDS FOR AUTHORIZATION
the metaphor BEARING THE NAME IS FUNCTIONING AS AN ELECT REPRESENTATIVE
(a subset of the metaphor THE SOCIAL WORLD IS THE PHYSICAL WORLD[29])

26. Kövecses, *Metaphor*, 245.
27. For a similar list of concepts in English relating to the hand, see ibid., 243.
28. For example, seals, branding, inscriptions, monuments, marriage contracts, etc.
29. That is, the epistemic nature of belonging and of representation are depicted in physical terms. See Kövecses, *Metaphor*, 255.

The conceptual metaphors and metonymies *available* to a speaker represent only one piece to the puzzle of motivation. Kövecses writes on the effects of physical, social, and cultural settings on a speaker's choice of metaphor, suggesting that together these exert the "pressure of coherence" on any given communicative event.[30] In this case, the journey motif was ideally suited for the narrative setting at Sinai. נשׂא שׁם is an unconventional expression arising from the inherent uniqueness of that event, motivated by a convergence of factors, including the revealed significance of YHWH's name, the conventional idioms for expressing a claim of ownership, the recounting of a physical journey through the wilderness, and Israel's formation as a people through the covenant at Sinai. Because the metaphor OBEDIENCE IS A JOURNEY is highly conventionalized, it is difficult to conceive of the life of faith/obedience without reference to forward movement (cf. Table 15).[31] This unique expression, נשׂא שׁם, which accesses the journey metaphor (in part) is especially fitting since the literary setting for this command in Exodus is the retelling of Israelites' journey to Canaan, during which their obedience to YHWH involved traversing the wilderness in the "sight" of the nations.[32] The wilderness narrative provided an arena in which the Israelites were clearly associated with YHWH and clearly in the purview of nations who were disposed to feel threatened, admiring, or skeptical.[33]

To think of election in these terms generates a field of associations (or entailments) and therefore expressions that would not otherwise be possible, such as profaning the name through immoral behavior or sanctifying the name through God-honoring behavior. How else could we account for these other expressions without acknowledging the conceptual metaphor ELECTION AS BRANDING or its corollary, NAME FOR REPUTATION, and the governing metaphor OBEDIENCE AS A JOURNEY?

Misinterpretation of the Metaphor

Metaphorical expressions based on conceptual metaphor are powerful communicative devices, but they come with inherent risks. The potential for misunderstanding is probably in inverse proportion to the semantic capital of a given metaphor; the more innovative the expression, the more thought provoking, and also the most likely to be "missed." Given the wilderness context, the NC was especially compelling and its imagery precisely appropriate. However, its saliency for future generations depended on their seeing themselves as sojourners at Sinai. In more-or-less settled

30. Ibid., 295–98.

31. On the conventionalization of metaphor, see Evans and Green, *Cognitive Linguistics*, 733–34.

32. This, too, is a metaphor: KNOWING IS SEEING, a subset of THE MIND IS THE BODY. The nations heard reports of Israel's travels but did not physically see them all transpire.

33. For example, Num 22:11.

eras, the potency of the language describing OBEDIENCE AS A JOURNEY may have diminished, resulting in greater risk of missing the point, and as a consequence reducing the perception of metaphorical expression נשׂא שׁם to an elliptical one.

The predilection toward connecting NAME with speech in the past is responsible for much of the misinterpretation of the NC. Proper recognition of the range of ways that NAME functioned historically—including metonymically and metaphorically—allows us to apprehend its true sense in the NC and avoid the pitfalls of some of the more common interpretations. All—NAME FOR REPUTATION, NAME FOR CLAIM TO OWNERSHIP, and NAME FOR AUTHORIZATION—are evident in the Sinai narratives and their near contexts.

The Concept of Name Bearing at Sinai

Given the multitude of potential motivations for the expression נשׂא שׁם, we will do well to examine the immediate context for analogues. In fact, the complex interaction of conceptual metaphor and metonymic expression is concretized in two distinct characters in the Sinai narratives of Exodus, each of which evinces a special connection with YHWH's "name." As such, either could shed further light on the concept of "name bearing" found in the NC. The first is the enigmatic reference to YHWH's envoy who led the Hebrews through the wilderness, of whom YHWH said, "My name is in him" (Exod 23:21). The second is Aaron, selected to become high priest and to "bear the names" of the Israelite tribes on his person and to wear the name of YHWH on his forehead as he entered the sanctuary (Exod 28:12, 29, 36–38). In order to assess the relevance of either figure to the interpretation of the NC, we must determine (as much as it is possible) his nature and function.

Exodus 23: YHWH's Envoy

The mention of YHWH's envoy seems abrupt and mysterious. Directly on the heels of the Book of the Covenant, several chapters of specific instructions regarding everything from agriculture to festivals and from bride prices to restitution, YHWH announced a change in topic with the deictic particle, "Look!" (הנה), followed by a verbless (participial) sentence (אנכי שׁלח מלאך).[34] In spite of the grammatical disjuncture, this section belongs conceptually with the covenant stipulations that precede it because it

34. On the disjunctive nature of verbless clauses in discourse, see Alviero Niccacci, "Workshop: Narrative Syntax of Exodus 19–24," in *Narrative Syntax and the Hebrew Bible: Papers of the Tilburg Conference 1996*, ed. Ellen van Wolde (Leiden: Brill, 2002), 167–202. On the "marked" character of a verbless clause with an extra constituent ahead of the subject, see Randall Buth, "Word Order in a Verbless Clause," in *The Verbless Clause in Biblical Hebrew: Linguistic Approaches*, ed. Cynthia L. Miller, *LSAWS* 1 (Winona Lake, IN: Eisenbrauns, 1999), 105.

continues to address the people as a whole. In Exod 24:1, YHWH addresses Moses directly, signaling a shift.[35]

Exodus 23:20–21

הנה אנכי שלח מלאך לפניך	Look, I am sending an envoy before you
לשמרך בדרך	to guard you along the way
ולהביאך אל־המקום	and to bring you to the place
אשר הכנתי	that I have determined.
השמר מפניו	Be on your guard before him[36]
ושמע בקלו	and listen to his voice.
אל־תמר בו	Do not rebel[3] against him
כי לא ישא לפשעכם	for he will not forgive your transgression
<u>כי שמי בקרבו</u>	**for my name is in him.**

The placement of this "envoy" pericope as the conclusion to the Covenant Code underscores the dynamic nature of obedience to YHWH and his representatives. A written code alone is insufficient for the life of faith. YHWH's vassals were expected to actively depend upon him as they left Sinai. According to Exodus 23, YHWH's envoy would provide at least four things for the Israelites: (1) protection on their journey (שמר; v. 20), (2) guidance to the land God promised them (v. 20, 23),[38] (3) ongoing instruction as they traveled (v. 22), and (4) leadership in battle after they entered the land (v. 23; cf. 33:2). Adding to the enigmatic nature of this passage is the reference to two other entities that YHWH promised to "send ahead" (שלח לפניך): terror and hornets (Exod 23:27–28). The former would cause confusion among the residents of Canaan, causing them to flee. The latter would

35. The change in addressee is signaled by the placement of the prepositional phrase ואל־משה before the finite verb אמר in 24:1. See Barry L. Bandstra, "Word Order and Emphasis in Biblical Hebrew Narrative: Syntactic Observations on Genesis 22 from a Discourse Perspective," in *Linguistics and Biblical Hebrew*, ed. Walter R. Bodine (Winona Lake, IN: Eisenbrauns, 1992), 123. For a discourse analysis of the Covenant Code that supports this delimitation (Exod 20:18–23:33), see Niccacci, "Workshop: Narrative Syntax of Exodus 19–24."

36. Or "on account of him"; *DCH* 8:483.

37. The MT reads תַּמֵּר, hiphil of מרר, "to be bitter." See *DCH* 5:493–94. However, the editors suggest an emendation to תֶּמֶר, hiphil of מרה, "to be rebellious (against)." See *DCH* 5:480. In no other passage is מרר followed by a ב prefix with pronominal suffix, but for מרה, see Ezek 20:8, 13, 21. Furthermore, LXX reads πείθει, "disobey." While not decisive, the proposed emendation seems reasonable.

38. Richter (*DH and Name Theology*, 54–55) identifies המקום here with "the place" of Deut 12. While המקום sometimes refers specifically to "the place YHWH will choose" as a central sanctuary, it is not always a technical term for sacred space (see Exod 3:5; 17:7; 20:24). Here it probably bears the same meaning as in Num 10:29: "the place of which YHWH said, 'I will give it to you,'" that is, the whole land of Canaan. Cf. Num 14:40; 20:5; Deut 1:31; 9:7; 11:5; 26:9. Note that the location had already been determined (*hiphil* of כון; v. 21; cf. Deut 12:5). Sarna (*Exodus*, 148) considers the possibility that the whole land was considered sacred.

drive out these inhabitants. However, in the following verses YHWH himself drives them out (vv. 29–30). The actions of YHWH's authorized representatives therefore merge with his own.[39]

For their part, the people were to be "on their guard" (*niphal* שמר; v. 21), obeying both YHWH and his agent (v. 22), and serving YHWH rather than the gods or peoples of Canaan (v. 24–25, 26). Note the word play: while the envoy was to "guard" (*qal* שמר; v. 20) the people, their responsibility was to "guard themselves" (*niphal* השמר; v. 21), making sure they maintained faithful obedience. Human submission and divine protection went hand in hand.

Most intriguing for this project are the two motivation statements in v. 21: "For he will not forgive your transgression (נשׂא לפשׁעכם), for my name is within him (שמי בקרבו)." Here נשׂא exhibits the lexicalized meaning, "forgive."[40] But *why* will YHWH's agent not forgive rebellion? Is it because God alone can forgive (cf. Exod 34:7a)? Or is it because he represents God, who takes sin seriously and will not overlook it (cf. Exod 34:7b)? If the second motivation clause is taken as a further explanation of the first, then the latter is more likely.[41] Because YHWH's name is "in" his agent, he functions

39. Similarly, YHWH's partnership with Israel is evident in vv. 29–31. First, YHWH says of the residents of Canaan, "I will drive them out" (v. 30). Then he explains, "I will deliver the inhabitants of the land into *your* hand and *you* will drive them out" (v. 31, emphasis mine). The envoy cannot have been Moses or Joshua. In Exod 32:34, God told Moses, "My envoy will go before you." The envoy also appears to Moses in Exod 3:2 and to the whole congregation in Exod 14:19, distinguished from the pillar of cloud. Moses is clearly not the envoy. Contra R. A. Cole, *Exodus*, TOTC (Downers Grove, IL: InterVarsity, 1973), 181. Likewise, nearing Jericho, Joshua encountered the envoy, who identified himself as the "captain of YHWH's army" (Josh 5:13–15). The agent is also distinguished from YHWH. Following the sin of the golden calf, YHWH told Moses, "I will send an envoy before you . . . but *I* will not go with you, because you are a stiff-necked people and I might destroy you on the way" (Exod 33:2–3, emphasis mine). In each of these cases, the agent is a distinct third party. Contra Durham (*Exodus*, 335), who suggests that YHWH is the envoy. López ("Identifying the 'Angel of the Lord' in the Book of Judges: A Model for Reconsidering the Referent in Other Old Testament Loci," *BBR* 20 [2010]: 4, 8) notes other ANE examples of messengers who spoke on behalf of a deity in first person and yet were addressed by the deity in second person. For a critical response to López, see Andrew S. Malone, "Distinguishing the Angel of the Lord," *BBR* 21 (2011): 297–314. Propp (*Exodus 19–40*, 287) concludes that the messenger is deliberately ambiguous, leaving God several options for how to lead his people into Canaan. For a strong argument highlighting the problems with seeing the messenger as the preincarnate Christ, see William Graham MacDonald, "Christology and 'The Angel of the Lord,'" in *Current Issues in Biblical and Patristic Interpretation: Studies in Honor of Merrill C. Tenney Presented by His Former Students*, ed. Gerald F. Hawthorne (Grand Rapids: Eerdmans, 1975), 324–35.

40. Lexicalization is evident because נשׂא is followed by לפשׁעכם, bringing the syntax into conformity with the verb סלח, which means "forgive" and is always followed by an object with a *lamed* prefix. For a fuller discussion, see p. 90 n. 157, above.

41. Houtman (*Exodus*, 3:274–75) concludes the opposite—that forgiveness is "solely YHWH's prerogative"—in part because after the golden calf incident YHWH extended forgiveness. However, he punished them for that sin (Exod 32:33–35).

Table 16. A Comparison of Priestly Garments[42]

(High-) Priestly Garments* בגדי־קדש	*Exod 28:4 Order of observation*	*Exod 28:6–43 Instructions for crafting*	*Exod 29:5–9 Instructions for dressing [priests]*	*Exod 39 Order of crafting*	*Lev 8:7–9 Order of dressing*
*breastpiece חשן	1	2	4	2	6
*ephod אפד	2	1	3	1	4
*band חשב			5		5
*robe מעיל	3	3	2	3	3
tunic כתנת	4	5	1 [1]	4	1
*turban מצנפת	5	6	6	5	7
*diadem ציץ		4	7	9	8
sash אבנט	6	7	[2]	8	2
[headgear] מגבעה	—	8	[3]	6	—
[breeches] מכנסי־בד	—	9	—	7	—

as an authorized representative, and therefore must treat sin with all the seriousness it deserves. God's envoy was not like a substitute teacher who had little power to stop the abuse of unwilling students. He would not tolerate rebellion in any form. To disobey him was as grievous as disobeying YHWH himself (cf. Josh 24:19–20).

The expression שמי בקרבו is unique to Exod 23:21; nowhere else is YHWH's name said to be "in" or "within" someone or something.[43] Based on the duties assigned to the envoy and the synthetic presentation of these activities with those of YHWH himself, we can safely assume that he functioned as YHWH's authorized representative in a way distinct from the nation of Israel. Because YHWH's name was "in" him, he acted in YHWH's stead.[44] Therefore it does not provide a direct analog or lexical connection to the NC. However, it is evident that the expression, "my name is in him," and the associated entailments of authority and representation draw on similar concepts.

42. The asterisk (*) indicates garments worn only by the high priest. Brackets [ ] indicate garments worn by ordinary priests.

43. It is possible that the author's choice of שְׁמִי בְּקִרְבּוֹ may have been influenced by sound patterning with the phrase וּשְׁמַע בְּקֹלוֹ in the previous line, linking the desired action with its motivation. On בקרבו as "within," see *DCH* 7:313–14. This is a strange preposition. This form is often found where a plural suffix might be expected (e.g., Gen 24:3; Num 14:11; Judg 1:30). However, in Hebrew "a people" or "a tribe" is grammatically singular. Analogous instances with regard to a single human subject include 1 Sam 25:37, 1 Kgs 3:28; Job 20:14; Ps 109:18; Isa 63:11; Hab 2:19; and Zech 12:1.

44. For an extended discussion of human or angelic figures who received the divine name, see Jarl E. Fossum, *The Name of God and the Angel of the Lord*, WUNT 36 (Tübingen: Mohr Siebeck, 1985), esp. pp. 87–106.

Exodus 28: YHWH's High Priest

At last we have occasion to explore the passage that shares with the NC both narrative context (Sinai) as well as linguistic expression (נשׂא שׁם). At first glance, the high priestly regalia has little in common with the NC—worn only by an elite cultic functionary, the ephod bore the literal inscriptions of tribal names. The ephod seems unrelated to the prohibition for every Israelite not to bear YHWH's name in vain. However, an extended exploration of this regalia along with its purpose, functional significance, and its place in the larger discourse will prove illuminating.

Aaron's high priestly garments distinguished him from every other Israelite, including other priests. While ordinary priests wore fine white linen breeches, caps, and tunics tied with an embroidered sash (Exod 28:39–43), Aaron's regalia also included a decorated blue robe, a golden ephod, and a breastpiece studded with gold and jewels. On his head he wore a fine turban with an engraved gold diadem. On only one occasion annually was Aaron to wear the plain linen garments of the common priesthood (Lev 16:4)[45]—namely, on the Day of Atonement when he entered the Most Holy Place. Otherwise Aaron donned his splendid wardrobe, a signal of his status and responsibility, comparable to royal garments of neighboring cultures.[46]

45. The linen of the priestly garments is variously described as בד or שׁשׁ. While שׁשׁ signifies an especially fine linen, בד does not necessarily connote a fabric of lesser quality. It may simply mean linen in general. The terms appear in apposition in 1QM7_{10}, and are used both together and interchangeably to describe the priestly attire (cf. the undergarments in Exod 28:42 [מכנסי־בד] and Exod 39:28 [מכנסי הבד שׁשׁ משׁזר]; or the tunic in Exod 28:39 [הכתנת שׁשׁ] and Lev 16:4 [כתנת־בד]). See also *DCH* 8:572. Contra Wenham, *The Book of Leviticus*, 230. Curiously, Haran (*Temples and Temple-Service in Ancient Israel: An Inquiry into Biblical Cult Phenomena and the Historical Setting of the Priestly School* [Winona Lake, IN: Eisenbrauns, 1985], 174) supposes that Aaron's garments for the Day of Atonement were of better quality than his regular linen vestments.

46. When we examine garments across the ANE spanning several millennia, a number of analogues from ancient Egypt and Mesopotamia stand out. Garments of comparable quality and style to Aaron's were typically associated with royal, priestly, or divine figures. Similarities in construction of Egyptian royal garments with the Israelite high priest include an ornamented headdress, several layers of clothing including a long tunic and decorative apron with a belt or sash, a wide collar, and (sometimes) bare feet. Mesopotamian royalty often wore short-sleeved, ankle-length tunics with aprons, fringes, and soft headpieces. Set as it was in the pre-Monarchic period of Israel's history, the instructions at Sinai included no official role for a king in the worship of YHWH, and nowhere was the clothing for an Israelite king prescribed. It is fitting that the regalia of the high priest would communicate the prestige and power normally reserved for royalty; after all, Aaron serves in the palace of the divine King.

On clothing in the ANE, see James Laver, *Costume in Antiquity* (London: Thames & Hudson, 1964); Eleanor Guralnick, "Fabric Patterns as Symbols of Status in the Near East and Early Greece," in *Reading a Dynamic Canvas: Adornment in the Ancient Mediterranean World*, ed. Cynthia S. Colburn and Maura K. Heyn (Newcastle, UK: Cambridge Scholars Press, 2008), 84–114; Eleanor Guralnick, "Neo-Assyrian Patterned Fabrics," *Iraq* 66 (2004): 221–32; Marie-Louise Nosch and C. Michel Nosch, eds., *Textile Terminologies*

Figure 11. Priestly garments (ordered according to Leviticus 8:7–9)

Cast as divine speech at Sinai, the instructions identify these as "sacred vestments" (בגדי־קדש), crafted "for dignity and for splendor" (לכבוד ולתפארת; Exod 28:2, 40), appropriate for the splendid tabernacle where God's glory was manifest.[47] As the most elaborately dressed Israelite, the high priest's status was unmistakable. Furthermore, the well-being of the entire nation rested on his shoulders, a fact made explicit by him bearing the onyx stones inscribed with the names of all 12 tribes.

Aaron's Regalia

Several passages describe these articles of clothing. Variations in the order of garments depend on the list's purpose (table 16, p. 152). Exodus 28:4 lists six garments in summary, in the order in which they would have been perceived. Exodus 28:6–43 offers detailed instructions for fashioning all nine items, proceeding from the costliest to the most common.[48] Exodus 39:1–31 describes the crafting of the nine garments in the order they were produced.[49] Leviticus 8:7–9 lists eight items in the order in which the high priest was clothed (fig. 11).[50] No list includes footwear; most likely

in the Ancient Near East and the Mediterranean Area from the 3rd to the 1st Millennium BC, Ancient Textiles 8 (Oxford: Oxbow, 2010); Cynthia S. Colburn, *Reading a Dynamic Canvas: Adornment in the Ancient Mediterranean World* (Newcastle, UK: Cambridge Scholars, 2008); Gillian Vogelsang-Eastwood, *Pharaonic Egyptian Clothing*, Studies in Textile and Costume History 2 (Leiden: Brill, 1993); A. Leo Oppenheim, "The Golden Garments of the Gods," *JNES* 8 (1949): 172–93; Elizabeth Riefstahl, *Patterned Textiles in Pharaonic Egypt* (Brooklyn: Brooklyn Institute of Arts and Sciences, 1944); Henry F. Lutz, *Textiles and Costume among People of the Ancient Near East* (Leipzig: Hinrichs, 1923).

47. NRSV takes בגדי־קדש as a hendiadys: "for glorious adornment." According to Deut 26:19, the whole nation would be exalted in splendor (תפארת). In Isaiah, this term was applied to the remnant of Israel (Isa 4:2; 46:13; 62:3) and to the temple (64:10).

48. Items 1 and 2 (breastpiece and ephod) from Exod 28:4 are reversed in the instructions that follow, perhaps because the breastpiece depends on the ephod to "hang" in place. The rest of the list in Exod 28:6–43 proceeds from the high priestly items that were most expensive and most difficult to make to those worn by all the priests.

49. Why this order differs from the instructions in Exod 28 is unclear.

50. My drawings in fig. 11 illustrate one possible design for these garments.

the priests were to officiate barefoot, as the appropriate response to "holy ground" (cf. Exod 3:5; Josh 5:15).[51]

Based on a careful reading of the tabernacle instructions, Haran notes three levels of quality in the workmanship of these articles of clothing: חשב, רקם, and ארג. The first two involved a combination of dyed wool and linen. Haran suggests that חשב fabric contained figures, especially cherubim, while רקם was a fine mixed fabric without design.[52] The word ארג, on the other hand, was a single-color unmixed fabric, either of wool or linen.[53]

While each article of Aaron's regalia could be studied on its own, this discussion will focus on the items relevant to this project: the ephod (no. 4), breastpiece (no. 6), and turban (no. 7) with its medallion (no. 8). Over time the Hebrew term אפד may have had more than one referent,[54] but in the priestly instructions the word applies to a type of apron made of fine linen material (שׁשׁ) woven with wool dyed blueish-purple, reddish-purple, and crimson in the חשב style.[55] In addition, craftsmen hammered out gold leaf and cut it into threads to work into the design, yielding an ornate and costly garment, perhaps similar to those worn by divine images in other ANE cultures.[56] Between the value of the gold and the exorbitant price of these

51. Contra Ziony Zevit ("Preamble to a Temple Tour," in *Sacred Time, Sacred Place: Archaeology and the Religion of Israel*, ed. Barry M. Gittlen [Winona Lake, IN: Eisenbrauns, 2002], 75), who assumes that priests were shod.

52. Most English translations assume the opposite, translating רקם as "embroidered" (NRSV, NIV, ESV, NLT, NJPS, NET).

53. Haran, *Temples and Temple Service*, 160–61.

54. For example, Samuel wears a linen ephod, though he is not the high priest (1 Sam 2:18). Haulotte (*Symbolique du Vêtement Selon la Bible*, Collection Théologie 65 [Paris: Aubier, 1966], 47, 50–51) suggests that the ephod itself evolved: a simple linen loincloth later became a long band wound above the waist and finally in the Postexilic Period a type of chest apron with 12 engraved stones. Alternatively, we could suppose that the range of meaning for אפד fluctuated over time. P. Jenson ("אֵפוֹד," *NIDOTTE* 1:476–77) suggests that "ephods were found in a variety of different forms, the more practical garments of a simple design and the more ceremonial types made of costly materials and heavily ornamented." All biblical examples are associated with the priesthood.

55. While precisely identifying the colors mentioned in ancient texts is difficult, both blueish-purple and reddish-purple dye were produced along the Mediterranean coast in the biblical period by processing the contents of two types of murex shells, on which, see King and Stager, *Life in Biblical Israel*, 160–61. These discoveries improve on Lutz's earlier suggestion that blue dye was derived from various plants, while purple-red came from henna leaves. See Lutz, *Textiles and Costume*, 77–80.

56. This technology is also attested in Assyrian royal embroidered robes. Lutz, *Textiles and Costume*, 97. See also *HALOT* 1:77. Hebrew אפד is related etymologically to the Old Assyrian *epattu*, a "costly garment," as well as the Hittite *ipantu*, which was worn by a divine image and either adorned with or made of silver. See Harold A. Hoffner, "Hittite Equivalents of Old Assyrian *kumrum* and *epattum*," *WZKM* 86 (1996): 154–56. Other possible analogs include the Ugaritic *ipd* and an apron-like garment associated with royalty/divinity in New Kingdom Egypt. See Bruce Wells, "Exodus," in *ZIBBCOT* 1:253–56.

dyes, the resulting fabric was a fitting choice both for the tapestries of the inner tabernacle and the high priestly garments.

Two shoulder straps and a decorated band (חשב-style) crafted from the same materials secured the אפד around the high priest's shoulders and waist over the blue robe and white linen tunic. Two engraved onyx stones mounted in gold rested on the shoulder straps, attached with gold corded chains to the breastpiece. Each bore the inscribed names of six of the Israelite tribes.

The breastpiece (חשן) was a decorated square pouch worn on the chest of the high priest containing the Urim and Thummim, which facilitated decision making.[57] In style it matched the אפד, woven (חשב-style) with gold, blueish-purple, reddish-purple, and crimson thread and fine white linen. The square measured a hand-breadth wide and was adorned with four rows of precious stones in gold settings.[58] Each bore the name of one of the Israelite tribes, engraved like a seal.[59] Gold corded chains were attached to gold rings at the top corners of the breastpiece and to the shoulder straps of the אפד, while a blue cord joined the breastpiece and אפד at the bottom corners. Of all the priestly garments, this one received the most attention in the priestly instructions. It is the costliest and most elaborate.

Around his head, the high priest wound a linen turban (מצנפת), ornamented with a gold medallion (ציץ) in front, fastened with a blue cord and engraved with the words "Holy, Belonging to YHWH" (קדש ליהוה; Exod 28:36–37).[60] His turban was superior to the caps (מגבעה) of ordinary priests.[61] The shape of the gold medallion is not specified, but the term ציץ can indicate a "blossom" or "flower."[62] It is described epexegetically as a "sacred crown" or "holy diadem" (נזר הקדש; Exod 29:6; cf. 39:30; Lev 8:9).

---

57. The use of the article indicates these were not innovations. So Sarna, *Exodus*, 181.

58. Each row may have featured a single color that varied in intensity from stone to stone. For discussion, see J. S. Harris, "The Stones of the High Priest's Breastplate," ed. John MacDonald, *ALUOS* 5 (1963): 40–62.

59. Harris (ibid., 43) posits that these ancient gemstones would have been cut flat or in rounded hemispheres rather than faceted as modern gems. The passage does not specify whether the engraving was intaglio (so that a clay impression could be read) or was to be read on the stone itself.

60. Given the difficulty of dying linen, the turban was likely white. Contra Wenham, *The Book of Leviticus*, 140. Ancient sources differ regarding the exact content and placement of the engraving. Josephus (*Ant.* 3.7, 6) says only "YHVH" was written in paleo-Hebrew script. I will say more on the meaning of this inscription below.

61. Turbans were associated with royalty (see Ezek 21:31; Isa 62:3), whereas a cap was worn by a bridegroom (Isa 61:10). So Haran, *Temples and Temple Service*, 170.

62. See Num 17:23; 1 Kgs 6:18–29. Note that in the latter passage ציץ refers to carved cedar blossoms plated with gold, decorating the interior of Solomon's temple alongside cherubim, gourds, and palm trees. According to Shabbat 63b, the ציץ was a narrow, oblong gold plate stretching from one ear to the other. However, Sarna notes that a floral diadem would not have been out of the question. Egyptian diadems featured a lotus flower. See Sarna, *Exodus*, 183. Propp (*Exodus 19–40*, 447) suggests a gold plate engraved with a flower and inscribed above or below the design.

Aaron's attire bears material similarities with the tabernacle furnishings.[63] The inner curtains of the tabernacle were woven of fine twisted linen and blueish-purple, reddish-purple, and crimson wool, with two cherubim woven into them (חשב-style; Exod 26:1). Similarly, the veil separating the holy place from the most holy place was woven of fine twisted linen and blueish-purple, reddish-purple, and crimson wool (again, חשב-style; Exod 26:31–33). These correspond in material to Aaron's outer garments, his ephod, breastpiece, and band. The loops to hang the curtains were made of blueish-purple wool, and clasped with gold (Exod 26:4–6), corresponding to Aaron's robe and the cords securing his breastpiece and diadem. Blueish-purple was the most expensive of the dyes.

The outer curtains were made of fine twisted linen (Exod 27:9–15),[64] comparable to the fine linen tunic under Aaron's robe. The screens for the entrance to the tent of meeting and the outer gate were made of blueish-purple, reddish-purple, and crimson with fine twisted linen (רקם-style; Exod 27:16), corresponding to Aaron's embroidered sash. The finest and most colorful fabrics decorated the inner sanctum of the tabernacle, with simpler fabric reserved for the outer courts. The screens were an exception. Entrances to the courtyard and tabernacle exhibited a higher quality than the rest of the perimeter, creating a more lavish East-West axis across sacred space.[65] While ordinary priestly garments corresponded in quality to the outer curtains of the courtyard, the workmanship of the high priestly vestments spanned the whole range from outer to inner furnishings. Haran observes that the high priestly garments inversely corresponded to the gradations of holiness of the tabernacle, with the garments most comparable to the ark worn on the outside and the most common garments underneath.[66]

Why is there so much detail on priestly garments in a book on the NC? A discourse analysis of the tabernacle instructions underscores two key elements, which receive more attention than any other articles: the ark and the ephod. The ark is the central object of worship and is associated with a textual climax regarding YHWH's presence among the Israelites (Exod 25:22). Its purpose is explicitly identified multiple times: to house the עדת, or "covenant tablets" containing the Decalogue (25:16, 21, 22). No comparable purpose statements are made with regard to any other tabernacle furniture or furnishings. Likewise, the instructions for making the ephod and breastpiece are very detailed compared to the other garments, and the engraving

63. So also Sarna, *Exodus*, 184.

64. The style of these curtains is unspecified, but a single-source fabric was normally designated as ארג.

65. Haran, *Temples and Temple Service*, 164–65.

66. Ibid. These gradations of workmanship also correspond to the value of the furniture at each level and the materials used to wrap them during transport. See ibid., 158–59. Propp (*Exodus 19–40*, 528) calls the high priest an "inside-out Tabernacle."

of the names is the climax of these instructions.[67] The depository of the stone tablets and the engraved names are thus the twin pinnacles of the narrative, inviting correlation.

Exodus 25:8 unveils the purpose for the construction of the tabernacle, its furnishings, and the priestly vestments: "And let them construct a sanctuary for me, *so that I may dwell among them*."[68] The tabernacle facilitated the presence of YHWH among his people. The magnificence of its furnishings was appropriate to the glory of the divine resident. Accordingly, the high priest was dressed to reflect his status as the prime functionary in the tabernacle. All the priestly garments were designed "for dignity and for splendor" (לכבוד ולתפארת; Exod 28:2, 40), and while the garments specifically set apart the men who wore them as priests (Exod 28:3), the high priestly garments far exceeded the rest. For the tabernacle to function properly as the cultic center of worship, the purity of priestly clothing had to be maintained.[69] Separation between the high priest and other priests and laypeople was emphasized by the prohibition of wool and linen blends in common clothing as well as the ban on personal use of the sanctuary recipes for anointing oil or incense (Exod 30:22–38).[70]

It was also made explicit by the words engraved on his medallion, קדש ליהוה, which may be translated "holy to YHWH"; "set apart for YHWH"; or "holy, belonging to YHWH." The noun + prepositional phrase appears sixteen times in the Hebrew Bible. Other items "set apart" as "belonging to YHWH" included the Sabbath (Exod 16:23; 31:15) and anything devoted to YHWH, such as a house, field, or tithe, which were then available for priestly use (Lev 27).[71] Deuteronomy 26:19 applies the phrase קדש ליהוה to the entire nation (cf. Exod 19:5), but the priests maintained distinction as cultic

67. For a discussion of the discourse structure of Exod 25–30, see Robert E. Longacre, "Building for the Worship of God: Exodus 25:1–30:10," in *Discourse Analysis of Biblical Literature: What It Is and What It Offers*, ed. Walter R. Bodine, Semeia (Atlanta: Scholars Press, 1995), 21–49. The purpose for these names will be discussed below.

68. Emphasis mine. The first verb (ועשו) retains the volitional force of the command in v. 2 (ויקחו), which results in a sense of purpose for the second *weqatal* verb (ושכנתי): "so that." See *IBHS* §39.2.2.

69. See M. E. Vogelzang, "Meaning and Symbolism of Clothing in Ancient Near Eastern Texts," in *Script Signa Vocis: Studies about Scripts, Scriptures, Scribes, and Languages in the Near East, Presented to J. H. Hospers by His Pupils, Colleagues and Friends*, ed. L. J. Vanstiphout et al. (Groningen: Forsten, 1986), 269. The seriousness of the role was underscored by instructions to wash hands and feet each time the priests entered the tent of meeting "that they may not die" (Exod 30:19–21).

70. The prohibitions of mixed substances are variously understood. Carmichael ("Forbidden Mixtures," *VT* 32 [1982]: 394–415) attributes the deuteronomic laws against mixing substances as a veiled critique of patriarchal history, alluding metaphorically to the stories of Genesis. Milgrom (*Leviticus 1–16*, 548–49) reads each law in relation to cultic separation. His interpretation is far more plausible than Carmichael's.

71. Firstborn sons also belonged to YHWH, but he accepted the Levites for service instead (Lev 27:26).

functionaries.[72] In each of these cases the *lamed* prefix indicates YHWH's possession of the entity via the link with God's personal name. It is set apart as YHWH's.

Aaron's Ordination

As noted above, the articles of priestly clothing are listed several times in Exodus and Leviticus, with different purposes for each list. Having considered their design and fabrication as expressed in Exod 28 and 39, we now consider the donning of these garments by the priests, prescribed in Exod 29 and carried out Lev 8. More exhaustive studies of these texts are available elsewhere.[73] My purpose here is to situate the high priestly garments in their ritual context in order to shed light on their significance.[74] Aaron and his sons could not simply don their new uniforms; they first had to be ritually qualified. The detailed procedure for their ordination lends further weight to the significance of their garments as well as their relevance to interpretation of the NC.

Victor Turner helpfully identifies three principal phases by which any given ritual achieves the desired effect: separation, liminality, and reintegration.[75] Passage through a liminal state, where the subject experiences loss, nakedness, or anonymity for a time, makes it possible for the initiate to leave behind the former life and undergo transformation. These stages are evident in the West Semitic high priestess' installation ceremony. She was chosen and anointed, thereby separating her from commoners. Then she was shaved, inducing a liminal state lasting up to nine days. After daily sacrifices, adornment, seven days of feasting, and a final procession from her father's house, she arrived at the temple to take up residence, an indication that the ritual was complete and she had begun her new role.[76]

---

72. For other instances, see Deut 7:6; 14:2, 21; Ezra 8:28; Isa 23:18; Jer 31:40; Ezek 48:14; Zech 14:20–21. Cf. Exod 22:30[31]; Lev 20:26; Num 3:12–13; 4 QInstr^{d} 81_{12}.

73. See, e.g., Gerald A. Klingbeil, *A Comparative Study of the Ritual of Ordination as Found in Leviticus* 8 and Emar 369 (Lewiston, NY: Edwin Mellen, 1998); Milgrom, *Leviticus 1–16*. Both authors argue that Lev 8 depends on Exod 29, and not the other way around. See ibid., 545; Klingbeil, *A Comparative Study of the Ritual of Ordination*, 105–7.

74. By "ritual," I refer to the "'conventional' action" prescribed by YHWH and undertaken by Moses to designate and ordain Aaron as high priest and his sons as priests. On the general problems associated with defining ritual, see Jack Goody, "Religion and Ritual: The Definitional Problem," *British Journal of Sociology* 12:2 (1961): 142–64.

75. For discussion, see, e.g., Victor Turner, "Liminality and *communitas*," 74–84 in, *Foundations in Ritual Studies: A Reader for Students of Christian Worship*, ed. Paul Bradshaw and John Melloh (Grand Rapids: Baker Academic, 2007). I do not suggest that the ritual itself had magical qualities. Rather, its efficaciousness depended on obedience to YHWH's command. See John Witvliet, "For Our Own Purposes: The Appropriation of the Social Sciences in Liturgical Studies," in *Foundations in Ritual Studies*, 17–42.

76. Daniel E. Fleming, *The Installation of Baal's High Priestess at Emar*, Harvard Semitic Studies 42 (Atlanta: Scholars Press, 1992), 63–65; 173–98. Also "The Installation of the Storm God's High Priestess," trans. Daniel Fleming, *COS* 1.222:427–31. On a smaller

Although the Israelite high priestly ordination ceremony is dissimilar to the West Semitic ritual in many ways, it includes all three defining marks of ritual, sharing several features with the West Semitic ritual: separation, anointing, sacrifices, adornment, and the use of sacred temple space.[77] First, Aaron and his sons were set apart from the people, selected to serve YHWH as priests (Lev 8:1–4). They spent seven days and nights at the entrance, or threshold (Latin: *limen*), of the tabernacle, separated from the community while not yet allowed to enter sacred space.[78] Noting their vulnerability to impurity during this liminal period, Milgrom explains, "Each day's rites will remove them farther from their former profane state and advance them to the ranks of the sacred, until they emerge as full-fledged priests."[79] As a transitional place between the sacred and the common, the doorway was the most appropriate venue for the seven-day vigil (Lev 8:33–35).[80]

During this liminal phase, Moses publically washed and re-clothed them in their sacred garments (Lev 8:6–9, 13), anointed them and the tabernacle (Lev 8:10–12), offered sacrifices, and sprinkled and smeared blood on them to consecrate them to YHWH (Exod 29:21; Lev 8:23–24, 30). It seems shocking that Moses deliberately poured oil and sprinkled blood on such carefully crafted and expensive garments. However, blood was an essential symbol, indicating that priest and tabernacle were set apart for YHWH's use and effectively cleansed by the sacrificial rites (Lev 4:5–7; 16:15).[81] Very little was

scale, daily temple rituals in Egypt in the 14th century BCE included removal of robes from the cult image, purification, and reclothing, followed by provision of food and "insignia." See A. Rosalie David, *Religious Ritual at Abydos (c. 1300 BC)* (Warminster: Aris & Phillips, 1973), 289. Cf. "Daily Ritual of the Temple of Amun-Re at Karnak," trans. Robert K. Ritner, *COS* 1.34:55–57. Even daily rituals such as this involved a period of liminality. On the cultic parallels between Israel, Mari, Emar, and the Horite-Hittite kingdom, see Israel Knohl, "P and the Traditions of Northern Syria and Southern Anatolia," in *Text, Time, and Temple: Literary, Historical and Ritual Studies in Leviticus*, ed. Francis Landy, Leigh M. Trevaskis, and Bryan D. Bibb (Sheffield: Sheffield Phoenix, 2015), 63–69.

77. Unlike the Hittite high priestess, who eventually proceeded from her father's house to the temple, Israel's high priest occupied the temple doorway for the entire ritual. His prescribed clothing was more comprehensive (hers included only jewelry and headdress).

78. Leviticus 1:5 describes the altar as being "at the entrance of the tent of meeting." From this, we can assume that Aaron and his sons were ordained somewhere in the courtyard, in an area where laypeople were allowed. Note that they placed their hands on the heads of the animals to be slaughtered, just as laypeople did (Lev 4:13–18). Richard E. Averbeck ("Tabernacle," in *DOTP*, 808) designates the entire courtyard area from the entrance of the outer curtains to the doorway into the holy place as the "entrance" of the tabernacle.

79. Milgrom, *Leviticus 1–16*, 538.

80. For a helpful discussion of liminal or transitional space, see Klingbeil, *A Comparative Study of the Ritual of Ordination*, 147, 319, 572.

81. On the cleansing properties of blood, see the helpful comparative study by Yitzhaq Feder, *Blood Expiation in Hittite and Biblical Ritual: Origins, Context, and Meaning*, SBLWAWSup 2 (Atlanta: SBL, 2011). On the significance of the dual anointing, see

required of initiates, except to wait and allow Moses to carry out YHWH's instructions.[82] Aaron and his sons merely laid their hands on the head of each sacrifice, identifying with their need for cleansing (Lev 8:14, 18, 22), and elevated an offering to dedicate it to YHWH (Lev 8:27).[83] Then they cooked and ate the meat with the bread (Lev 8:31–32). The sacrifices Moses offered on their behalf were also transitional, including some features of well-being offerings and others of holy offerings.[84] Moses ate some, but not all, of the meat usually designated for the priests, in keeping with his own transitional role (Lev 8:26).[85] The purpose of the seven-fold offerings was purification and consecration of the initiates (Exod 29:14, 21) as well as to please YHWH (Exod 29:18, 25).

After carefully following YHWH's ritual instructions, Aaron and his sons were allowed to approach the sanctuary to begin their duties לפני יהוה ("before YHWH").[86] On the eighth day, the priests performed the first set of sacrificial rites on behalf of the community (Lev 9:1–21). At the conclusion of this important work, Aaron approached the congregation to pronounce the blessing, an act that confirmed his mediatorial role and elevated status as well as the efficacy of the sacrifices (Lev 9:22–23). With this third phase, reintegration, the ritual was complete. YHWH's response confirms this.[87] Only after this blessing did God's glory appear and fire consume the offerings (Lev 9:23–24a). The people's visceral response included shouts of joy and falling facedown (9:24b).

Exodus 29:44–46 prescribes this ordination ritual and identifies its overall purpose: "So I will consecrate the tent of meeting and the altar and

Michael Hundley, *Keeping Heaven on Earth: Safeguarding the Divine Presence in the Priestly Tabernacle*, FAT 2/50 (Tübingen: Mohr Siebeck, 2011), 78–80.

82. For a statistical analysis showing Moses' responsibility for 45.45% of the action in this ritual and Aaron's only 29.09%, see Gerald A. Klingbeil, *Bridging the Gap: Ritual and Ritual Texts in the Bible*, BBRSup 1 (Winona Lake, IN: Eisenbrauns, 2007), 192–93.

83. On תנופה as an "elevation" rather than a "wave" offering, see Milgrom, *Leviticus 1–16*, 464–65, 469–73. The idiom מלא יד ("ordain"; Exod 29:9), which only appears in context of priestly ordination, may derive from this practice of placing certain ritual elements "upon the palms" of the priests (על כפי אהרן ועל כפי בניו; Lev 8:27) for them to offer. "Ordination" is explicitly linked with these sacrificial elements in Lev 8:28; cf. Exod 29:26–29. Propp (*Exodus 19–40*, 452) notes a lexical parallel from Mari, *mullû qātam*, which means "fill the hand(s), hand over, entrust" [*CAD* M/1 187] and connotes "a divine commissioning, a transfer of authority from a god to a sacred human."

84. Milgrom, *Leviticus 1–16*, 527.

85. Ibid., 531.

86. The phrase "before YHWH" (לפני יהוה) usually refers to acts that occur in and around the tabernacle. Exodus 27:21 specifies an act done "*outside* the curtain that is before the covenant tablets" as "before YHWH" (cf. Exod 40:23). In addition to rituals enacted in the holy place, those done in the courtyard or entrance to the tabernacle were "before YHWH" (Exod 29:11, 23–25, 42). However, because the divine presence was not limited to the tabernacle, on occasion events outside sacred space were "before YHWH" (Gen 27:7; Exod 16:9; Lev 23:40; Num 10:9; Deut 6:25; 29:9).

87. For discussion, see Hundley, *Keeping Heaven on Earth*, 90.

Table 17. Stated Purposes for the High Priestly Garments in Exodus 28

Reference	*Signal*	*Article of Clothing*	*Purpose*
Exod 28:12	וְנָשָׂא	inscribed shoulder stones	"so that Aaron may **bear their names** before YHWH on his two shoulders *as a memorial*"
Exod 28:29	וְנָשָׂא	inscribed chest stones	"so that Aaron may **bear the names of the Israelites** on the breastpiece of decision over his heart when he enters the holy place *as a memorial* before YHWH regularly"
Exod 28:30	וְנָשָׂא	Urim and Thummim	"so that Aaron may **bear the decision of the Israelites** over his heart before YHWH regularly"
Exod 28:38	וְנָשָׂא	inscribed gold medallion	"so that Aaron may **bear the iniquity of the holy [offerings]** that the Israelites consecrate, for all their holy gifts, *that they may be acceptable* before YHWH"

will consecrate Aaron and his sons to serve me as priests. Then I will dwell among the Israelites and be their God. They will know that I am YHWH their God, who brought them out of Egypt so that I might dwell among them. I am YHWH their God." In order for YHWH to dwell among the people rescued from Egypt, the cultic furniture, tabernacle furnishings, and cult functionaries had to be consecrated, set apart for the task of facilitating God's presence among the Israelites.

Aaron's Role

Aaron's garments were more than decoration. They were essential. Without them, he could not rightly perform the rituals assigned to him as high priest.[88] Alongside the furniture and curtains of the tabernacle, Moses ritually anointed Aaron and his regalia in order to set each apart for cultic service. Aaron's garments were his means of consecration. In Exod 28:3, YHWH instructed Moses, "Make sacred garments for your brother Aaron *to give him dignity and honor*." The garments are "*for his consecration, so that* he may serve me as priest" (28:4b, emphasis mine). The splendor of his attire not only qualified him for service but signified his indispensability to the tabernacle.

Form begets function.[89] Aaron was not permitted to dishevel his hair or tear his clothes in mourning because that would constitute a defilement or disruption of the cultic apparatus itself (Lev 10:6; 21:10).[90] Stated positively, Aaron's regalia signaled his role as chief facilitator of the covenant

88. So also ibid., 73–75.
89. For discussion, see Haran, *Temples and Temple Service*, 212.
90. So also Houtman, *Exodus*, 3:467.

relationship between YHWH and Israel.[91] As such he bore several weighty responsibilities, each of them related to his mediatorial role. Exodus 28 explicitly declares the purpose for several of his garments, usually signaled by the Hebrew prefixed preposition ל or the prefixed conjunction ו.[92] Four times in Exodus 28, a *weqatal* form of נשׂא identifies an active purpose for Aaron's regalia.[93] In each case, the verb נשׂא identifies what Aaron will carry on his person as he fulfills his duties (table 17).

First, on his breastpiece and shoulders the high priest bore the names of each tribe "as a memorial" (לזכרן) to YHWH when entering the holy place (Exod 28:12, 29). The grammatical construction in v. 12, אבני זכרן לבני ישׂראל, could indicate either that the shoulder stones are a reminder *for* the Israelites, or a memorial *pertaining to* the Israelites—that is, a reminder for YHWH. Clarification immediately follows; that the stones are said to be worn לפני יהוה (28:12b) suggests that YHWH is the primary one who "remembers."[94] Verse 29 confirms this conclusion by specifying the location of the "memorial"—namely, the holy place, which was off-limits for laypeople.[95]

The inclusion of all twelve tribal names ensured that members of each tribe would continue to have access to YHWH via the high priest's ministry. In previous generations YHWH had indicated the choice of one son over another to inherit the covenant promises (Jacob over Esau; Isaac over Ishmael; Gen 21:12; 26:2–5; 28:10–15). By extending the covenant promises to all twelve of Jacob's sons, the promise of descendants "as numerous as the stars in the sky" began to be realized (Gen 15:5; Exod 1:1–7). Therefore, Aaron

91. This role began in Egypt, when YHWH appointed Aaron as Moses' spokesman: "[Aaron] indeed shall speak for you to the people; he shall serve as a mouth for you, and you shall serve as God for him" (Exod 4:16; NRSV).

92. Eleven purpose clauses in Exod 28 are introduced by ל, 10 by ו, and 2 without a grammatical signal (vv. 12 and 32). Purpose statements in Exod 29 and 39 are less relevant here because they mostly concern sacrifices rather than garments.

93. Each carries the force of an imperative, instructing the Israelites in the proper design and wearing of priestly clothing. For a discussion of the prefix-conjugation verb as a statement of purpose or result, see *IBHS* §34.6. The three other purposive *weqatals* in Exod 28 relate to the blue cords on the breast piece ("so that the breastpiece will not swing out from the ephod"; v. 28), the placement of the Urim and the Thummim ("and it shall be over Aaron's heart"; v. 30), and the bells on the hem of his robe ("so that he may not die; v. 35). None of these denotes an active duty for Aaron.

94. Cassuto (*Exodus*, 377) suggests that the shoulder stones faced upward so YHWH could read them. However, both sets of stones were designated לפני יהוה. Houtman (*Exodus*, 3:476) helpfully suggests the shoulder stones bring the Israelites to YHWH's attention.

95. On the other hand, Joshua instructed the Israelites to make a heap of stones in the middle of the Jordan River to commemorate their crossing into Canaan, with one stone representing each of the 12 tribes. These stones were also called "stones of remembrance" (האבנים האלה לזכרון לבני ישׂראל, Josh 4:7; cf. אבני זכרן לבני ישׂראל, Exod 28:12), signaling that all 12 of the tribes had a share in the land. These stones in the Jordan apparently reminded the Israelites of their unity. The shoulder stones of the high priest may have carried a dual connotation—reminding the tribes of their brotherhood and reminding YHWH of his covenant commitment to them.

bore all 12 names as "representative of the entire community."[96] YHWH remembered them collectively on the shoulder stones, and as individual tribes on the chest stones.[97]

It is also significant that these names were engraved on gemstones rather than embroidered or affixed in some other way. While the text does not indicate the reason for the use of gemstones, their inherent value would have signaled the importance of the tribes to YHWH. The stones were also engraved like a seal (פתוחי חותם; Exod 28:21), perhaps underscoring Aaron's representative function with the virtual "signature" of each tribe, or their delegated authority. Aaron's representative role is reinforced by the fact that the tribal leaders provided the gemstones (Exod 35:27; cf. 16:22; Num 1:44).[98] Each had a share in his ministry.

Second, Aaron carried the (means of) decision (אל־חשן המשפ) for the Israelites inside the pouch of his breastpiece (v. 30). These stones, called Urim and Thummim, enabled him to discern the will of YHWH regarding particular situations.[99] Mystery shrouds these stones; we cannot be certain exactly how they functioned, and a full exploration is outside the scope of this project. However, it is clear that the high priest was responsible to seek guidance from YHWH, a role authorized by his wearing of the ephod and breastpiece לפני יהוה. Significantly, the means for decision making hung "over his heart" (על־לב; v. 30). In Hebrew, the לב was the seat of understanding and decision making.[100] Aaron's decision "before YHWH"—that is, the decision submitted to YHWH's guidance—was then binding for the whole community, further underscoring Aaron's representative role.

Third, because of the gold medallion on Aaron's turban, inscribed with YHWH's name, he bore iniquity arising from any failure to follow YHWH's instructions regarding the sanctuary—that is, "the iniquity of the consecrated things" (את־עון הקדשים; Exod 28:38; cf. Num 18:1).[101] Significantly,

96. Sarna, *Exodus*, 179–80.

97. On the two sets of gemstones, see Propp, *Exodus 19–40*, 524.

98. So also ibid., 438. In Num 7:2, the "leaders of Israel" (נשיאי ישראל) are further defined as "heads of their fathers' household" (ראשי בית אבתם) and listed by name in vv. 11–34, one נשיא per tribe. Cf. Houtman, *Exodus*, 2:346, 3:353; Sarna, *Exodus*, 224.

99. Most scholars assume the stones were cast like lots to achieve binary results. That the Israelites were already familiar with these stones prior to these instructions is evident from the direct article attached to "Urim and Thummim" (את־האורים ואת־התמים). So Cornelis Van Dam, *The Urim and Thummim: A Means of Revelation in Ancient Israel* (Winona Lake, IN: Eisenbrauns, 1997). The words אורים and תמים appear to be related to "light" (אור) and "perfection" (תמים), which may offer a clue for how they operated. Van Dam ("אורים," in *NIDOTTE* 1:330) suggests the presence of "a confirmatory sign of a special or miraculous light" and argues that a prophetic component was also likely (see, e.g., 1 Sam 10:22). See also Houtman, *Exodus*, 3:495.

100. See, e.g., Gen 6:5. Alex Luc, "לֵב," *NIDOTTE* 2:749–54.

101. See Schwartz, "Bearing of Sin," 16. Contra Houtman (*Exodus*, 3:516), who posits that the gold medallion enabled the high priest to *avoid* bearing iniquity. Propp (*Exodus 19–40*, 448–49) agrees that Aaron bore Israel's sin only until Yom Kippur.

the form of the inscription involved the *lamed inscriptionis*, which was also used on seals and inscriptions to indicate the authorization of the owner.[102] The high priestly medallion indicated that he belonged to YHWH and was set apart, authorized for cultic service.

Exodus 28:38

והיה על־מצח אהרן	A	And it shall be upon Aaron's forehead,
ונשא אהרן את־עון הקדשים	B	so Aaron shall bear the sin of the consecrated things
אשר יקדישו בני ישראל		that the sons of Israel shall consecrate
לכל־מתנת קדשיהם		for all their consecrated gifts,
והיה על־מצחו תמיד	A′	and it shall be upon his forehead continually,
לרצון להם לפני יהוה	B′	for their acceptance before YHWH.

The chiastic structure of this verse highlights the explicit purpose for the medallion: to authorize Aaron to deal with sin to maintain Israel's acceptance before YHWH. The one "holy to YHWH" was responsible to maintain the holiness of YHWH's holy place.[103] Aaron's authorization to bear sanctuary-related sin erased the communal effects of individual defiance.[104]

Leviticus 22:2 reinforces this conceptual link between YHWH's name (written on the gold medallion), which indicated the divine claim to ownership of the high priest, and the holy offerings. YHWH warned the high priest to "treat with awe" the holy offerings lest he "profane [his] holy name."[105] Priestly responsibilities inside the sanctuary included a charge to keep the lamps burning in the tabernacle and keep everything in order (Exod 27:21), to burn perpetual incense on the altar in the Holy Place (Exod 30:7–8), and to perform sacrifices and offerings on behalf of the people (Lev 1–7). Should the priests fail to follow God's instructions regarding sacred offerings, sin would accrue on the holy diadem, thus "profaning" the name (Exod 28:38; cf. Ezek 20:39). Careful maintenance of the cult would ensure that YHWH's name was honored.

102. See discussion above, p. 72. See also Propp, *Exodus 19–40*, 524–25.

103. According to Milgrom (*Leviticus 1–16*, 1033–34), the sin of the community defiled the sanctuary incrementally, and the Day of Atonement (or "Purgation") was needed to cleanse the sanctuary of the effects of those sins annually. Cf. Schwartz, "Bearing of Sin," 21. Here the sins are specifically connected to "the sacred offerings that the Israelites consecrate as any of their sacred gifts" (הקדשים אשר יקדישו בני ישראל לכל־מתנת קדשיהם; Exod 28:38; cf. Num 18:1). However, Aaron's role in the Day of Atonement ceremony reinforced his personal responsibility to bear guilt for all of Israel's sins. While the first goat purged the sanctuary of accumulated sin, Aaron transferred the guilt he personally bore to the scapegoat, who physically removed it. For a defense of this interpretation, see Nobuyoshi Kiuchi, *The Purification Offering in the Priestly Literature: Its Meaning and Function*, JSOTSup 56 (Sheffield: Sheffield Academic, 1987), 143–56.

104. Lam (*Patterns of Sin*, 22–23) also notes the theological link between Aaron's headdress and his role.

105. "Aaron and his sons" need not refer to all the priests. It can designate Aaron and any of his descendants who serve as high priest, as in Exod 28:4, where the phrase appears in relation to the high priestly garments.

The Levitical instructions imply that iniquity gradually accumulated at the sanctuary, requiring an annual purgation ceremony known as Yom Kippur, or the Day of Atonement (Lev 16).[106] On that day, Aaron made atonement by offering sacrifices and smearing blood on the altar of incense just outside the Most Holy Place and sprinkling it over the ark (Exod 30:10; Lev 16:18). Curiously, Aaron was *not* to wear the most elaborate of his official vestments (breastpiece and ephod) when it would seem most appropriate to do so—while entering the Most Holy Place. He wore them only when performing regular sacrifices and maintaining service in the Holy Place, implying that his representation of Israel to God pertained to the sacrificial system and the ongoing maintenance of the cult; he did not "bear the names" of the sons of Israel into the Most Holy Place. When he appeared in the Most Holy Place on the most holy day, he had to come humbly, without status or pretense, and in so doing symbolize Israel's undeserved access to YHWH's presence.[107] Most importantly, Aaron's diadem signified what was true of the entire nation—namely, that they were "holy, belonging to YHWH." On that basis, he appealed to YHWH for forgiveness of their sin. To wear only ארג garments (cf. Exod 39:27), which corresponded to the outer curtains of the tabernacle courtyard, concretized Aaron's mediatory role. He brought the outer courtyard into the inner sanctum, representing every Israelite as he approached YHWH. On regular days, Aaron did the reverse, in effect wearing the elaborate furnishings of the Most Holy Place as he moved about the Holy Place and the courtyard, representing the glory of

106. Milgrom, *Leviticus 1–16*, 1033–34. The ritual is initially cast as a response to the sins of Aaron's sons, Nadab and Abihu, which polluted the sanctuary. See ibid., 1011.

107. Alban Cras (*La symbolique du vêtement dans la Bible: Pour une théologie du vêtement*, Lire la Bible [Paris: du Cerf, 2011], 34) suggests that wool garments (dyed cloth) were prohibited because the high priest should not carry death when he approached the living God. However, wool need not imply death, since sheep are normally sheared without killing them. Furthermore, a prohibition of animal fibers would be strange, since the curtains of the most holy place were woven of dyed wool and the outside was covered with ram and fine goatskin leather (ערת תחשים). On the translation of תחש as dyed leather, see N. Kiuchi, "תַּחַשׁ," *NIDOTTE*, 4:287.

Ezekiel's temple vision introduced striking innovations to the priestly system. Milgrom (*Ezekiel's Hope*, 168–69) suggested that because of his complicity with Israel's idolatry, the high priest had been permanently removed from temple service. Changes to temple furniture and the religious calendar may be attributed to his absence. The Day of Atonement, which required high priestly action, disappeared or was subsumed under another festival, with its activities relegated to ordinary priests (Ezek 44:17–31). The lamps, ark, and incense altar of the temple, formerly maintained by the high priest, also disappeared. Similarly, priestly and Levitical duties were reorganized to reflect the punishment of those who had not served faithfully. Only Zadokites were permitted to serve as priests, while other Levites were demoted to temple guards or assistants (Ezek 44:11). Ibid., 169. Consequently, Ezekiel never mentioned the high priestly vestments (note Ezek 21:31). Only pure white linen tunics, turbans, and undergarments were permitted in the holy precinct, perhaps to safeguard its purity. Even the sash was disallowed, given its blend of wool and linen.

YHWH to ordinary priests and laypeople via richly colored and ornamented fabrics, gold, and gemstones. This interpenetration of spheres was an essential component of Aaron's ministry.[108]

However, in addition to his plain linen garments, on the Day of Atonement Aaron also wore his turban (מצנפת; Lev 16:4).[109] Without his other splendid garments to distract, Aaron's turban would have been more noticeable. It is fitting that the day designed to purge the sanctuary of accumulated sin is the day on which Aaron's costume featured the turban—the article of clothing that uniquely designated Aaron as sin-bearer for the tabernacle. During the ritual, Aaron placed his hands on the head of a goat, confessing the sins of the community and thereby transferring their iniquity from himself to the goat. While Aaron had "borne iniquity" (נשׂא עון) all year within the tabernacle, the goat then "bore iniquity" (נשׂא עון) into the wilderness, signifying the permanent physical removal of those sins and their effects from the sanctuary.[110] The Day of Atonement was the unique occasion annually where such cleansing occurred. Naturally, the responsibility for this ritual rested on the high priest alone. Aaron's careful enactment of this rite benefitted the entire nation, but by wearing YHWH's name on his forehead, he especially represented YHWH, dealing definitively with the defiling effects of human sin.[111]

108. Milgrom (*Leviticus 1–16*, 1016–17) suggests that Aaron dressed in plain linen to signify his entrance into the divine council. However, he does not consider the correspondences with the tabernacle furnishings.

109. Although the gold medallion is not mentioned in Lev 16, the only turban (מצנפת) named among the holy garments of Exod 28 is that worn by the high priest, which was decorated with the gold medallion. Regular priests wore a simple cap, or מגבעה.

110. The requirement of *two* goats on this day underscores the significance of his substitutionary role. The slaughtered goat purified the sanctuary, while the live goat bore Aaron's guilt away from the holy place. See Kiuchi, *Purification Offering*, 150–53. For a recent proposal that the one who led the goat into the wilderness was a criminal, see Raymond Westbrook and Theodore J. Lewis, "Who Led the Scapegoat in Leviticus 16:21?" *JBL* 127 (2008): 417–22. Some scholars posit a dual meaning for נשׂא עון where in some contexts it means that a person is weighed down with guilt while on other occasions it denotes the removal of that guilt. See Schwartz, "Term or Metaphor: Biblical *nōśē ʿāwōn/pešaʿ/ḥeṭ*," 168, 170; Schwartz, "Bearing of Sin," 10. However, if that were the case here, no Day of Atonement would have been necessary because the high priest would have already "borne away" any guilt. On the contrary, the goat bore the iniquity just as Aaron had done all year. The difference is that it left the premises, bearing the sin far from sacred space so that it no longer interfered with the covenant relationship. The difference is not due to a hidden lexical differentiation but rather a spatial one.

111. Haran (*Temples and Temple Service*, 212) suggests that Aaron could not possibly have worn his elaborate regalia while slaughtering animals, because it was heavy, awkward, and precious. He argues further that, since other priests could also offer sacrifices, Aaron's regalia would be meaningless here. If he is correct, this would also explain why Aaron did not wear the ephod, belt, and breastpiece on the Day of Atonement. However, Aaron performed his first set of sacrifices in Lev 9 directly following his seven-day ordination ceremony, when he first donned his regalia (Lev 8). This ritual text carefully

Within the complex of passages about the high priest's clothing and official duties, one more significant task calls for comment—the blessing.[112] The blessing relates to Aaron's regalia in two ways: (1) He first pronounced the blessing as the culmination of his initial day in uniform (Lev 9:22–23).[113] Aaron's vestments authorized him to give the blessing as YHWH's select representative. (2) In the act of blessing the people, Aaron conferred YHWH's name upon them, as Num 6:27 makes explicit. While Aaron literally bore YHWH's name on his forehead, the people, having been blessed, bore an invisible brand by virtue of their covenant relationship with him.

Numbers 6:23–27

דבר אל־אהרן ואל־בניו לאמר	"Speak to Aaron and to his sons, saying,
כה תברכו את־בני ישׂראל	'Thus you are to say to the Israelites;
אמור להם	say to them,
יברכך יהוה וישׁמרך	"May YHWH bless you and protect you.
יאר יהוה פניו אליך ויחנך	May YHWH smile at you and be gracious to you.
ישׂא יהוה פניו אליך וישׂם לך שׁלום	May YHWH show you favor and grant you peace."'
ושׂמו את־שׁמי על־בני ישׂראל	So **they shall set my name on the Israelites,**
ואני אברכם	and I myself will bless them."

This prescription appears immediately before the description of the offerings for the tabernacle dedication (see Num 7:1), suggesting that this blessing was integral to proper tabernacle service. The blessing itself audibly proclaimed the name of YHWH three times and linked it with God's covenantal commitment to them—expressed as blessing, protection, grace, favor, and peace.[114] The Masoretes separated each line of the blessing with

prescribes each step of the process, including his clothing, without mentioning that Aaron was to remove his vestments before beginning his work. Moreover, Aaron did not work alone; he had help performing the sacrifices and he may not have done much of the messy labor (Lev 9:9, 12–13, 18–20). The instructions for sin offerings in Lev 4 signal the representative role of the priest on another level. There, the sacrificial animal required for unintentional *priestly* sin—a bull—was identical to that required for the unintentional sins of the *whole community* (Lev 4:3). Although a priest was only one person, since he represented the entire community, the magnitude of the required reparation equaled that of the whole community (Lev 4:13–14). However, when a single Israelite sinned unintentionally, whether ruler or commoner, the required sacrifice was less costly: a goat rather than a bull (Lev 4:22–23, 27–28). We need not assume he was unadorned.

112. Deuteronomy 10:8 and 21:5 either reflect the extension of this privilege to all the Levites or could be read as a summary of Levitical (including Aaronide) duties. Since Aaron was a son of Levi, his duties could also be considered "Levitical."

113. Given the cultic context and the divine theophany that follows the blessing, this was most likely the so-called "Aaronic blessing" prescribed in Num 6:24–26. See Christopher Wright Mitchell, *The Meaning of BRK "To Bless" in the Old Testament*, SBLDS 95 (Atlanta: Scholars Press, 1987), 97. According to Milgrom (*Leviticus 1–16*, 587), the following Jewish texts assume this as well: *Sipra,* Millu'im Shemini 30; *b. Sota* 38a; *y. Ta'an.* 4:1.

114. On the structure and significance of the blessing, see Milgrom, *Numbers*, 50–52, 360–62. On the antiquity of this blessing (based on metric analysis), see David Noel Freedman, "The Aaronic Benediction (Numbers 6:24–26)," in *No Famine in the Land: Stud-*

a ס, setting it apart as a distinct utterance; furthermore, they framed the whole blessing with ס and פ. These markers testify to the ongoing ritual significance of the text. The blessing functioned as an act of oral branding, affixing the divine name (שׂמו את־שׁמי על) upon the people who consequently belonged to YHWH by using an expression reminiscent of the idiom לשׂום שׁמו שׁם.[115] This variation of a standard idiom for claim to ownership suggests that its metaphorical qualities are fully activated for this unique occasion (or that the passage predates lexicalization). In either case, the association of YHWH's name with Israel is deliberate, not incidental or subconscious, and commemorates the inauguration of their covenant relationship.

The gold medallion worn by the high priest and inscribed with YHWH's name thereby functioned as a visual lexicon for Israel's vocation as bearers of that name. As the one authorized to bless the people in YHWH's name, the high priest symbolized their collective status while providing an organic link between the concepts of possession and representation. At the same time, the physicality of the high priestly bearing of names reinforced the journey metaphor. By entering into covenant with YHWH and receiving the blessing, the Israelites as a whole were set apart and identified as God's, appointed to represent YHWH. The interconnectedness of priest and people, vestments and blessing, cannot be overlooked.[116] Both high priest and people were said to be "holy, belonging to YHWH" (Exod 28:29; Deut 7:6; 14:2, 21; 26:18–19). Aaron's ministry embodied the sacred juncture between two worlds, facilitating their interaction by maintaining the covenant apparatus.[117] Dressed in the splendor of the Most Holy Place before the people

ies in Honor of John L. McKenzie, ed. James W. Flanagan and Anita Weisbrod Robinson (Missoula, MT: Scholars Press, 1975), 35–48.

115. Milgrom (*Numbers*, 52) suggests that Num 6:27 may indicate a physical prophylactic but acknowledges that most think it refers to a figurative wearing of the name or its invocation through the blessing. For a concrete interpretation, see Bar-Ilan, "They Shall Put My Name"; Jacobs, "The Body Inscribed," 11–13. The Ketef Hinnom amulets attest to the antiquity of the Aaronic blessing. For discussion, see G. Barkay et al., "The Amulets from Ketef Hinnom: A New Edition and Evaluation," *BASOR* 334 (2004): 41–71.

116. Baruch 5:2–3 makes an intriguing typological connection between Aaron's high priestly garments and Israel as a royal priesthood: "Put on the robe of righteousness from God, place the diadem of the glory of the everlasting upon your head, for God will show your brilliance to everything under heaven." Here, the whole nation is pictured as returning from exile wearing priestly robes and the high priestly turban or diadem (here, "the everlasting glory").

117. An Egyptian analogy may shed further light on Aaron's cultic vocation. Lorton notes a complicated system of mutual representation in the Egyptian cult, involving an interpenetration of personality. The officiant in the cult was identified by name as the god being served, resulting in a seemingly redundant ritual whereby the god served and sustained himself so that he would live to sustain the people. In his example, the priest to the god Horus was himself renamed Horus, in hopes that Horus would favor the people, who were also represented by the priest. See David Lorton, "The Theology of Cult Statues in Ancient Egypt," in *Born in Heaven, Made on Earth: The Making of the Cult Image in the Ancient Near East*, ed. Michael B. Dick (Winona Lake, IN: Eisenbrauns, 1999), 135. This

and in plain linen before YHWH, Aaron's wardrobe exemplified his mediatorial role. Aaron's responsibilities began when he donned the clothing and ended at death, when his garments were transferred to his son, Eleazar (Num 20:28). On the annual Day of Atonement, Aaron removed his elaborate outer garments—all but his turban—to appear as a common priest in the holy of holies, but with special authorization to address the problem of accumulated sin. As representative of the entire nation, it is only natural that the high priest would bear the divine name, because he represented and even embodied Israel's collective vocation as those "called by his name."

The Occasion of Bearing YHWH's Name

All that remains for this project is to explore the circumstances by which the Israelites were drawn into covenant with YHWH and to identify their resulting vocation. I have limited this discussion as much as possible to passages in the Sinai narratives (Exod 19–Num 10) and their immediate literary framework (Exod 1–18; Num 10–36). At the end, I suggest ways that Deuteronomy builds on this theme.

Ritual at Sinai

The liminality of Israel's experience at Sinai has already been mentioned. The first two key elements of ritual, separation and liminality, are readily apparent.[118] God first brought his people out of Egypt, physically separating them from their former way of life so they were prepared to embrace a new identity as his people. But what ritual(s) occurred here to justify the application of ritual theory to these chapters? Ronald Hendel views the entire journey from Egypt to Canaan as a rite of passage.[119] However, he still isolates the events at Sinai as ritually significant. One rite has already been discussed above in conjunction with the priestly ordination: the priestly blessing. Another is the covenant ratification ceremony in Exod 24.

The first feature to emphasize is that Sinai itself was not "sacred space." The biblical notion of sacred space is not geographically fixed. "Holy ground" is dependent upon the presence of YHWH, and is therefore dynamic and transitory.[120] Thus, the ritual at Sinai is appropriate not because of geography, but because of the theophany that Israel has just experienced

---

Egyptian example may be analogous to Aaron's role in the Israelite cult. Inscribed with YHWH's name on his forehead, Aaron represented YHWH to the people, blessing them in YHWH's name. But he also represented the people to YHWH, causing YHWH to remember them by wearing their names on his breastpiece and shoulders. As YHWH's representative, did Aaron also represent YHWH to YHWH (by wearing his medallion on the Day of Atonement) and the people to themselves, reminding them of their covenant status? If so, this interpenetration of roles and identities affirmed his mediatorial position.

118. See above, pp. 123 and 159.

119. Hendel, "Sacrifice as a Cultural System," 375.

120. For discussion, see Sara Japhet, "Some Biblical Concepts of Sacred Place," in *Sacred Space—Shrine, City, Land: Proceedings of the International Conference in Memory of Joshua*

there. The second feature to highlight is that Exod 24 is literarily bound with what precedes it. The giving of the Decalogue and the Book of the Covenant at Sinai (Exod 20–23) is framed by a theophany on either side (Exod 19 and 24).[121] On both occasions, Moses spoke to Israel on Yhwh's behalf (19:7, 24:3), followed by the people's unanimous acceptance (19:8a, 24:3, 7). The repetition of their covenant commitment was verbatim and increasingly emphatic. In both cases, the invitation to approach God was followed by a restriction (19:20–24; 24:1–2). The offer of a covenant relationship in 19:5–6 corresponds to its ratification in writing in 24:7. Clearly, these events are parallel.[122] The ritual in Exod 24:3–8 is further framed by a command-fulfillment schema in vv. 1–2 and 9–11, where the leaders are invited to ascend the mountain to worship Yhwh.[123] That scene demonstrates the efficacious nature of the covenant. When they first arrived, the people were strictly warned not to approach the mountain (19:12–13; 20–24); after the ceremony their representatives were invited to ascend the mountain and see God (24:1–2; 9–11).

The ritual in Exod 24 involved several key components: an altar, stone pillars, sacrifices, blood, and efficacious words. The ceremony concluded with a ritual meal before Yhwh on the mountain, attended by Moses, Aaron and his sons, and the elders, and an invitation to Moses to approach God and receive the stone tablets. Each of these components deserves mention.

First, Moses built an altar (מזבח) and set up pillars (מצבה). Pillars such as these were used in the ANE to memorialize a divine encounter (e.g., Gen 28:10–22) or bear witness to a covenant (Gen 31:44–54). They also could mark a cult site (Exod 23:24; Lev 26:1). All three functions are evident here. The number twelve is significant because it assures each tribe that it is represented in the covenant ceremony.[124] As we saw above, the 12 gemstones

Prawer, ed. Benjamin Z. Kedar and R. J. Zwi Werblowsky (Jerusalem: Israel Academy of Sciences and Humanities, 1998), 55–72.

121. The grammatical shift in 24:1, where Moses is identified as the addressee of Yhwh's discourse, parallels Yhwh's speaking to Moses directly in ch. 19.

122. For other parallels, see Dozeman, *Exodus*, 562–63.

123. Whether this mountain scene included a covenant meal is disputed. Houtman (*Exodus*, 3:295–96) argues that the statement in 24:10, "they saw God, and they ate and drank" means "they saw God and lived to tell about it." Cf. Eccl 3:13. However, the elders may have eaten the portion of the fellowship offering reserved for the worshiper (v. 5). Covenants often involved a meal (see Gen 26:30; 31:46; Exod 18:12). Cf. Dozeman, *Exodus*, 566; Sarna, *Exodus*, 153.

124. Moses and the elders instructed the people to recapitulate this ritual at Shechem. There they were to erect an unspecified number of "large stones" (here, אבנים rather than מצבה) on which they were to write the Torah. They were also to build a stone altar (מזבח) and offer burnt (עולת) and fellowship offerings (זבחת שלמים), eating before Yhwh, just as Moses and the elders at Sinai (Deut 27:1–8). For discussion, see Block, "'What Do These Stones Mean?'" Curiously, the account of the actual event in Shechem mentions only one large stone and no altar, sacrifice, or meal (Josh 24:26). However, at the Jordan crossing (Josh 4), 12 stones represent the 12 tribes and serve as a perpetual reminder of Yhwh's

on the high priest's ephod reinforced this idea, providing a visual reminder long after the Israelites left Sinai.

As prescribed in Exod 20:24–25, the altar provided the staging ground for two types of sacrifices, עלות, or "burnt offerings," and זבחים שלמים, or "fellowship offerings" (24:5). These directly fulfilled Moses' request to Pharaoh for permission to sacrifice to YHWH in the wilderness (Exod 10:25; cf. 18:12).[125] As its name implies, the עלה sacrifice was burned entirely, signifying that it belonged wholly to YHWH. The זבח שלם was a celebratory offering; its meat would have been eaten by the people or their representatives.[126] The blood became a sign of the covenant, like the Passover blood on Hebrew doorposts. It would remain visible on the altar as a "tangible sign of the remembrance and the corresponding blessing."[127] The splattering (זרק) of the blood on both the altar and the people was highly significant, because only in one other ritual, also at Sinai, was blood applied to both altar and people: the priestly ordination (Lev 8:23–24, 30).[128] At that time blood was sprinkled (נזה) on Aaron, his garments, his sons, and their garments.[129] Already we have seen that because of his garments, Aaron embodied the whole nation of Israel, bearing the names of each tribe. Here we discover that his ordination, occurring some time later in the narrative sequence, mirrored the consecration of all the people as they entered into a covenant with YHWH. The gravity of both events was reinforced by the advent of YHWH's glory (Exod 24:9–18; Lev 9:23–24).

Finally, we consider the efficacious words by which the covenant was enacted. The ceremony began with Moses' recital, apparently from memory, of all that YHWH had said up to that point (presumably the Decalogue [כל־דברי יהוה] and what would later be called the Book of the Covenant [כל־המשפטים]; 24:3a). The people's response was complete and unanimous: "All the people answered with one voice, 'All that YHWH has spoken we will do'" (v. 3b). Then Moses recorded YHWH's words, performed the sacrifices,

---

power. The repeated mention of the priests (vv. 3, 9, 10, 11, 15, 17, 18), as well as the inclusion of both circumcision and Passover (Josh 5:2–12), suggest the ritual significance of this act.

125. Unfortunately, the same sacrifices were offered to the golden calf (Exod 32:6).

126. For more on the sacrifices, see Milgrom, *Leviticus 1–16*, 172–77, 217–25.

127. Hendel, "Sacrifice as a Cultural System," 387.

128. As noted by Dozeman (*Exodus*, 562). On one other occasion, blood was sprinkled on a person, as a way of reinstating to the covenant community those with a defiling skin disease (Lev 14:1–32). For that situation, it was not sprinkled on the altar. The practice was likely intended to mimic the high priestly ordination and thereby evoke the concept of the entire nation as a "kingdom of priests" (Exod 19:6). Here, physical defilement prompted the need for reconsecration and readmittance. Cf. Averbeck, "אָשָׁם," *NIDOTTE* 1:563. Contra Milgrom (*Leviticus 1–16*, 839, 855), who supposes the blood is in this case apotropaic.

129. Cf. Exod 29:21, where the rite was prescribed. Typically, the verb for applying blood to the altar is זרק, while application of blood to people involves נזה. However, in the covenant ratification ceremony, the blood is "splattered" on the people (זרק; Exod 24:8).

and read the written terms of the covenant to the people, now called "the covenant document" (ספר הברית; v. 7). This recitation, too, elicited an affirmative response, using identical language to 19:8: "Everything YHWH has said we will do," with an additional verb for emphasis, "and we will be obedient" (ונשמע; 24:7). Given their consent, Moses concluded the covenant ceremony by splattering them with blood and saying, "Look, the blood of the covenant which YHWH has made with you in accordance with all these words" (24:8).[130]

The links with Exod 19 are significant. There Israel's new identity and purpose as YHWH's redeemed covenant partner were elaborated:

> You yourselves have seen what I did to the Egyptians, how I carried you on eagle's wings and brought you to myself. So now, if you will indeed obey my voice and keep my covenant, then you will be my treasured possession (סגלה) out of all the peoples. Though all the earth is mine, you will be my kingdom of priests and holy nation. (Exod 19:4b–6a)

Keeping the covenant would reflect a vocation consistent with Israel's election. She would become YHWH's סגלה, or treasured vassal.[131] Furthermore, the holiness of the entire nation would facilitate a priestly function in relation to other nations.[132] Like the priests, their preparation for the theophany and covenant instructions of chs. 20–23 involved consecration, washing their clothes, and abstaining from sexual intimacy (19:10–15).[133] The significance of these rituals at Sinai cannot be overestimated.

Israel's "Regalia"

As a kingdom of priests (Exod 19:5), Israel's wardrobe included several hints of their priestly status.[134] As already discussed, their sprinkling

130. Significantly, though several elements of this ritual correspond to the priestly ordination ceremony, as ordinands the priests are silent. Aaron speaks only when bestowing the blessing (Lev 9:22–23). This seems to underscore his mediatorial role, taking the accent off him personally and focusing attention on YHWH's words. As a member of the community, Aaron has already voiced his affirmation of the covenant stipulations. His ordination merely sets him apart to facilitate that covenant.

131. On the ANE background to this term, see above, p. 118.

132. For more on Israel's vocation, see below, pp. 147–179.

133. During ordination, priests were consecrated with oil, washed, and reclothed (Lev 8:6–13). Their presence at the tabernacle entrance for seven days precluded sexual relations.

134. Surprisingly, circumcision was not the sign (אות) of this covenant at Sinai (cf. Gen 17:11). On the contrary, it was apparently not practiced in the wilderness. Moses himself seemed reluctant to perform the surgery (Exod 4:25). Of all the Sinai regulations only Lev 12:3 prescribed it, and only as a corollary to the primary issue (namely, purification after childbirth). Not until after Moses' death, under Joshua's leadership, were adult males circumcised as preparation for entering Canaan (Josh 5:2–5). And so, while in other eras circumcision functioned as a covenant sign, for the wilderness generation the functional covenant sign (אות) was Sabbath observance (Exod 31:13). For discussion, see Daniel I.

with blood marked them as covenant members (Exod 24:8). Then, during the wilderness journey after Sinai, when Israel's willingness to obey was severely tested, YHWH instructed them to make tassels for the corners of their garments (Num 15:38). The tassels were to contain a blueish-purple thread (תכלת), the same color worn by the priests, resulting in a combination of linen and dyed wool that was otherwise prohibited for common use.[135] These tassels reminded the Israelites to exhibit holiness by obeying YHWH's commands (Num 15:39–40). Since in other ANE cultures tassels were a status symbol, worn primarily by kings, deities, and warriors, they may also have illustrated Israel's special standing as YHWH's treasure.[136] At the very least they provided a tangible reminder of their calling to be a "kingdom of priests" (Exod 19:6).

But Israel wore something invisible as well: YHWH's name. At Sinai YHWH declared himself to be Israel's God, calling Israel "mine" (והייתם לי; Exod 19:5), and instituting the priestly blessing, whereby Aaron and his successors would regularly "place his name" on Israel (Num 6:27). Through the priests' proclamation YHWH would continually remind Israel that he had claimed her as his own. The covenant link between YHWH and his people, mediated by the priest who bore both of their names, was regularly reaffirmed. That claim to ownership was memorialized in the expression נקרא שם על and it justified the designation of Israel as עם־קדש ליהוה ("a holy people, belonging to YHWH").[137] Israel was the people over whom YHWH's name had been proclaimed, marking them as his special people and chosen representatives.[138]

The notion that YHWH's name is something to be worn also underlies the later practice of wearing phylacteries. Phylacteries, or *tefillin*, concretized the Deuteronomic command to "bind [the commands] as a sign on your hand, and fix them as an emblem between your eyes" (Deut 6:8).[139] For Jews

Block, "Hearing Galatians with Moses: An Examination of Paul as a Second and Seconding Moses" (unpublished paper), 13–18. Also noted by Jacobs, *The Body as Property*, 28–29.

135. See Jacob Milgrom, "Of Hems and Tassels: Rank, Authority and Holiness Were Expressed in Antiquity by Fringes on Garments," *BAR* 9/3 (1983): 61–65; Vogelzang, "Meaning and Symbolism of Clothing."

136. Stephen Bertman, "Tassled Garments in the Ancient East Mediterranean," *BA* 24:4 (1961): 128.

137. See Block, "No Other Gods," 244. The latter phrase matched the inscription on the high priestly medallion (Deut 26:19; cf. Exod 28:36, קדש ליהוה). The high priest embodied what YHWH intended his people to be.

138. Chris Wright (*The Mission of God*) offers a full exploration of the theme but does not bring it in conversation with the NC. John Goldingay (*Old Testament Theology*, vol. 3: *Israel's Life* [Downers Grove, IL: IVP Academic, 2009]) mentions "bearing the name" throughout his volume on OT ethics. For a brief but helpful introduction to the topic, see Daniel I. Block, "Bearing the Name of the LORD with Honor," in *How I Love Your Torah, O LORD! Studies in the Book of Deuteronomy* (Eugene, OR: Cascade, 2011), 61–72; idem, "Privilege of Calling."

139. For a thorough discussion of the contents, shape, and ANE analogues for the *tefillin*, see Keel, "Zeichen der Verbundenheit."

in later centuries, the phylacteries physically represented not only the Torah, but also the very name of God. Since the design and wrapping of phylacteries mimicked the consonants of YHWH's epithet Shaddai, they were to be worn only by the righteous.[140] For Deut 28:10, Targum Pseudo-Jonathan reads, "Then all the nations of the earth shall see that the Lord's name *is inscribed already on the tefillim that is (you carry) on you* and they will be afraid of you."[141] This text provides relatively early evidence (ca. 400–450 CE) that phylacteries were thought to represent God's name, which was literally to be worn.[142]

We cannot be certain how early or how widespread these ideas were. According to Meir Bar-Ilan, this scattered evidence of concretization points to a ritual whereby the priests literally wrote YHWH's name on the foreheads of those they blessed.[143] However, these practices probably arose from the shared conceptual metaphor ELECTION AS BRANDING rather than from a concrete priestly ritual. As with the NC, the injunction to tie the commandments on arms and foreheads has a clear metaphorical basis. The metaphor readily explains the unique expression in the NC as well as its concretization in various practices.

Israel's Role among the Nations

The exit of the Hebrews from Egypt was punctuated by reminders of God's covenant with Abraham and his promise to give him the land of Canaan (Exod 2:24; 3:6, 15–16; 4:5; 6:3–5, 8; 13:5). YHWH's deliverance was the fulfillment of that Abrahamic promise, including its international dimension (Gen 12:2–3):

> I will make you into a great nation and I will bless you;
> I will make your name great and you will be a blessing.
> I will bless those who bless you, and whoever curses you I will curse
> And all peoples on earth will be blessed through you.

The repeated articulation of Abraham's name throughout the exodus event evoked this promise. Even Balaam, a foreigner, acknowledged its

140. Braude, *Pesikta Rabbati: Discourses for Feasts, Fasts, and Special Sabbaths*, 22.5; 458. See Rabinowitz, "Teffilin," *EJ* 19:578, and discussion above, p. 39.

141. Ernest Clarke, trans., *Targum Pseudo-Jonathan: Deuteronomy*, ArBib 5B (Collegeville, MN: Liturgical Press, 1998), 74–75, emphasis his.

142. Similarly, Targum Pseudo-Jonathan specifies the mark placed on Cain (Gen 4:15) as "a letter from the great and glorious name." Noted by Philip S. Alexander, "Jewish Aramaic Translations of Hebrew Scriptures," in *Mikra*, 231–32.

143. Bar-Ilan, "They Shall Put My Name"; idem, "Magic Seals." However, John Barton (*The Nature of Biblical Criticism*, 1st ed. [Louisville: Westminster John Knox, 2007], 98 n. 60) sees Deut 6:8 as metaphorical. Elsewhere, Bar-Ilan ("Writing in Ancient Israel, Part Two: Scribes and Books in the Late Second Commonwealth and Rabbinic Period," in *Mikra*, 27) argues that although tattoos were prohibited in Lev 19:28, Jews marked the body with ink to ward off evil by indicating their divine servitude. Cf. Jacobs, "The Body Inscribed," 11–13; Jacobs, *The Body as Property*, 222.

lasting potency, pronouncing, "May those who bless you be blessed and those who curse you be cursed!" (Num 24:9b). The frame around the Sinai narratives reinforces this theme. Pharaoh himself requested a blessing from the Hebrews, hinting at the fulfillment of YHWH's desire that Egypt would know he was God (Exod 12:32; cf. 7:5; 9:14, 16, 29; 14:4, 18; Num 33:3–4). Jethro, a Midianite priest, concluded, "Blessed be YHWH who delivered you from the hand of the Egyptians and from the hand of Pharaoh . . . Now I know that YHWH is greater than all the gods" (Exod 18:10–11). As we have seen, concern for YHWH's international reputation underlay Moses' plea for mercy (Exod 32:12; Num 14:13–16; cf. Num 22:6).

Though the missional dimension of Israel's election was not fully developed at Sinai, YHWH clearly indicated Israel's intended role to be a kingdom of priests and holy nation, and he elucidated the means to that end—obedience to covenant stipulations (Exod 19:5–6).[144] The essence of their vocation was to be "distinguished from all the (other) peoples" by the presence of YHWH among them (Exod 33:16). Naturally, then, Leviticus makes the most insistent link between YHWH's name and Israel's role. As the Holiness Code illustrates, Israel's separation from the nations required distinctive behavior, diet, and dress (Lev 11:44; 19:2; 20:24–26).[145] She was to imitate YHWH's holiness. When she failed to do so, YHWH's name was profaned. Since YHWH's ultimate purpose in choosing Israel was to declare his grace and power to the nations, her disobedience to the commands at Sinai interfered, sending the wrong message about YHWH's character.[146] Israel's redemption from slavery had missional implications—the nations were watching (Lev 26:45).[147]

Leviticus 19 offers a poignant example of the connection between YHWH's character and the behavior expected of his people. A long list of regulations covering every conceivable area of life (speech, dress, agriculture, worship, sexual ethics, etc.) is punctuated with the statement "I am YHWH" (vv. 3, 4, 10, 12, 14, etc.), emphasizing *imitatio dei* as the basis for Is-

144. Numbers 20:14–17 offers a rare example of Israel's oral testimony to foreigners after Sinai. Preuss (*OT Theology*, 1:25) connects election with obedience in his proposed center for Old Testament theology.

145. Cf. Exod 8:19[23]; 11:7. In the context of covenant renewal (Josh 8:30–35; 24:1–28), Joshua exhorted the Israelites to maintain distinction from the nations by refusing to worship their gods or to marry their women (Josh 23:7, 12). The theological significance of the covenant renewal at Mt. Ebal and Mt. Gerazim is rooted in the patriarchal narratives. Both Abraham and Jacob had built altars there (Gen 12:6–7; 33:18–20). Moses had instructed Joshua to build an altar there as well (Deut 27:4–5). See David M. Howard, *Joshua*, NAC 5 (Nashville: Broadman & Holman, 1998), 212–13.

146. For a fuller discussion, see John T. Strong, "Israel as a Testimony to YHWH's Power: The Priest's Definition of Israel," in *Constituting the Community: Studies of the Polity of Ancient Israel in Honor of S. Dean McBride Jr.*, ed. John T. Strong and Steven S. Tuell (Winona Lake, IN: Eisenbrauns, 2005).

147. Cf. Levine, *Leviticus*, 192.

rael's ethic. The entire series is prefaced by the rationale, "You shall be holy, for I, YHWH your God, am holy" (19:2). Recognition of the idea that Israel bore YHWH's name explains why the two should be connected. Just as the high priest was קדש ליהוה (Exod 28:37), so, too, was Israel:

Leviticus 20:26

והייתם לי קדשים	You shall be **set apart as mine** [or "**holy, belonging to me**"],
כי קדוש אני יהוה	because I, YHWH, am holy
ואבדל אתכם מן־העמים	and I have separated you from the peoples
להיות לי	to be mine.

The appearance of the prepositional phrase לי, the 1st-person pronominal equivalent of ליהוה, underscores that Israel belonged to YHWH, while the explicit mention of separation (בדל) clarifies the nature of holiness as being "set apart." As the high priest was set apart from his compatriots for YHWH's service in the tabernacle (Lev 21:8), so Israel was set apart for his service on a global scale.[148]

Deuteronomy develops this theme more fully, calling the next generation of Israelites "a people of [YHWH's] special possession" (עם נחלה; Deut 4:20; cf. 9:29),[149] his "holy" and "treasured people" (עם סגלה, ליהוה עם קדוש; Deut 7:6; 14:1–2, 21; 28:9), chosen from among all the nations (Deut 10:15). Deuteronomy makes clear that election always involves selection from among other candidates. The Hebrew verb בחר identifies four entities in Deuteronomy that YHWH selected to carry out his purposes. First, the people of Israel are described as those chosen "out of all the peoples" (מכל העמים; Deut 7:6; 10:15; 14:2) to obey his decrees and be his holy nation, a living object lesson of his character. Second, God promised to choose a place for his name "out of all your tribal allotments" (מכל־שבטיכם), which would function as a central sanctuary to serve the whole nation (Deut 12:5, 14).

148. Tension between these two is evident in Num 16:3–7.

149. The Hebrew Bible employs נחלה to refer to the land of Israel as YHWH's property and the covenant people as YHWH's special possession. Though cognate languages offer equivalents for the former, the application to people is unique to Biblical Hebrew. See Harold O. Forshey, "The Construct Chain *naḥalat YHWH / ʾelōhîm*," *BASOR* 220 (1975): 51–53. Cf. Daniel I. Block, *Gods of the Nations*, 76–79. Wildberger (*Jahwes Eigentumsvolk: Eine Studie zur Traditionsgeschichte und Theologie des Erwählungsgedankens*, ATANT 37 [Zurich: Zwingli, 1960], 77–78) suggests that נחלה replaced the rarer סגלה. However, נחלה never appears with the other covenant titles from Exod 19:5–6, as one might expect if it replaces סגלה. The other titles are as rare as סגלה. Furthermore, סגלה also appears in postexilic texts (Ps 135:4 and Mal 3:17), making it less likely that it was replaced. Forshey ("*Segulah* and *Nachalah* as Designations of the Covenant Community," *Hebrew Abstracts* 15 [1974]: 85–86) suggests that the application of סגלה to the covenant people is an exilic development of the word נחלה. Alternatively, נחלה may represent a more modest way of talking about Israel's status in prayer or public address (e.g., Moses' plea for YHWH to accept Israel again as his possession [ונחלתנו] following the sin of the golden calf [Exod 34:9]). Cf. Deut 4:20; 9:26, 29; 32:9; 1 Kgs 8:51, 53; 2 Kgs 21:14; Isa 19:25; 47:6; 63:17; Jer 10:16; 51:19; Joel 2:17; 4:2[3:2]; Mic 7:14, 18; Ps 28:9; 33:12; 74:2; 78:62, 71; 94:5, 14; 106:5, 40.

Third, the people were permitted to choose a king "from the midst of your brothers" (מקרב אחיך), who would model humble obedience to *Torah* (Deut 17:15–20). Fourth, Yhwh chose the tribe of Levi "out of all your tribes" (מכל־שבטיך) to minister in Yhwh's name (Deut 18:5). In each case, whether nation, place, king, or priest, the selection was from among other potential candidates, but the chosen were designated to serve the rest.

Two passages in particular highlight Israel's vocation in relation to other nations—a role linked to Yhwh's claim on her, though not explicitly with the expression נשׂא שׁם. The first utilizes the phrase from the high priestly medallion, applying it to the people as a whole (עם־קדשׁ ליהוה), and the second includes the standard idiom for claim to ownership (נקרא שׁם על).

Deuteronomy 26:18–19

ויהוה האמירך היום	And Yhwh has had you declare yourselves this day
להיות לו לעם סגלה כאשר	to be his treasured people, just as he said to you,
דבר־לך	so you shall keep his commands,
ולשׁמר כל־מצותיו	and he shall set you high over all the nations
ולתתך עליון על כל־הגוים	that he has made, **for praise, for fame, and for**
אשׁר עשׂה לתהלה ולשׁם ולתפארת	**honor,**
ולהיתך עם־קדשׁ ליהוה אלהיך	and to be **a people holy to Yhwh** your God,
כאשׁר דבר	just as he said.

In this declarative speech act, Yhwh appointed a new generation as his treasured vassal so that the nations would see Israel and honor Yhwh (Cf. Deut 4:6–8; 28:1).[150] The performative or perlocutionary dimension of Yhwh's statement, signaled by the *hiphil* form of אמר, enacted the appointment of a new generation of Israelites as his vassal. Deuteronomy described these intentions for Israel using three vivid words: "And he will set you high over all the nations that he has made, for *praise*, for a *name*, and for *splendor*" (לתהלה ולשם ולתפארת; v. 19, emphasis mine). Like the high priestly garments, designed "for glory and splendor" (לכבוד ולתפארת; Exod 28:2, 40), so Israel's obedience would be like a splendid garment, inspiring the admiration of all nations.[151] The echoes of these lexemes from the instructions regarding the high priest underscore Israel's role as a kingdom of priests, bearing Yhwh's name among the nations just as the high priest bore Yhwh's name among

150. For a full discussion of this passage as a declarative speech act, see Stephen Guest, "Deuteronomy 26:16–19 as the Central Focus of the Covenantal Framework of Deuteronomy" (Ph.D. diss., Southern Baptist Theological Seminary, 2009). Cf. McConville, *Deuteronomy*, 384–85. On speech-act theory, see Kevin J. Vanhoozer, *Is There a Meaning in This Text? The Bible, the Reader, and the Morality of Literary Knowledge* (Grand Rapids: Zondervan, 1998), 209. On עם סגלה see Greenberg, "Hebrew *s^e^gullā*: Akkadian *sikiltu*"; Davies, *Royal Priesthood*, 54–60.

151. Jeremiah twice echoed this phrase, expressing Yhwh's renewed plan to make them "my people, for *fame*, and *praise*, and *splendor*" (לעם ולשם ולתהלה ולתפארת; Jer 13:11, emphasis mine; cf. Jer 33:9). In spite of their initial failure, Jeremiah envisioned a day when Yhwh would heal his people and forgive their sin while the nations watched.

his people. To honor him by keeping covenant would paradoxically result in their own fame as well.[152]

Deuteronomy 28:9–10

יקימך יהוה לו לעם קדוש	YHWH will establish you as his holy people
כאשר נשבע־לך	just as he promised you on oath
כי תשמר את־מצות יהוה אלהיך	if you keep the commands of YHWH your God
והלכת דרכיו	and walk in his ways
וראו כל־עמי הארץ	and all the peoples of the earth will see
כי שם יהוה נקרא עליך	that **YHWH's name has been proclaimed over you**
ויראו ממך	and they will fear you.

Because of YHWH's declared ownership of Israel, indicated by the standard idiom נקרא שם על, her obedience to his commands would make the nations tremble. Israel's covenant was enacted in the public eye. YHWH's name upon Israel and her allegiance to him implied his protection and blessing (cf. Num 6:24).[153] While these passages from Deuteronomy do not employ the expression נשׂא שם, they provide the clearest evidence of Israel's vocation resulting from YHWH's claim on her.

Conclusion: Election to Representation

What has become clear is that covenantal election is not merely a status indicating the "chosen."[154] The events at Sinai made explicit the election of Abraham's descendants, the Hebrews, as his covenant people for broader purposes. Election is the means by which God intended to mediate his blessing to the nations (cf. Gen 12:1–3). The Sinai narratives do not stress this dispersion of blessing; Israel had yet to learn how to be YHWH's people. However, in being his holy people, they eventually found their vocation in relation to the nations. The potency of their witness depended on the scrupulousness of their obedience. Suzanne McDonald calls it "election to representation," rightly recognizing these active and functional dimensions of election.[155]

---

152. Cf. 2 Sam 7:9, 13. Note the conceptual metonymy, NAME STANDS FOR REPUTATION. The ambiguity is intentional. With the praise of one comes the praise of the other. The echo of this passage in Deut 28:1–14 further underscores that Israel will receive recognition; the nations will fear her, and she will be the "head" rather than the "tail" (vv. 10, 13). Furthermore, Zeph 3:19–20 is explicit that fame and praise is given *to Israel* by YHWH: כי־אתן אתכם לשם ולתהלה בכל עמי הארץ.

153. See Tigay, *Deuteronomy*, 260.

154. The theological conversation regarding "election" is long and littered with corpses. I do not intend to join the fray, except to suggest that Israel's covenant ratification at Sinai confirmed her status as God's chosen people and implied a vocation for which she was responsible. See above, p. 60 n. 44.

155. Suzanne McDonald, *Re-imaging Election: Divine Election as Representing God to Others and Others to God* (Grand Rapids: Eerdmans, 2010), 191. Though McDonald's project focuses on *imago dei*, her conclusions about the dynamic nature of election

In ch. 4, I argued that the phrase נקרא שם על is a lexicalized expression indicating ownership through vocal declaration, and as such it sometimes operates interchangeably with the other idioms indicating ownership, such as לשכן שמו שם, לשום שמו שם, and להיות שמו שם. Most of these are widely distributed in both cultic and non-cultic contexts. The application of several of these idioms to the same entities suggests a convergence of concepts.

This is not true of the NC's נשׂא שם. It is not widely distributed, appearing only in the Decalogue, the description of the high priestly breastpiece, and in Ps 16:4. We have no evidence for its lexicalization or application to other contexts. It appears to be a unique expression, created for this occasion to impress upon the Israelites the solemnity of their calling as YHWH's people. It draws on the conceptual framework underlying the other NAME-idioms, activating the idea that YHWH lays claim to what he owns through verbal BRANDING, and that his subjects' obedience is like a JOURNEY in the sight of the nations. As a result, his reputation is bound up with the fate of what he owns.

Israel's status as YHWH's possession is obvious. At Sinai, he revealed himself and called Israel his "kingdom of priests" and "treasured possession" (סגלה), a title normally reserved for vassals (Exod 19:5–6).[156] In a momentous ritual, and with their full knowledge of what it entailed, Israel formally entered into covenant with YHWH (Exod 24). The priestly blessing provided a regular opportunity to commemorate her election by reinforcing the oral act of branding (Num 6:27), whereby the whole nation could be called "a people holy to YHWH" (עם־קדשׁ ליהוה) mirroring the high priestly inscription (Deut 26:19; cf. Exod 28:36; Lev 19).

Though indicative of Aaron's elite status in characteristic ancient Near Eastern fashion, the high priest's garments also symbolized Israel's national vocation. They indicated Aaron's special role, having been selected to represent the whole nation by wearing their names before YHWH, and to remind Israel of her holy vocation by wearing YHWH's name among them. While Aaron was to maintain the holiness of the tabernacle, offering sacrifices for sin and thereby facilitating the presence of God among his people, the people were to be holy as well, their behavior worthy of fame, praise, and honor in the sight of other peoples so that YHWH's presence among them would be a source of blessing rather than judgment. Failure on either part brought guilt and, as a result, profaned the holy name of YHWH.

Interpreting the NC representationally has significant ethical consequences. Instead of limiting application to a particular type of speech, the

---

corroborate the results of this project. She writes from a Reformed perspective, affirming the major tenets of Reformed theology, including "God's eternal electing decision" and his absolute sovereignty (ibid., xiii). However, her insights about the dynamic nature of that election apply equally well to those who prefer to discuss election in terms of God's saving acts within history.

156. For a fuller discussion, see Davies, *Royal Priesthood*.

representational reading encompasses *everything* God's people do or say. No area of life is untouched by this command because Israel "bears the name" in everything she does. Just as the other constitutional documents treat matters of diet and dress, economics and agriculture, purity and justice, cult and society, war and festivals, marriage and family, so the NC implies that covenant members may not claim allegiance to YHWH without carrying out his divine will in all these areas. However, while the range of behavior is much broader than traditional interpretations of the NC suggest, the subjects of that behavior are limited. The NC—read representationally—embodies the heart of what it means to be a member of the covenant community, set free from slavery to another and brought into YHWH's service, having been "branded" by a new sovereign. Israel's role is missional, intended to demonstrate to the nations the gracious character and power of God through unflinching obedience to his commands.

Translation of the NC into English

How then should the NC be translated into English? *The Oxford English Dictionary* traces the English idiom "to take . . . in vain" to the Latin Vulgate of Exod 20:7 (*assumere nomen Dei in vanum*), rendered literally.[157] In English, the idiom "to take God's name in vain" has come to mean "to use or utter (the name of God) lightly, needlessly, or profanely."[158] This idiom reflects popular understanding of the NC. However, as we have seen, "take" is an inadequate and misleading translation of the Hebrew נשׂא.[159] "You shall not bear the name of YHWH, your God, in vain" does justice to the Hebrew, to its literary, historical, and theological contexts, as well as to the way the English language works, providing a satisfying alternative to the traditional translations. "Bearing the name" also retains the connection with the underlying conceptual metaphors ELECTION AS BRANDING and OBEDIENCE IS A JOURNEY, leaving room for fruitful theological reflection.

Appendix

Semantic Overlap between נשׂא and λαμβάνω

Table 18. Passages Where נשׂא Is Translated by λαμβάνω[1]

LXX [MT]	*Meaning*	*Notes*
Gen 21:18	take up (a child)	
Gen 27:3	take up (weapons)	
Gen 31:17	lift up (wives and children)	to mount them on camels
Exod 20:7 (2x)	bear the name	
Exod 28:23 [29]	bear the names	
Exod 30:12	register people	MT: lift up the heads LXX: take the computation
Lev 5:1	bear sin	
Lev 5:17	bear sin	
Lev 7:8 [18]	bear sin	
Lev 16:22	bear sin	The scapegoat carries it off.
Lev 17:16	bear sin	
Lev 19:8	bear sin	
Lev 19:15	show favoritism	lit., lift the face of
Lev 19:17	bear sin	
Lev 22:9	bear sin	
Lev 24:15	bear sin	
Num 1:2	register people	
Num 1:49	register people	elliptical, "head" is missing
Num 3:40	register people	
Num 4:2	register people	
Num 4:22	register people	
Num 5:31	bear sin	
Num 9:13	bear sin	

1. Table 18 lists all 157 passages where נשׂא is translated by λαμβάνω in the LXX (according to HCRS). The vast majority (unless otherwise noted) involve Hebrew *qal* stems. *Niphal* is passive; *hiphil* is causative; *piel* means "to maintain support" or "carry away" (cf. *HALOT* 1:726–27). The Aramaic *peal* means "to take" (*HALOT* 2:1934). Light shading indicates the lifting or bearing of something tangible. Dark shading indicates the bearing of something intangible, such as sin, reproach, or the name. Other idioms—registering people, taking a wife, showing favoritism, or lifting up a lament—remain unshaded.

Num 11:12	carry (Israel)	נשׂא occurs twice, translated by λαβὲ and ἆραι. λαμβάνω occurs twice, for נשׂא and הרה ("conceive" = ἐν γαστρὶ ἔλαβον).
Num 14:34	bear sin	
Num 16:15	carry off/take away (donkey)	i.e., steal
Num 18:1 (2x)	bear sin	
Num 18:22	bear sin	
Num 18:23	bear sin	
Num 18:32	bear sin	
Num 26:2	register people	
Num 30:16	bear sin	
Num 31:26	register people	i.e., plundered people and animals
Num 31:49	register people	
Deut 5:11 (2x)	bear the name	
Deut 12:26	take/bring (an offering)	
Josh 4:8	take up/carry (12 stones)	
Judg 9:48	take up (bundle of brush)	
Judg 16:31	take up/carry (dead body)	
Judg 21:23	take (wives)	
Ruth 1:4	take (wives)	
1 Sam 17:20 (A)	get up/arise	
1 Sam 17:34	steal/carry off (a lamb)	
2 Sam 5:21	take away/carry off (idols)	
2 Sam 14:14	take away (a life)	= banish someone from God's presence
2 Sam 17:13	carry/bring (ropes)	*hiphil*
2 Sam 23:16	carry (water)	
1 Kgs 8:31	lift up (a curse or oath)	or Heb. נשׁא (to be a creditor) for נשׂא. The LXX presumes the former.
2 Kgs 3:14	show favor	lit., lift the face (MT), receive the face (LXX)
2 Kgs 4:36	take/carry away (son)	
2 Kgs 4:37	take/carry away (son)	
2 Kgs 7:8	steal/carry off (plunder)	
2 Kgs 9:25	carry away (corpse)	
2 Kgs 19:4	lift up (a prayer)	
2 Kgs 20:17	take away/carry off	*niphal;* goods into exile

2 Kgs 23:4	take away/carry (ashes)	
1 Chr 10:9	take away/carry off (head)	from Saul's dead body
1 Chr 10:12	take away/carry off (corpses)	
1 Chr 11:18	take/carry (water)	
1 Chr 15:15	carry (the ark)	
1 Chr 16:29	take/bring (an offering)	
1 Chr 18:11	take/carry off (silver / gold)	
1 Chr 21:24	lift up (offering)	MT: lift up (offering) LXX: take (what is yours)
1 Chr 23:22	take (wives)	
1 Chr 27:23	register people	
2 Chr 5:4	carry (the ark)	
2 Chr 6:22	lift up (a curse or oath)	or Heb. נשׁא (to be a creditor) for נשׂא. LXX presumes the former
2 Chr 13:21	take (wives)	
2 Chr 16:6	take (stones)	λαμβάνω occurs twice, for לקח and נשׂא
2 Chr 24:3	take (wives)	
Ezra 1:4	supply (silver/gold)	*piel;* "support with"
Ezra 5:15	carry away (vessels)	Aramaic *peal;* "to take"
Ezra 9:2	take (wives)	
Ezra 9:12	take (wives)	
Ezra 10:44	take (wives)	
Neh 2:1	take/carry (wine)	
Neh 13:25	take (wives)	
Job 34:31	bear (sin?)	נשׂא lacks an object
Job 42:8	show favor	
Ps 14:3 [15:3]	take up (a reproach)	
Ps 23:4 [24:4]	lift up (soul)	
Ps 23:5 [24:5]	receive (a blessing)	
Ps 80:3 [81:3]	lift up (a song)	
Ps 81:2 [82:2]	show favoritism	to sinners
Ps 115:4 [116:13]	lift up (cup of salvation)	
Ps 138:9 [139:9]	arise (on wings)	ἀναλαμβάνω
Ps 138:20 [139:20]	show favor	
Ecc 5:14	bring/carry (anything)	
Ecc 5:18	accept (their lot)	
Isa 2:4	take up/lift up (sword)	
Isa 8:4	carry away/seize (wealth)	
Isa 14:4	take up (a taunt)	

Isa 15:7	carry away (possessions)	
Isa 22:6	bear (quiver)	
Isa 38:21	take (lump of figs)	
Isa 39:6	take away/carry off (possessions)	*niphal*
Isa 40:24	carry off (princes)	ἀναλαμβάνω – in the wind
Isa 41:16	carry off (mountains)	in the wind
Isa 57:13	carry off (idols)	in the wind
Jer 9:9	take up (weeping and wailing)	
Jer 9:17	take up (a lamentation)	
Jer 15:15	bear reproach	
Jer 30:24 [49:29]	carry off/take (camels)	
Jer 38:19 [31:19]	bear disgrace	
Jer 52:17	carry off/take (bronze)	
Jer 52:31	show favor	
Ezek 4:4	bear sin	
Ezek 4:5	bear sin	
Ezek 4:6	bear sin	
Ezek 10:7	take	
Ezek 14:10	bear sin	
Ezek 18:19	bear sin	
Ezek 18:20 (2x)	bear sin	
Ezek 19:1	take up (a lament)	
Ezek 23:35	bear wickedness and fornication	i.e., consequences for
Ezek 23:49	bear sinful idolatry	i.e., consequences for
Ezek 26:17	take up (a lament)	
Ezek 27:2	take up (a lament)	
Ezek 27:32	take up (a lament)	
Ezek 28:12	take up (a lament)	
Ezek 29:19 (A)	carry off/take (plunder)	
Ezek 32:2	take up (a lament)	
Ezek 32:24	bear disgrace	MT: bear disgrace LXX: receive torment
Ezek 32:30 (A)	bear disgrace	MT: bear disgrace LXX (A): receive torment LXX: Bear (ἀποφέρω) torment
Ezek 33:25 (A)	lift up (your eyes)	MT: lift up your eyes LXX (A): 'lift' your eyes LXX: [missing]

Ezek 36:7	bear disgrace	MT: bear disgrace LXX: receive dishonor
Ezek 38:13	carry off/take away (silver/ gold)	
Ezek 39:10	carry/take (wood)	
Ezek 39:26	bear disgrace	MT: bear disgrace LXX: receive dishonor
Ezek 44:10	bear sin	
Ezek 44:12 (A)	bear sin	MT: bear sin LXX (A): bear sin LXX: missing
Ezek 44:13	bear disgrace	
Ezek 45:11	carry/hold (a tenth)	i.e., contain
Dan 11:12	carry off (crowd)	*niphal* MT: ההמון LXX: συναγωγήν LXX (TH): ὄχλον
Hos 4:8	lift up (his soul)	= desire
Hos 5:14	carry off/take (judah)	
Hos 13:1	accept (regulations)	MT: he exalted (*qal*) Syr.: he was exalted (*niph*)
Hos 14:3	bear (away) sin	plea for YHWH's forgiveness
Amos 4:2	take away/carry off (exiles)	*piel*
Amos 5:1	lift up (a lament)	
Amos 6:10	take up/carry (corpse)	
Jonah 1:15	take/seize/pick up (jonah)	
Micah 2:4	take up (a taunt)	
Micah 6:16	bear reproach	
Hab 1:3	(strife/contention) arise	MT: (strife/contention) arise LXX: receive [a reward]
Hab 2:6	take up (a taunt)	
Zeph 3:18	bear (reproach)	MT: burden [מַשְׂאֵת] (of reproach) LXX: bear (a reproach)
Hag 2:12	take/carry (meat)	
Zech 6:13	bear (honor)	MT: bear (honor) LXX: receive (divine power)
Mal 1:8	show favor	
Mal 1:9	show favor	
Mal 2:3	seize	
Mal 2:9	take away/carry off (you)	

Bibliography

Alexander, Philip S. "Jewish Aramaic Translations of Hebrew Scriptures." Pages 217–54 in *Mikra: Text, Translation, Reading and Interpretation of the Hebrew Bible in Ancient Judaism and Early Christianity*, edited by Martin Mulder. Peabody, MA: Hendrickson, 2004.

Alexander, T. Desmond. *From Paradise to the Promised Land: An Introduction to the Main Themes of the Pentateuch*. Grand Rapids: Baker, 1998.

Alexander, T. Desmond and David W. Baker, eds. *Dictionary of the Old Testament: Pentateuch*. Downers Grove, IL: InterVarsity, 2003.

Allen, Leslie C. *Psalms 101–150*. WBC 21. Waco, TX: Word, 1983.

Alster, Bendt. "The Instructions of Urninurta and Related Compositions." *Orientalia* 60 (1991): 141–57.

Alt, Albrecht. *Essays on Old Testament History and Religion*. Translated by R. A. Wilson. Garden City, NY: Doubleday, 1967.

Alter, Robert. *The Art of Biblical Poetry*. New York: Basic Books, 1985.

Ambrosiaster. *Commentaries on Galatians–Philemon*. Translated by Gerald Lewis Bray. ACT. Downers Grove, IL: IVP Academic, 2009.

Anderson, A. *The Book of Psalms: Psalms (1–72)*. Vol. 1. NCBC. Grand Rapids: Eerdmans, 1981.

Anderson, Gary A. *Sin: A History*. New Haven, CT: Yale University Press, 2009.

Aquinas, Thomas. *The Commandments of God: Conferences on the Two Precepts of Charity and the Ten Commandments*. Translated by Laurence Shapcote. London: Burns, Oates & Washbourne, 1937.

______. "The Moral Precepts of the Old Law (1267–73)." Pages 51–60 in *The Ten Commandments: The Reciprocity of Faithfulness*, edited William P. Brown. Louisville: Westminster John Knox, 2004.

______. *ST.* 61 vols. Westminster: Eyre & Spottiswoode, 1964–81.

Assmann, Jan. *The Search for God in Ancient Egypt*. Translated by David Lorton. Ithaca, NY: Cornell University Press, 2001.

Augustine. *Sermons II (20–50) on the Old Testament*. Edited by John E Rotelle. Translated by Edmund Hill. WSA 3/2. Brooklyn, NY: New City, 1990.

______. *Sermons V (148–183) on the New Testament*. Edited by John E. Rotelle. Translated by Edmund Hill. WSA 3/5. New Rochelle, NY: New City, 1992.

Averbeck, Richard E. "Tabernacle." *DOTP* 807–27.

Avigad, Nahman, and Benjamin Sass. *Corpus of West Semitic Stamp Seals*. 2nd ed. Jerusalem: Israel Academy of Sciences and Humanities, 1997.

Balz, H., and G. Schneider, ed. *Exegetical Dictionary of the New Testament.* ET. Grand Rapids: Eerdmans, 1990–93.

Bandstra, Barry L. "Word Order and Emphasis in Biblical Hebrew Narrative: Syntactic Observations on Genesis 22 from a Discourse Perspective." Pp. 109–24 in *Linguistics and Biblical Hebrew*, edited by Walter R. Bodine. Winona Lake, IN: Eisenbrauns, 1992.

Bar-Ilan, Meir. "Magic Seals upon the Body among Jews in the First Centuries CE." *Tarbiz* 57 (1987): 37–50 (Hebrew).

______. "'They Shall Put My Name upon the People of Israel.'" *HUCA* 60 (1989): 19–31 (Hebrew).

______. "Writing in Ancient Israel, Part Two: Scribes and Books in the Late Second Commonwealth and Rabbinic Period." Pages 21–38 in *Mikra: Text, Translation, Reading and Interpretation of the Hebrew Bible in Ancient Judaism and Early Christianity*, edited by Martin Mulder. Peabody, MA: Hendrickson, 2004.

Barkay, G., A. G. Vaughn, M. J. Lundberg, and B. Zuckerman. "The Amulets from *Ketef Hinnom*: A New Edition and Evaluation." *BASOR* 334 (2004): 41–71.

Barr, James. *Comparative Philology and the Text of the Old Testament*. Oxford: Clarendon, 1968.

Barré, Michael L. "Mesopotamian Light on the Idiom *nāśāʾ nepeš*." *CBQ* 52 (1990): 46–54.

Barton, John. *The Nature of Biblical Criticism*. 1st ed. Louisville: Westminster John Knox, 2007.

______. *Reading the Old Testament: Method in Biblical Study*. Rev. ed. Louisville, KY: Westminster John Knox, 1996.

Bartor, Assnat. *Reading Law as Narrative: A Study in the Casuistic Laws of the Pentateuch*. AIL 5. Atlanta: SBL, 2010.

Beckman, Gary M. "International Law in the Second Millennium." Pages 753–74 in vol. 1 of *A History of Ancient Near Eastern Law*, edited by Raymond Westbrook. Leiden: Brill, 2003.

Beckman, Gary M., and Harold A. Hoffner. *Hittite Diplomatic Texts*. SBLWAW 7. Atlanta: Scholars Press, 1999.

Berlin, Adele. *The Dynamics of Biblical Parallelism*. Rev. ed. Grand Rapids: Eerdmans, 2008.

Berliner, A., ed. *Targum Onkelos*. Berlin: Gorzelanczyk, 1884.

Berman, J. *Created Equal: How the Bible Broke with Ancient Political Thought*. New York: Oxford University Press, 2008.

______. "CTH 133 and the Hittite Provenance of Deuteronomy 13." *JBL* 130 (2011): 25–44.

Bertman, Stephen. "Tassled Garments in the Ancient East Mediterranean." *BA* 24:4 (1961): 119–28.

Biddle, Mark E. *Deuteronomy*. SHBC. Macon, GA: Smyth & Helwys, 2003.

Birch, Bruce C., Walter Brueggemann, Terence E. Fretheim, and David L. Peterson. *A Theological Introduction to the Old Testament*. 2nd ed. Nashville: Abingdon, 2005.

Blenkinsopp, Joseph. *Ezra–Nehemiah*. OTL. Louisville: Westminster John Knox, 1998.

______. *Isaiah 56–66*. AB 19B. New York: Doubleday, 2003.

______. *The Pentateuch: An Introduction to the First Five Books of the Bible*. ABRL. New York: Doubleday, 1992.

Bloch-Smith, Elizabeth. "Solomon's Temple: The Politics of Ritual Space." Pages 83–94 in *Sacred Time, Sacred Place: Archaeology and the Religion of Israel*, edited by Barry M. Gittlen. Winona Lake, IN: Eisenbrauns, 2002.

Block, Daniel I. "Bearing the Name of the LORD with Honor." Pages 61–72 in *How I Love Your Torah, O LORD! Studies in the Book of Deuteronomy*. Eugene, OR: Cascade, 2011.

______. "Bearing the Name of the LORD with Honor: A Homily on the Second Command of the Decalogue (Exodus 20:7; Deuteronomy 5:11)." *BSac* 168 (2011): 20–31.

______. *The Book of Ezekiel: Chapters 1–24*. Grand Rapids: Eerdmans, 2005.

______. *The Book of Ezekiel: Chapters 25–48*. Grand Rapids: Eerdmans, 2003.

______. "Covenance: A Whole Bible Perspective." Paper presented at the Annual Meeting of the ETS, Baltimore, MD, November, 2013.

______. "The Decalogue in the Hebrew Scriptures." Pages 1–27 in *The Decalogue through the Centuries*, edited by Jeffrey P. Greenman and Timothy Larsen. Louisville: Westminster John Knox, 2012.

______. *Deuteronomy*. NIVAC. Grand Rapids: Zondervan, 2012.

______. *For the Glory of God: Recovering a Biblical Theology of Worship*. Grand Rapids: Baker Academic, 2014.

______. *The Gods of the Nations: Studies in Ancient Near Eastern National Theology*. 3rd ed. Eugene, OR: Wipf & Stock, 2013.

______. *The Gospel according to Moses: Theological and Ethical Reflections on the Book of Deuteronomy*. Eugene, OR: Cascade, 2012.

______. "The Grace of Torah: The Mosaic Prescription for Life (Deut 4:1–8; 6:20–25)." Pages 1–20 in *How I Love Your Torah, O LORD!: Studies in the Book of Deuteronomy*. Eugene, OR: Cascade, 2011.

______. "Hearing Galatians with Moses: An Examination of Paul as a Second and Seconding Moses." Unpublished paper.

______. *How I Love Your Torah, O Lord! Studies in the Book of Deuteronomy*. Eugene, OR: Cascade, 2011.

______. "In the Tradition of Moses: The Conceptual and Stylistic Imprint of Deuteronomy on the Patriarchal Narratives." Unpublished paper presented at Andrews University, Berrien Springs, MI, April 3, 2016.

______. "No Other Gods: Bearing the Name of Yhwh in a Polytheistic World." Pages 237–71 in *The Gospel according to Moses: Theological and Ethical Reflections on the Book of Deuteronomy*. Eugene, OR: Cascade, 2012.

______. "The Privilege of Calling: The Mosaic Paradigm for Missions (Deut 26:16–19)." Pages 140–61 in *How I Love Your Torah, O Lord! Studies in the Book of Deuteronomy*. Eugene, OR: Cascade, 2011.

______. "Reading the Decalogue Right to Left: The Ten Principles of Covenant Relationship in the Hebrew Bible." Pages 21–55 in *How I Love Your Torah, O Lord! Studies in the Book of Deuteronomy*. Eugene, OR: Cascade, 2011.

______. "The View from the Top: The Holy Spirit in the Prophets." Pages 175–207 in *Presence, Power, and Promise: The Role of the Spirit of God in the Old Testament*, edited by David G. Firth and Paul D. Wegner. Downers Grove, IL: IVP Academic, 2011.

______. "'What Do These Stones Mean?' The Riddle of Deuteronomy 27." *JETS* 56:1 (2013): 17–41.

______. "'You Shall Not Covet Your Neighbor's Wife': A Study in Deuteronomic Domestic Ideology." Pages 137–68 in *The Gospel according to Moses: Theological and Ethical Reflections on the Book of Deuteronomy*. Eugene, OR: Cascade, 2012.

Boer, P. A. H. de. "Numbers 6:27." *VT* 32 (1982): 1–13.

Bonaventure. *St. Bonaventure's Collations on the Ten Commandments*. Translated by Paul J. Spaeth. St. Bonaventure, NY: Franciscan Institute, 1995.

Borgen, Peder. "Philo of Alexandria as Exegete." Pages 114–43 in *A History of Biblical Interpretation*, vol. 1: *The Ancient Period*, edited by Alan J. Hauser and Duane F. Watson. Grand Rapids: Eerdmans, 2003.

Bosman, Hendrik. "Adultery, Prophetic Tradition, and the Decalogue." Pages 267–74 in *The Ten Commandments: The Reciprocity of Faithfulness*, edited William P. Brown. 1st ed. Louisville: Westminster John Knox, 2004.

Botterweck, G. J., and H. Ringgren, eds. *Theological Dictionary of the Old Testament*. Translated by J. T. Willis, G. W. Bromiley, and D. E. Green. 15 vols. Grand Rapids: Eerdmans, 1994–2006.

Bradshaw, Paul, and John Melloh, eds. *Foundations in Ritual Studies: A Reader for Students of Christian Worship*. Grand Rapids: Baker Academic, 2007.

Branden, Albertus van den. "Le Décalogue." *BeO* 33:2 (1991): 93–124.
Braude, William G., trans. *Pesikta Rabbati: Discourses for Feasts, Fasts, and Special Sabbaths*. Yale Judaica 28. New Haven, CT: Yale University Press, 1968.
Braulik, Georg. "The Sequence of the Laws in Deuteronomy 12–26 and in the Decalogue." Pages 313–35 in *A Song of Power and the Power of Song: Essays on the Book of Deuteronomy*, edited by Duane Christensen, translated by L. M. Maloney. SBTS 3. Winona Lake, IN: Eisenbrauns, 1993.
Breuer, Mordechai. "Dividing the Decalogue into Verses and Commandments." Pages 291–330 in *The Ten Commandments in History and Tradition*, edited by Ben-Zion Segal, translated by Gershon Levi. Jerusalem: Magnes, 1990.
Brichto, Herbert Chanan. *The Problem of "Curse" in the Hebrew Bible*. JBL Monographs 13. Philadelphia: SBL, 1963.
Briggs, Charles, and Emilie Briggs. *A Critical and Exegetical Commentary on the Book of Psalms*. 2 vols. ICC. Edinburgh: T&T Clark, 1906.
Brooks, Roger. *The Spirit of the Ten Commandments: Shattering the Myth of Rabbinic Legalism*. San Francisco: Harper & Row, 1990.
Brown, William P. "The Didactic Power of Metaphor in the Aphoristic Sayings of Proverbs." *JSOT* 29 (2004): 133–54.
______. "'Here Comes the Sun!': The Metaphorical Theology of Psalms 15–24." Pages 259–77 in *The Composition of the Book of Psalms*, edited by Erich Zenger. BETL 238. Leuven: Peeters, 2010.
Brown, William P., ed. *The Ten Commandments: The Reciprocity of Faithfulness*. Louisville: Westminster John Knox, 2004.
Broyles, Craig C. *Psalms*. NIBCOT. Peabody, MA: Hendrickson, 1999.
Bruckner, James K. *Exodus*. NIBCOT. Peabody, MA: Hendrickson, 2008.
Brueggemann, Walter. *Theology of the Old Testament: Testimony, Dispute, Advocacy*. Minneapolis: Fortress, 2005.
Budge, E. A. Wallis. *The Book of the Dead: The Papyrus of Ani*. New York: Dover, 1967.
Bullinger, E. W. *Figures of Speech Used in the Bible*. Grand Rapids: Baker, 1968.
Burkitt, F. C. "The Hebrew Papyrus of the Ten Commandments." *JQR* 15 (1903): 392–408.
Buth, Randall. "Word Order in a Verbless Clause." Pages 79–108 in *The Verbless Clause in Biblical Hebrew: Linguistic Approaches*, edited by Cynthia L. Miller. LSAWS 1. Winona Lake, IN: Eisenbrauns, 1999.
Byargeon, Rick W. "Echoes of Wisdom in the Lord's Prayer (Matt 6:9–13)." *JETS* 41 (1998): 353–65.
Calvin, John. *Harmony of the Pentateuch 2*. Translated by Charles Williams Bingham. *CC* 2. Grand Rapids: Baker, 1979.
______. *Institutes of the Christian Religion*. Edited by John T. McNeill. Translated by Ford Lewis Battles. LCC 20. Philadelphia: Westminster, 1967.
______. *John Calvin's Sermons on the Ten Commandments*. Translated by Benjamin W. Farley. Grand Rapids: Baker, 1980.
Carmichael, Calum M. "Forbidden Mixtures." *VT* 32 (1982): 394–415.
______. *The Laws of Deuteronomy*. Ithaca, NY: Cornell University Press, 1974.
______. *The Origins of Biblical Law: The Decalogues and the Book of the Covenant*. Ithaca, NY: Cornell University Press, 1992.
______. *The Ten Commandments*. Oxford: Oxford Centre for Postgraduate Hebrew Studies, 1983.
Cassuto, Umberto. *A Commentary on the Book of Exodus*. Translated by Israel Abrahams. Jerusalem: Magnes, 1967.
Cathcart, Kevin J., and Robert P. Gordon, trans. *The Targum of the Minor Prophets*. ArBib 14. Wilmington, DE: Michael Glazier, 1989.

Chapot, Frédéric. "Réflexions antiques sur la structure du Décalogue: Entre appropriation et rationalisation." Pages 29–47 in *Le Décalogue au miroir des Pères*, edited by Rémi Gounelle and Jean-Marc Prieur. Cahiers de Biblia Patristica 9. Strasbourg: Université Marc Bloch, 2008.

Childs, Brevard S. *The Book of Exodus: A Critical, Theological Commentary*. OTL. Philadelphia: Westminster, 1974.

Chilton, Bruce, trans. *The Isaiah Targum*. ArBib 11. Collegeville, MN: Liturgical Press, 2005.

Christensen, Duane. *Deuteronomy 1:1–21:9*. 2nd ed. WBC 6A. Nashville: Thomas Nelson, 2001.

Cicero. *In Verrum*. Edited by Albert Clark. Translated by William Peterson. Oxford Classical Texts, 1917. Cited 7 June 2013. Online: http://www.perseus.tufts.edu.

Clarke, Ernest, trans. *Targum Pseudo-Jonathan: Deuteronomy*. ArBib 5B. Collegeville, MN: Liturgical Press, 1998.

Claissé-Walford, Nancy de, Rolf A. Jacobson, and Beth LaNeel Tanner. *The Book of Psalms*. NICOT. Grand Rapids: Eerdmans, 2014.

Clement of Alexandria. *Paedagogus* 3.79.1. Translated by Claude Modésert and Chantal Matray. SC 158. Paris: du Cerf, 2008.

______. *Stromata*. Edited by Otto Stählin. *Clemens Alexandrinus* 2. GCS 15. Leipzig: Hinrichs, 1906.

______. *Stromata*. Translated by A. Cleveland Coxe. *ANF*. Peabody, MA: Hendrickson, 1996.

Clements, Ronald E. *Old Testament Theology: A Fresh Approach*. Atlanta: John Knox, 1978.

Clines, David J. A. *Interested Parties: The Ideology of Writers and Readers of the Hebrew Bible*. JSOTSup 205. Sheffield: Sheffield Academic, 1995.

______, ed. *Dictionary of Classical Hebrew*. Sheffield: Sheffield Academic, 1993–2011.

Coats, George W. *Rebellion in the Wilderness: The Murmuring Motif in the Wilderness Traditions of the Old Testament*. Nashville: Abingdon, 1968.

Coffin, Fulton Johnson. "The Third Commandment." PhD diss., University of Chicago, 1898.

______. "The Third Commandment." *JBL* 19 (1900): 166–88.

Coffman, James Burton. *The Ten Commandments: Yesterday and Today*. Westwood, NJ: Revell, 1961.

Cohn, Robert L. *The Shape of Sacred Space: Four Biblical Studies*. AAR Studies in Religion 23. Chico, CA: Scholars Press, 1981.

Colburn, Cynthia S. *Reading a Dynamic Canvas: Adornment in the Ancient Mediterranean World*. Newcastle, UK: Cambridge Scholars, 2008.

Cole, R. A. *Exodus*. TOTC. Downers Grove, IL: InterVarsity, 1973.

Collins, John J. *Introduction to the Hebrew Bible*. Minneapolis: Fortress, 2004.

Collins, Raymond F. "Ten Commandments." *ABD* 6:383–87.

Collon, Dominique. *First Impressions: Cylinder Seals in the Ancient Near East*. Chicago: University of Chicago Press, 1988.

Conklin, Blane. *Oath Formulas in Biblical Hebrew*. LSAWS 5. Winona Lake, IN: Eisenbrauns, 2011.

Cook, Stanley A. "A Pre-massoretic Biblical Papyrus." *Proceedings of the Society of Biblical Archaeology* (1903): 34–57.

Cooke, G. A. *A Critical and Exegetical Commentary on the Book of Ezekiel*. ICC. Edinburgh: T&T Clark, 1951.

Craigie, Peter. *The Book of Deuteronomy*. NICOT. London: Hodder & Stoughton, 1976.

______. *Psalms 1–50*. 2nd ed. WBC. Nashville: Nelson Reference & Electronic, 2004.

Crane, Ashley S. *Israel's Restoration: A Textual-Comparative Exploration of Ezekiel 36–39*. VTSup 122. Leiden: Brill, 2008.

Cras, Alban. *La symbolique du vêtement dans la Bible: Pour une théologie du vêtement*. Lire la Bible. Paris: du Cerf, 2011.

Cross, Frank Moore. *Canaanite Myth and Hebrew Epic: Essays in the History of the Religion of Israel*. Cambridge, MA: Harvard University Press, 1973.

Cross, Frank Moore, and Richard J. Saley. "Phoenician Incantations on a Plaque of the Seventh Century BCE from Arslan Tash in Upper Syria." Pages 265–69 in *Leaves from an Epigrapher's Notebook: Collected Papers in Hebrew and West Semitic Palaeography and Epigraphy*. HSS 51. Winona Lake, IN: Eisenbrauns, 2003.

Crüsemann, Frank. *Bewahrung der Freiheit: Das Thema des Dekalogs in sozialgeschichtlicher Perspektive*. Kaiser Traktate 78. Munich: Chr. Kaiser, 1983.

______. *The Torah: Theology and Social History of Old Testament Law*. Translated by A. W. Mahnke. Minneapolis: Fortress, 1996.

Crystal, David. *The Cambridge Encyclopedia of the English Language*. New York: Cambridge University Press, 1995.

Currid, John. *A Study Commentary on Exodus*, vol. 2: *Exodus 19–40*. EPSC. Webster, NY: Evangelical Press, 2000.

Cyprian. *Testimonies*. Edited by A. Cleveland Coxe. Translated by Ernest Wallis. Ante-Nicene Fathers 5. Peabody, MA: Hendrickson, 2004.

Dahood, Mitchell. *Psalms I: 1–50*. AB. Garden City, NY: Doubleday, 1965.

______. *Psalms II: 51–100*. AB. Garden City, NY: Doubleday, 1968.

______. *Psalms III: 101–50*. AB. Garden City, NY: Doubleday, 1970.

Dana, Joseph. "The *'Piyyuṭ'* on the Ten Commandments Ascribed to Saadiah Gaon." *JQR* n.s. 86/3–4 (1996): 323–75.

Dandamaev, Muhammad A. *Slavery in Babylonia: From Nabopolassar to Alexander the Great (626–331 B.C.)*. Edited by M. A. Powell and D. B. Weisberg. Translated by V. A. Powell. DeKalb, IL: Northern Illinois University Press, 1984.

Danker, F. W., W. Bauer, W. F. Arndt, and F. W. Gingrich. *Greek–English Lexicon of the New Testament and Other Early Christian Literature*. 3rd ed. Chicago: University of Chicago Press, 2000.

David, A. Rosalie. *Religious Ritual at Abydos (c. 1300 BC)*. Warminster, UK: Aris & Phillips, 1973.

Davies, Graham. "Some Uses of Writing in Ancient Israel in the Light of Recently Published Inscriptions." Pages 155–74 in *Writing and Ancient Near Eastern Society: Papers in Honour of Alan R. Millard*. LHBOTS 426. New York: T&T Clark, 2005.

Davies, Graham, ed. *Ancient Hebrew Inscriptions*. 2 vols. Cambridge: Cambridge University Press, 1991 and 2004.

Davies, John. *Royal Priesthood: Literary and Intertextual Perspectives on an Image of Israel in Exodus 19.6*. JSOTSup 395. New York: Continuum, 2004.

Demsky, Aaron, and Meir Bar-Ilan. "Writing in Ancient Israel and Early Judaism." Pages 1–20 in *Mikra: Text, Translation, Reading and Interpretation of the Hebrew Bible in Ancient Judaism and Early Christianity*, edited by Martin Mulder. Peabody, MA: Hendrickson, 2004.

DeRouchie, Jason S. "Counting the Ten: An Investigation into the Numbering of the Decalogue." Pages 93–125 in *For Our Good Always: Studies on the Message and Influence of Deuteronomy in Honor of Daniel I. Block*, edited by Jason S. DeRouchie, Jason Gile, and Kenneth J. Turner. Winona Lake, IN: Eisenbrauns, 2013.

______. "Making the Ten Count: Reflections on the Lasting Message of the Decalogue." Pages 415–40 in *For Our Good Always: Studies on the Message and Influence of Deuteronomy in Honor of Daniel I. Block*, edited by Jason Gile, Kenneth J. Turner, and Jason S. DeRouchie. Winona Lake, IN: Eisenbrauns, 2013.

DeSilva, David A. *Introducing the Apocrypha: Message, Context, and Significance*. Grand Rapids: Baker Academic, 2002.

Dhorme, Édouard. *Les Religions de Babylonie et d'Assyrie*. Les anciennes Religions orientales 2. Paris: Presses Univeritaires de France, 1949.

Dietrich, M., O. Loretz, and J. Sanmartín, eds. *The Cuneiform Alphabetic Texts from Ugarit, Ras Ibn Hani, and Other Places.* Münster: Ugarit-Verlag, 1995.

______. *Die keilalphabetischen Texte aus Ugarit.* M. AOAT 24/1. Neukirchen-Vluyn: Neukirchener Verlag, 1976.

Dillard, Raymond, and Tremper Longman. *An Introduction to the Old Testament*. Grand Rapids: Zondervan, 1994.

Dirksen, Peter B. "The Old Testament Peshitta." Pages 255–97 in *Mikra: Text, Translation, Reading and Interpretation of the Hebrew Bible in Ancient Judaism and Early Christianity*, edited by Martin Mulder. Peabody, MA: Hendrickson, 2004.

Donner, H., and W. Röllig, eds. *Kanaanäische und aramäische Inschriften.* 2nd ed. Wiesbaden: Harrassowitz, 1966–69.

Dougherty, Raymond Philip. *The Shirkûtu of Babylonian Deities*. YOS 5–2. New Haven: Yale University Press, 1923.

Doxey, Denise M. "Names." *OEAE* 2:490–92.

Dozeman, Thomas B. *Commentary on Exodus*. ECC. Grand Rapids: Eerdmans, 2009.

Driver, G. R. "Notes on the Psalms II: 73–150." *JTS* 44 (1943): 12–23.

______. *Semitic Writing: From Pictograph to Alphabet*. 3rd ed. London: Oxford University Press, 1976.

Duke, Rodney K. "Form and Meaning: Multi-layered Balanced Thought Structures in Psalm 24:4." *TynBul* 62:2 (2011): 215–32.

Dulaey, Martine. "Le Décalogue, les tables de la Loi et la catéchèse." Pages 49–63 in *Décalogue au miroir des Pères*. Strasbourg: Université Marc Bloch, 2008.

Dumbrell, W. J. *Covenant and Creation: A Theology of Old Testament Covenants*. Eugene, OR: Wipf & Stock, 2009.

Dumermuth, F. "Zur deuteronomischen Kulttheologie und ihren Voraussetzungen." *ZAW* 70 (1958): 59–98.

Durham, John. *Exodus*. WBC. Waco, TX: Word, 1987.

Ebeling, Erich, Bruno Meissner, and Michael P. Streck, eds. *Reallexikon der Assyriologie.* Berlin: de Gruyter, 1932–2011.

Eichrodt, Walther. *Theology of the Old Testament*. Translated by J. A. Baker. OTL. Philadelphia: Westminster, 1961.

Ellis, Richard S. *Foundation Deposits in Ancient Mesopotamia*. YNER 2. New Haven, CT: Yale University Press, 1968.

Elßner, Thomas R. *Das Namensmißbrauch-Verbot (Ex 20,7 / Dtn 5,11): Bedeutung, Entstehung und frühe Wirkungsgeschichte*. ETS 75. Leipzig: St. Benno, 1999.

Epstein, I., ed. and trans. *Babylonian Talmud.* 35 vols. London: Socino, 1935–52.

Evans, John Frederick. "An Inner-Biblical Interpretation and Intertextual Reading of Ezekiel's Recognition Formulae with the Book of Exodus." Th.D. diss., University of Stellenbosch, 2006.

Evans, Vyvyan, and Melanie Green. *Cognitive Linguistics: An Introduction*. Mahwah, NJ: L. Erlbaum, 2006.

Feder, Yitzhaq. *Blood Expiation in Hittite and Biblical Ritual: Origins, Context, and Meaning*. SBLWAWSup 2. Atlanta: SBL, 2011.

Fensham, F. Charles. *The Books of Ezra and Nehemiah*. NICOT. Grand Rapids: Eerdmans, 1982.

Ferry, Joëlle. "Le Décalogue, une loi pour l'homme?" *Transversalités* 80 (December 2001): 155–70.

Feuer, Avrohom Chaim. *Sēfer Tehillîm: A New Translation with a Commentary Anthologized from Talmudic, Midrashic and Rabbinic Sources*. Brooklyn: Mesorah, 1995.

Field, Fridericus. *Origenis Hexaplorum*. Vol. 1. Hildesheim: Olms, 1964.

Fischer, Irmtraud. *Wo ist Jahwe? Das Volksklagelied Jes 63,7—64,11 als Ausdruck des Ringens um eine gebrochene Beziehung*. Stuttgart: Katholisches Bibelwerk, 1989.

Fishbane, Michael. *Biblical Interpretation in Ancient Israel*. Oxford: Clarendon, 1988.

Fitzmyer, Joseph A. *The Aramaic Inscriptions of Sefire*. Biblica et Orientalia 19. Rome: Pontifical Biblical Institute, 1967.

Fleming, Daniel E. *The Installation of Baal's High Priestess at Emar*. Harvard Semitic Studies 42. Atlanta: Scholars Press, 1992.

Flesher, Paul, and Bruce Chilton. *The Targums: A Critical Introduction*. Waco, TX: Baylor University Press, 2011.

Fohrer, Georg. *Das Buch Hiob*. KAT 16. Gütersloh: Mohn, 1963.

______. *Ezechiel*. HAT 13. Tübingen: Mohr Siebeck, 1955.

Forshey, Harold O. "The Construct Chain *naḥalat YHWH / ʾelōhîm*." *BASOR* 220 (1975): 51–53.

______."*Segulah* and *Nachalah* as Designations of the Covenant Community." *Hebrew Abstracts* 15 (1974): 85–86.

Fossum, Jarl E. *The Name of God and the Angel of the Lord*. WUNT 36. Tübingen: Mohr Siebeck, 1985.

Foster, Benjamin R. *Before the Muses: An Anthology of Akkadian Literature*. 2nd ed. Bethesda, MD: Capital, 1996.

Fowler, Jeaneane D. *Theophoric Personal Names in Ancient Hebrew: A Comparative Study*. JSOTSup 49. Sheffield: JSOT, 1988.

Fox, Michael V. *Proverbs 10–31*. AB 18B. New Haven: Yale University Press, 2009.

Fox, Nili S. "Marked for Servitude: Mesopotamia and the Bible." Pages 267–78 in *A Common Cultural Heritage: Studies on Mesopotamia and the Biblical World in Honor of Barry L. Eichler*, edited by Grant Frame, Erle Leichty, Karen Sonik, Jeffrey Tigay, and Steve Tinney. Bethesda, MD: Capital Decisions Ltd., 2011.

Freedman, David Noel. "The Aaronic Benediction (Numbers 6:24–26)." Pages 35–48 in *No Famine in the Land: Studies in Honor of John L. McKenzie*, edited by James W. Flanagan and Anita Weisbrod Robinson. Missoula, MT: Scholars Press, 1975.

______. *The Nine Commandments: Uncovering the Pattern of Crime and Punishment in the Hebrew Bible*. New York: Doubleday, 2000.

______, ed. *Anchor Bible Dictionary*. 6 vols. New York: Doubleday, 1992.

Freedman, H., and Maurice Simon, eds. *Midrash Rabbah*. 3rd ed. New York: Soncino, 1983.

Fretheim, Terence E. *The Pentateuch*. Edited by Gene M. Tucker. Interpreting Biblical Texts. Nashville, TN: Abingdon, 1996.

Frood, Elizabeth. *Biographical Texts from Ramessid Egypt*. SBLWAW 26. Atlanta: SBL, 2007.

Geerlings, Wilhelm. "The Decalogue in Augustine's Theology." Pages 106–17 in *The Decalogue in Jewish and Christian Tradition*, edited by Henning Graf Reventlow and Yair Hoffman. LHB/OTS 509. New York: T&T Clark, 2011.

Gentry, Peter J., and Stephen J. Wellum. *Kingdom through Covenant: A Biblical-Theological Understanding of the Covenants*. Wheaton, IL: Crossway, 2012.

Gerstenberger, Erhard. *Psalms: Part 1 with an Introduction to Cultic Poetry*. Vol. XIV. FOTL. Grand Rapids: Eerdmans, 1988.

Gibson, Arthur. *Biblical Semantic Logic: A Preliminary Analysis*. London: Sheffield Academic, 2001.

Gill, David W. *Doing Right: Practicing Ethical Principles*. Downers Grove, IL: IVP, 2004.

Goldenstein, Johannes. *Das Gebet der Gottesknechte: Jesaja 63,7–64,11 im Jesajabuch*. Neukirchen-Vluyn: Neukirchener Verlag, 2001.

Goldingay, John. *Daniel*. WBC 30. Nashville: Thomas Nelson, 1996.

______. *Isaiah*. NIBCOT. Peabody, MA: Hendrickson, 2001.

______. *Old Testament Theology, Vol. 3: Israel's Life*. Downers Grove, IL: IVP Academic, 2009.

______. *Psalms 1–41*. BCOT. Grand Rapids: Baker Academic, 2006.

______. *Psalms 90–150*. BCOT. Grand Rapids: Baker Academic, 2008.

Goody, Jack. "Religion and Ritual: The Definitional Problem." *British Journal of Sociology* 12:2 (1961): 142–64.

Görg, Manfred. "Missbrauch des Gottesnamens." *BN* 16 (1981): 16–17.

Graupner, Axel. "Die zehn Gebote im Rahmen alttestamentlicher Ethik: Anmerkungen zum gegenwärtigen Stand der Forschung." Pages 61–95 in *Weisheit, Ethos und Gebot: Weisheits- und Dekalogtraditionen in der Bibel und im frühen Judentum*. Biblisch-Theologische Studien 43. Neukirchen-Vluyn: Neukirchener Verlag, 2001.

Graves, Michael. "Vulgate." Pages 278–89 in vol. 1A of *Textual History of the Bible*. Edited by Emanuel Tov and Armin Lange. Leiden: Brill, 2016.

Gray, Alison Ruth. "Psalm 18 in Words and Pictures: A Reading through Metaphor." PhD diss., Selwyn College, 2012.

Grayson, A. Kirk. *Assyrian Rulers of the Early First Millennium BC I (1114–859)*. RIMA 2. Toronto: University of Toronto Press, 1991.

Greenberg, Moshe. "Decalogue (The Ten Commandments)." *EJ* 5:520–25.

______. "Hebrew *s*[e]*gullā* : Akkadian *sikiltu*." *JAOS* 71 (1951): 172–74.

______. "Some Postulates of Biblical Criminal Law." Pages 283–300 in *A Song of Power and the Power of Song: Essays on the Book of Deuteronomy*, edited by Duane Christensen. SBTS 3. Winona Lake, IN: Eisenbrauns, 1993.

Greene-McCreight, Kathryn. "Restless until We Rest in God: The Fourth Commandment as Test Case in Christian 'Plain Sense' Interpretation." Pages 223–36 in *The Ten Commandments: The Reciprocity of Faithfulness*, edited William P. Brown. 1st ed. Louisville: Westminster John Knox, 2004.

Greengus, Samuel. "Law; Biblical and ANE Law." *ABD* 4:242–52.

Greenstein, Edward L. "The Rhetoric of the Ten Commandments." Pages 1–12 in *The Decalogue in Jewish and Christian Tradition*, edited by Henning Graf Reventlow and Yair Hoffman. LHBOTS 509. New York: T&T Clark, 2011.

Gruber, Mayer I. *Rashi's Commentary on Psalms*. BRLJ 18. Boston: Brill, 2004.

Guest, Stephen. "Deuteronomy 26:16–19 as the Central Focus of the Covenantal Framework of Deuteronomy." PhD diss., Southern Baptist Theological Seminary, 2009.

Guillaume, A. "Is 44:5 in the Light of the Elephantine Papyri." *ExpTim* 32 (1920): 377–79.

Gunkel, Hermann. *Die Psalmen: übersetzt und erklärt*. 4th ed. HKAT. Göttingen: Vandenhoeck & Ruprecht, 1926.

Guralnick, Eleanor. "Fabric Patterns as Symbols of Status in the Near East and Early Greece." Pages 84–114 in *Reading a Dynamic Canvas: Adornment in the Ancient*

Mediterranean World, edited by Cynthia S. Colburn and Maura K. Heyn. Newcastle, UK: Cambridge Scholars, 2008.

______. "Neo-Assyrian Patterned Fabrics." *Iraq* 66 (2004): 221–32.

Hall, John R. Clark, ed. *A Concise Anglo-Saxon Dictionary for the Use of Students*. New York: Macmillan, 1894.

Hallo, William, and K. Lawson Younger, eds. *Context of Scripture*. 3 vols. Leiden: Brill, 2003.

Hamilton, Victor P. *Exodus: An Exegetical Commentary*. Grand Rapids: Baker Academic, 2011.

Hanhart, Robert, ed. *Tobit*. Septuaginta: Vetus Testamentum Graecum 8/5. Göttingen: Vandenhoeck & Ruprecht, 1983.

Haran, Menahem. *Temples and Temple-Service in Ancient Israel: An Inquiry into Biblical Cult Phenomena and the Historical Setting of the Priestly School*. Winona Lake, IN: Eisenbrauns, 1985.

Harman, Allan M. *Deuteronomy: The Commands of a Covenant God*. Focus on the Bible. Ross-shire, Scotland: Christian Focus, 2007.

______. "The Interpretation of the Third Commandment." *RTR* 47 (1988): 1–7.

Harn, Roger van, ed. *The Ten Commandments for Jews, Christians, and Others*. Grand Rapids: Eerdmans, 2007.

Harrelson, Walter J. *The Ten Commandments and Human Rights*. Rev. ed. Macon, GA: Mercer University Press, 1997.

Harris, J. S. "The Stones of the High Priest's Breastplate." Edited by John MacDonald. *ALUOS* 5 (65 1963): 40–62.

Harris, R. L., and G. L. Archer, Jr., eds. *Theological Wordbook of the Old Testament*. 2 vols. Chicago: Moody, 1980.

Hartley, John E. *Leviticus*. WBC 4. Dallas: Word, 1992.

Hartman, Louis F. "God, Names of." *EJ* 7:672–78.

Hatch, E., and H. A. Redpath. *Concordance to the Septuagint and Other Greek Versions of the Old Testament*. 2 vols. Oxford, 1897. Supplement, 1906; reprinted, Graz, Austria: Akademische Druck, 1954.

Haulotte, Edgar. *Symbolique du Vêtement Selon la Bible*. Collection Théologie 65. Paris: Aubier, 1966.

Hauser, Alan J., and Duane F. Watson, eds. *A History of Biblical Interpretation*, vol. 1: *The Ancient Period*. Grand Rapids: Eerdmans, 2003.

Heim, Knut Martin. *Poetic Imagination in Proverbs: Variant Repetitions and the Nature of Poetry*. BBRSup 4. Winona Lake, IN: Eisenbrauns, 2013.

Hendel, Ronald S. "Sacrifice as a Cultural System: The Ritual Symbolism of Exodus 24,3–8." *ZAW* 101 (1989): 366–90.

Henry, Matthew. *Matthew Henry's Commentary on the Whole Bible*. Peabody, MA: Hendrickson, 1991.

Hestrin, Ruth, and Michal Dayagi-Mendeles. *Inscribed Seals: First Temple Period Hebrew, Ammonite, Moabite, Phoenician and Aramaic from the Collections of the Israel Museum and the Israel Department of Antiquities and Museums*. Jerusalem: Israel Museum, 1979.

Hess, Richard S. "Hebrew Psalms and Amarna Correspondence from Jerusalem." *ZAW* 101 (1989): 249–65.

______. *Israelite Religions: An Archaeological and Biblical Survey*. Grand Rapids: Baker Academic, 2007.

Hilaire of Poitiers. *Sur Matthieu I* 4,23. Translated by Jean Doignon. SC 254. Paris: du Cerf, 2007.

Hirsch, David H., and Nehama Aschkenasy. "Translatable Structure, Untranslatable Poem: Psalm 24." *Modern Language Studies* 12:4 (1982): 21–34.

Höffken, Peter. *Das Buch Jesaja: Kapitel 40–66*. Neuer Stuttgarter Kommentar Altes Testament 18. Stuttgart: Katholisches Bibelwerk, 1998.

Hoffner, Harold A. "Hittite Equivalents of Old Assyrian *kumrum* and *epattum*." *WZKM* 86 (1996): 154–56.

Hoftijzer, J., and K. Jongeling, eds. *Dictionary of the North-West Semitic Inscriptions*. 2 vols. Leiden: Brill, 1995.

Holladay, William L. *Jeremiah 1: A Commentary on the Book of the Prophet Jeremiah Chapters 1–25*. Hermeneia. Minneapolis: Fortress, 1986.

Holmes, Michael. *The Apostolic Fathers: Greek Texts and English Translations*. 3rd ed. Grand Rapids: Baker Academic, 2007.

Hornung, Erik. *Conceptions of God in Ancient Egypt: The One and the Many*. Translated by John Baines. Ithaca, NY: Cornell University Press, 1971.

Hossfeld, Frank-Lothar. *Der Dekalog: Seine späten Fassungen, die originale Komposition und seine Vorstufen*. Göttingen: Vandenhoeck & Ruprecht, 1982.

Houtman, Cornelis. *Exodus*. Translated by Sierd Woudstra. HCOT. Leuven: Peeters, 2000.

Howard, David M. *Joshua*. NAC 5. Nashville: Broadman & Holman, 1998.

Howe, Bonnie. *Because You Bear This Name: Conceptual Metaphor and the Moral Meaning of 1 Peter*. BIS 81. Boston: Brill, 2006.

Huehnergard, John, and Harold Liebowitz. "The Biblical Prohibition against Tattooing." *VT* 63 (2013): 59–77.

Huffmon, Herbert B. "Contrasting Juridical Conceptions in Ancient Near Eastern Treaties and Covenants." Paper presented at the Annual Meeting of the SBL, Chicago, IL, November 2012.

______. "The Fundamental Code Illustrated: The Third Commandment." Pages 205–12 in *The Ten Commandments: The Reciprocity of Faithfulness*, edited by William Brown. Louisville: Westminster John Knox, 2004.

Hundley, Michael. *Keeping Heaven on Earth: Safeguarding the Divine Presence in the Priestly Tabernacle*. FAT 2/50. Tübingen: Mohr Siebeck, 2011.

______. "To Be or Not To Be: A Reexamination of Name Language in Deuteronomy and the Deuteronomistic History." *VT* 59 (2009): 533–55.

Hwang, Jerry. *The Rhetoric of Remembrance: An Investigation of the "Fathers" in Deuteronomy*. Siphrut 8. Winona Lake, IN: Eisenbrauns, 2012.

Ibn Ezra. *Commentary on the Pentateuch: Exodus (Shemot)*. Translated by H. Norman Strickman and Arthur M. Silver. New York: Menorah, 1996.

Ishmael. *Mekhilta according to Rabbi Ishmael: An Analytical Translation*. Translated by Jacob Neusner. BJS 148. Atlanta: Scholars Press, 1988.

Jackson, B. S. "The Ceremonial and the Judicial: Biblical Law as Sign and Symbol." *JSOT* 30 (1984): 25–50.

Jacob, Benno. *The Second Book of the Bible: Exodus*. Translated by Walter Jacob. Hoboken, NJ: Ktav, 1992.

Jacobs, Sandra. *The Body as Property: Physical Disfigurement in Biblical Law*. LHBOTS 582. London: Bloomsbury, 2014.

______. "The Body Inscribed: A Priestly Initiative?" Pages 1–16 in *The Body in Biblical, Christian and Jewish Texts*, edited by Joan E. Taylor. LSTS 85. London: Bloomsbury, 2014.

James, T. G. H. *Hieroglyphic Texts from Egyptian Stelae, etc.* Part 9. London: Trustees of the British Museum, 1970.

Janzen, Waldemar. *Exodus*. Believers Church Bible Commentary. Scottdale, PA: Herald, 2000.

______. *Old Testament Ethics: A Paradigmatic Approach*. Louisville: Westminster John Knox, 1994.

Japhet, Sara. *I and II Chronicles: A Commentary*. OTL. Louisville: Westminster John Knox, 1993.

______. "Some Biblical Concepts of Sacred Place." Pages 55–72 in *Sacred Space—Shrine, City, Land: Proceedings of the International Conference in Memory of Joshua Prawer*, edited by Benjamin Z. Kedar and R. J. Zwi Werblowsky. Jerusalem: Israel Academy of Sciences and Humanities, 1998.

Jastrow, Marcus. *A Dictionary of the Targumim, the Talmud Babli and Yerushalmi, and the Midrashic Literature*. 2nd ed. Peabody, MA: Hendrickson, 2006.

Jenni, E., and C. Westermann, eds. *Theological Lexicon of the Old Testament.* Translated by M. E. Biddle. 3 vols. Peabody, MA: Hendrickson, 1997.

Jenson, Philip Peter. *Graded Holiness: A Key to the Priestly Conception of the World.* JSOTSup 106. Sheffield: Sheffield Academic, 1992.

Jindo, Job Y. *Biblical Metaphor Reconsidered: A Cognitive Approach to Poetic Prophecy in Jeremiah 1–24*. HSM 64. Winona Lake, IN: Eisenbrauns, 2010.

______. "Toward the Poetics of the Biblical Mind: Language, Culture, and Cognition." *VT* 59 (2009): 222–43.

Jobes, Karen, and Moises Silva. *Invitation to the Septuagint*. Grand Rapids: Baker Academic, 2005.

Johnstone, William. "From the Sea to the Mountain: Exodus 15,22–19,2: A Case-Study in Editorial Techniques." Pages 245–63 in *Studies in the Book of Exodus: Redaction, Reception, Interpretation*, edited by Marc Vervenne. BETL 126. Leuven: Leuven University Press, 1996.

Jones, C. P. "Stigma: Tattooing and Branding in Graeco-Roman Antiquity." *JRS* 77 (1987): 139–55.

Josephus, Flavius. *Jewish Antiquities.* Translated by H. St. J. Thackeray. LCL 242. Cambridge, MA: Harvard University Press, 1998.

Joüon, Paul, and T. Muraoka. *A Grammar of Biblical Hebrew*. Rome: Pontifical Biblical Institute, 2006.

Kaiser, Walter C. *Toward Old Testament Ethics*. Grand Rapids: Zondervan, 1983.

Kalluveettil, Paul. *Declaration and Covenant: A Comprehensive Review of Covenant Formulae from the Old Testament and the Ancient Near East*. AnBib 88. Rome: Pontifical Biblical Institute, 1982.

Keck, Leander E., ed. *The New Interpreter's Bible Commentary.* 12 vols. Nashville: Abingdon, 1994–2003.

Keel, Othmar. "Zeichen der Verbundenheit: Zur Vorgeschichte und Bedeutung der Forderungen von Deuteronomium 6,8 f. und Par." Pages 159–240 in *Mélanges Dominique Barthélemy: Études Bibliques Offertes A L'Occasion de son 60 Anniversaire*, edited by P. Casetti, O. Keel, and A. Schenker. OBO 38. Göttingen: Vandenhoeck & Ruprecht, 1981.

Keel, Othmar, and Christoph Uehlinger. *Gods, Goddesses, and Images of God in Ancient Israel.* Translated by Thomas H. Trapp. Minneapolis: Fortress, 1998.

Kellermann, Ulrich. "Der Dekalog in den Schriften des Frühjudentums: Ein Überblick." Pages 147–226 in *Weisheit, Ethos und Gebot: Weisheits- und Dekalogtraditionen in der Bibel und im frühen Judentum*. Biblisch-Theologische Studien 43. Neukirchen-Vluyn: Neukirchener Verlag, 2001.

Kessler, Werner. "Die literarische, historische und theologische Problematik des Dekalogs." *VT* 7 (1957): 1–16.

Kilchör, Benjamin. *Mosetora und Jahwetora: Das Verhältnis von Deuteronomium 12–26 zu Exodus, Levitikus und Numeri*. BZABR 21. Wiesbaden: Harrassowitz, 2015.
King, Philip J. *Jeremiah: An Archaeological Companion*. Louisville: Westminster John Knox, 1993.
King, Philip J., and Lawrence E. Stager. *Life in Biblical Israel*. LAI. Louisville: Westminster John Knox, 2001.
Kitchen, Kenneth A. *On the Reliability of the Old Testament*. Grand Rapids: Eerdmans, 2006.
Kitchen, Kenneth A., and Paul J. N. Lawrence. *Treaty, Law and Covenant in the Ancient Near East*. 3 vols. Wiesbaden: Harrassowitz, 2012.
Kittel, G., and G. Friedrich, eds. *Theological Dictionary of the New Testament*. Translated by G. W. Bromiley. 10 vols. Grand Rapids: Eerdmans, 1964–76.
Kiuchi, Nobuyoshi. *The Purification Offering in the Priestly Literature: Its Meaning and Function*. JSOTSup 56. Sheffield: Sheffield Academic, 1987.
Klein, Michael L. *The Fragment-Targums of the Pentateuch according to Their Extant Sources*. 2 vols. AnBib. Rome: Pontifical Biblical Institute, 1980.
______. *Genizah Manuscripts of Palestinian Targum to the Pentateuch*. 2 vols. Cincinnati: Hebrew Union College Press, 1986.
Klein, Ralph W. *1 Samuel*. WBC. Nashville: Thomas Nelson, 1983.
______. *2 Chronicles: A Commentary*. Hermeneia. Minneapolis: Fortress, 2012.
Kline, Meredith G. *Treaty of the Great King: The Covenant Structure of Deuteronomy: Studies and Commentary*. Grand Rapids: Eerdmans, 1963.
______. "The Two Tables of the Covenant." *WTJ* 22 (1960): 133–46.
Klingbeil, Gerald A. *Bridging the Gap: Ritual and Ritual Texts in the Bible*. BBRSup 1. Winona Lake, IN: Eisenbrauns, 2007.
______. *A Comparative Study of the Ritual of Ordination as Found in Leviticus 8 and Emar 369*. Lewiston, NY: Edwin Mellen, 1998.
Klopfenstein, M. A. *Die Lüge nach dem Alten Testament*. Zürich: Gotthelf, 1964.
Knafl, Anne K. "Deuteronomy, Name Theology and Divine Location." Paper presented at the Annual Meeting of the SBL, Atlanta, GA, November 2010.
______. "Forms of God, Forming God: A Typology of Divine Anthropomorphism in the Pentateuch." PhD diss., University of Chicago, 2011.
Knight, Douglas. *Law, Power, and Justice in Ancient Israel*. LAI. Louisville: Westminster John Knox, 2011.
Knight, George A. F. *Theology as Narration: A Commentary on the Book of Exodus*. Edinburgh: Handsel, 1976.
Knohl, Israel. "P and the Traditions of Northern Syria and Southern Anatolia." Pages 63–69 in *Text, Time, and Temple: Literary, Historical and Ritual Studies in Leviticus*, edited by Francis Landy, Leigh M. Trevaskis, and Bryan D. Bibb. Sheffield: Sheffield Phoenix, 2015.
Koehler, L., W. Baumgartner, and J. J. Stamm, *The Hebrew and Aramaic Lexicon of the Old Testament*. Translated and edited under the supervision of M. E. J. Richardson. 2 vols. Boston: Brill, 2001.
Kopf, Lothar. "Das arabische Wörterbuch als Hilfsmittel für die hebräische Lexikographie." *VT* 6 (1956): 286–302.
Kövecses, Zoltán. *Metaphor: A Practical Introduction*. 2nd ed. Oxford: Oxford University Press, 2010.
Kraus, Hans-Joachim. *Psalms 1–59*. CC. Minneapolis: Fortress, 1993.
Kugel, James L. *The Bible as It Was*. Cambridge, MA: Belknap, 1997.
______. *The Idea of Biblical Poetry: Parallelism and Its History*. Baltimore: Johns Hopkins University Press, 1998.

Kuntz, Paul Grimley. *The Ten Commandments in History: Mosaic Paradigms for a Well-Ordered Society*. Edited by Thomas D'Evelyn. Emory University Studies in Law and Religion. Grand Rapids: Eerdmans, 2004.

Kutsch, Ernst. *Verheissung und Gesetz: Untersuchungen zum sogenannten "Bund" im Alten Testament*. BZAW 131. New York: de Gruyter, 1973.

Lakoff, George, and Mark Johnson. *Metaphors We Live By*. Chicago: University of Chicago Press, 1980.

Lam, Joseph. *Patterns of Sin in the Hebrew Bible: Metaphor, Culture, and the Making of a Religious Concept*. Oxford: Oxford University Press, 2016.

______. Review of Gary A. Anderson, *Sin: A History*. *RBL* (2010).

Lambert, W. G. *Babylonian Wisdom Literature*. Oxford: Clarendon, 1960.

______. "*Dingir.šà.dib.ba* Incantations." *JNES* 33 (1974): 267–322.

Laroche, E., ed. *Catalogue des textes hittites.* Etudes et commentaries 75. Paris: Klincksieck, 1971.

Lauinger, Jacob. "Esarhaddon's Succession Treaty at Tell Tayinat: Text and Commentary." *JCS* 64 (2012) 87–123.

______. "Some Preliminary Thoughts on the Tablet Collection in Building XVI from Tell Tayinat." *Journal of the Canadian Society for Mesopotamian Studies* 6 (2011): 5–14.

Lau, Wolfgang. *Schriftgelehrte Prophetie in Jes 56–66: eine Untersuchung zu den literarischen Bezügen in den letzten elf Kapiteln des Jesajabuches*. Berlin: de Gruyter, 1994.

Laver, James. *Costume in Antiquity*. London: Thames & Hudson, 1964.

LeFebvre, Michael. *Collections, Codes, and Torah: The Re-characterization of Israel's Written Law*. LHBOTS 451. New York: T&T Clark, 2006.

Lehmann, M. R. "Biblical Oaths." *ZAW* 81 (1969): 74–92.

Lenzi, Alan, ed. *Reading Akkadian Prayers and Hymns: An Introduction*. ANEM 3. Atlanta: SBL, 2011.

Levine, Baruch A. *Leviticus*. JPS Torah Commentary. Philadelphia: Jewish Publication Society, 1989.

______. *Numbers 1–20*. AB 4A. New Haven, CT: Yale University Press, 1993.

Levtow, Nathaniel B. *Images of Others: Iconic Politics in Ancient Israel*. BJSUCSD11. Winona Lake, IN: Eisenbrauns, 2008.

Lewis, Theodore J. "ʿAthtartu's Incantations and the Use of Divine Names as Weapons." *JNES* 70:2 (2011): 207–27.

Liddell, H. G., R. Scott, and H. S. Jones, *A Greek-English Lexicon.* 9th ed. with revised supplement. Oxford: Clarendon, 1996.

Liebermann, F. *Die Gesetze der Angelsachsen*. Scientia Aalen, 1960.

Lohfink, Norbert. "Kennt das Alte Testament einen Unterschied von 'Gebot' und 'Gesetz'? Zur bibeltheologischen Einstufung des Dekalogs." *JBTh* 4 (1989): 63–89.

______. *Theology of the Pentateuch: Themes of the Priestly Narrative and Deuteronomy*. Translated by L. M. Maloney. Minneapolis: Fortress, 1994.

Longacre, Robert E. "Building for the Worship of God: Exodus 25:1–30:10." Pages 21–49 in *Discourse Analysis of Biblical Literature: What It Is and What It Offers*, edited by Walter R. Bodine. Semeia. Atlanta: Scholars Press, 1995.

Longman, III, Tremper, and David E. Garland, eds. *The Expositor's Bible Commentary*. Grand Rapids: Zondervan, 2006–12.

López, René A. "Identifying the 'Angel of the Lord' in the Book of Judges: A Model for Reconsidering the Referent in Other Old Testament Loci." *BBR* 20 (2010): 1–18.

Lorton, David. "The Theology of Cult Statues in Ancient Egypt." Pages 123–210 in *Born in Heaven, Made on Earth: The Making of the Cult Image in the Ancient Near East*, edited by Michael B. Dick. Winona Lake, IN: Eisenbrauns, 1999.

Lundbom, Jack R. *Jeremiah 1–20*. AB 21A. New York: Doubleday, 1999.

Lunn, Nicholas. *Word-Order Variation in Biblical Hebrew Poetry: Differentiating Pragmatics and Poetics*. Waynesboro, GA: Paternoster, 2006.

Lust, Johan. *A Greek-English Lexicon of the Septuagint*. Stuttgart: Deutsche Bibelgesellschaft, 1992.

______. "Textual Criticism of the Old and New Testaments: Stepbrothers?" Pages 15–31 in *New Testament Textual Criticism and Exegesis: Festschrift J. Delobel*, edited by A. Denaux. BETL 161. Leuven: Leuven University Press, 2002.

Luther, Martin. "Admonition to Peace." In *The Christian in Society III*. Edited and translated by Robert C. Schultz. *LW* 46:24. Philadelphia: Fortress, 1967.

______. "On the Jews and Their Lies." In *The Christian in Society IV.* Edited by Franklin Sherman. Translated by Martin H. Bertram. *LW* 47. Philadelphia: Fortress, 1971.

______. "A Simple Way to Pray." In *Devotional Writings II*. Edited by Gustav K. Wiencke. Translated by Carl J. Schindler. *LW* 43. Philadelphia: Fortress, 1968.

______. "Ten Sermons on the Catechism, 1528." Pages 141–43 in *Sermons I*. Edited and translated by John W. Doberstein. *LW* 51. Philadelphia: Muhlenberg.

Lutz, Henry F. *Textiles and Costume among People of the Ancient Near East*. Leipzig: Hinrichs, 1923.

MacDonald, William Graham. "Christology and 'The Angel of the Lord.'" Pages 324–35 in *Current Issues in Biblical and Patristic Interpretation: Studies in Honor of Merrill C. Tenney Presented by His Former Students*, edited by Gerald F. Hawthorne. Grand Rapids: Eerdmans, 1975.

Macho, Alejandro Díez, trans. *Neophyti 1: Targum Palestinense MS de la Biblioteca Vaticana, Tomo II: Éxodo*. Textos y Estudios Consejo de Redacción 8. Madrid: Consejo Superior de Investigaciones Científicas, 1970.

______. *Neophyti 1: Targum Palestinense MS de la Biblioteca Vaticana, Tomo V: Deuteronomio*. Textos y Estudios 11. Madrid: Consejo Superior de Investigaciones Científicas, 1978.

Magness-Gardiner, Bonnie. "Seals." *OEANE* 4:509–12.

Maimonides. *Sefer Ha-Mitzvoth of Maimonides*. Translated by Charles B. Chavel. New York: Soncino, 1967.

Malone, Andrew S. "Distinguishing the Angel of the Lord." *BBR* 21 (2011): 297–314.

Markl, Dominik. *Der Dekalog als Verfassung des Gottesvolkes: die Brennpunkte einer narrativen Rechtshermeneutik des Pentateuch in Exodus 19–24 und Deuteronomium 5*. Freiberg: Herder, 2007.

Marshall, J. W. "Decalogue." *DOTP* 171–82.

Mathews, Kenneth. *Genesis 11:27–50:26*. NAC. Nashville: B&H, 2005.

McBride, S. Dean. "The Deuteronomic Name Theology." PhD diss., Harvard University, 1969.

McCann, J. Clinton. "The Book of Psalms." In vol. 4 of *NIB*. Nashville: Abingdon, 1996.

McCarthy, Dennis J. *Treaty and Covenant: A Study in Form in the Ancient Oriental Documents and in the Old Testament*. AnBib 21A. Rome: Pontifical Biblical Institute, 1978.

McComiskey, Thomas. "Zechariah." Pages 1003–244 in *The Minor Prophets: An Exegetical and Expository Commentary*, edited by Thomas McComiskey. Grand Rapids: Baker Academic, 2009.

McComiskey, Thomas, ed. *The Minor Prophets: An Exegetical and Expository Commentary*. Grand Rapids: Baker Academic, 2009.

McConville, J. G. *Deuteronomy*. AOTC. Downers Grove, IL: InterVarsity, 2002.

______. "God's 'Name' and God's 'Glory.'" *TynBul* 30 (1979): 149–63.

McDonald, Suzanne. *Re-imaging Election: Divine Election as Representing God to Others and Others to God*. Grand Rapids: Eerdmans, 2010.

McNeile, A. H. *The Book of Exodus*. 3rd ed. WC. London: Methuen, 1931.

Mendenhall, George E. "The Conflict between Value Systems and Social Control." Pages 169–80 in *Unity and Diversity: Essays in the History, Literature and Religion of the Ancient Near East*, edited by H. Goedicke and J. J. M. Roberts. Baltimore: Johns Hopkins University Press, 1975.

______. *Law and Covenant in Israel and the Ancient Near East*. Pittsburgh: Presbyterian Board of Colportage, 1955.

Mendenhall, George E., and Gary A. Herion. "Covenant." *ABD* 1:1179–202.

Merrill, Eugene H. *Deuteronomy*. NAC. Nashville: Broadman & Holman, 1994.

Merwe, Christo H. J. van der, Jackie A. Naudé, and Jan H. Kroeze. *A Biblical Hebrew Reference Grammar*. Biblical Languages: Hebrew 3. New York: Sheffield, 2002.

Mettinger, Tryggve N. D. *The Dethronement of Sabaoth: Studies in the Shem and Kabod Theologies*. Translated by Frederick H. Cryer. ConBOT 18. Lund: Gleerup, 1982.

Meyers, Carol L. *Exodus*. New Cambridge Bible Commentary. New York: Cambridge University Press, 2005.

Meyers, E. M., ed. *The Oxford Encyclopedia of Archaeology in the Near East*. New York: Oxford University Press, 1997.

Milgrom, Jacob. "The Desecration of YHWH's Name: Its Parameters and Significance." Pages 69–81 in *Birkat Shalom: Studies in the Bible, Ancient Near Eastern Literature, and Postbiblical Judaism Presented to Shalom M. Paul on the Occasion of His Seventieth Birthday*, edited by Chaim Cohen et al. Winona Lake, IN: Eisenbrauns, 2008.

______. *Leviticus 1–16*. AB 3. New York: Doubleday, 1991.

______. *Leviticus 17–22*. AB 3A. New York: Doubleday, 2000.

______. *Leviticus 23–27*. AB 3B. New York: Doubleday, 2001.

______. *Numbers [Ba-midbar]*. JPS Torah Commentary. Philadelphia: Jewish Publication Society, 1990.

______. "Of Hems and Tassels: Rank, Authority and Holiness Were Expressed in Antiquity by Fringes on Garments." *BAR* 9/3 (1983): 61–65.

Milgrom, Jacob, and Daniel I. Block. *Ezekiel's Hope: A Commentary on Ezekiel 38–48*. Eugene, OR: Cascade, 2012.

Millard, Alan R. "The Corpus of West Semitic Stamp Seals: Review Article." *IEJ* 51 (2001): 76–87.

______. "Königssiegel." *RlA* 6:135–40.

______. "Owners and Users of Hebrew Seals." *Eretz Israel* 26 (1999): 129–33.

Miller, Patrick D. *Deuteronomy*. Int. Louisville: John Knox, 1990.

______. "The Place of the Decalogue in the Old Testament and Its Law." *Int* 43 (1989): 229–42.

______. *The Ten Commandments*. Int. Louisville: Westminster John Knox, 2009.

______. "Ten Commandments." *NIDB* 5:517–22.

Mitchell, Christopher Wright. *The Meaning of BRK "To Bless" in the Old Testament*. SBLDS 95. Atlanta: Scholars Press, 1987.

Moberly, Walter. "Exodus." *DTIB* 211–16.

Morenz, Siegfried. *Egyptian Religion*. Translated by Ann E. Keep. Ithaca, NY: Cornell University Press, 1973.

Morschauser, Scott. "Do Not Look to Egypt? On an Alternative to Joshua Berman's 'CTH 133 and the Hittite Provenance of Deuteronomy 13.'" Unpublished manuscript.

Motyer, J. A. *The Message of Exodus: The Days of Our Pilgrimage*. Downers Grove, IL: InterVarsity, 2005.

Mowinckel, Sigmund. *Psalmenstudien I*. Amsterdam: Schippers, 1961.

Mulder, Martin J. "Baal-Berith." *DDD* 141–44.

______, ed. *Mikra: Text, Translation, Reading and Interpretation of the Hebrew Bible in Ancient Judaism and Early Christianity*. Peabody, MA: Hendrickson, 2004.

Muraoka, T. *A Greek-English Lexicon of the Septuagint*. Leuven: Peeters, 2009.

______. *A Greek-Hebrew/Aramaic Two-Way Index to the Septuagint*. Leuven: Peeters, 2010.

Na'aman, Nadav. "Hezekiah's Fortified Cities and the 'LMLK' Stamps." *BASOR* 261 (1986): 5–21.

Nelson, Richard D. *Deuteronomy: A Commentary*. OTL. Philadelphia: Westminster, 2002.

Neusner, J., ed. *The Mishnah: A New Translation*. New Haven, CT: Yale University Press, 1988.

Neusner, J., ed. and trans. *Jerusalem Talmud*. 35 vols. Chicago: University of Chicago Press, 1989.

______. *Mekhilta according to Rabbi Ishmael: An Analytical Translation*. BJS 148. Atlanta: Scholars, 1988.

Newsom, Carol A. "A Maker of Metaphors: Ezekiel's Oracles against Tyre." Pages 191–204 in *"The Place Is Too Small for Us": The Israelite Prophets in Recent Scholarship*, edited by R. P. Gordon. SBTS 5. Winona Lake, IN: Eisenbrauns, 1995.

Niccacci, Alviero. "Workshop: Narrative Syntax of Exodus 19–24." Pages 167–202 in *Narrative Syntax and the Hebrew Bible: Papers of the Tilburg Conference 1996*, edited by Ellen van Wolde. Leiden: Brill, 2002.

Nielsen, Eduard. *The Ten Commandments in New Perspective*. London: SCM, 1968.

Nosch, Marie-Louise, and C. Michel Nosch, eds. *Textile Terminologies in the Ancient Near East and the Mediterranean Area from the 3rd to the 1st Millennium BC*. Ancient Textiles 8. Oxford: Oxbow, 2010.

Noth, Martin. *The Deuteronomistic History*. 2nd ed. JSOTSup 15. Sheffield: Sheffield Academic, 1991.

______. *Exodus: A Commentary*. Translated by J. S. Bowden. OTL. Philadelphia: Westminster, 1962.

Oelsner, Joachim, Bruce Wells, and Cornelia Wunsch, "Neo-Babylonian Period." Pages 911–74 in *A History of Ancient Near Eastern Law*, edited by Raymond Westbrook. Vol. 2. Leiden: Brill, 2003.

Opificius, R. "Gottessiegel." *RlA* 3:576–80.

Oppenheim, A. Leo. "The Golden Garments of the Gods." *JNES* 8:3 (1949): 172–93.

Osiek, Carolyn. *The Shepherd of Hermas: A Commentary*. Hermeneia. Minneapolis: Fortress, 1999.

Oswalt, John. *The Book of Isaiah: Chapters 40–66*. NICOT. Grand Rapids: Eerdmans, 1998.

Otto, Eckhart. "Der Dekalog in den deuteronomistischen Redaktionen des Deuteronomiums." Pages 95–108 in *Die Zehn Worte: der Dekalog als Testfall der Pentateuchkritik*, edited by Michael Konkel, Christian Frevel, and Johannes Schnocks. QD 212. Freiburg im Breisgau: Herder, 2005.

———. *Theologische Ethik des Alten Testaments*. Theologische Wissenschaft. Stuttgart: Kohlhammer, 1994.

Pardee, Dennis. "A New Ugaritic Song to *ʿAṯtartu* (RIH 98/02)." Pages 27–40 in *Ugarit at Seventy-Five*, edited by K. Lawson Younger Jr. Winona Lake, IN: Eisenbrauns, 2007.

Parpola, Simo. "International Law in the First Millennium." Pages 1047–66 in *A History of Ancient Near Eastern Law*, edited by Raymond Westbrook. Vol. 2. Leiden: Brill, 2003.

Parpola, Simo, and Kazuko Watanabe. *Neo-Assyrian Treaties and Loyalty Oaths*. SAA 2. Helsinki: Helsinki University Press, 1988.

Patmore, Hector. "The Shorter and Longer Texts of Ezekiel: The Implications of the Manuscript Finds from Masada and Qumran." *JSOT* 32 (2007): 231–42.

Paton, Lewis. "The Meaning of Exodus XX. 7." *JBL* 22 (1903): 201–10.

Patrick, Dale. "Law in the OT." *NIDB* 3:602–14.

———. *Old Testament Law*. Atlanta: John Knox, 1985.

Paul, Shalom M. *Amos: A Commentary on the Book of Amos*. Hermeneia. Minneapolis: Fortress, 1991.

———. *Isaiah 40–66: Translation and Commentary*. ECC. Grand Rapids: Eerdmans, 2012.

———. *Studies in the Book of the Covenant in the Light of Cuneiform and Biblical Law*. VTSup 18. Leiden: Brill, 1970.

Payne, Annick. *Iron Age Hieroglyphic Luwian Inscriptions*. SBLWAW 29. Atlanta: SBL, 2012.

Pelikan, J., and H. T. Lehmann, eds. *Luther's Works.* 55 vols. Philadelphia: Fortress, 1955–86.

Perdue, Leo G. *The Collapse of History: Reconstructing Old Testament Theology*. Overtures to Biblical Theology. Minneapolis, MN: Fortress, 1994.

Peshitta: The Old Testament in Syriac according to the Peshitta Version. Peshitta Institute. Leiden: Brill, 1977.

Peters, Albrecht. *Ten Commandments*. Translated by Holger K. Sonntag. Commentary on Luther's Catechisms. St. Louis: Concordia, 2009.

Phillips, Anthony. *Ancient Israel's Criminal Law: A New Approach to the Decalogue*. New York: Schocken, 1970.

———. *Essays on Biblical Law*. JSOTSup 344. New York: Sheffield Academic, 2002.

Philo. *On the Decalogue.* Translated by F. H. Colson. LCL 320. Cambridge, MA: Harvard University Press, 1937.

Plato. *The Statesman*. Translated by Harold N. Fowler. LCL 164. Cambridge, MA: Harvard University Press, 1925.

———. *Symposium.* Translated by W. R. M. Lamb. LCL 166. Cambridge, MA: Harvard University Press, 1925.

Pleins, J. David. *The Social Visions of the Hebrew Bible*. Louisville: Westminster John Knox, 2001.

Pliny the Younger. *Letters.* Translated by Betty Radice. LCL 55. Bibliotheca Teubneriana, Schuster, 1952; Cambridge, MA: Harvard University Press, 1969. Cited 7 June 2013. Online: http://www.perseus.tufts.edu.

Polycarp. *To the Philippians.* In *The Apostolic Fathers*, edited and translated by Michael W. Holmes. Grand Rapids: Baker Academic, 2007.

Preuss, Horst Dietrich. *Old Testament Theology*. Translated by Leo G. Perdue. 2 vols. OTL. Louisville: Westminster John Knox, 1995.

Pritchard, J. B. *Ancient Near Eastern Texts Relating to the Old Testament.* 2nd ed. Princeton, NJ: Princeton University Press, 1955.

Propp, William H. C. *Exodus 19–40*. AB 2A. New York: Doubleday, 2006.

Rabinowitz, Louis Isaac. "Teffilin." *EJ* 19:577–80.

Rad, Gerhard von. *Deuteronomy: A Commentary*. Translated by Dorothea Barton. OTL. Philadelphia: Westminster, 1966.

______. *Studies in Deuteronomy*. Translated by David Stalker. Chicago: Regnery, 1953.

Radner, Ephraim. "Taking the Lord's Name in Vain." Pages 77–94 in *I Am the Lord Your God: Christian Reflections on the Ten Commandments*, edited by Carl E. Braaten and Christopher R. Seitz. Grand Rapids: Eerdmans, 2005.

Ramban. *Commentary on the Torah: Exodus*. Translated by Charles B. Chavel. New York: Shilo, 1973.

Redford, Donald B., ed. *The Oxford Encyclopedia of Ancient Egypt*. New York: Oxford University Press, 2001.

Reiner, Erica. *Šurpu: A Collection of Sumerian and Akkadian Incantations*. AfO 11. Osnabrück: Biblio, 1970.

Rendtorff, Rolf. *The Canonical Hebrew Bible: A Theology of the Old Testament*. Translated by David E. Orton. TBS 7. Leiden: Deo, 2005.

Reventlow, Henning Graf. "The Ten Commandments in Luther's Catechisms." Pages 132–47 in *The Decalogue in Jewish and Christian Tradition*, edited by Henning Graf Reventlow and Yair Hoffman. LHBOTS 509. New York: T&T Clark, 2011.

Richter, Sandra L. *The Deuteronomistic History and the Name Theology: lĕšakkēn šĕmô šām in the Bible and the Ancient Near East*. BZAW 318. Berlin: de Gruyter, 2002.

______. *The Epic of Eden: A Christian Entry into the Old Testament*. Downers Grove, IL: IVP Academic, 2008.

______. "The Place of the Name in Deuteronomy." *VT* 57 (2007): 342–66.

______. "Placing the Name, Pushing the Paradigm: A Decade with the Deuteronomistic Name Formula." Pages 64–78 in *Deuteronomy in the Pentateuch, Hexateuch, and the Deuteronomistic History*, edited by Konrad Schmid and Raymond F. Person Jr. Tübingen: Mohr Siebeck, 2012.

Rieder, David, ed. *Pseudo-Jonathan: Targum Jonathan Ben Uziel on the Pentateuch*. Jerusalem: Salomon's, 1974.

Riefstahl, Elizabeth. *Patterned Textiles in Pharaonic Egypt*. Brooklyn: Brooklyn Institute of Arts and Sciences, 1944.

Roberts, Alexander, and James Donaldson, eds. *The Ante-Nicene Fathers*. 1885–87. 10 vols. Peabody, MA: Hendrickson, 1994.

Rose, Martin. "Names of God in the OT." *ABD* 4:1001–11.

Rosenbaum, M., and A. M. Silbermann, trans. *Pentateuch with Targum Onkelos, Haphtaroth and Prayers for Sabbath and Rashi's Commentary*. London: Shapiro, Vallentine & Co., 1948.

Rotelle, John E., ed. *Works of Saint Augustine*. Hyde Park, NY: New City, 1990–2009.

Roth, M. *Law Collections from Mesopotamia and Asia Minor*. SBLWAW 6. Atlanta: Scholars Press, 1995.

Sabatier, Pierre. *Bibliorum Sacrorum latinæ versiones antiquæ seu Vetus Italica*. Regis Typographum & Bibliopolam, 1743.

Sailhamer, John. *The Pentateuch as Narrative: A Biblical-Theological Commentary*. Grand Rapids: Zondervan, 1995.

Sakenfeld, Katharine, ed. *New Interpreter's Dictionary of the Bible*. Nashville: Abingdon, 2006–9.

Sänger, Dieter. "Tora für die Völker—Weisungen der Liebe: Zur Rezeption des Dekalogs im frühen Judentum und Neuen Testament." Pages 97–146 in *Weisheit, Ethos und Gebot: Weisheits- und Dekalogtraditionen in der Bibel und im frühen Ju-*

dentum. Biblisch-Theologische Studien 43. Neukirchen-Vluyn: Neukirchener Verlag, 2001.

Sarna, Nahum. *Exodus [Shemot]*. JPS Torah Commentary. Philadelphia: Jewish Publication Society, 1991.

Schmidt, Werner H. *Die Zehn Gebote im Rahmen alttestamentlicher Ethik*. Edited by Holger Delkurt and Axel Graupner. EdF 281. Darmstadt: Wissenschaftliche Buchgesellschaft, 1993.

Schökel, Luis Alonso. *A Manual of Hebrew Poetics*. Subsidia Biblica 11. Rome: Pontifical Biblical Institute, 1988.

Schüngel-Straumann, Helen. *Der Dekalog: Gottes Gebote?* SBS 67. Stuttgart: KBW, 1973.

Schwartz, Baruch J. "The Bearing of Sin in Priestly Literature." Pages 3–21 in *Pomegrantes and Golden Bells*, edited by D. Wright, D. N. Freedman, and A. Hurwitz. Winona Lake, IN: Eisenbrauns, 1995.

______."Term or Metaphor: Biblical *nōśē ʿāwōn/pešaʿ/ḥeṭ*." *Tarbiz* 63 (1994): 149–71 (Hebrew).

Schwienhorst-Schönberger, Ludger. "Das Verhältnis von Dekalog und Bundesbuch." Pages 57–75 in *Die Zehn Worte: der Dekalog als Testfall der Pentateuchkritik*, edited by Michael Konkel, Christian Frevel, and Johannes Schnocks. QD 212. Freiburg im Breisgau: Herder, 2005.

Schultz, W. *Das Deuteronomium*. Berlin: Schlawitz, 1859.

Shafer, Ann. "Assyrian Royal Monuments on the Periphery: Ritual and the Making of Imperial Space." Pages 133–59 in *Ancient Near Eastern Art in Context: Studies in Honor of Irene J. Winter by Her Students*, edited by Jack Cheng and Marian H. Feldman. CHANE 26. Leiden: Brill, 2007.

Simpson, J. A., and E. S. C. Weiner. *The Oxford English Dictionary*. 2nd ed. 20 vols. Oxford: Clarendon, 1989.

Singer, Itamar. *Hittite Prayers*. SBLWAW 11. Atlanta: SBL, 2002.

Skolnik, Fred, and Michael Berenbaum, eds. *Encyclopaedia Judaica*. 2nd ed. 16 vols. Detroit: Thomson Gale, 2007.

Smith, Craig A. "Criteria for Biblical Chiasms: Objective Means for Distinguishing Chiasms of Design from Accidental and False Chiasm." PhD diss., University of Bristol, 2009.

Smith, J. Payne, ed. *A Compendious Syriac Dictionary*. Winona Lake, IN: Eisenbrauns, 1998.

Smith, Mark S. *The Pilgrimage Pattern in Exodus*. JSOTSup 239. Sheffield: Sheffield Academic, 1997.

Smith, Mark S., and Simon B. Parker, eds. *Ugaritic Narrative Poetry*. SBLWAW 9. Atlanta: Scholars Press, 1997.

Soden, W. von, ed. *Akkadisches Handwörterbuch*. 3 vols. Wiesbaden: Harrassowitz, 1965–1981.

Sokoloff, Michael. *A Dictionary of Jewish Palestinian Aramaic of the Byzantine Period*. Dictionaries of Talmud, Midrash and Targum 2. Ramat-Gan: Bar Ilan University Press, 1990.

Soncino, Rifat. "Law; Forms of Biblical Law." *ABD* 4:252–54.

Soulen, R. Kendall. "The Blessing of God's Name." Pages 47–61 in *The Ten Commandments for Jews, Christians, and Others*, edited by Roger van Harn. Grand Rapids: Eerdmans, 2007.

______. *The Divine Name(s) and the Holy Trinity: Distinguishing the Voices*. Louisville: Westminster John Knox, 2011.

Sparks, Kenton L. *Ancient Texts for the Study of the Hebrew Bible: A Guide to the Background Literature*. Peabody, MA: Hendrickson, 2005.

Speiser, E. A. *Genesis*. AB 1. New York: Doubleday, 1964.

Sperber, Alexander, ed. *The Bible in Aramaic Based on Old Manuscripts and Printed Texts*, vol. 1: *The Pentateuch according to Targum Onkelos*. Leiden: Brill, 1959.

Stamm, J. J. *The Ten Commandments in Recent Research*. Translated by M. E. Andrew. SBT 2/2. Naperville, IL: Allenson, 1967.

Staples, W. E. "The Third Commandment." *JBL* 58 (1939): 325–29.

Stec, David, ed. *The Targum of Psalms*. ArBib 16. Collegeville: Liturgical Press, 2004.

Stolper, Mathew. "Inscribed in Egyptian." Pages 133–43 in *Studies in Persian History: Essays in Memory of David M. Lewis*, edited by Maria Brosius and Amélie Kuhrt. Achaemenid History 11. Leiden: Nederlands Instituut voor het Nabije Oosten, 1998.

Stott, John R. W. *Basic Christianity*. Grand Rapids: Eerdmans, 2008.

Strawn, Brent A., ed. *The Oxford Encyclopedia of the Bible and Law*. Oxford: Oxford University Press, 2015.

Strong, John T. "Israel as a Testimony to YHWH's Power: The Priest's Definition of Israel." Pages 89–106 in *Constituting the Community: Studies of the Polity of Ancient Israel in Honor of S. Dean McBride Jr.*, edited by John T. Strong and Steven S. Tuell. Winona Lake, IN: Eisenbrauns, 2005.

Surls, Austin D. *Making Sense of the Divine Name in the Book of Exodus: From Etymology to Literary Onomastics*. BBRSup 17. Winona Lake, IN: Eisenbrauns, 2017.

Swift, Edgar, ed. *The Vulgate Bible*, vol. 1: *The Pentateuch, Douay Rheims Translation*. Dumbarton Oaks Medieval Library. Cambridge, MA: Harvard University Press, 2010.

Tal, Abraham. "The Samaritan Targum of the Pentateuch." Pages 189–216 in *Mikra: Text, Translation, Reading and Interpretation of the Hebrew Bible in Ancient Judaism and Early Christianity*, edited by Martin Mulder. Peabody, MA: Hendrickson, 2004.

______. *The Samaritan Targum of the Pentateuch: A Critical Edition*, part 1: *Genesis, Exodus*. Vol. 4. Texts and Studies in the Hebrew Language and Related Subjects. Tel-Aviv: Tel-Aviv University, 1980.

______. *The Samaritan Targum of the Pentateuch: A Critical Edition*, part 2: *Leviticus, Numeri, Deuteronomium*. Vol. 5. Texts and Studies in the Hebrew Language and Related Subjects. Tel-Aviv: Tel-Aviv University, 1981.

Tal, Abraham, and Moshe Florentin, eds. *The Pentateuch: The Samaritan Version and the Masoretic Version*. Tel Aviv: The Haim Rubin Tel Aviv University Press, 2010.

The Talmud of the Land of Israel: A Preliminary Translation and Explanation. Chicago: University of Chicago Press, 1989.

Tawil, Hayim ben Yosef. *An Akkadian Lexical Companion for Biblical Hebrew: Etymological-Semantic and Idiomatic Equivalents with Supplement on Biblical Aramaic*. Jersey City, NJ: Ktav, 2009.

Tertullian. *Against Praxeas*. Translated by Ernest Evans. Great Britain: Constable, 1948.

______. *On Idolatry*. Translated by J. H. Waszink and J. C. M. Van Winden. SVG 1. New York: Brill, 1987.

Thayer, Joseph Henry, trans. *Greek-English Lexicon of the New Testament*. 4th ed. Edinburgh: T&T Clark, 1901.

Theodoret of Cyrus. *The Questions on the Octateuch: On Genesis and Exodus*. Edited by John F. Peiruccione. Translated by Robert C. Hill. LEC 1. Washington, DC: Catholic University of America Press, 2007.

Thomas, D. Winton. *Documents from Old Testament Times*. New York: Harper & Row, 1958.

Tigay, Jeffrey H. *Deuteronomy [Devarim]*. JPS Torah Commentary. Philadelphia: Jewish Publication Society, 1996.

______. "Israelite Religion: The Onomastic and Epigraphic Evidence." Pages 157–94 in *Ancient Israelite Religion: Essays in Honor of Frank Moore Cross*, edited by Patrick D. Miller Jr., Paul D. Hanson, and S. Dean McBride. Philadelphia: Fortress, 1987.

Toorn, K. van der, B. Becking, and P. W. van der Horst, eds. *Dictionary of Deities and Demons in the Bible*. 2nd ed. Leiden: Brill, 1999.

Tov, Emanuel. *Textual Criticism of the Hebrew Bible*. 2nd rev. ed. Minneapolis: Fortress, 2001.

______. *Textual Criticism of the Hebrew Bible*. 3rd rev. ed. Minneapolis: Fortress, 2012.

Troxel, Ronald. *LXX-Isaiah as Translation and Interpretation: The Strategies of the Translator of the Septuagint of Isaiah*. Boston: Brill, 2008.

Uhlig, Torsten. *The Theme of Hardening in the Book of Isaiah*. FAT 2/39. Tübingen: Mohr Siebeck, 2009.

Van Dam, Cornelis. *The Urim and Thummim: A Means of Revelation in Ancient Israel*. Winona Lake, IN: Eisenbrauns, 1997.

Vandier, Jacques. *La Religion Égyptienne*. Les anciennes Religions orientales 1. Paris: Presses Univeritaires de France, 1944.

VanGemeren, Willem A. *New International Dictionary of Old Testament Theology and Exegesis*. 5 vols. Grand Rapids: Zondervan, 1997.

______. "Psalms." *EBC* 5:1–880.

Vanhoozer, Kevin J. *Is There a Meaning in This Text? The Bible, the Reader, and the Morality of Literary Knowledge*. Grand Rapids: Zondervan, 1998.

______, ed. *Dictionary for Theological Interpretation of the Bible*. Grand Rapids: Baker, 2005.

Van Seters, John. "'Comparing Scripture with Scripture': Some Observations on the Sinai Pericope of Exodus 19–24." Pages 111–30 in *Canon, Theology and Old Testament Interpretation: Essays in Honor of Brevard S. Childs*, edited by G. M. Tucker. Philadelphia: Fortress, 1988.

Vaughn, Andrew G. *Theology, History, and Archaeology in the Chronicler's Account of Hezekiah*. ABS 4. Atlanta: SBL, 1999.

Vaux, Roland de. "Le lieu que Yahvé a choisi pour y établir son nom." Pages 219–28 in *Das ferne und nahe Wort: Festschrift L. Rost*, edited by Fritz Maass. Berlin: Alfred Töpelmann, 1967.

______. "Review of 'Jahwes Eigentumsvolk: Eine Studie zur Traditionsgeschichte und Theologie des Erwählungsgedankens.'" *RB* 71 (1964): 115–17.

Veijola, Timo. "Das dritte Gebot (Namenverbot) im Lichte einer ägyptischen Parallele." *ZAW* 103 (1991): 1–17.

Verhoef, Pieter. *The Books of Haggai and Malachi*. NICOT. Grand Rapids: Eerdmans, 1987.

Vogelsang-Eastwood, Gillian. *Pharaonic Egyptian Clothing*. Studies in Textile and Costume History 2. Leiden: Brill, 1993.

Vogelzang, M. E., and W. J. van Bekkum. "Meaning and Symbolism of Clothing in Ancient Near Eastern Texts." Pages 265–84 in *Script Signa Vocis: Studies about Scripts, Scriptures, Scribes, and Languages in the Near East, Presented to J. H. Hospers by His Pupils, Colleagues and Friends*. Edited by L. J. Vanstiphout, K. Jongeling, F. Leemhuis, and G. J. Reinink. Groningen: Forsten, 1986.

Vogt, Peter T. *Deuteronomic Theology and the Significance of Torah: A Reappraisal*. Winona Lake, IN: Eisenbrauns, 2006.
Vos, Geerhardus. *Biblical Theology: Old and New Testaments*. Carlisle, PA: Versa, 2007.
Vroom, Jonathan. "Recasting *Mišpāṭîm*: Legal Innovation in Leviticus 24:10–23." *JBL* 131 (2012): 27–44.
Wagenaar, Jan. "Crossing the Sea of Reeds (Exod 13–14) and the Jordan (Josh 3–4): A Priestly Framework for the Wilderness Wandering." Pages 461–70 in *Studies in the Book of Exodus: Redaction, Reception, Interpretation*, edited by Marc Vervenne. BETL 126. Leuven: Leuven University Press, 1996.
Wagner, A. J. "An Interpretation of Exodus 20:7." *Int* 6 (1952): 228–29.
Waltke, Bruce K., and M. O'Connor. *An Introduction to Biblical Hebrew Syntax*. Winona Lake, IN: Eisenbrauns, 1990.
Walton, John H. *Ancient Near Eastern Thought and the Old Testament: Introducing the Conceptual World of the Hebrew Bible*. Grand Rapids: Baker Academic, 2009.
______. "The Decalogic Structure of the Deuteronomic Law." Pages 93–117 in *Interpreting Deuteronomy*, edited by David G. Firth and Philip S. Johnston. Nottingham: Apollos, 2012.
______. "Deuteronomy: An Exposition of the Spirit of the Law." *GTJ* 8:2 (1987): 213–25.
______. "Interpreting the Bible as an Ancient Near Eastern Document." Pages 298–327 in *Israel: Ancient Kingdom or Late Invention*, edited by Daniel I. Block. Nashville: Broadman & Holman, 2008.
Walton, John H., ed. *Zondervan Illustrated Bible Background Commentary: Old Testament.* 5 vols. Grand Rapids: Zondervan, 2009.
Watson, Thomas. *The Ten Commandments*. Rev. ed. London: Banner of Truth, 1965.
Weber, Robertus, and Roger Gryson, eds. *Biblia Sacra: Iuxta Vulgatum Versionem*. 5th ed. Stuttgart: Deutsche Bibelgesellschaft, 2007.
Webster's New World College Dictionary. Edited by Michael Agnes. 4th ed. Cleveland: Wiley, 2008.
Weinfeld, Moshe. "Covenant." *EJ* 5:249–53.
______. "Covenant Making in Anatolia and Mesopotamia." *JANES* 22 (1993): 135–39.
______. "The Decalogue: Its Significance, Uniqueness, and Place in Israel's Tradition." Pages 4–9 in *Religion and Law: Biblical-Judaic and Islamic Perspectives*, edited by E. B. Firmage, B. G. Weiss, and J. W. Welch. Winona Lake, IN: Eisenbrauns, 1990.
______. *Deuteronomy 1–11*. AB 5. New York: Doubleday, 1991.
______. *Deuteronomy and the Deuteronomic School*. Oxford: Oxford University Press, 1972.
Weiss, Andrea L. *Figurative Language in Biblical Prose Narrative: Metaphor in the Book of Samuel*. VTSup 107. Leiden: Brill, 2006.
Wells, Bruce. "Exodus." *ZIBBCOT* 1:160–283.
Wenham, Gordon J. *The Book of Leviticus*. NICOT. Grand Rapids: Eerdmans, 1979.
______. "Deuteronomy and the Central Sanctuary." *TynBul* 22 (1971): 103–18.
______. *Genesis 16–50*. WBC. Dallas: Word, 1994.
______. "Law." *DTIB* 441–46.
Westbrook, Raymond. "The Character of Ancient Near Eastern Law." Pages 1–90 in *A History of Ancient Near Eastern Law*, edited by Raymond Westbrook. Vol 1. Leiden: Brill, 2003.
Westbrook, Raymond, ed. *A History of Ancient Near Eastern Law*. 2 vols. Leiden: Brill, 2003.

Westbrook, Raymond, and Theodore J. Lewis. "Who Led the Scapegoat in Leviticus 16:21?" *JBL* 127 (2008): 417–22.

Westbrook, Raymond, and Bruce Wells. *Everyday Law in Biblical Israel: An Introduction*. Louisville: Westminster John Knox, 2009.

Westerholm, Stephen. "Law in Early Judaism." *NIDB* 3:587–94.

Westermann, Claus. *Elements of Old Testament Theology*. Atlanta: John Knox, 1982.

Wevers, John William, ed. *Deuteronomium*. Septuaginta: Vetus Testamentum Graecum 3/2. Göttingen: Vandenhoeck & Ruprecht, 1977.

______. *Exodus*. Septuaginta: Vetus Testamentum Graecum 2/1. Göttingen: Vandenhoeck & Ruprecht, 1991.

______. *Leviticus*. Septuaginta: Vetus Testamentum Graecum 2/2. Göttingen: Vandenhoeck & Ruprecht, 1986.

Wildberger, Hans. *Jahwes Eigentumsvolk: Eine Studie zur Traditionsgeschichte und Theologie des Erwählungsgedankens*. ATANT 37. Zurich: Zwingli, 1960.

Williams, Ronald. *Hebrew Syntax: An Outline*. 2nd ed. Toronto: University of Toronto Press, 1976.

Williamson, H. G. M. *1 and 2 Chronicles*. NCBC. Grand Rapids: Eerdmans, 1982.

Wilson, Ian. "Merely a Container? The Ark in Deuteronomy." Pages 212–49 in *Temple and Worship in Biblical Israel*, edited by John Day. New York: T&T Clark, 2007.

______. *Out of the Midst of the Fire*. SBLDS 151. Atlanta: Scholars Press, 1995.

Wolfson, Elliott R. "Circumcision and the Divine Name: A Study in the Transmission of Esoteric Doctrine." *JQR* 78 (1987): 77–112.

Work, Telford. *Deuteronomy*. BTCB. Grand Rapids: Brazos, 2009.

Wright, Christopher. *The Mission of God: Unlocking the Bible's Grand Narrative*. Downers Grove, IL: IVP Academic, 2006.

______. *Old Testament Ethics for the People of God*. Downers Grove, IL: IVP Academic, 2004.

Young, Edward J. *The Book of Isaiah*. NICOT. Grand Rapids: Eerdmans, 1974.

Younger, K. Lawson, Jr. *A Political History of the Arameans: From Their Origins to the End of their Polities*. Atlanta: SBL, 2016.

Zadok, Ran. "Names and Naming." *OEANE* 4:92–96.

Zernecke, Anna Elise. "A Shuilla: Ishtar 2, 'The Great Ishtar Prayer.'" Pages 257–90 in *Akkadian Prayers and Hymns: An Introduction*, edited by Alan Lenzi. ANEM 3. Atlanta: SBL, 2011.

Zevit, Ziony. "Preamble to a Temple Tour." Pages 73–81 in *Sacred Time, Sacred Place: Archaeology and the Religion of Israel*, edited by Barry M. Gittlen. Winona Lake, IN: Eisenbrauns, 2002.

Ziegler, Joseph. *Duodecim prophetae*. Septuaginta: Vetus Testamentum Graecum 13. Göttingen: Vandenhoeck & Ruprecht, 1984.

______, ed. *Jeremias, Baruch, Threni, Epistula Jeremiae*. 2nd ed. Septuaginta: Vetus Testamentum Graecum 15. Göttingen: Vandenhoeck & Ruprecht, 1976.

Zimmerli, Walther. *Ezekiel 1*. Translated by Ronald E. Clements. Hermeneia. Philadelphia: Fortress, 1979.

______. *I Am Yahweh*. Edited by W. Brueggeman. Atlanta: John Knox, 1982.

______. *Old Testament Theology in Outline*. Translated by David E. Green. Edinburgh: T&T Clark, 1978.

Zipor, M. A. "Some Notes on the Origin of the Tradition of the Eighteen *tiqqûnê sôperîm*." *VT* 44 (1994): 77–102.

Index of Authors

Index of Scripture

Deuterocanonical Literature

New Testament